'This is essential reading for all those interested in Soviet film. Dobrenko with his fresh approach and non-standard mix of examples confounds many of the clichés about the subject.'
Professor Katerina Clark, Yale University

'Professor Dobrenko's absorbing new study of Stalin period cinema shows how films set in the past, from historical epics to versions of literary classics to narratives of the Revolutionary struggle were required to adapt 'history' to the evolving political demands of the present. Witty and nuanced, drawing on a broad range of sources, the book combines unprecedented attention to hitherto neglected films with exciting new insights into classics of Soviet cinema.'
Professor Julian Graffy, University College London

For Maya Iosifovna Turovskaya.
In memory of Neya Markovna Zorkaya

STALINIST CINEMA AND THE PRODUCTION OF HISTORY
MUSEUM OF THE REVOLUTION

Evgeny Dobrenko
Translated by Sarah Young

YALE UNIVERSITY PRESS
New Haven and London

Published 2008 in the United Kingdom by Edinburgh University Press Ltd and in the United States by Yale University Press.

Typeset in 10/12.5 pt Sabon by Servis Filmsetting Ltd, Manchester
Printed in the United Kingdom

Library of Congress Control Number: 2008920599
ISBN 978-0-300-14160-3 (hardcover : alk. paper)

A catalogue record for this book is available from the British Library.

The paper in this book meets the guidelines for permanence and durability of the Committee on Production Guidelines for Book Longevity of the Council on Library Resources.

10 9 8 7 6 5 4 3 2 1

CONTENTS

History does not break down into stories but into images.

Walter Benjamin

INTRODUCTION: HISTORY
DEGREE ZERO

CINEMA AND HISTORY: DISCOURSES OF LEGITIMISATION

It is not the literal past that rules us: it is images of the past.

George Steiner

From Steiner's maxim, used here as an epigraph, one might conclude that the 'literal past', being something definite, stands opposed to 'images of the past' as something mysterious and undefined. It is, however, the other way round; 'images' turn out to be something that is quite tangible, verbalised and visualised, while the 'literal past' is no more than a construct, created with the help of these 'images'. In essence, history is also 'images of the past', which 'rule us'. Frequently (and under Stalinism, the subject of this book, always), history is the past, constructed and served by the authorities, who are attempting to curtail the experience of the 'literal past' by packaging it into a literary narrative. In the era of the media revolution, literature is transformed into film, which in its turn engenders (or transforms) the historical image. The focus of this book is not the history of the cinema, but its role in the production of history and the conversion of the present and experience into history, mechanisms of transfer, and what is located between history and the past. We are therefore referring not so much to 'propaganda' through art, as to the culture-forming function of these artefacts. Cinema, as the most constitutive and advanced artistic practice in Stalinist culture, is examined here in its role as institution for the production of history.

This book is about how Stalinist art works with time, the past and memory, but it is simultaneously also about Stalinist art per se, understood not so much as a style, but as a grandiose political-aesthetic project which completes the revolutionary project. Here we have the 'quiet haven' of revolutionary culture; the attempt to 'leap out of history' itself, in its turn, proves to be history. This is the Museum of the Revolution. This museum is not only Stalinist, but also of the post-Soviet era, transformed into the museum of its own history, so as to be able to live in (and with) it. Post-Soviet culture cannot escape from this system of images of the past for the very reason that history comes together with ready-made images, just as thought comes with speech. This is why a contemporary analysis of the origins of these images is so important. Their domain is in the Soviet past.

With the disintegration of the Soviet Union, Soviet identity also fell apart, while history, created for the production, reproduction and preservation of this identity, began to melt before one's eyes, not only reawakening earlier traumas, but also opening new wounds. The past, without finding formation and explanation in the new historical doctrine, was poured out into mass consciousness with new traumas. 'The end of a beautiful era', the disintegration of a 'Great Power', the wounding of 'national pride', were accompanied by a growth within the mass consciousness of undigested (historically unformed) layers of the past. *Perestroika* and the end of communism which followed it brought with them not only economic 'shock therapy', but also a painful shock in mass consciousness; a situation was created in which society, suffering the painful experience of an identity crisis, was forced once more to consume the past, open and full of traumas, without historicising anaesthetic.

This history-anaesthetic is pure mythology, apparently overcoming time itself. But, as Claude Lévi-Strauss noted, myth is also a social machine for destroying time or, as Roland Barthes put it, a 'dehistoricising mechanism'.[1] If in the historical narrative the reader/viewer should read only a symbol of the grandeur of Russia, then in the image projected from the pages of the novel or from the screen, he or she should discard the reality included in it. 'Reality' proves to be irrelevant. The 'image' is instrumentalised and loses for the consumer all referentiality.

'Battling with myth', with the help of the historian's traditional arsenal, is a task beyond one's strength. In the final analysis, documents, eye-witness accounts – that is, 'archives' – do not so much 'reproduce' the past as act as fuel for the present, which identifies itself in the mythology of the past; every era has its 'past', although they are all 'the same' ('the literal past'). 'History, not only as a narrative, is an artefact and a construct, but also in its social function it frequently stands as a product of the artistic practices at the centre of this book, be they verbal (the historical novel or official document) or visual (the film or picture). Moreover, the latter, in a paradoxical way, prove to be closer to strictly historical narrative.[2]

As Pierre Sorlin observed, 'History is not pre-existent to the film, it is produced by it . . . [I]t is not a reality used by the film; it has to be rebuilt and the result of the reconstruction is never reliable.'[3]

The path the reader faces through this book – from word to cinema image – demands certain preliminary considerations. Why has cinema in particular been chosen ahead of other historicising artistic practices? As we know, early in the pre-Enlightenment period, sculpture held first place in historicising art;

in its place came the picture, and in the nineteenth century this was replaced by the historical novel. In the twentieth century, the cinema mimicked this relay race. The 'screen' is transformed into one of the key concepts of the end of the twentieth century, in a similar way to such epoch-making categories as the 'window' of the Renaissance or the 'mirror' of mannerism and the Baroque. The birth of this chronotope of 'screen adaptation' led to the conception of the world by contemporary man being mediated by the screen. The concept of 'screen culture' (as a form of 'virtual reality') has today become particularly topical. The problem, however, lies in the fact that the birth of this culture is not so much the result of the postmodern view of the world, but rather a technological product. Precisely in this capacity, the expansion of the screen coincided with the boom in totalitarian ideologies and manipulating political technologies. One can definitely assert that the structuring of the new feeling of social space and of behaviour within this milieu is not in the least the product of the 'postmodern sensibility', but rather the product precisely of modernism and of political reaction to it (fascism and communism).

In this sense, Valery Podoroga's observation is interesting, as he noted that precisely as a result of the realisation of the huge ideological potential of the cinema, the artistic experiment from which cinematography was born effectively came to nothing: 'the cinematographer enters into the era of visual narration, it works more and more with the language of the consciousness of the mass viewer, with all the mythology and ideological stereotypes he has assimilated.'[4] In other words, the very language of the cinematographer is ever more converted into the new functions of screen action; forming social stereotypes, it is itself projected and set out by them. The cinematographer 'strives only to reproduce what its fault-finding master/viewer considers to be reality'; it is, rather, 'not a window into the world', 'but truly a screen, a colourless surface, on to which are imprinted the visual images of the consciousness, seeing itself'.[5] When the director's task is reduced to only 'narrating history', the social function of cinematographer is altered; it is important that 'the mass viewer, sitting in his seat in a darkened auditorium, knows it [this history – E. D.], takes it as his own, as the result of the activities of his own consciousness.'[6] In other words, the cinematographer legitimises the image being projected on to the viewer, turning it into an internalised image for the viewer.

In this way, the screen is not what reveals but what conceals. Its main characteristic is its opacity, which guarantees the very event of the film. In this it is similar to a mirror, the reflective function of which is guaranteed by its opacity. This metamorphosis does not occur without consequences for mass consciousness; in effect it is as though the cinematographer 'adapts from us reality with the illustrated word'. Through this estranged screen, reality not only leaves man in the world of ideological fantasies and images, but also 'seizes our senses by means of total prostheticisation'; the product of screen culture, 'the man who sees and hears not because he has eyes and ears, but because he has at his disposal specific audiovisual systems . . . in fact finds himself at their disposal.'

More than that, 'consciousness itself a global prosthesis, bring us closer to reality, which exists only in the imagination of the newest electronic systems.'[7]

At the same time, reading history from the screen itself relies not so much on the content of the information as on its morphology. As Marc Ferro notes, 'film is valuable not only because of what it reveals but also because of the socio-historical approach that it justifies':[8]

> It is easy to think that film is not suited to represent past reality and that at best its testimony is valuable only for the present; or that, aside from documents and newsreels, the reality it offers is no more real than the novel's. I think this is untrue and that, paradoxically, the only films that do not manage to surpass film's testimony concerning the present are films about the past: historical reconstructions.[9]

In other words, true 'historical reality' lies not in the subject (representations of the past) but precisely in the time of production; that is, the historical film does in fact construct history, but it also 'reflects' above all the time of its production. *Alexander Nevsky* says much more to us about 1938 than it does about the thirteenth century. In this way, in films (novels) about the past created in the Stalin era, we can read much more about the Stalin era than we can about the eras which these films (novels) were meant to 'reflect'.

Meanwhile, the illusion of 'reflection' remained the most important aim of Stalinist art. The attraction to film was there defined as functional-stylistic. The inevitable and total historicism of Stalinism was linked exactly with its total 'realism'; the 'truth of life' (or the 'truth of history') had to shine from the screen with the unfading light of the mimetic.

Cinema corresponded most fully with the very nature of Stalinist art; the Stalinist *Gesamtkunstwerk* required a synthesis of the arts, and precisely cinema turned out to be amenable to the synthesis of literature, the theatre, music and painting. Searches in this direction were actively carried out in the 1930s, and were at the centre of thinking about the cinema at this time.[10] Cinema authorised the age-old dichotomy of word and image, formulated in the following way by Ankersmit:

> [I]t could be claimed that the medium of language and that of painting are so different that, despite the mimetic nature of both word and picture, we cannot really speak of a rapprochement between word and picture. Precisely the difference in medium creates an unbridgeable gap between word and picture . . . painting offers a coordination of objects in its representation of the word and is therefore *sui generis* suitable for representing the spatial aspects of reality. By contrast, language, prose or poetry cannot be surveyed in a single glance; reading is temporal process and language is therefore suitable for the representation of temporary processes.[11]

Only in film can both these strategies work together, which turned cinema into the most effective medium of ideological and historical representation. In Stalinism, 'cinema becomes the medium of "history" itself, of the historical myth being created.'[12]

Stalinism was exceptionally sensitive to the problem of consumption and assimilation, in addition to the formation of ideology. Occupied with the ideological constructing – via history – of its own legitimacy and new Soviet identity, it relied on the cinema, seeing in this 'most important of the arts' the most effective form of propaganda and 'organisation of the masses', of which Lenin and Stalin spoke. Stalin directly managed Soviet cinematography and devoted an enormous amount of attention to it.[13]

At the same time the literary component cannot be eliminated from the effective representation of history. The word yields to censorship more easily than the visual image. (A graphic example of this is the story of the screenplay and film of *Ivan the Terrible*; the screenplay, approved by Stalin, was implemented by Eisenstein in such a way that the ideological task of the film was completely subverted.) As Oksana Bulgakowa has shown:

> [T]he reduction of the cinema to a medium of conservation and translation meant in practice a disdain for film depictions and an assumption that they could not (should not) have an independent semantics. All incidences of censorship are linked with the literary editing of the screenplay, directed at monitoring the dialogue and checking the text being transmitted.[14]

Konstantin Simonov describes in his memoirs a noteworthy scene. In 1940, on Stalin's orders, the film *The Law of Life* (*Zakon zhizni*) was banned, and the author of the screenplay, Alexander Avdeenko, was subjected to acute criticism. After a meeting of the Central Committee, Stalin was asked what should be done with the directors, Alexander Stolper and Boris Ivanov, who were in fact present. Stalin, carelessly turning his fingers in the air to show how film revolves in a camera, observed, 'And who are they? They only turned the reels on what he wrote for them.'[15]

The status of the word increased enormously in Stalinist cinema. As a result of this, the film screenplay is endowed with the status of an independent literary work; it is declared 'the basis of the film'. This is why montage is also understood now not as a means of organising space, time and rhythm, nor as a fundamental structural principle of cinematographic narrative (as it was understood in the 1920s), but as a device, destroying conventional narrative. The directors who were experimenting in the 1920s with specific film-narrative structures, Eisenstein and Vertov, were declared 'plotless', which in the new understanding had the same meaning as 'unideological'.[16] 'The plot of a work', noted the then head of Soviet cinema, Shumyatsky, 'is the constructed expression of its ideas. The plotless form . . . is powerless to express any significant ideas.'[17]

And so, the plot . . .

Between the Word and the Cinematic Image: Museum and (De)construction of the Past

The Museum, instead of being circumscribed in a geometrical location, is now everywhere, like a dimension of itself.

Jean Baudrillard, *Simulations*

We are living in an era of crisis of the Grand Historical Narrative. Yet the more actively the process of re-evaluation occurs, the clearer becomes the connection of the traditional historical narrative with the worked-out and effective mechanisms of political, ideological and cultural domination, the power of this narrative over the sphere of the 'political unconscious', filled with social anxiety, fear before the unknown and, precisely, before the future. This anxiety gives birth to the fantasy of the future, which has as its aim mastery of the realm of the unknown. In the nineteenth and twentieth centuries to this fantasy was added 'faith in science' (such as, for example, the Marxist 'historical laws' or 'scientific communism'). In order to master the future, it is necessary, in the first place, to turn it into the past (as it is based on the 'known', the past does not scare), and, second, to sacrifice the present (which turns out from this future-directed perspective to be irrelevant, as everything is done 'for the bright tomorrow' and 'for future generations').

Yet if the twentieth century proved anything, it was the great self-sufficiency of the present and the great deception of the future. The present was the main sacrifice of the twentieth century; all totalitarian regimes worked for the 'future', trying to calm the social anxieties and fears before them through rationalisation or mystique. The famous 'abolition' by Stalin of Hegel's law of negation of the negation left without an answer the question of what there would be 'after communism'; the horizon of expectations was directed towards the past, in so far as there was already nothing to 'expect' in the future. Stalin introduced a new temporality: the concluded future (a kind of future pluperfect). In order to free the ground for this new future, the present was shifted into the past, and the future-directed future was transformed into the present, as a result of which the present itself underwent complete de-realisation. The completed construction of the past turns out anew to be an ideal, a model for the future (either as a direct projection or 'in reverse'). The same role which was played by the future in revolutionary culture was played in Stalinist culture by the past. While in revolutionary culture the future is a source of legitimacy, within Stalinist culture it is itself in need of legitimising.

By modelling the past, culture models the future, but the twentieth century, the century of the cult of progress and the future, proved to be the era of the cult of the past. In Stalinism, as Vladimir Paperny noted,

> The future, transformed into eternity, is so homogenous and immutable that in essence nothing can be seen in it, it is even pointless to look

there – culture's glance is constantly turned backwards, as if swung around 180°. The present moment turns out to be already not the starting point of history, but rather its finale. Culture begins to be interested in the path by which it came to the present moment, begins to be interested in history . . . The basic content of culture 2 [that is, Stalinist culture – E. D.] becomes its own history, and from there history becomes the basic genre of culture 2.[18]

But in a paradoxical way, the twentieth century also turned out to be the century of previously unforeseen idolatry – of the future, that is, of its own fear. In the conditions of the mass society and terror of the twentieth century, social fantasising fulfilled an important therapeutic function.

It cannot be ruled out that necrosis is an essential feature of these societies. Be that as it may, too many tranquillisers, antidepressants and other psychotropic drugs are introduced into the social organism. Partly for this reason, societies based on terror are soon worn down. They produce much more history than they can consume. This surplus of history can be likened to high cholesterol levels, leading to atherosclerosis, cardiovascular disease and premature ageing.

Old age is memory. Here, however, we are dealing with a desire not to remember. This is linked not only with the traumatic past, but also with the fact that a part of the terror on which these societies are based is the terror of history. A strategy of these societies is the logical exchange of social memory with history. Memory is trauma; history is therapy. In the artificial memory created via the historical narrative, there occurs a removal of social traumatics via the historicisation of experience: that is, the construction of the past. The cost of this therapeutic procedure is alienation of the past. It is precisely here that history directly meets with literature; as Roland Barthes noted in *Writing Degree Zero*, 'the teleology common to the Novel and to narrated History is the alienation of the facts.'[19] History proves to be a protective dam against memory, which it is required to congeal and verbalise in the images of history. If memory is a procedure of selection, then history is a procedure of conceptualisation and alienation of what has been experienced (memory). History is neither a collection nor even a selection of events. Nor is it a collection of interpretations of these events, but rather a system of techniques and optics which produces the events themselves from the past and give them the very status of events. In other words, history can be conceived as the alienated past, as transformed social experience. (Memory is personal; history is social.) In this capacity, not only does it not articulate the traumatics of real experience, but it also serves to de-realise the past and memory. In fact, the oft-noted obsession these societies have with 'historicism' is the product of their 'amnesia'.

The museum is the adequate materialisation of this obsession. If history is the concentrated past, then the museum is materialised history. The past in it is depersonalised, since the museum has almost no link with memory. It is a perfect machine for the maintenance of ready-made mythology and the alienation of the past. The museum is above all not a collection but a composition – a conception of the past, an ideological montage. The fundamental characteristic of all the functions of the museum is the appropriation of history; by appropriating objects the museum also appropriates their historical connotations. Scattered and gathered anew in the museum, the world transforms the museum into the ideal mythogenic space. The first museum (as the concept is now understood) was founded by the French Convention of 1793 at the Louvre. From this one should consider not only the history of the museum in the modern era, but also the link between the museum and the guillotine. The Revolution invented the guillotine and turned palaces into museums, having first looted them. The museum is the guillotine of history. It is the ideal machine for working with the Revolution; as the heads of revolutionaries go under the guillotine, the Revolution itself becomes a 'memorial of the past'. The museum simultaneously destroys and exhibits the past. The very process of destruction occurs via its exhibiting. Stalinist culture destroys the Revolution via its exhibiting and reworking.

Stalinism's relation to the Russian Revolution is practically the same as that of present-day France to the French Revolution. On the bicentenary of the Revolution, Jean Baudrillard wrote:

> [C]ommemoration . . . signifies the absence of something. Thus within the domain of the political imaginary, the bicentennial signifies the definitive end of the French Revolution. The act of oblivion takes on two forms: on the one hand, the slow or violent extermination of memories; on the other, the spectacular promotion, that is to say the migration of history into the space of advertising . . . We are in the process of fabricating for ourselves, with the help of many advertising images, a synthetic memory which stands in place of a primal scene, or founding myth, and which especially allows us to take leave of the actual, historical event of the Revolution. The Revolution is no longer on the agenda in France today.[20]

From this Baudrillard concludes that commemoration marks the end of history, since we can no longer produce 'an original history';[21] the place of celebration is the place in which the new revolution can no longer happen, because it would destroy the very idea of commemoration and ceremonies. As a result, revolution may never take place. A 'vision' and spectacle of history replace 'original history'. The same could be said of the Russian Revolution in the Stalinist era.

In Soviet history two apparently contradictory tendencies lived side by side: on the one hand, the battle against the museum; on the other, total museumification. Leftist artists, following the words of Vladimir Mayakovsky, declared 'it's time bullets rang out against museum walls.' At the other pole, the proletarian poet Vladimir Kirillov, in the name of the 'new beauty', appealed, 'burn

Raphael, destroy museums, trample on flowery art.' The symbol of the link between these two streams, the avant-garde and the proletarian, was an inscription made by Mayakovsky in a book given to Kirillov: 'To a comrade in arms in the battle against Raphaels.' But, in a paradoxical way, by smashing up the museum, revolutionary culture prepared the ground for its own growth within it.

The avant-garde's relationship to the museum was somewhat more complex than simple 'hatred of the past'. In essence, the museum is a place not of preservation, but, like a crematorium, of destruction; the technology of preservation, when verified, turns out in fact to be the technology of destruction. The hatred felt in revolutionary culture for the museum can be explained by its formalism, which did not allow one to see the social function of this institution; in preserving the form of the past, the museum destroys its content. And the more effectively it does the former, the more inevitable becomes the latter.

The strategy of revolutionary culture, being absolutely negative, meant that this culture was unarmed when it came face to face with its heir, Stalinist culture, which turned everything into a museum. As Boris Groys observed,

> Stalinist aesthetics in essence preserved the same aim [as the avant-garde – E. D.] – overcoming the difference between art and life. But it began to resolve this problem not by means of destroying the museum, and by means of its own kind of aesthetic equalisation of the museum exhibition and media external to the museum via the physical fulfilment of this medium by art, undifferentiated from museum [art] . . . Wielding control over both reality and its representation in art, the communist leadership proved to be in a position to make art auto-referential and thereby embody the dream of the avant-garde of identity of the signifying and the signified. In such art contemplation and practice coincide, which, in turn, completely erases the border between the space of the museum and the space beyond it.[22]

This guaranteed a profound link between Stalinism and the museum on the level of organisation of the aesthetic field: 'Totalitarianism is the creation of a single, total, visual space, in which the borders between art and life, between the museum and practical life, between contemplation and action, disappear.'[23]

Historically, Stalinism believed itself above all to be 'the legitimate heir and continuer' of the revolutionary past and Marxist ideas. This in earnest brings Stalinism closer to the museum, which is based on the cult of legacy, and is in its way an institution for the legitimisation of the rights of legacy. This is why the revolutionary past was subjected to particularly intense museumification under Stalinism. It turns out, however, that between the two strategies used in relation to it – destruction and museumification – there is in fact no gap at all. Museumification acts as one form of destruction, in so far as the only thing that is not acceptable to Stalinism is the 'living past'. 'Living', for it, is the 'living dead' – a museum exhibit. It is no accident that the first 'historical' building opened by Stalin was the mausoleum for the 'eternally living' Lenin. There then followed Stalin's famous letter in the newspaper *Proletarskaia revoliutsiia* (*Proletarian Revolution*), in which he called historians 'grave-diggers' and 'archive rats'.

Between the archive and the museum there is a quite complex link. Archives (under the control of the KGB during the Soviet period) were closed, while museums, as public spaces, were open. In effect, the museum was the justification for the closed nature of the archive, or, to be more accurate, it was the open part of the archive; it contained and displayed precisely that part of the archive which it was advantageous to display. In this sense, the museum can be understood as a filtered archive. If the archive is the basis of the historian's work in the restoration of the past, then the museum is the basis for official myth and the institution for the installation of the artificial past.

But there is here also a strictly social context. The unsettled life of the 1930s – when millions of people found themselves in a social dynamic unprecedented in Russia's history, migrating to cities, living in hostels, barracks and communal apartments, when the traditional links and historical memory were disintegrating before one's eyes – begins to run up against the reconstructed idea of 'legacy' and the 'historical past', which had been expelled from everywhere in the 1920s. This process, usually described as a process of mass 'accustoming' to the past, was in fact a process of alienation. In the end, the 'legacy', which the masses did not have at their disposal in the unsettled nature of their everyday lives, was turned into something official and sublime. The very idea of 'legacy' and the perception of the world through this idea are closely linked to the commodification of history, the substitute of memory with artefacts, which then constitute this 'legacy'. This, in its turn, gave rise to:

> the interpretation of the past through an artifactual history which partly obscures the social relations and struggles which underlay that past; the belief that the past is to be understood through pastiched images and stereotypes which convert that past into simple narratives and spectacles; the belief that history is turned into heritage and made safe, sterile and shorn of danger, subversion and seduction; and the overall loss of belief in a historical subject which is seeking its own redemption will bring about a universal redemption of humankind.[24]

It is precisely here that we encounter the cinema – this museum of the post-industrial era and the communication revolution; the linearity of the museum is overcome in the historical film through the reanimation of dead people and objects. 'Reanimated' does not, of course, mean 'alive'. Rather, it means 'definitively dead'; depriving the exhibit of authenticity, the film profanes history. At the same time, cinema differs from the museum in that it produces the image, while the museum exhibit produces pure 'knowledge' and appeals to reality. But both the image and the exhibit lie in the same ideological matrix, in the same network for the production of meaning, in which 'knowledge' constructs reality itself. The problem, it appears, is linked to the very genre of the historical film. In contrast to musical, drama or science fiction, it appeals directly to reality; in it 'real historical figures' are acting, in it 'real historical events' take place, and, finally, in it history is materialised. And here the connection between the museum and art is also revealed; like historicising art, the museum does not so much generate knowledge as simulate the past. While the museum operates as a witness, film produces a reality to which only it can bear witness.

But as obvious as the closeness of the historicising strategies of the museum and cinema is, their fundamental differences are also apparent. Cinema, being based on 'mechanical reproduction', is a product of the industrial era and mass society. With the museum, on the other hand, the main issue is authenticity. One could say that the museum fetishises the authenticity of the objects on show, while art is occupied with creating new and – by definition – fictitious objects. It is precisely in the museum that the dichotomy of the authenticity of the object and its artificial representational context reaches its greatest point of tension. And only in art is this dichotomy cancelled out. Thus, in the historical film and novel, the artificial turns out to be both the 'object' itself in the form of an ideologeme (such as 'Ivan the Terrible was a harsh but wise ruler'; 'Peter the Great was a progressive historical figure' and so on) and its representation. In a sense, art turns out to be more historical than the museum, which concentrates on the object in itself and not on history. Art, on the other hand, is occupied by history, not the object, and itself produces authenticity.

The Soviet museum of history is a kind of metaphor for those transformations which the past underwent in the process of de-realisation in Soviet ideological doctrine. In the end, the museum is a unique 'universal space of representation'.[25] In its other function, the 'museum negotiates a nexus between cultural production and consumption.'[26] This museum is only a container (a structure and objects), the content of which is created by visitors themselves. Being an institution of representation par excellence, the museum is also a space of discipline. It intersects with disciplines (art, history, archaeology, science, anthropology, literature and so on), creating a well-ordered, normalised, classified, surveyed world. The connection of the museum with technologies of disciplining and dominating lie in the very nature of this institution, which produces 'a monologic discourse dominated by the authoritative cultural voice of the museum'.[27] It is precisely here, in the field of this authoritative voice, that there is created what, referring to those institutions involved in producing and circulating meanings about the past, Michael Bommers and Patrick Wright have called the 'public historical sphere'. These institutions – museums, historical novels, bioepics, documentaries and so on – play their role in enacting 'a publicly instituted structuring of consciousness'.[28]

As Tony Bennett shows in *The Birth of the Museum*, the staged past is a 'culturally organized text', and it produces 'textually organized meanings whose determinations must be sought in the present'.[29] At the same time this turns the museum into one of the most perfect mechanisms for ideological manipulation. It is a space in which 'the rhetoric of power embodied in the exhibitionary complex – a power made manifest not in its ability to inflict pain but by its ability to organise and co-ordinate an order of things and to produce a place for the people in relation to that order'.[30] In this sense the museum is the reverse side of the two-faced Janus of power. It is not surprising, therefore, that its other side is . . . the prison:

> If the museum and the penitentiary thus represented the Janus face of power, there was none the less – at least symbolically – an economy of effort between them. For those who failed to adopt the tutelary relation to the self promoted by popular schooling or whose hearts and minds failed to be won in the new pedagogic relations between state and people symbolised by the open doors of the museum, the closed walls of penitentiary threatened a sterner instruction in the lessons of power. Where instruction and rhetoric failed, punishment began.[31]

Even if this Foucaultian reading of the social function of the museum seems an exaggeration, the link between the Stalinist museumification of the past and the Gulag seems in no way to be a simple chronological coincidence.

The main functions of the museum are collection, conservation and exhibition. In this sense museumification is the process of selection of what has been constituted as 'history' (collection), the assembly from this selection of a coherent picture of the world (conservation), and the advancement of this picture into the space beyond the museum (exhibition). In these functions the museum carries out the important social function of reforging the past into an ideologically coherent narrative.[32]

Legitimising the past, the museum asserts the status quo, urging people to be reconciled to their positions within the 'correct' and 'naturally formed' world. In this capacity, the museum's function, as Kevin Walsh notes, is the 'naturalization of power'.[33] In the course of legitimisation of the institutionalised past, not only does interest in the past decline sharply, but so does people's access to it. The museum replaces the archive, about which Stalin wrote directly in his letter to the journal *Proletarskaia revoliutsiia*, calling on historians to write an illuminating history of the Party from the point of view of 'Bolshevik axioms', rather than from any sources found in archives. The wider the doors of the museum are opened, the more firmly are the doors of the archive shut. In this way, the museum proves to be an institution of 'historical amnesia', while its main function is 'distancing people from their pasts', rather than bringing them closer to it.[34]

The very idea of the museum, from its foundations linked with ideas of progress, industrialisation and urbanisation, must be understood first and foremost as an idea of order and institutionalised knowledge. In the final analysis, the museum is an institution of control over the past. By placing an authentic object in an artificial context, creating a shop-window from the past, the museum produces power – 'the power of the gaze, an ability to observe, name and order, and thus control'.[35] Here, however, it is worth bearing in mind that the function of the museum is derived from the function of historical narrative, which it serves. The deep kinship of the museum and history lies not so much in their closeness of function, but in terms of writing.

Michel de Certeau suggested that:

> Writing speaks of the past only in order to inter it. Writing is a tomb in the double sense of the word in that, in the very same text, it both honors and eliminates. Here the function of language is to introduce through *saying* what can no longer be *done* . . . But unlike other artistic and social 'tombs,' here taking the dead or the past back to a symbolic place is connected to the labor aimed at creating in the present a place (past or future) to be filled, a 'something that must be done.' Writing gathers together the products of this labor. In this way it liberates the present without having to name it. Thus it can be said that writing makes the dead so that the living can exist elsewhere. More exactly, it receives the dead that a social change has produced, so that the space opened by this past can be marked, and so that it will still be possible to connect what appears with what disappears . . . A society furnishes itself with a present time by virtue of historical writing. The literary founding of this space thus rejoins the labors that historical practice had brought about.
>
> As a substitute for the absent being, an enclosure of the evil genius of death, the historical text plays a performative role. Languages allows a practice to be situated in respect to its *other*, the past. In fact, in itself it is a practice . . . Through its performativity, historiography fills the lacuna that it represents; it uses this locus to impose upon the receiver a will, a wisdom, and a lesson. In sum, narrativity, the metaphor of performative discourse, finds its support precisely in what it hides: the dead of which it speaks become the vocabulary of a task to be undertaken.[36]

History itself from this perspective turns out to be 'a discourse about the past that has the status of being the discourse of the dead . . . History becomes the myth of language. It manifests the very condition of discourse: a death.'[37] And here we reach the dead-end of the historical narrative: 'For to speak of the dead means to deny death and almost to defy it. Therefore speech is said to "resuscitate" them. Here the word is literally a lure: history does not resuscitate anything.'[38]

In essence, we have arrived at the realisation of one of the most radical utopias of Russian culture – Nikolai Fyodorov's 'Philosophy of the Common Cause', based on the idea of the resurrection of one's dead ancestors. Fyodorov wrote a great deal on the museum. (He even dedicated a special work to this theme, 'The Museum, Its Meaning and Purpose'.) For Fyodorov, the museum was akin to the cemetery, the basis of the 'Common Cause'. In his philosophy, the cemetery plays the role of a true cathedral, and therefore in Fyodorov's philosophy, likening the museum to the cemetery was the highest praise. He wrote of museums in the following terms: 'special cemeteries, called museums',[39] 'higher than the museum there is only the grave' (p. 576), 'museums must be united and turned into a cathedral' (p. 326). More than that, 'every museum must have in its foundation a book' (p. 444); it is 'only a varied illustration to a book' (p. 446).

Did Fyodorov have in mind historical narrative? Quite probably, if one takes into account those ideological functions which history fulfilled. In the end, according to Fyodorov, 'The museum is a depiction of the true, the actual, that which must be' (p. 466). Precisely such a past, as it 'must be', is produced by the official historical narrative. The museum, although not yet fully mature, in Fyodorov's terms, in its understanding of its role as a cemetery (p. 492), had to become, like Stalinism itself, a true *Gesamtkunstwerk*:

> The idea, acting with all artistic means, neither separated by space, nor broken off by time, acting educationally, unites art, gathers all artists in a single cathedral [sobor] for all the arts, in a single temple-museum, which unifies in itself all arts. (p. 459)

In this temple the museum must reject collecting things and concentrate instead on the resurrection of the dead: 'The museum is not a collection of things, but a gathering [sobor] of people; its work consists not in the accumulation of dead things, but in the resurrection to life of the remains of those who have died, in the restoration of the dead' (p. 587). Stalinism opposes the museum of this necrophiliac utopia as its own kind of secularised cathedral. If the ideal, perfect museum is the cemetery of the past, then the Stalinist museum is the true cemetery of the Revolution.

NOTES

1. Roland Barthes, *The Eiffel Tower, and Other Mythologies*, trans. Richard Howard, New York: Noonday, 1979, p. 145.
2. On history as an instrument in the creation of national myths, see Eric Hobsbawm, Terrence Ranger (eds), *The Invention of Tradition*, Cambridge: Cambridge University Press, 1983; Linda Colley, *Britons: Forging Nation 1707–1837*, London: Pimlico, 1992; Robert Gildea, *The Past in French History*, New Haven, CT: Yale University Press, 1994; Stefan Collini, *English Pasts*, Oxford: Oxford University Press, 1999; Robert Foster, *The Irish Story: Telling Tales and Making it Up in Ireland*, London: Penguin, 2001; Michel-Rolph Trouillot, *Silencing the Past: Power and the Production of History*, Boston, MA: Beacon, 1995.
3. Pierre Sorlin, *The Film in History: Restaging the Past*, Oxford: Basil Blackwell, 1980, p. 170.
4. Roundtable 'Kinematograf i kul'tura', *Voprosy filosofii*, 1990, No. 3, p. 24.

5. Ibid., p. 25.
6. Ibid., p. 25.
7. Ibid., p. 25.
8. Marc Ferro, *Cinema and History*, Detroit: Wayne State University Press, 1988, p. 29.
9. Ibid., p. 47.
10. See A. Piotrovskii, 'Kinofikatsiia iskusstv', *Kinovedcheskie zapiski*, 1998, No. 40, p. 221, and also books by I. I. Ioffe, *Sinteticheskaia istoriia iskusstv: Vvedenie v istoriiu khudozhestvennogo myshleniia*, Leningrad, 1933; *Sinteticheskoe izuchenie iskusstva i zvukovoe kino*, Leningrad, 1937; *Muzyka sovetskogo kino: Osnovy muzykal'noi dramaturgii*, Leningrad, 1938.
11. F. R. Ankersmit, 'Statements, Texts and Pictures'. In Frank Ankersmit and Hans Kellner, *A New Philosophy of History*, Chicago: University of Chicago Press, 1995, p. 215.
12. Oksana Bulgakova, 'Sovetskoe kino v poiskakh "obshchei modeli"'. In Khans Giunter, Evgenii Dobrenko (eds), *Sotsrealisticheskii kanon*, St Petersburg: Akademicheskii proekt, 2000, p. 152.
13. See G. Mar'iamov, *Kremlevskii tsenzor: Stalin smotrit kino*, Moscow: Kinotsentr, 1992.
14. Bulgakova, 'Sovetskoe kino v poiskakh "obshchei modeli"', p. 150.
15. Konstantin Simonov, 'Glazami cheloveka moego pokoleniia', *Znamia*, 1988, No. 4, pp. 71–2.
16. Bulgakova, 'Sovetskoe kino v poiskakh "obshchei modeli"', p. 150.
17. Boris Shumiatskii, 'Tvorcheskie zadachi templana', *Sovetskoe kino*, 1933, No. 11, pp. 6–7.
18. Vladimir Papaernyi, *Kul'tura 2*, Moscow: Novoe literaturnoe obozrenie, 1996, pp. 45, 46.
19. Roland Barthes, *Writing Degree Zero*, New York: Noonday, 1991, pp. 32–3.
20. Jean Baudrillard, 'Revolution and the End of Utopia'. In Jean Baudrillard, *The Disappearance of Art and Politics*, New York: St Martin's, 1992, p. 233.
21. Ibid., p. 234.
22. Boris Grois, 'Bor'ba protiv muzeia, ili Demonstratsiia iskusstva v totalitarnom prostranstve'. In Marina Balina, Evgenii Dobrenko, Iurii Murashov (eds), *Sovetskoe bogatstvo: Stat'i o kul'ture literature, i kino*, St Petersburg: Akademicheskii proekt, 2002, pp. 48–9.
23. Ibid., p. 37.
24. John Urri, 'How Societies Remember the Past'. In Sharon Macdonald, Gordon Fyfe (eds), *Theorizing Museums*, Oxford: Blackwell, 1996, p. 52.
25. Boris Grois, *Kommentarii k iskusstvu*, Moscow: Khudozhestvennyi zhurnal, 2003, p. 33.
26. Sharon Macdonald, 'Introduction'. In Sharon Macdonald, Gordon Fyfe (eds), *Theorizing Museums*, Oxford: Blackwell, 1996, p. 4.
27. E. Hooper-Greenhill, *Museums and the Shaping of Knowledge*. London: Routledge, 1992, p. 103.
28. Michael Bommers, Patrick Wright, ' "Charms of residence": The Public and the Past'. In *Making Histories: Studies in History, Writing and Politics*, London: Hutchinson, 1982, p. 266.
29. Tony Bennett, *The Birth of the Museum: History, Theory, Politics*, London: Routledge, 1995, p. 130.
30. Ibid., p. 67.
31. Ibid., p. 87.
32. See Kevin Walsh, *The Representation of the Past: Museums and Heritage in the Post-Modern World*, London: Routledge, 1992, pp. 1–3.
33. Ibid., p. 99.
34. Ibid., pp. 93, 176.

35. Ibid., p. 32.
36. Michel de Certeau, *The Writing of History*, New York: Columbia University Press, 1988, pp. 101–2.
37. Ibid., p. 46.
38. Ibid., p. 47.
39. Nikolai Fedorov, *Sochineniia*, Moscow: Mysl', 1982, p. 317. Further references to this edition are given in the text in parentheses.

I. THE DIALECTICS OF THE POPULAR MONARCHY

[I]f historical science is to be a real science, it can no longer reduce the history of social development to the actions of kings and generals, to the actions of 'conquerors' and 'subjugators' of states, but must above all devote itself to the history of the producers of material values, the history of the labouring masses, the history of peoples.

History of the Communist Party of the Soviet Union (Bolsheviks).
Short Course[1]

[I]n order not to err in politics, one must look forward, not backward.

History of the Communist Party of the Soviet Union (Bolsheviks).
Short Course[2]

HISTORY, LOOKING FORWARD

In the 'golden kernel' of the *Short Course*, the renowned 'philosophical chapter', 'On dialectic and historical materialism', Stalin explained how the Marxist dialectic must be applied to history in order to 'save the science of history from becoming a jumble of accidents and an agglomeration of most absurd mistakes'. Once 'the world is in a state of constant movement and development', everything must be looked at 'historically'; that is, there are no 'eternal laws or social systems', and that which is progressive today will be reactionary tomorrow and so on.[3]

This 'historical dialectic' is based on the principle which Michel de Certeau would later call 'temporalisation'. It is precisely this, suggests de Certeau, which produces historical narrative itself and creates 'historical perspective', which 'authorizes the operation which, from the same place and within the same text, substitutes conjunction for disjunction and holds contrary statements together'. Temporalisation thus 'allows a sum of contradictions to be held together without the need for resolving them'.[4] (De Certeau brings in the idea of 'good' and 'bad' weather as an example. It is sufficient to temporalise these two contradictory assertions for the contradiction to be cancelled out: 'the weather's good today'; 'yesterday the weather was bad.') This is the procedure Stalin called dialectic.

On the one hand, its narrative-generating character attracts attention to itself. From this perspective the historical narrative is a meeting place of history and logic; but on the other hand, it is characterised as an 'authorising operation', directed in the final analysis at legitimising the assertion containing 'two contradictory assertions'. (Stalinism constantly needed temporality/historicism in order to impart coherence to its doctrine, and regularly combined mutually exclusive assertions.)

Legitimacy, according to Max Weber, is supported on three bases: tradition (the authority of the 'eternal yesterday': that is, customs, habits, traditions), charisma (the authority of the 'extraordinary personal gift') and, finally, 'legality' (the authority of rational establishments, institutions and laws).[5] The very genre of the historical novel and film, which had its heyday in the 1930–40s, appeals to the 'eternal yesterday', restoring (or establishing?), articulating and visualising the 'customs, habits and traditions of the past'. Practically all these works related to the biographical variety of historical genres; that is, at their centre there was always a charismatic leader, be it Pugachev or Razin, Peter the Great or Ivan the Terrible, Suvorov or Nakhimov. Finally, they all appealed to the rational 'laws of history' and to 'legal' institutions which had 'arisen historically' (the monarchy, the State, the army, the navy and so on).

As we have already seen, 'the laws of history', immutably working for the legitimisation of the regime, stood at the centre of the Soviet world. Shaped according to the copy book of 'historical materialism', this construct bypassed 'humanisation' in Stalinist culture via an appointed executor of the 'will of history' (that is, the 'historical personality'), whether the 'progressive tsar', the 'great commander', the 'marshal of the popular masses' or the 'leader of all of progressive humanity'. As Mikhail Allenov noted, legitimacy here was constructed on a constant appeal to prototypes, to Lenin and Marx, acting

> as images traced on 'tablets of stone', dictated from above by history itself. History is the true god, the idol of the system. Its designs are fulfilled in the image of socialism. Everything that is accomplished in it is accomplished on the stage of history, illuminated by the light of historical materialism. Historical materialism is the centre of the ideological universe.[6]

History, in so far as its design is absolutely realised (although often with hindsight) has an entirely miraculous character. Belief in the miracle of the historical augury is rationalised by historical determinism, the very rhetoric of which transforms history into a machine of correct prophecies.

This [notes Allenov] is the technique of selection and weeding out of historical facts for the sake of ease of interpretation, and interpreting what remains to one's own credit and justification. But in so far as justification can issue from an instance which is invested with unlimited confidence, it is necessary constantly to force and support the authority of the prophet – history. Falsification of history is therefore a function of its apologetics.[7]

Stalinism thus does not simply 'use' history. History proves to be precisely the basis of the legitimacy of Stalinism, and the adjustment of 'historical images' to fit their 'historical prototypes' becomes almost the main occupation of historicising writing. The historicising aspect of Stalinist art is found consequently to be the reverse side of socialist realism's lacquering practices – of the production novel or the *kolkhoz* poem; just as the latter form the 'image' of Soviet reality, the historicising texts (the historical novel, the biographical or historical-revolutionary film) form their 'prototype', undoubtedly fully conforming to the present of 'real socialism'.

In this Stalinism was only continuing the tradition of Western historiography, in which, as de Certeau notes, 'intelligibility is established through a relation with the other; it moves (or "progresses") by changing what it makes of its "other" – the Indian, the past, the people, the mad, the child, the Third World.'[8] The continually changing 'objective law' was declared the 'Great Other of History' in Stalinism; each new victor is pronounced here 'progressive agent' (to conform to 'historical necessity'), whilst this progressiveness is not exhausted by the victory of the next 'progressive agent'. Slavoj Žižek defined this type of understanding of history as 'evolutionary idealism',[9] seeing here the specifics of the legitimisation of the leader's power. If the traditional king was legitimised by a supra-social, external power (God, nature, the mystical past and so on), then the leader does not need external support for his legitimisation; he is the leader in so far as he is only the expression and embodiment of the interests and desires of the masses, he is the executor of their will.

> Here [writes Žižek] the basic deception consists in the fact that the Leader's point of reference, the instance to which he is referring to legitimise his rule (the People, the Class, the Nation) does not exist – or, more precisely, exists only through and in its fetishistic representative, the Party and its Leader . . . the People and the 'real People' exist only in so far as they are embodied in their representative, the Party and its Leader . . . the People always support the Party because any member of the People who opposes Party rule automatically excludes himself from the People.[10]

Thus in the process of the legitimisation of power not only is the subject of power constructed, but also its object. The 'dialectic synthesis' must take place, as usual, between the 'thesis' and the 'antithesis'. The subject and object of power, permanently acting on one another, prove to be tightly bound together.

This power cannot exist without that subject ('the People'), but also that very subject ('the People') cannot be constituted and exist outside this power; 'the People' can be formed, turned into itself only in the process of the legitimisation of power. They create each other.

History cannot function as an ideological reality outside art. Historicising art paints 'historical reality' in pictures and personalities. According to Soviet aesthetics, the viewer goes to the cinema to 'become acquainted with reality'. And not simply to become acquainted: 'The viewer, going to the cinema to learn, to become acquainted with reality, demands from his art the true and full, detailed representation of life,'[11] whilst 'the historical and artistic truth are fused together for us.'[12] Just as here there is no difference between history and art, nor is there any difference between past and present. And this is why Sergei Eisenstein, undertaking production of *Alexander Nevsky*, insisted that 'the role of the historical film is colossal precisely in connection with the creation of contemporary films, and generalising the experience of the historical film, it is worth always bearing in mind that this is also material for a contemporary film.'[13] He was echoed by one of the leading Soviet poets, Alexei Surkov:

> [T]he work of art dedicated to the historical past is authentic and effective when it not only enriches the viewer or reader with knowledge about the past, but also gives rise in them to analogies with the contemporary world, to thoughts about the present.[14]

But of course, the connection between historicising art and the Soviet present was realised not only 'in connection with' 'analogy'. History is the best method of rationalising the present, and is therefore the most effective means of legitimising it. All the fundamental strategies of legitimisation work here in astonishing harmony. Terry Eagleton attributed the following to their number: the promotion of beliefs and values which are congenial to the spirit of the dominant power (such as the ideas of the strong State, the centralisation of power, the justification of violence and terror, which stand at the centre of Soviet historicising art); naturalising and universalising such beliefs so as to render them self-evident and apparently inevitable (such as the 'kindness and peace-loving nature of Russians'; the 'freedom-loving character of the Russian people'; Russia's 'friendship between nations', evidence of which is certainly present in any work on a historical theme); denigrating ideas which might challenge the power (for example, the entire circle of ideas linked with 'Westernism', any kind of allusion to the superiority of the West or to Russia's dependence on Western goods and technical achievements); excluding rival forms of thought, perhaps by some unspoken but systematic logic (such as, for example, the militancy of the Stalinist view of the past, in which any 'civility' is discredited as 'spinelessness', if not treachery); and, finally, obscuring social reality (such as, for example, the erosion of class-based conflicts in representations of pre-revolutionary Russia, where the peasants worship their progressive and forward-thinking princes, or soldiers their commanders).[15]

It was precisely in the Middle Ages and on its very borders with the New Era that Stalinism sought and found the demanded 'analogy with the present' and that Soviet historicising art solved the main problems – of the State, power and violence. Intensely scrutinising the Middle Ages, Stalinism hit upon the key characters of Russian history – Alexander Nevsky and Minin and Pozharsky, Ivan the Terrible and Peter the Great, Razin and Pugachev. And on the contrary, the New Era, the nineteenth century, turned out to be suitable only for representation in the cinema of 'progressive figures of Russian science' (Popov, Zhukovsky, Pirogov), music (Glinka, Rimsky-Korsakov, Mussorgsky) and literature (Belinsky). This intense interest in the Middle Ages is characteristic of exactly the second half of the 1930s and the first half of the 1940s; the intensive forming of the Soviet nation was taking place precisely in the years of the Great Terror and the war. And, on the contrary, biographical films about public figures from Russian culture in the nineteenth century were made in the postwar era.

The new historical doctrine formed in Stalinist Russia in the middle of the 1930s, by virtue of the nature of 'historical knowledge' in the 'land of the socialist victory', was directed above all at legitimising the already stagnating regime. It continued to assert its succession over earlier Marxist doctrine ('The genealogy of the Revolution – that is where you will find the profound content of the best works of the Soviet historical genre'[16]); its centre, however, proved to be not legitimisation of the Revolution (as in Pokrovsky) but, on the contrary, legitimisation of the State.

Karamzin concluded the key work of Russian historiography, *The History of the Russian State*, with the words, 'The people's history belongs to the tsar.' The 'people's history' is wrapped up in the 'history of the State' and both 'belong to the tsar'. In the new doctrine this 'ownership' of history by power is fully realised, with Soviet historicising art understanding that, as Shklovsky noted in 1939, 'the question of the Soviet historical film is first of all a question of mastering history.'[17]

It is not surprising therefore that in Stalinism history is not considered a 'withdrawal from the present'. On the contrary, it is turned into the most topical possible occupation. In the second half of the 1930s, the situation which had taken shape in the previous decade, when there existed 'various scholastic theories about the withdrawal of almost all historical novelists from contemporary life', was sharply criticised. Now it seemed that, for example, Chapygin's *Razin* bore witness precisely not to a 'withdrawal', but to the writer's 'proximity to revolutionary reality'.[18] The same proved to be true not only for a novel about a popular uprising, but also for a novel about . . . a tsar. As has now been firmly established, 'A. Tolstoy's *Peter* was born not of withdrawal, but of the author's proximity, his rapprochement with the revolutionary present.'[19] Such is the 'historical dialectic' of Stalinism, for which temporalisation is not even needed. Here the weather is simultaneously good and bad. Here the historical hero is progressive and reactionary at the same time. Here 'withdrawal into history' and 'entrance into the present' are one and the same thing. In this world the waves of the dialectic roll off each other without washing away the sand or cancelling out anything. Here 'negation' does not 'negate', but coexists. This dialectic, which knows no development, is fit only for Stalinist logicality, building up a certain 'synthesis', a 'sense of the historical past'.

Thesis . . .

The first Russian feature film, released on 15 October 1908, was the 'historical drama', *Stenka Razin*. The movie was in complete conformity with the general tendency of the birth of the cinema in different countries. The first films were part of mass culture, which not only was a reflection of the basic features of the national character and national mythology, but also found a lively response from the viewer from the masses, be that to the fairytale plays and comedies of Louis Lumière's *Watering the Gardener* (*L'Arroseur arrosé*), the first French film; to the technically innovative and genre-creating first American film, *The Great Train Robbery*, by Edwin Porter; to *The Last Days of Pompeii* and other pompous historical productions by Arturo Ambrosio, the first Italian films. But rather than a fairytale comedy, a technical action movie or a grandiose historical show, it was a historical melodrama which began the history of Russian cinema, the screening of a national legend, at the centre of which lay the victory of the collective principle, of the ideals of the Cossack outlaws and the 'fraternity of the simple people' – the paradigmatic features of the 'Russian national character' which was distinctively refracted later in Soviet cinema.[20]

At the heart of *Stenka Razin* lay a famous folk song about a Cossack *ataman* who fell in love with a Persian princess and then, suspecting her of betrayal, drowned her in a river. At the centre of the plot is a 'band of robbers' making merry with their *ataman*. His love for the foreign princess places his fidelity to the 'Cossack brotherhood' in doubt. A conspiracy brews. They accuse the princess of betrayal (although the authority of the *ataman* is not placed in doubt). They make him tipsy and give him a forged letter, in which the princess makes a declaration of love to her beloved Persian prince, Hasan. In rage and to the rejoicing of the 'gang', the *ataman* throws the Persian princess in the river, which had to signify the triumph over passion and a full return to the 'men's brotherhood' and the 'struggle for freedom'.

The song about how Stepan Timofeevich Razin sailed in decorated boats 'from the island to the channel' remains to this day one of the most popular in Russia. Thousands of pages of books, articles and textbooks have been written on the uprising under Razin's leadership. Great popularity was enjoyed by three long novels written about him in Soviet times – Alexey Chapygin's *Razin Stepan*

(1926–7; the 1939 film *Stepan Razin* was based on this); Stepan Zlobin's *Stepan Razin* (1951, for which the author received the Stalin prize in that year); and, finally, Vasily Shukshin's 1971 novel, *I Came to Give you Freedom* (*Ia prishel dat' vam voliu*), from which he also hoped to produce a film.

The popular epic preserved the image of Razin as 'brooding about the poor' and 'not bowing down to the rich'. Before the Revolution Stenka Razin was called none other than a 'thief', a brigand, the ringleader of bandits, robbers and murderers who were gathering under the banner of this Don Cossack drunkard and boor, who proclaimed himself not only the people's leader-*ataman*, but also the 'head of the personal guard of Tsar Alexei Mikhailovich and Tsarevich Alexei'; but Soviet historiography turned him into the 'people's hero-protector', the brave 'leader of the popular masses', full of 'unbending faith in the justice of the popular cause'.

Depicting 'the peasant uprising under the leadership of Stepan Razin', Soviet historiography was not in a position to answer the question of against whom the Cossacks were 'rising', as they had always been free people, were not involved in agriculture, lived by raids, robbery and warfare, had self-government and were not subject to the power of the Tsar in the seventeenth century. It was also unclear against what they were waging war. According to the Soviet interpretation, it was 'for the freedom of the serfs', who ran away in large numbers from central Russia to join the Cossacks. It is known, however, that the conflict actually arose from a run-of-the-mill robbery; it began with the capture of a convoy of ships belonging to the Tsar, the patriarchy and rich merchants in 1667. After pillaging, Razin travelled down the Volga to Persia, whence he returned with rich spoils. On his return he plundered the Volga and the Don, devastating and pillaging settlements, towns and monasteries on his way. His 'army' (in essence, a band of robbers) grew from little gangs, runaway serfs, bonded slaves and convicts, vagrants, Chuvash, Tatars and the like. The geography and speed of the uprising were explained by the pressure and dissatisfaction on the side of the forever growing 'popular masses', who envied Razin's booty and were greedy for their own share. As a result, Razin moved up the Volga, but after defeat at Simbirsk was seized by 'rich Cossacks' and brought to Moscow, where in 1671 he was put to death near the Place of Execution in Red Square.

Razin proved to be not only the successful leader of an ill-assorted brigand army, but also a popular hero who was turned by his death on the scaffold into a martyr. The real Razin was in fact born to a rich family of 'loyal' Cossacks. We know that he was a heavy drinker, unbelievably coarse, and actively participated in fisticuffs. The wild debaucheries and reckless drunken merriment of the *Razintsy* and the *ataman* himself became part of the myth, as did the brutal means of conducting battles used by Razin and his captains, the savagery and criminal habits of the Cossack outlaws, who were involved in looting, robbery, rape and murder. In the Soviet interpretation all this was painted as 'class struggle', the actions of the *Razintsy* were declared to be a 'peasant war against the feudal order', and Razin himself was 'an outstanding organiser of the popular masses and a talented military leader'. Although it was admitted that 'Razin did not have a clear political programme' and 'shared the tsarist illusions of the peasantry', this did not stop him becoming, according to Lenin's definition, one of the 'champions of the mutinous peasantry, [who] laid down his life in the struggle for freedom'. The Razin myth placed the gloomy atmosphere of 'tsarist-*boyar* Moscow' in opposition to the 'revolutionary element', the oppressed people and the noble visage of the revolutionary hero – the young, handsome, freedom-loving and strong *ataman*; it opposed execution and torture with the humanism of the 'leader of the people' and the fearlessness of the broad mass of insurgents. This was how Razin would remain in popular memory.

Soviet cinema actively worked with this 'memory', forming it and not simply preserving this or that character, but carefully selecting and transforming them to conform with the required picture of the past (of the so-called 'historical truth'). It is interesting that, even in Pokrovsky, for all his class rigour, the 'popular uprisings' of the seventeenth and eighteenth centuries did not at all enjoy support. In the second half of the 1930s, with the creation of a whole series of films about peasant uprisings and their leaders, the picture began to change. On screen there appeared one after the other Pavel Petrov-Bytov's *Pugachev* (1937), Mikhail Chiaureli's *Arsen* (1937), Georgy Tasin's *Karmeliuk* (1939), Ivan Pravov and Olga Preobrazhenskaya's *Stepan Razin* (1939) and Yakov Protazanov's *Salavat Iulaev* (1940). They 'reflected' (that is, created) the picture of the 'revolutionary struggle of the peasant masses'. The repudiation of Pokrovsky led to class uprisings being turned into national uprisings, but their leaders lacked many of the 'conflicts of class interests' that had earlier been ascribed to them.

The story of Razin is paradigmatic. All these uprisings differed in Soviet art in terms of time, names of characters, 'social basis', geography and changes of tsar (be it Alexei Mikhailovich or Catherine II), but preserved their familiar schema: the oppressed people (who have strength, beauty and the love of peace on their side), the oppressors (caricature-ugly, flabby, displaying a slavish mentality, savage malice and craftiness) and a popular leader (all thoughts of the people, freedom and the radiant future), with obligatory attributes – the hero's wife and children, torture chambers, conspirator-traitors and the death of the 'people's defender' on the scaffold, preceded by his passionate monologue, addressed to the people who have grown dumb in sorrow and anger.

In the depiction of the people in films about peasant uprisings (here I will dwell on only two: Pravov and Preobrazhenskaya's *Stepan Razin* and Petrov-Bytov's *Pugachev*), it is not only the appearance of the 'people' which attracts attention – the emaciated faces of the convicts in stocks, the hard-labour convicts shackled in fetters, the exhausted look of the peasants and the serfs dressed in unbelievable rags, and so on – but above all the status of the 'popular leader', who is here a 'champion of the people' and spokesman for their aspirations. The fact that the '*atamans*' belonged to the Cossack 'bosses' is in general not mentioned. It was sufficient for Razin to come from a 'Cossack circle' and, addressing the 'poor of the Don' and the 'runaway peasants', to declare, 'Your sorrows are my sorrows' and 'We will achieve a free life. The land will be ours – Cossacks', peasants'!' for everyone to go over to his side, while on his opponent's side – the chief Cossack *ataman* Kornei – there was nobody left. This creates the impression that among the 'Cossack outlaws' everything was truly decided by the 'poor folk of the Don' and the 'runaway peasants', whilst the idea that the land can be 'ours' – belonging to the 'Cossacks' and the 'peasants' simultaneously – suggests an absence of difference between the Cossacks and peasants. (The very Razin uprising was qualified in Soviet historiography as 'Cossack-peasant' – an oxymoron similar to the 'feudal-bourgeois revolution'.) At another stage, after the seizure of Astrakhan, Razin addresses the 'people' with the promise that the 'urban poor will till the *boyars*' land for themselves'. This erosion of class boundaries was the first sign of the repudiation of the class approach. If 'Cossacks' and 'peasants' are the same thing, if there is no boundary between the 'urban poor' (which has to suggest 'poor artisans') and 'peasants', then society is divided not into classes but into two unequal groups: the hated oppressors (who in *Pugachev* all speak Russian with pronounced German accents) and the ennobled oppressed. (Thus, for the role of Razin an actor from the Maly Theatre was chosen who had emphatically noble features and correct pronunciation; this was Andrei Abrikosov, who subsequently took on the roles of Gavrila Oleksich in *Alexander Nevsky* and Fyodor Kolychev/Metropolitan Philip in *Ivan the Terrible*, both by Eisenstein.)

One can say that the fundamental aim of the representation of the so-called 'peasant wars' in Stalinist cinema is to erase class differences between the Cossacks and the peasantry. Just as in *Razin* it is always emphasised that the hero is '*ataman* to the runaway serfs', so in *Pugachev* the fact that the hero belongs to the 'Cossack upper class' is constantly glossed over, and on the contrary it is constantly emphasised that he is the 'tsar of the common people and peasant farmers', that he, 'the peasant tsar, gathered together a 100,000-strong army of insurgents'. Pugachev himself addressed 'the people' with an appeal to join battle for 'our free land, gained with our own blood'. In *Razin*, Stepan, after the pillaging of the Persian campaign, declares that 'the campaign [against Persia – E. D.] began to find the truth'. And now 'we will go through Russia with fire, and find the truth!'

Even the 'Persian princess', it turns out, is entangled in this 'search for the truth'. The scene of her famous drowning appears thus. After an argument about who will win her, Stepan addresses his captains, who unanimously reply, 'She's yours!' 'Mine?' cries Razin. 'Well, alright then! More than anything I love you, Mother Volga. Accept a gift from the Don Cossacks!' And he throws the princess, who, it seems, has sunk in a semi-conscious state in his embraces, overboard. 'Did you think I'd trade you for a woman?' he says to the *atamans*. 'No! We'll blaze with fire throughout Rus'. Not with robbery, but mutiny! Let's smash the *boyars* and install our own, peasant, Cossack truth in Rus'!' And thus for the entire duration of the film, Razin addresses both the inhabitants of seized towns and his own forces with appeals such as: 'Forward to freedom! For a free life!'; 'Fight for the dependent people!'; 'March on Moscow – burn the deeds of enslavement!' and so on. Even the songs in *Pugachev* and *Razin* sound neither sad nor daring; they are not about famous princesses thrown overboard, but rather speak of 'the people's anger' with the refrain: 'We will win our freedom and tear out the *voevody* at their roots.' Where exactly the Cossacks are here, the peasants, the *streltsy* or the landowners, is impossible to say definitely.

Soviet art of the second half of the 1930s returns to the era of pre-Marxist 'sociology'. Social history is turned before one's eyes into national history. When the history of classes, social groupings and political-economic structures is taken out of it, the operative concept became not 'class' but 'the people': that is, strictly speaking, 'the nation'. The ethnic aspect of this 'nation' is also extremely important; 'the people' includes the oppressed of all ethnic groups of that time in Russia/USSR (besides Cossacks and Russians, Bashkirs, Tatars, Kalmyk, Chuvash, Mordvinians, Mari, Kazaks and Kirghiz took part in uprisings), whilst the Germans and the French represented the camp of the oppressors. This ethnic moment allows understanding of the specifics of the nation being modelled. Its locus – the 'motherland' – constitutes the main difference between Stalinist patriotic culture and revolutionary culture. Possessing a higher legitimising power, this concept is constructed within Stalinist culture with particular care.

The status of the 'peasant uprising' constitutes a particular problem. On the one hand, it was 'spontaneous' (although that condemned it to defeat); on the other, it demanded a certain dose of 'consciousness' (after all, this is a 'peasant uprising' or even a 'war', and not a 'revolt'). Meanwhile, 'distortions' took place continually, which served as a basis for criticism. The way in which the uprising is represented in *Stepan Razin*, wrote one critic, means that it can be perceived as 'not an uprising at all, but robbery on the high road, a thieves' attack by bandits and lovers of profit'. In the film 'you hear quite enough foul language, but do not see any difference between Stepan Razin and any Volga river pirate (*ushkuiniki*).'[21]

Maintaining a balance in the consciousness of the leader of the uprising and his followers was also required. The focus of criticism was therefore that Razin himself was too conscious, whilst the *Razintsy* lacked consciousness:

> Razin alone suddenly begins to understand that the Russian people are demanding from the renowned *ataman* a great deed. A meeting of the people in Astrakhan reveals this to him. Well, and the *Razintsy* themselves? What are they thinking about? Apparently, nothing. In the best case they are staying silent and obediently following their *ataman*. How can a popular movement be portrayed like that! How can the *Razintsy* be depicted like that, when, if not all, then many of them were spokesmen of the thoughts and will of the people, and organisers of their assault![22]

The leader proves to have been torn away from the *Razintsy* who are known to him, who in their turn themselves take up the role of the avant-garde of the 'popular masses' (in the manner of the party).

In *Pugachev* matters turned out to be even more complicated. For some, Pugachev seemed too conscious – almost a revolutionary. (Viktor Shklovsky ironically said that in the film he was playing the role of Commissar Furmanov.[23]) For others, on the contrary, he was too spontaneous, and the film itself was 'oversimplified':

> The absence in parts of Pugachev's army of a single clear notion of what they must achieve should not have prevented the filmmakers seeing in the peasant movement a mature political idea, and in Pugachev himself the range not only of the daring, formidable and 'adroit', but also of the statesman. But this (the main thing!) is decidedly not in the film! The guides and leaders of the people appear in the main with a sort of unreal, 'hail-fellow-well-met'-type manner.[24]

The fine balance of the socialist-realist dialectic of spontaneity and consciousness was not subject to articulation. When there was discussion of how to depict peasant uprisings and their leaders, critics appealed to . . . the epic:

> The people in songs and folktales have always held dear to them the image of Stepan Timofeevich Razin, who, before he began the struggle, was a long time in giving birth to the great idea. In songs it is said that Stepan's idea is kept by the cliffs on the Volga. And there is the profound thought that the people along the whole of the middle and lower reaches of the Volga call their cliffs, hills and burial mounds by the name Stepan. Hundreds of them, the tallest and most beautiful, climbing above the valley of the great Russian river, recall the fact that Stepan's thoughts and deeds are the thoughts and deeds of all working people, all the poor, all those injured in the past by social injustice, all those who in a profound way gave birth to a dream of a happy life for the people and fought for it.[25]

This is the mystical-vague 'image of the popular hero' that the critic wanted to see revealed in the film.

The release of *Razin* was preceded by crushing reviews (including one in *Pravda*). The film was called 'quasi-operatic' and 'pseudo-patriotic'. Shklovsky noted, apropos of this, that 'between the *Razintsy* and the view you sense there is an invisible orchestra, because the whole thing is an opera.'[26] Pudovkin came to the defence of the picture. He justified its 'operatic' nature with the fact that the director, 'creating the film, gave himself the aim of communicating historical events and the image of Razin as they are reflected in popular songs . . . and folklore'.[27] Pudovkin explained the particularly criticised scene with the Persian princess by suggesting that, although 'this story is almost certainly a fabrication', 'the deepest idea of this poetic fabrication' consists in the fact that it 'in simple, clear and perhaps even naïve form gives the artistic image of a man who, without a moment's doubt, sacrifices his personal happiness for the common good.'[28]

Pudovkin develops the theme of 'naivety' further:

> [T]he naivety and credulity of Razin, who does not see enemies in the peasant army, are not features of this character alone. All the people with whom Razin comes into contact are infected with credulity. It is the same spontaneity and disorganisation characteristic of historical conditions of that time. This, it would seem, is the pivotal meaning of Stepan Razin's personal naivety.[29]

Translating from the language of 1938, Razin's 'naivety' signified the 'irresponsibility of leaders' who did not see 'enemies who had wormed their way into their confidence'.

By explaining everything with the logic of the class struggle and economic interest, Marxism deprives history of intrigue. Two things could impart historical narrative with a plot: conspiracy and melodrama. In the situation in the second half of the 1930s, when conspiracies were being discussed in practically every paper, the historical film intensively exploited mass paranoia – the morbid interest in conspiracies and the susceptibility of mass consciousness to the conspiratorial view of political events. In *Pugachev*, as in *Razin*, conspiracy plays a key role in the development of the action. Both films begin and end in torture chambers. *Razin* opens with the scene of the death of the hero's brother under torture, with his verbal testament to his brother Stepan: 'There will be no life on earth, if we do not seize it from the *boyars* and *voevody*.' The film ends with the interrogation under torture of Razin, wounded on the field of battle, by the traitor Fyodor Shpyn, who betrays him more than once, but whom the 'naïve' Razin forgives and admits on to his staff.

The same story is repeated in Pugachev as well, in the headquarters where the traitor hides and the conspiracy ripens. As a result the insurgent army ends up surrounded by tsarist forces, and in the end Pugachev himself, like Razin, is handed over to the Tsar by 'rich Cossacks', which is the logical conclusion of a plot constructed from beginning to end on a conspiracy. *Pugachev* opens with a caption informing the reader that Catherine II came to power as the result of a conspiracy – the murder of Peter III. In the very first scene in the prison, in which Pugachev appears, in response to a call to escape, he says: 'It's not escaping that's needed, it's knowing who to go with.' This enigmatic remark is then explained: 'for tsar Peter III. He is alive and wants to give the land to the peasants'. Having witnessed a riot in the prison, Pugachev, like Lenin in Romm's film *Lenin in October* (*Lenin v Oktiabre*), says to the camera: 'It's time to begin.' There later follows a scene with the Cossack *atamans*, who have gathered a treasury and an army for Pugachev, so that he can proclaim himself tsar: 'We have decided on our own tsar to stand in the place of the tsarina,' the Cossack *atamans* say to Pugachev. Pugachev does not understand why this charade is necessary. His aims are quite different: 'The down-trodden poor have tired of waiting. The *boyars* have strangled the people', he says. (It is not clear from this why the *atamans* start to wage war for the sake of the 'down-trodden poor'.) His ways of achieving his aims are also different: 'We can achieve our freedom without the tsar's throne.' (Here Pugachev does not define precisely whose 'freedom' he intends to achieve.) The conflict with the conspirators is marked out from the very start. It is concluded with the plot by the Cossack colonels, who decide to give Pugachev up to the authorities. His last words at liberty are: 'Traitors! You want to buy your lives with my head.' As repositories of evil, the *atamans* in both films are deprived of any kind of individuality. (Shklovsky notes apropos of this that the Cossack colonels do not have roles or characters: 'they are distinguished from each other only by their beards.'[30]) The heroes have no 'roles or characters' either, although both of them, wounded but not broken, die just like Chapaev.

The Chapaevan revolutionary impulse is hardened into the operatic poses of the heroes of these historical films. Thus ten years after the publication of Alexei Chapygin's book, a critic wrote that:

> [I]n the pages of the novel Razin acts as a decisive defender of the lower orders of the peasantry and the Cossacks, as the real hero of a peasant uprising, shaking the gentry's serf-based state . . . Razin's prophecies were imbued with a profound faith that the battle they had begun would in the end be crowned with victory, that there would come a time, and in the ruins of the nobles' empire there would take shape a new, free life, when the people would be liberated from slavery.[31]

And although Chapygin's contribution was interpreted as 'directly combat-[ting] the Menshevik interpretation of the role of the peasantry in the history of the class struggle',[32] the novel was the product of a totally different era, and that is why Razin in the novel was in any case far from sugar-coated (which of course did not stop Chapygin modernising his hero, making him godless and tsar-hating, both impossible in the seventeenth century). At the end of the novel Razin directly foretells the Soviet epoch:

> Cut me to shreds, don't waver! You won't be able to extinguish the fire over the whole of Rus' – not by water, not by blood. And from that fire, tsar's devils, sooner or later, I don't know, but your end will come! Every folktale, every song on the river Volga will tell that I am alive . . . and will come again! I will come to tear to pieces all the tsar's deeds, to throw off bondage from the poor, and to tear off your heads, big-bellied devils! I will fling those heads of yours together with the tsar into the Moscow river, you swine![33]

What distinguishes this Razin from the film hero, created from a screenplay by the same Chapygin, is his speech. (It is known that Razin was terribly foul-mouthed.) In the novel he speaks in such a way that the *voevoda* torturing him, coming out of the torture chamber, is distressed: 'Ugh, what a sweat! He's not a man! He's Satan! That's barking, not words! I can't show His Majesty this interrogation report – I should burn it!'[34]

The screen Razin answers the question of the *boyar* torturing him about buried treasure and treasure houses with a monologue: 'The treasure is not in the earth. It is on the earth. The treasure is the whole of the Russian people. You won't extinguish the fire throughout Rus' with blood or water! The people will rip your heads off!' From the dais before his execution he addresses the weeping people who have filled Red Square with the words: 'Forgive me, people of Russia! I came for you! Don't forget me, good people!' In response the crowd answers resoundingly: 'We won't forget!' At the end of *Pugachev* this scene is repeated. This time Pugachev, with candles in his hands, addresses the crowd and his executioners with the words: 'You cannot force the people to be silent! They will again gather strength! Do not submit, my friends!' And, as if in reply, his wife exhorts her son, 'Remember this, son!'

The other salvation from the all-explaining 'class conflicts' of Marxist narrative was melodrama. It is interesting that, although the families of the heroes play important roles in the plots of both films, they are not the focus of the heroes' interest. In *Razin*, the hero's wife Alyona appears with her child before the viewer immediately after the scene with the Princess, with whom Razin, we must suggest, has betrayed his wife. Then for some reason she turns up in besieged Astrakhan and dies under torture. For all this, in both *Razin* and *Pugachev* the wives display qualities that are indeed heroic, begging their husbands to take them with them and remaining faithful to them to the last moment. Not so with the men. Pugachev, like Razin, having found his Princess, is transformed into a 'tsar', marries anew and, settling down with his 'Tsarina' (with a living wife and three children), maintains his loyalty to both spouses. But his real wife ends up, of course, in the *boyars'* torture chambers, and at the end of the film she is present at the execution of her bigamist husband, maintaining her fidelity to him.

But the main problem is that these films do not support a positive image of power. Tsar Alexei Mikhailovich appears at the very end of *Razin*, as if in answer to the enumeration of the ever-growing number of new 'peasant uprisings' blazing throughout Rus' (here someone is 'stirring up the people', there 'the mob is agitating,' 'arson' here, 'rebellion' there and so on) to declare: 'Serfs seek the truth. There is no serfs' truth! There should not be!' Catherine II appears at the very end of *Pugachev* to demand that her retinue 'catch the thief'. The astonishing similarity of the ends of both films is emphasised in the final scene of the execution of the hero by the use of the same scenery of Red Square, the Kremlin and the Place of Execution; Pugachev pronounces his passionate monologue before the silenced people on the very same spot where a hundred years before him Razin pronounced his (and where 150 years later Stalin would pronounce his 'Vow' in Chiaureli's film).

One can say that the 'people' are always right, while authority (in the person of the tsar) is less consistent; if Alexei Mikhailovich or Catherine II did not possess historical legitimacy, then Peter the Great, Georgy Saakadze or Ivan the Terrible were, on the contrary, 'historically progressive'. The 'tsarist theme' in Soviet historical film appears simultaneously with the theme of 'the people'; *Peter the First* came out in 1937, the same year as *Pugachev*. Moreover, this is not an equation of valency in which both pictures must 'counterbalance' the new historical construction. The 'tsar series' (to which was also attached a series of films about 'great Russian military leaders') was to be perceived as a kind of antithesis of the 'people' theme. Therefore films about the leaders of 'popular uprisings' were appraised from this 'tsarist' perspective:

> The release of a film like *Pugachev* even two years ago might have been assessed as a positive phenomenon. Now, after the significant achievements of our cinematography in work on historical themes, after the release by the very same Lenfilm of the first part of *Peter the First*, a picture which is correctly selecting the path of the development of the Soviet historical film, *Pugachev* cannot be spoken of as a new success in the development of the historical genre.[35]

A real 'positive synthesis' had to be born from precisely these 'significant achievements'. If not for the specifics of the Stalinist dialectic, in which the 'law of the negation of the negation', demonstrably not referred to by Stalin in the *Short Course*, was revoked.

ANTITHESIS . . .

In the preparations for the film *Peter the First* (*Petr pervyi*), the greatest problem proved to be the search for an actor to take on the role of Peter. Nikolai Simonov, who eventually played him in the film, was fifteenth on the list of candidates for the role, but made it after a screen test. The actor was good in every way except one; externally he did not resemble a single one of the twenty-five known representations of Peter. And then Alexei Tolstoy said: 'If Simonov plays Peter, it is he who will be remembered – he will be the twenty-sixth, most famous portrait of the great reformer.'[36] An experienced writer and courtier, Tolstoy was proved correct; Peter has remained in mass consciousness exactly as he appeared on screen. But the twenty-sixth portrait of Peter was above all an ideological construct; for all his external dissimilarity, he was ideally cut out according to the ideological template of the second half of the 1930s.

Of all the characters in the Stalinist historical masquerade, Peter was undoubtedly the most incontrovertible figure. He is not a mythologised, prehistoric, semi-legendary, epic, saintly Alexander Nevsky; nor is he an Ivan the

Terrible, controversial from the point of view of the historic consequences of his reign; nor a David Bek (Amo Bek-Nazarov's *David Bek* was released in 1944), who in the eighteenth century raised the Armenians (with the help of the Russian army) to an uprising against the Persians and 'liberated Armenia' in such a way that it became part of Russia; nor yet a Georgy Saakadze (Mikhail Chiaureli's *Georgy Saakadze* was produced in 1942–3), who, in the 'battle for the unification of Georgia' in the seventeenth century, on the contrary, led the Persian army, ravaging the country. As distinct from these important characters from national history, Peter the Great alone proved to be the 'father' of the nation, the figure from whom we begin to count the New Era in the history of Russia.

This factor turned the film about Peter (beginning production in 1935, it became, essentially, the first historical film of the Stalin period) into a kind of 'birth of the nation' epic, which the director himself understood very well, asserting that, 'the historical alteration of features of the national character, the enrichment and development of its best qualities, the forming of the psychological mentality of the people especially powerfully proclaims itself and reveals itself at critical turning points,'[37] to which the Petrine reign is related. One could say that without the historicising art of the 1930s the birth of the Soviet nation would have been impossible. Films like *Peter* depicted not only the 'historical perspective', but also a 'genetic picture' of the new Soviet nation. Peter's 'young Russia' and Stalin's 'industrialised Russia' entered into dialogue, about which Alexei Tolstoy said: 'In spite of their difference in aims, Peter's epoch and ours have in common a kind of riotous power, with explosions of human energy and will.'[38] Attained by Peter through 'inevitable sacrifice', 'the greatness of our Fatherland' – as a higher value – was directly projected on to the Stalinist industrial revolution and ideological campaign to reinforce the 'greatness' of the new, Soviet Fatherland. The audience received in the film a screen for the projection of a new identity – of the very same Other, through whom the 'time connection' was renewed; in the film not only was Peter's epoch 'brought up to date', but the Soviet viewer himself was 'historicised', receiving all the capacity and density of the past and historical dimension.

Peter has remained one of the most contradictory figures in Russian history, and as such was found at the crossroads of the geopolitical self-positioning of the new 'Soviet Fatherland'. On the one hand, Peter had a revolutionary-industrialising Western impulse, which was close to early Stalinism; on the other, Peter-the-conqueror, the 'gatherer of lands' and creator of the regular Russian army, fitted in well with the political realities of the end of the 1930s. Having spent the whole of his life writing about Peter, Alexei Tolstoy was constantly shifting in his assessment of the Tsar – from exclusively negative in 1916–18, 1921 and 1928, in *The Delusion (Navazhdenie)*, *Peter's Day (Den' Petra)*, *The First Terrorists (Pervye terroristy)* and the play *On the Rack (Na dybe)*; to positive, in the novel *Peter the First*; and then, in the screenplay and film, to an apologia; and finally, in the last editions of his play about Peter, to idealisation.

Official doctrine, although much less interested in Peter-the-revolutionary and much more enthusiastic about 'State-building', was moving in the same direction (although from the opposite end). The meeting point was the middle of the 1930s; a pure product of the rejection of Pokrovsky – the new Peter – appeared on screen. It is worth noting, however, that Tolstoy the novelist and Tolstoy the screenwriter were working with different materials; the novel ends with the 'defeat of Narva', while the film only begins at this point.[39] This is one of the rare occasions when the writer does not screen the novel itself, but 'adds' its sequel with the screenplay and film, the course of working on new material in fact changing his conception of the hero. Comparing the novel and film, R. Messer wrote: 'In the film the historical-biographical motifs have fallen away and at the forefront is placed the civic idea of the significance of Peter's deeds for the creation of the might of the Russian State.'[40] Viktor Shklovsky, who moved in the same ideological vector as Tolstoy (but from the opposing side), noted that in the novel and film 'we have before us not so much an analysis of the Petrine era as an apologia for Peter. With such an understanding of history, we are obliterating time!'[41]

In this new Peter the image which had lived in Russian historiography for the preceding two centuries (including in the Marxist tradition) died. The new historicism of the authors of the film was immediately detected by film critics, who wrote that *Peter the First* 'is a film of great historical truthfulness', becoming 'a new stimulus to the development of historical science and historical art', and even 'outstripping historical science' in so far as it rejects the 'anti-historical conception of the Pokrovsky school' and 'placed it in opposition to the correct understanding of the progressive role of Peter in Russian history'.[42] At this point *Pravda* wrote:

> Not a degenerate and not a reckless playboy, as Peter has been portrayed many times, and not a blind 'instrument of commercial capital', as he has been presented in the writings of vulgar-sociological 'historians', but the genuinely great personality of that epoch, and it was that very epoch that the makers of the film *Peter I* intended to show.[43]

Simonov himself, having played Peter, said: 'We decided to create the image not of a sickly degenerate of the imperial family, not of debauchery and drunkenness, as Peter has often been portrayed, but of the most powerful public figure and reformer of his epoch.'[44] The recurring theme of the 'degenerate' came from Pokrovsky. Now features of 'sickly degeneracy' by inheritance were given to . . . Peter's son, Alexei. Interestingly, Pudovkin, appearing at a discussion of part two of the picture at the *Dom kino* and admiring Cherkasov's work on the image of Alexei, also called Peter's son 'this degenerate'.[45]

Alexei in the film is not only a degenerate and 'feeble-minded', but also a truly infernal villain and traitor to the State. History, understood as a conspiracy, dictated its 'historically correct' plot. The conspiracy ripens in part one of the film, and in part two the action is based completely on this. Here on the one hand are operating internal enemies – obscurantists, hysterical religious women, holy fools, who see the antichrist in the Tsar, and *boyars*, who are against the reforms because of their own privileged positions and desires not to have to pay in to the treasury to support Peter's reforms and wars, and see their salvation in Alexei. On the other hand, there are external enemies – that is, Europe (England, France, Sweden, the Roman monarchy) – who do not wish to see Russia strengthened. The internal enemy joins up with the external; the conspiracy ripens by attracting foreign armies, spies and traitors to the State. Again the torture chambers appear – as familiar in the seventeenth century (by 'analogy with the present') as in 1937 (the year in which part one of the film was screened) – as the environment of the 'nation-building'.

It is not surprising, therefore, that in the film Peter is presented primarily as a warrior. Battles begin and end every part of the film. The film opens with Peter's words, 'The war has only just begun,' and ends with the sea battle and final victory over the Swedes and celebration of the 'eternal peace' of the treaty of Nystad. But when military aims are relegated to second place, Tolstoy turns Peter into a merchant, a manufacturer, a capitalist, lessening and removing into the background in every possible way the 'serfdom aspect' of Peter's reforms. Thus Peter appeared in the novel (the first volume of which came out in 1930, the second in 1934). This was still a time when Pokrovsky's conception dominated Soviet historiography.

Pokrovsky's idea of 'trade capitalism' came to take the place of the traditional conception, according to which Russia in the seventeenth century experienced feudalism. Legitimisation of the 'proletarian revolution' urgently demanded a 'proletariat' (preferably 'mature') and the 'capitalism' which gave rise to it, but in so far as it first arrived in the 1860s, after the abolition of serfdom, it was too late. Thus the special 'social-economic structure' introduced by Pokrovsky, 'trade capitalism', with the merchants as an advancing power in the socio-political life of the country, beginning in the seventeenth century, became generally accepted. In Tolstoy's novel, where the idea is advanced that as far back as the sixteenth century politics were defined by the tsars as 'the interests of the arising trade capital', Pokrovsky's conception is perfectly distinct. One should not think, however, that this conception was completely alien to Stalinism. Only some of its implications were unacceptable, but the conception itself is alive in the film. The attempt to make Peter into the father of the Russian bourgeoisie (and he invariably appears in the film surrounded by the 'third estate', while the *boyars* are always presented satirically), and not the monarch of the feudal state and empire of the gentry, had the aim of turning him into a kind of Russian Napoleon. In this projection the Bolsheviks were acting not simply as modernisers of the country, but – as real socialists, in any case – as legitimate heirs of his bourgeois reforms.

This ideological capital (the 'analogy with the present') had its price. The rejection of Pokrovsky signified rejection not only of the tradition of assessing the character of Peter, but also of sociological analysis; in the film, there is simply no class criticism levelled at tsarism at all. The film can be viewed as an apologia for tsarism. The historical conflict which was earlier seen in the 'class struggle' is here transferred into the plot, psychologised and personalised. It acquired not class, but national dimensions; precisely the 'cinematographic scenes of the conflict between Peter and Alexei consolidated in mass consciousness the perception of it as the confrontation of old and new Russia.'[46] The 'tsarist' series and the 'people's' series existed, it would seem, in different ideological realities; the focus of one was the 'State', while the focus of the other was the 'people'. But in so far as both the one and the other were only ideological constructs (and this State of course was nothing like that depicted in *Peter*; this people was nothing like that conveyed to the audience of *Pugachev*), they proved to be correlated on the level of the already familiar 'historical dialectic'. In the film there is no opposition between the Tsar and the people. The sources of the people's misery are revealed quite plainly – not autocracy at all, but inert villain-*boyars*, thieving governors and *voevody*, blood-drinking factory owners and embezzling bureaucrats. He addresses them with the threatening, 'You have grown fat! I will not give you any peace!', but immediately forgives his closest friend Menshikov, who has stolen two and a half million from the State treasury. The adventurism, embezzling and bribe-taking of Peter's 'finest' are shown to be humorously smoothed over thanks to Mikhail Zharov, who was chosen for this role.

The story of the serf Fedka is a very good example of the parallel existence of two apparently different pictures of the past. Beaten by his master and running away from him, becoming a soldier and being sent into hard labour, almost dying in Demidov's mines and finally escaping to the Don and becoming an *ataman* of the Cossack outlaws, he not only does not rise up against Peter, but also gives up the envoy from the *boyars*, who had been dispatched by Tsarevich Alexei and incited to rise up against the Tsar, to the crowd to be torn apart. He did not 'forgive his master'; he intended to 'achieve the truth', but in this proves to be completely the opposite of Razin and Pugachev. Interestingly, the Razin theme arises several times in Peter; moreover, it sounds quite neutral, as the theme of the 'glorious past of the people'. The operatic *Stepan Razin*, released simultaneously with part two of *Peter*, fully conformed to the goal of the museumisation of the 'history of the people'.

The Tsar absorbs the people into himself. He is himself the embodiment of the 'national character'; deprived of any subtlety (which is given in abundance to his son Alexei), Peter is as straightforward as a peasant, as strong as a *bogatyr*, as spirited as the people. He does everything himself – he shoots and measures his strength against recruits, quarrels with peasants and leads soldiers into attack, storms a fortress under fire, works in a smithy and trades with foreign merchants, saves people during a flood and works as a river pilot. His infectious laughter, his open smile, the simplicity of his behaviour, his coarse practical jokes, the people around him – simple sailors, soldiers, blacksmiths and merchants – make him a real 'representative of the people'. And the people respond to him with love; crowds stand devotedly in front of his palace when Peter is ill and greet him enthusiastically wherever he appears. Such a tsar does not need the people. He is the people himself. The tsar becomes the incarnation of the people.

Even Peter's speech fully corresponds to the current political rhetoric of 1939. The screen Peter declares to the Roman ambassador (on the very eve of the signing of the Molotov-von Ribbentrop pact): 'Not for war, but for ever-lasting peace have we returned to our ancient Baltic ancestral lands.' Addressing the members of the Senate before his son's death sentence, he accuses him of betraying the State in almost the exact same words which filled the newspapers during the Moscow show-trials: 'European states hate us and are endeavouring to return us to our old, base way of living, and divide us into provinces and principalities.' Similar invective was directed at the leaders of the opposition, who were 'selling the Motherland lock, stock and barrel' and 'trying to return power to the landowners and capitalists' by Stalin's General Prosecutor, Vyshinsky. A kind of paraphrase of the popular proverb from the era of mass terror, 'when the wood's felled, the chips fly,' is put into Peter's mouth: 'It was broadly intended. There was no time to feel pity.'

But all the same, Peter's 'modernisation' consisted not in the fact that he uttered these words that were necessary in 1939, but in the fact that, in essence, he is acting here not so much like a tsar as like a leader. The tsar is legitimised through supra-social powers, whilst Peter demonstratively rejects dependence on them – he slighted both the church (and in doing so disregards his own divine legitimacy) and the *boyars* and nobility (to all intents and purposes undermining the basis of his legitimacy in tradition and the past). He is established as the expression and embodiment of the interests of the people, the executor of the historical will. 'For the Fatherland I will not spare my own life,' he says to his son. Appealing to his troops before the Battle of Poltava, Peter says: 'Do not think that you are fighting for Peter, you're fighting for the State entrusted to Peter.' But at the end of the film, on the joyful day when the 'everlasting peace' is signed, when the Senate confers on him the name 'Father of the Fatherland', he addresses the people, who are rapturously attentive to him: 'I was strict with you, my children, but I was not strict for myself, but because Russia was dear to me.'

Tolstoy understood very well that he was extolling not a tsar but a hero-leader, for 'the idea, philosophy, grandiose flight of popular strength – none of this is expressed in little or accidental heroes. You comprehend and interpret them only through the maximally large, central, key points, which defined figures of the epoch,' as Tolstoy wrote in the article 'The Writer's Thoughts' in 1937.[47] His Peter is a typical populist leader, strengthening the State and army, fighting against reaction and embezzlement, and loved by the people. It is impossible not to love a tsar like that. This sort of autocracy cannot be hated. All the earlier contradictions of Peter's historical activity are removed. He is always thinking of the greatness of Russia. Conforming to this logic, Soviet criticism began to assert something unthinkable even in the first half of the 1930s: that 'the "barbaric methods" of government in the conditions of the Petrine era were caused by historical necessity.'[48]

Authors were so carried away by this 'necessity' that even the most benevolent critic was obliged to defend the 'people':

> [B]estial, unshaven, with vacant faces and glazed-over eyes, Demidov's serf-folk must willy-nilly represent the Russian peasantry. The director had to show the disastrous situation of the peasantry at that time. But behind their lack of culture, their downtroddeness and savagery, he lost the fundamental qualities which have never altered in the Russian people: inner dignity, love of work, courage and humour . . . The free Don Cossacks in the film are also bestial and dim . . . Historical films released by Soviet cinematography must speak to their audience of the greatness of the Russian people. Part two of *Peter* shows this very well in isolated specimens of the people. The people itself as a mass is shown in a wrong, vulgar way.[49]

Critics agreed, however, that depicting the people's happiness (instead of the 'oppression of the people' under tsarism) fully conformed to the new historical task of asserting the 'greatness of Russia'. 'What is remarkable in these scenes of the people's mass labour?' asked a reviewer in *Iskusstvo kino* in 1937. And he answers:

> We remember how the right renegade Bukharin slandered the great Russian people when he accused them of stagnation, laziness, oblomovism. The picture gives a graphic answer to this counter-revolutionary slanderous attack. The film opposes the sluggishness and backwardness of the powers of reaction with the creative power of the Russian people.[50]

Be that as it may, the images of the people and power produced by Soviet art were the result of ideological techniques used in the twentieth century in order to legitimise the leader. These techniques are also distinctive in that they are connected with a strong dose of inevitable romanticism. While the king or tsar did not require romantic attire for his legitimisation (their legitimacy does not result from their personal qualities; its sources are supra-social), the leader needs a romantic aureole. A leader is a romantic hero who has been given power. The 'romanticism' of this hero, of course, is always the pure product of artistic make-up and ideological manipulation, in so far as a real leader, as a rule, is a sober pragmatist, a pitiless and cunning politician, who could not, however, be shaped without historico-legitimising art. Stalin's words about the Russian people being used to a strong tsar are well known. Usually they are projected on to the figure of Stalin, who constructed the image of the leader on the basis of the representational practices employed in autocracy. In fact, it is not that the leader is transformed into a tsar in the Stalin era, but entirely the opposite – the tsar is transformed into a leader. And it is on this projection that their 'similarity' is constructed.

Soviet historicising art developed (and thus must be understood) in the paradigm and logic of the development of mass societies. At its centre stands a mutual relationship between the masses and power and the status of agents as the real 'driving forces' of twentieth-century history, and not at all Marxist sociology, based on the concept of classes, which was rejected, along with the classes themselves, in the 1930s. Tsars, princes (*boyars*), troops, merchants, 'the people' . . . the 'historical forces' on this stage had nothing in common with 'social classes' or 'economic relations'. The only referent for these ideological constructs was the Soviet political consciousness. The historical film depicted, to all intents and purposes, a classless society; here 'the people' are an obedient mass in the hands of the adored tsar-leader, and the leader is the 'flesh from the flesh of the people'. Soviet society is structured in exactly the same way as Russian society, as depicted in *Peter*, or Georgian society, in *Georgy Saakadze*. It can be said that the Soviet historical film gives the most adequate picture of it. In this sense it can be acknowledged as the most realistic genre, 'historically veracious' in its reflection of Soviet reality. This picture is far from simple, and the lines of separation and attraction are nowhere near where they were with the class approach.

Georgy Saakadze, by Stalin's chief court director, Chiaureli, presents us with Georgia in the seventeenth century. Having been broken up into principalities, Georgia was not in a position to defend itself from the Turks and Persians laying waste to it. Tsar Luarsab II was weak and fully dependent on the princes, who were weaving conspiracies and selling the country to its aggressors. Commander Saakadze appeals to the Tsar to unite the country for its defence: 'A united force is invincible. Let it under your sceptre forge the whole of Georgia!' But the Tsar is weak. He knits his brows threateningly, declaring that he will not become Suleiman's vassal and will not bow down to the Persian Shah, Abbas, but all the same goes to the slaughter, and before the eyes of the whole court the Persians drag his sister off to Persia by force. The weak Tsar understands that the princes are destroying the country; however, he does not want to break off with them. In the film there is no explanation for this. It remains to suggest that it is a question of the personality of the monarch, who was weak-willed and easily led. Here the theme of Ivan the Terrible arises; Saakadze persuades Tsar Luarsab in the name of the unification of the country to tame the princes. 'I do not want to spill the blood of Georgians, like Ivan the Terrible,' replies Luarsab. Saakadze does not agree: 'He was named "Terrible" because he tamed the obstinate aristocracy,' and as a positive example he brings in the Persian Shah, Abbas, who cut off the heads of recalcitrant *khans*. To Luarsab's question of what the people will say, Saakadze replies: 'The life-blood of the people of Georgia has long been pouring out under the princes' yoke.

The people will follow you to strengthen the kingdom.' The people, in other words, are on the side of Ivan the Terrible. When the news reaches the princes that Saakadze has convinced the Tsar to collect money from them to construct a fortress for the defence of Georgia, Prince Shadiman says that Saakadze 'wants to throw us into a dungeon, like the Russian *boyars*', or 'put us to death, like the *khans* in Iran'.

There is therefore nothing surprising in the fact that the princes banish Saakadze from Georgia; he goes into the service of the Persian Shah, for whom he conquers Afghanistan, Baghdad and India, after which he decides to raise an army to march on Georgia. His plan is to lead the Persians not against 'the people' but against the princes, and with the help of the Persian forces to bring them to submission. 'Let the Persians sack the princes' castles,' he says. But the Persians behave in a completely inexplicable way; they burn villages, churches and monasteries, kill the old, rape the women, and (exactly like the 'Teutonic and Livonian knights' in *Alexander Nevsky*) throw children on to fires and drive away the inhabitants, but do not touch the princes' castles (where there are riches and spoils for them). Shah Abbas makes a deal with the princes that they will hand over the Tsar to him. The Shah's actions would have been logical (having weakened the tsardom, he would with ease also destroy the princes) if they had not been so transparent; the fact was that the princes themselves, depicted in the film as treacherous and corrupt, cannot but understand what is going on (all the more so, as the Persians want to drive the Georgians into Persia, and colonise Georgia with Persians). Meanwhile, the princes act quite suicidally, by helping the Persians. Saakadze acts just as suicidally; the cunning and treacherous commander hopes that, by leading the Persian forces into Georgia, he will be able to 'not permit the destruction of the country by the Persians'. As a result, having smashed the Persian army (with the help of 'the people'), Saakadze saves 'Georgia': that is, in fact . . . the princes (in so far as the Tsar has been handed over to the Persians and there is now nobody left to 'unite' the country). The whole absurdity of the plot was in no way the product of the defects of the screenplay. Their sources lie within the Stalinist conception of the social structures of feudal society itself.

If the 'reactionary' nature of the Russian *boyars* was explained by their 'obscurantism' and adherence to old patriarchal culture, the behaviour of the Georgian princes is inexplicable. The chief villain, Prince Shadiman, betrays the Tsar on the battlefield, and (being the leader of the Georgian forces!) is very worried that the Georgians might win . . . Together with the other princes, he goes over to the side of the Persian Shah; whilst simultaneously begging the Tsar to make an alliance with the Turks and in the end compelling him to surrender to the Persians, he slips poison into a cup which he gives the Tsarina. The princes are depicted as a group of conspirators, turncoats and traitors to the State, who desire the defeat of their own country. One can only suggest that these infernal scoundrels were necessary as a counterbalance to the absolute good embodied in the romantic hero Saakadze.

After Stalin's death Chiaureli was accused of not creating the image of a 'national hero', of not answering the question of which class forces Saakadze was representative, as he strove to limit the powers of the feudal lords, the social circle he represented, of creating a tragic romantic loner-hero, fighting for the unification of country and out of touch with 'the people'. All this led to the extolling and justification of the hero and the 'cult of personality'.[51] Saakadze behaves like a model romantic loner, and the principle of 'the hero and the crowd' is fulfilled in the film. In answer to his wife's appeal to give up the risky Georgian campaign, Saakadze declares: 'It's too late. The die is cast . . . I know it's difficult for a man to live when his name is cursed by the people. But I will bear it all in the name of their happiness. He who cuts a path through impregnable rocks is always alone.'

What unites *Peter* and *Saakadze* is the status of the hero (the transformation of the Tsar into a leader) and his relationship to the masses and the princes (*boyars*). In both cases this is a particularly 'classless' and precisely a national approach, based both on the mutual love of the Tsar and the people, alike in opposing the oppressors (princes, *boyars*), and on a virtual apologia of tsarism. But if in *Peter* the focus is on the 'gathering of lands' and wars over new/old territories, then at the centre of *Saakadze* is the 'unification of the country'. The task of 'unification' itself seems completely abstract, in so far as the princes display astonishing short-sightedness; they cannot fail to understand that in burning the villages and driving out the people and cattle, Shah Abbas is effectively destroying their own prosperity (indeed everything belongs to them), and they believe his promise to preserve their power, although it is clear that only unification can save them.

No so with Saakadze. He looks on everything in terms of 'class', but this is class character of a particular kind, with the Tsar and the people at one pole, and the princes at the other. In this loss of contact between the Tsar and the princes the model of ideal (Soviet) power shows through. The Tsar is not the head of a feudal state but the incarnation of 'the people': that is, in effect, the leader. The totalitarian revision of Marxist class character leads in Stalinist art to the revision of feudalism. The tsars here are dealing with only one category – 'the people'. ('In your name, my people, I am leaving you, my people,' declares Luarsab, addressing some sort of void in front of the camera, as if he is speaking to God.) Feudalism turns out to be bad only because power here has been seized by the princes (*boyars*), whose legitimacy is based on a 'historically obsolete' tradition. The legitimacy of the Tsar himself (in so far as he comes out in opposition to the church and the princes) is based on charisma and 'conformity with the laws of history' (which appears in the form of the rationalised will, using the words of Saakadze himself, of 'the eternally young people'). If power is taken away from the princes and given to the 'tsar' (that is, the leader), history will begin to develop 'progressively'. (According to this logic Peter's son, Alexei, who wishes to seize the throne and to this end is prepared to lead a foreign army into Russia, is a traitor and a State criminal, while

Saakadze is a hero, in so far as the former is reactionary and the latter is historically progressive.) Saakadze acts out the role of a 'third force' – neither a prince nor the tsar/people. When Tsar Luarsab abandons Georgia and the Persians have been banished from the country, Saakadze sends a missive to Teimuraz Kakhetinsky, summoning him to the Georgian throne. His letter begins with the words: 'The people and Georgy Saakadze appeal to you.' As leader, Saakadze proves to be the guarantee that the will of the people ('historical necessity') is fulfilled, and vows to rest only 'when a single strong tsar surrounds our kingdom with a chain of impregnable fortresses'.

As in the case of Peter the Great and Ivan the Terrible, 'the image of Georgy Saakadze, an outstanding State figure, has been distorted by bourgeois Georgian historians.'[52] The military commander, who led the Persian forces into the country in order to conquer the Georgian throne, had to appear as a hero, who at the beginning of the seventeenth century wished to unite Georgia, subordinating the feudal lords to a single, centralised power.

Feudalism in this perspective looks not so much like a 'natural stage of historical development' as a kind of perverted form of historically progressive authoritarianism. The mission of the Tsar is to correct a mistake, wresting power from the *boyars* who had seized it. We are dealing with the already familiar concept of 'class character': 'the people' against 'the oppressors'. From this perspective, Saakadze's class consciousness is only the substantiation of the national aim: 'We must be above love and hate. Forget everything personal. That is what the Motherland demands! The Motherland demands! Happy is he whose heart beats for the Motherland.' Saakadze is, above all, a charismatic national leader. The people greet him in raptures, even when he enters at the head of the Persian army. ('Our dear Georgy has returned to us! Has the sun really lit up the path for us again?!') But when villages burn and folk perish, 'the people' endure terrible suffering and curses are directed at Saakadze. However, one word from him, one vow ('I swear by the life of my children to give all my blood for my long-suffering people') is sufficient for the whole army and all 'the people' to follow him. (After *Georgy Saakadze*, Chiaureli also went on to shoot the film *The Vow* (*Kliatva*), in which another charismatic Georgian leader would say literally the same thing to 'the people' in 1924.)

There was much that was topical in the film, which was released in the most critical years for the country. As one great Soviet critic wrote:

> The great contribution by the authors of the screenplay and the director Chiaureli was that they were not afraid to show in all fullness and power both the greatness of Saakadze and his mistakes. They showed Saakadze in the crown of victory and Saakadze wounded in battle. They show the hero steadfastly accepting both the love of the people and their anger. The strength of the passion and profound sorrow experienced by Saakadze win us over, force us to forgive his mistakes, to love him and believe in him.[53]

But it was not of the sorrows of the Georgians in the seventeenth century, nor of Saakadze's mistakes or of love and belief in him that the audience in 1942–3 was thinking, but of another Georgian altogether. It was not of Saakadze that the viewers thought when they saw on the screen in 1942 a charismatic leader with a strong Georgian accent, appealing: 'Raise the people to holy war!', 'The enemy will not trample our soil!' And the great Georgian actor Akaky Khorava did not only create the image of Saakadze, 'beautifully communicating his enormous inner strength, his purposefulness, his external reserve, at times immobility, behind which was hidden enormous spirit'.[54] And even the motif of sacrificing the favourite son 'for the Motherland and the triumph of the cause' – following Peter the Great, Ivan the Terrible and Georgy Saakadze – in no way needed highlighting. (It was at exactly this time that semi-official rumours began to circulate about the fact that Stalin's son, Yakov, was in German captivity and the leader, it was claimed, had refused to exchange him for Field Marshal Paulus, who had just been captured at Stalingrad.)

All these 'analogies with the present' Stalin, of course, could not have foreseen when a year before the start of the war he had become interested in the idea of a film about Georgy Saakadze, a cruel and treacherous commander who took no account whatsoever of his victims. Stalin was presented with two scripts: one by the famous Georgian writer, Georgy Leonidze, the other by Anna Antonovskaya and Boris Cherny (adapted from Antonovskaya's six-volume novel, *The Great Mouravi*). Stalin rejected Leonidze's script, approving Antonovskaya and Cherny's, announcing that it 'could qualify as one of the best works of Soviet cinematography' on condition that 'historical truth were restored'. The point was that Stalin did not like the end of the future film – Saakadze's triumph. Apparently, 'such a good prince' could not be victorious. (As we know, Stalin changed the ending of Eisenstein's *Alexander Nevsky*, where the hero died from poisoning, declaring that 'such a good prince could not die like that.'[55]) Stalin explained in detail the 'screenwriters' error':

> In fact, as history tells us, Saakadze's policy, although progressive from the point of view of the future perspective of Georgia, was defeated (and Saakadze himself perished) because Georgia at the time of Saakadze was not yet mature enough for such a policy: that is, unification into a single state by means of assertion of tsarist absolutism and the liquidation of the power of the princes. The reason is clear: the princes and feudalism were stronger, and the Tsar and the court weaker, than Saakadze supposed. Saakadze sensed this internal weakness of Georgia and conceived of the idea of concealing it by calling an external (foreign) force to battle. But the power of the external factor could not compensate for the country's internal weakness. What happened is well known. In the situation of these insoluble contradictions in policy, Saakadze had to suffer – and indeed did suffer – a defeat.[56]

Colossal resources (especially for war-time) were allocated to the making of the film. The production was luxurious: enormous crowd scenes, magnificent scenery, sumptuous sets, grandiose architecture – everything working towards the creation of a monumental picture. Not even a film, but an epic.

> Freed by necessity from the details of historical life, the film to a greater extent [than the novel – E. D.] acquired features of heroic monumentalism. Its scale, having decreased in time, seems to grow in size. It is not a story, but a narrative poem . . . The epic features are consistent throughout the whole production; some scenes are like magnificent historical engravings,

wrote the chief court journalist, David Zaslavsky, in the pages of *Pravda* on 13 September 1942, when the fate of the country was being decided at Stalingrad. Khorava's Saakadze,

> the image of a great and wise military leader, . . . is majestic. He is genuinely the hero of popular legend. Hence there is also a certain theatricality, as if from the novel to the screen the artistic image has also passed through the stage.[57]

The same would be said some years later about Eisenstein's *Ivan the Terrible*.

Stalin wrote his opinion on the script for *Georgy Saakadze* on 11 October 1940, and three months later Eisenstein was commissioned to make a film about Ivan the Terrible. The theme was called by Zhdanov 'absolutely paramount' and 'a priority'. Both films were guaranteed particularly favourable conditions. The results of these simultaneously commissioned films proved to be diametrically opposed and equally unprecedented. Stalin conferred on *Georgy Saakadze* two Stalin prizes – for each part taken separately – while part one of *Ivan the Terrible* was awarded the Stalin prize first class, but the second was publicly denounced and banned.

BLOW-UP . . .

Ivan the Terrible is a phenomenon which goes beyond the boundaries of cinema proper. This film-event, which became the culmination of the relationship of one of the greatest artists of world cinematography with Soviet power, posed with unusual force, profundity and audacity fundamental questions about power. Examining it in the context of the history of one of the genres of Soviet cinema – the historical film – would be like examining *War and Peace* as a 'historical novel'. A work of such a scale exists within its genre, it seems, only to challenge it.

And after all, the 'cult of personality' (and Eisenstein occupied in Soviet cinema – by virtue of the scale and significance of his work in world cinematography – such an important place that he had long himself been transformed into a kind of romantic loner-hero) was of benefit to no one. From the huge amount of literature on Eisenstein one can pick out a few dozen works specially devoted to *Ivan the Terrible*; however, the film is almost always considered either in the context of the general glorification of Ivan the Terrible under Stalin (the cultivation of patriotism, allusions to the present – legitimisation of the terror, annexation of the Baltic states and so on),[58] or strictly from the point of view of film studies,[59] or in the context of the evolution of the work and ideas of the Master,[60] and in relation to his opposition to official doctrine and the political orders of the leader.[61] Moreover, neither the conceptually historical (and not only topically political) substance of the doctrine, nor the historical imagination of the leader himself is in practice examined. Meanwhile, it not only had, as we have seen, its own history, but was also 'dialectically contradictory'. Stalin reasoned in the logic of transformation and contradiction of this doctrine, and his 'horizon of expectations' was formed corresponding to this logic. And not only logic: before *Ivan the Terrible* the Soviet historical-biographical film had in effect developed a genre, a figurative and conceptual canon. Stalin was also reasoning within this canon when he commissioned the film from Eisenstein.

However, Eisenstein himself was not simply familiar with this canon, but in *Alexander Nevsky* was one of those who formed it (rehabilitating himself in the eyes of the leader – he was therefore far from being the last choice when Stalin commissioned him to make *Ivan*). More than that, as the crowning point of the 'tsarist series', *Ivan the Terrible* cannot be understood outside this tradition. Meanwhile, to examine Eisenstein in the context of the work of his colleagues in the guild of the 'masters of the Soviet historical genre' has to this day been considered almost blasphemous. The very combination of Eisenstein's name with that of Pravov, Preobrazhenskaya, Petrov or Chiaureli is perceived as a monstrous perversion of scales, and examining *Ivan the Terrible* in the context of the tradition of *Razin* or *Saakadze* even now seems like an impossibly strained interpretation.

In the films of the 'tsarist series' preceding *Ivan the Terrible* (even if we are talking only of *Peter* and *Saakadze* examined above), the entire plot construction of Eisenstein's film is already laid in place. All these characters (whether Peter, Saakadze or Ivan) were previously 'distorted by bourgeois historiography'. *Saakadze*, in the words of Pyotr Pavlenko, 'a fundamental historical canvas . . . sustained in the severe tones of the historical annals',[62] was from the start conceived in two parts. *Peter the First*, like *Ivan*, was in general conceived as a three-part epic film. In part one of all these films the conspiracy only begins to take shape, while part two is already fully based on the *boyars'* (princes') conspiracy. The poisoning of the Tsar's wife by the conspirators in *Saakadze* corresponds to the poisoning of Ivan's wife. The death of the son – guilty but 'feeble-minded' (in *Peter*), or innocent (Georgy Saakadze's son, Paata, whom Shah Abbas keeps hostage and whose severed head he sends to

Saakadze) – is transformed in *Ivan* into the death at the hands of a secretly dispatched assassin of the 'feeble-minded' and innocent Vladimir Staritsky. The murder scene concludes with the mother's insanity; Veriko Andzhaparidze as Saakadze's wife Rusudan with her son's head in her hands, having lost her mind from grief, finds direct parallel in the scene of Efrosinya Staritskaya, having lost her mind from grief, singing a lullaby over the body of her son. Even the dances of Saakadze's troops in carnival masks recall the famous dances of the *oprichniki* in *Ivan*. Just as there is an argument between the Tsar and the Patriarch, with curses which are sent by the highest orders of the clergy to the ruler (in both *Peter* and *Saakadze*), the same scenes are found in *Ivan*. *Ivan*, so to speak, synthesises the fundamental problems of *Peter* (at the centre of which is resolving a geopolitical problem; *Ivan* part one is devoted to this) and *Saakadze* (at the centre of which lie unification and centralisation, to which part two of *Ivan* is devoted). One could bring in a great many other parallels (right up to motifs: the severely ill Tsar and the behaviour of those around him; the poisoned Tsarina on her death bed and so on); *Ivan the Terrible* preserves the very atmosphere of the Soviet historical film, alternating court scenes and mass battle scenes, in surroundings of gloomy stone palaces and torture chambers, in a theatrical and operatic atmosphere.

These parallels serve to emphasise especially that the greatness of Eisenstein consists not in the fact that he 'discovered' these narrative strands (they were so common in historical films that Stalin, reading the script, did not notice the director's agenda), but in the fact that, while remaining within the framework of the genre's conventions, he was able to blow them apart. Outside this tradition it is impossible to position *Ivan the Terrible* correctly within the ideological landscape of late Stalinism and understand the significance of what Eisenstein accomplished.

The most serious attempt to analyse conceptually the rehabilitation of Ivan the Terrible in the Stalin period has been undertaken by Kevin Platt and David Brandenberger. They came to the conclusion that different agents – Party bureaucrats, historians and artists – worked in different modes of representation, both on the level of temporality (the Party apparatus and artists strived towards allegory, historians towards the 'historical dialectic') and on the level of narrative construction (Party bureaucrats and historians required a heroic-romantic narrative, while artists produced tragedy). It is precisely the heroic-romantic plot, Platt and Brandenberger suggest, that responds to the demands of power:

> The prominence of this archetypical plot in Soviet public discourse is of course a direct consequence of the foundational status of another romance story in Soviet political mythology: the revolutionary transformation of tsarist Russia into the socialist motherland. Thus the party hierarchy's approach to Ivan the Terrible may be summarized as an allegorical view of the past emplotted as a romance.[63]

Power did not need tragedy (and it is precisely to this that Stalin's reproach-comparison of Eisenstein's Ivan with Hamlet points):

> The romantic and tragic visions of Ivan, when refracted through the prism of historical allegory, communicate vastly differing messages with regard to the Soviet present. Both ultimately contributed to the legitimation of dictatorial rule and terror, yet they served this cause in different ways. Romance tells of the triumph of the human spirit over all, demonstrating simply that our destiny is to realize the transcendent order on earth. Those who oppose this grand calling can only be enemies, to be crushed with no regret. On the other hand, while the tragedy may also end in triumph, it tells the story of the noble sacrifices which lie along the path to redemption. While we are called to look, with Ivan, toward the great ideals which lie beyond the horizon, we also feel his agony as he loses family and friends, sacrificing his own flesh and blood to his historical mission.
>
> It is not hard to understand why the party hierarchy preferred the former emplotment over the latter. In the Soviet 40s, the romance of Ivan the Terrible was fully compatible with the ongoing propaganda campaign to mythologize the present as a scene of triumph over internal and external enemies, the elements, and time itself under the leadership of a prescient *vozhd'*. Yet the attraction of the artistic establishment to the tragic vision of history is less easily comprehended. It may be that, in the tradition of earlier treatments of Ivan or in pursuit of purely artistic goals, artists like Tolstoy and Eisenstein adopted the genre without full consideration of its allegorical implications for the present. This reckless move led to personal catastrophe and political impasse: the implication that the Soviet experiment might be viewed as a tragedy was something the party hierarchy found intolerable, no matter how noble the sacrifice, nor how great the eventual victory. Socialist construction, the war, the leader, and the enemy could only be presented in the triumphant, grandiose pose of the romance.[64]

In other words, according to Platt and Brandenberger, power denies tragedy's capacity for creating a positive picture, through which the audience might identify the present. That is, tragedy could not work within the basic function of Soviet historicising art: allegory. Here we are dealing with that very same isolation of Eisenstein within the sphere of 'related' material of which we spoke earlier.[65] It is worth remembering that, simultaneously with *Ivan* (by Eisenstein and A. Tolstoy), *Georgy Saakadze* was created, which had its plot altered by Stalin himself from a heroic-romantic film to a tragic one. Stalin demanded alteration of the script so that, instead of Saakadze's triumph at the end, there followed his defeat (according to 'historical truth', of course). Chiaureli's film was received in an unprecedentedly positive manner, and was declared beforehand by Stalin to be 'one of the best works of Soviet cinematography'.

It is also difficult to believe that such an experienced courtier as Alexei Tolstoy, who so successfully worked with historical allusions throughout his entire artistic life, did not think through the consequences of the choice of genre. As regards Eisenstein, for him the choice was definitely conscious, and consciously ambiguous, which cannot, of course, have escaped the attention of his contemporaries. Even the semi-official Soviet writer, Leonid Sobolev, during a discussion of part two, did not refrain from suspecting Eisenstein of conscious deviation from the 'tragedy' being proclaimed:

> Although Grozny swears that he's doing everything in the name of the people, in the name of the future, in the name of an outlet in the Baltics, I see something different, that this man remains on the throne and wants to cut down his enemies . . . When Basmanov says, 'Burn, burn down the house,' this is destruction not in the name of the people, not in the name of the historical future, but in the name of sadism inherent in people; they like to kill, to burn down houses.[66]

Stalin sensed exactly this as well, comparing Eisenstein's *oprichniki* to the Ku Klux Klan. The 'explanation' (and with it justification) of Russian history (through sacrifices and tragedy) issuing from the film was also placed in doubt by Eisenstein's contemporaries. During the same discussion Ivan Pyrev noted apropos of this:

> As a Russian man it's hard for me to watch a film like this. I cannot accept it because I become ashamed of my past, of the past of our Russia, ashamed of this great sovereign, Grozny, who was the unifier and first progressive tsar of our Russia.[67]

As we can see, such ideologically sensitive viewers as Pyrev saw that the problem was not at all in the 'tragedy'.

The system of historical projections within Stalinism was more complex than Platt and Brandenberger suggest, when they assert that only the direct heroic-romantic plot could be deemed an adequate form for historical allegory. Precisely because allusionary projections in Stalinism were complex, the ambivalence which Eisenstein managed to advance, or in the language of those years, to 'drag in' (protashchit') in his film became possible. According to Platt and Brandenberger, although everyone – Party *apparatchiks*, historians and artists – was dissatisfied with each other, they were all working for the 'common cause':

> Stalinist cultural agents intentionally promoted competing conceptions of the Ivan narrative, repeatedly clashing over the myth's use as a political metaphor . . . while it is undeniable that some representations of Ivan IV deviated significantly from the official line, we see this as indicative of a

diversity of opinion concerning Ivan and his relevance to Stalinist society, rather than evidence of wilful subversion on the part of the Soviet elite.[68]

Because different cultural agents had differing, so to speak, aesthetic views on the problem of the representation of the rehabilitated Tsar, the whole campaign, the authors suggest, in the end collapsed.

From this perspective, Eisenstein's film not only is not a dissident work but, on the contrary, contains a distinctive justification of Stalinism:

> Such a tragic vision of the recent past might have expressed both the necessity and the agony of the preceding two decades, providing a more psychologically apt representation of Soviet history than romance . . . Even today, the film's tragic vision retains its appeal. Ultimately, this is not hard to understand, as Eisenstein's retelling of Russian history as a noble tragedy – a series of necessary, yet agonizing sacrifices – must remain compelling for those within contemporary society who wish to remember the criminal bloodletting of the revolution and the Soviet era while also celebrating the triumphs of industrialization and the Second World War.[69]

Following this logic, it is impossible to understand, however, why the same popularity was not enjoyed by the no less 'tragic' plays of Alexei Tolstoy or *Georgy Saakadze*, which were created simultaneously with *Ivan the Terrible* and swiftly removed from the repertoire after Stalin's death (precisely at the time when the second part of *Ivan* was released). The point is obviously that Eisenstein's last film not only contained a pseudo-tragic stratum, but also concealed much more complex subtexts and authorial intentions. Therefore it ought not to be read only in the context of the work of Eisenstein himself (as occurs in the vast majority of works about him), or in the context of the specific campaign for the rehabilitation of Ivan the Terrible (as do Platt and Brandenberger).

It has become commonplace to assert that *Ivan the Terrible* stands out from the run of historical films because the director is interested in the theme of power. Indeed, if the theme of *Alexander Nevsky* was patriotism, then the theme of *Ivan* is statehood (or rather 'nation-building'). And, after all, it is not so much the 'theme of power' which excites the director, as the theme of absolute power. Strictly speaking, *Ivan* represents, in its own way, the filming of a Machiavellian fantasy projected on to Russian history of the sixteenth century and simultaneously on to the Stalinist Terror. As Bernd Uhlenbruch commented, apropos of this:

> After the victory over Hitler, it was historically proven that Stalin had succeeded in completing Grozny's work. Instead of now creating a historical parable of the apotheosis of Stalin, Eisenstein filmed, in part two, a cryptogram of the internal state of the Party in the 1930s and 1940s.[70]

Eisenstein approached this task fully prepared. In his films of the 1920s, the director conceived of history in terms of class; neither *Strike (Stachka)*, *Battleship Potemkin (Bronenosets Potemkin)* nor *October (Oktiabr')* was a purely historical metaphor, although they were devoted to history and actively participated in the creation of the mythology of the Revolution. Eisenstein moved towards a conscious mythologisation of history in *Bezhin Meadow* (Bezhin lug) and particularly in *Alexander Nevsky*. And after all, this was the same artist who dreamt of 'producing' a screen adaptation of Marx's *Capital* . . .

Ivan the Terrible was guilty of many ideological sins. The main thing that turned events linked with *Ivan* into a political scandal was, so it seems, not so much the dissident 'dragging in' of every possible unforeseen allusion, but the creation of a situation in which, for criticism to be voiced, it was necessary for matters to be articulated which could not be articulated in the Stalinist epoch. Eisenstein drew back the boundaries of made-to-order analogies and historical allusions so that they not only had an effect opposite to that which was expected, but also created a situation in which the audience found itself by necessity articulating what was beyond articulation in this culture.

Yu. Yuzovsky recounted how happy Eisenstein was when he told him that he had seen in the film an allusion to *Boris Godunov*:

> Lord, can you really see it? What happiness, what happiness! Of course, Boris Godunov: 'For six years I've reigned peacefully, but there's no happiness in my soul.' I couldn't make such a picture without the Russian tradition, without the great Russian tradition, the tradition of conscience. Violence can be explained, it can be legitimised, it can be substantiated, but it can't be justified, then redemption's needed, if you're a man . . . That's, therefore, what it is – the motif of redemption and not doubt, not Hamlet – that's the European tradition, but Boris Godunov's the Russian tradition. But I can imagine how I. V. [Joseph Vissarionovich Stalin – E. D.] resisted. How? He embodies triumphant victory over the conquered enemy, and I make him pay for that with this 'there's no happiness in my soul', that's right, no happiness, triumph, power. I understand his anger at this dissatisfied hint, reproach . . . He was aggrieved that he was suspected of weakness, but it's not weakness.[71]

Eisenstein was, of course, being cunning; he understood that 'I. V.' 'was aggrieved' not at all at these innocent hints. It is sufficient to read the works of Stalin the polemicist (with the Mensheviks before the Revolution, with the opposition in the 1920s, his irate performance at the bloody plenums of the Central Committee in the second half of the 1930s) to be convinced of the leader's rare ability to read into his opponents the most unbelievable political 'distortions' and 'mistakes', of his capacity for the most refined casuistry and tendency to unnatural heights of suspiciousness. No, Stalin was not 'aggrieved' – he had simply read accurately the analogies posed in the film, the same ones which contemporaries were afraid to acknowledge to themselves. Vsevolod Vishnevsky reproduces in his diaries a conversation with Alexander Dovzhenko about part two of *Ivan the Terrible*:

> [S]ome sort of hints, parallels with the present . . . It's strange, Vsevolod . . . either Eisenstein is naïve, or . . . I don't know. But a film like that about a Russia like that, the Kremlin, would be incredible agitation against us. And that final monologue about the right of the tsar to be above morality . . . Grozny is talking to the camera . . . From the author . . . There's something not good in all this.[72]

This terror at the necessity of articulating what both interlocutors, of course, understood (and what they understood both Eisenstein and Stalin also doubtless understood) was the basic explosive effect produced by the film. Eisenstein arranged everything so that his attitude to the Tsar and the *boyars'* opposition remained ambivalent. According to Uhlenbruch's observation: 'Eisenstein's films and his self-criticism are excellent examples of his techniques of subversion. In the film itself, it is a refusal of a second interpretation, the questioning of motives by which the viewers and censors are irritated.'[73]

In the course of the campaign against part two of the film it became necessary to articulate the most pointed questions (as a result of which the campaign for the adulation of Ivan the Terrible found itself on the edge of collapse). Eisenstein's colleagues not only had to admit in private discussions that instead of the commissioned and, correspondingly, expected historical legitimisation of Stalinism, Eisenstein had created a 'tragedy of power'. For all this, all critics were compelled to construct their argument with Eisenstein by demonstrating the disparity between what Eisenstein was supposedly trying to show (the progressive nature of the Tsar and the *oprichniki* and so on) and that which actually ('through naivety', 'unconsciously' or 'through ignorance', as the resolution of the Central Committee asserted) 'appeared' in the film. It is clear, meanwhile, that precisely what the director, who was suffering from neither naivety nor inexperience, wanted did actually appear in the film.

The rhetoric of censure of the film could not in these conditions have been constructed otherwise than by contrasting 'what ought to have been' and 'how it worked out'. As a result, the very historical reality was revealed which official myth was strenuously trying to hide. This occurred not only behind the scenes but also in public. The critic Yurenev wrote:

> They tried to convince us that Ivan's politics were progressive, but there are no politics in the film, if you exclude the court intrigues. They tried to convince us that the battle with the *boyars* had a social, political character, but the explanation given for this hatred, this battle, is psychophysiological; the childhood of Ivan is shown, when this pale, sickly and

nervous lad, who looks as though he has just stepped out of an icon, frightened and tormented by the coarse *boyars*, who have sown in his heart cruelty and eternal hatred towards them. They tried to convince us that Grozny's state apparatus was progressive, but showed the *oprichniki* raving in masks, drunken, bawling songs about murder, about blood, parading themselves first in red, then in black monks' robes. Finally, they tried to convince us that all Grozny's thoughts and feelings were directed towards the people. But what can the great Russian people have in common with a psychopath, dreadful and pitiful, as Grozny is depicted in part two of the film?[74]

The first part of the construction ('They tried to convince us') sounds ambiguous: as if it is a question of someone – not Eisenstein – trying to convince us of the positive side of Ivan, while the film shows something completely different. It is difficult to imagine anything more destructive for this apologist mythology, based on the removal of every contradiction in the image of Ivan the Terrible, than this opposing construction itself, at this very moment, when the apologist plays of Alexei Tolstoy and Solovyov were showing in the most prominent theatres in the land (including MKhAT, the Maly, Vakhtangov, the Leningrad and many provincial theatres), when many thousands of copies of books by historians (Vipper, Smirnov, Bakhrushin) were being published with apologetics for Ivan, along with articles in central newspapers and also literary works, from the three-volume novel by Valentin Kostylev to Ilya Selvinsky's 'tragedy in verse'.

And what 'analogies with the present' cannot be found in *Ivan*! The alliance with England against the 'Germans and Livonians', which definitely recalls the 'Teutonic and Livonian knights' from *Alexander Nevsky*; Vladimir Staritsky/the buffoonish Tsar/the dispatched assassin – Kirov/Nikolaev; Kurbsky, escaping to Poland/Trotsky, living in exile; even the conversation between Ivan and Kurbsky during the taking of Kazan (about the fact that Kurbsky did not like the Tsar's powder) recalls the conflict between Stalin and Bukharin.[75] To the list of similar analogies one could also add the very logic of the Tsar's relations with his allies and enemies. In part one Ivan's friends, Kurbsky and Kolychev, stay the hand of Malyuta Skuratov, who wants to kill the Tsar; in part two, when the Tsar no longer has either the treacherous Kurbsky or Kolychev at his side, the closest associates of the Tsar, Malyuta and Fyodor Basmanov, stay the hand of the unsuccessful regicide, Pyotr Volynets; in part three Eisenstein was going to show the death of Malyuta and the murder (on Ivan's order) of Fyodor Basmanov, and Pyotr Volynets becomes the only person close to the Tsar. This logic reproduces Stalin's ascent to power: with Zinoviev and Kamenev against Trotsky; with Bukharin and Rykov against Zinoviev and Kamenev; then against the 'right opposition' and so on. Furthermore, the repentance and treachery of the *oprichniki*, planned for part three of the film, in effect presenting the *oprichnina* as a 'murderously corrupt institution',[76] could not but remind the audience of the fate of

Yagoda, and then Ezhov and so on. The analogies were so ambiguous, and the conspiracy plot so reversible, that it was already impossible to say definitively who in the film are the conspirators, who has provoked whom, and where conspiracy has ripened and where counter-conspiracy. One of the participants in the discussion on part two of the film at the State committee for cinematography said, as an example, that Malyuta was 'also a kind of conspirator, just against the *boyars*'.[77] Others asserted directly that the *boyars* fell victim to the terror initiated by Grozny and the *oprichniki*.

In his justification Eisenstein said that he was trying to show the 'contradictions' of the Tsar, but in the first place, as Maureen Perrie shows, 'the extent to which Ivan Grozny had become identified with Stalin by the late 1940s [was such] that criticisms of Grozny, however mild, might be read as an allegorical attack on the Soviet leader';[78] in the second place, the task before the director was actually quite different. This was formulated quite precisely by the very same Leonid Sobolev:

> We have in some way to reconcile our people to understand Ivan the Terrible and love him, because this historical character did much that was good for the State . . . We have to love the *oprichnina* because the people in the name of the greater progressive good did many good things.[79]

Eisenstein understood his task perfectly well,[80] and for this reason set himself the aim of de-historicising the hero (as Pushkin had done in *Boris Godunov*) in order to raise the plot above historical everydayness and political topicality to the level of a 'tragedy of power'. Meanwhile, the allegorism of the Soviet historical film is a product of the very complex balance of the plot narrative and the visual image; it cannot shoulder too strong a historicisation (in so far as it must leave space for historical allusions), but nor can it bear de-historicisation (in so far as 'generalisation' reveals too strongly those aspects of 'historical reality' which not only must not be articulated, but whose reading becomes an act of dangerous dissidence).

Undoubtedly, Eisenstein was taking a deliberate risk. He was counting on the internal logic of the work of historical analogy. On the one hand, he was assuming recognition. Yuzovsky recalls his conversation with Eisenstein. Apropos of *Ivan the Terrible* Zhdanov said to him:

> History is a lesson, and the people must comprehend this lesson – whoever does not understand will understand; allusion, analogy is the aim of the picture, so that everybody can learn, Eisenstein summarised. Everything around must be recognised, I will not go into the depths of the centuries in order to drag out this or that figure, on the contrary, I will take my contemporaries and pull them into the depths of the centuries, in fact I was told – analogy, but you know it is an fascinating task for an artist, I think – analogy, analogy, I walk – analogy, analogy,

I look – analogy, analogy. All my acquaintances and all the people I know, all the people everybody knows, are transformed in my imagination, their clothes are changed, their behaviour, movement, even their appearance is transformed by film, but they still remain as they are.[81]

On the other hand, as Igor Mantsov commented, what we see on the screen are only

chimeras, symbols, foreshortenings of POWER. Identification is impossible . . . No identification can occur with any of the characters. I am not allowed inside. POWER is not shared with me . . . Only characters, great plans, stopping time. Only voices, only rhetoric, cancelling action, dramatic construction and psychology. Rhetoric befriends POWER. We are offered pseudodialogues. A kind of collective speech which to animate the action has been divided up between the characters.[82]

In these conditions the mildest of all possible accusations became an accusation of the 'unrussianness' of the picture – an accusation which was at the time grave, but all the same much milder than the accusation of being 'anti-Soviet':

Mikhail Romm: 'All this is something un-Russian. It is some sort of disguised Spain, transplanted in Potylikha . . . The Fiery Furnace scene is somehow strange: like painted Chinamen, or *skomorokhs* playing Chaldeans.'[83]

Leonid Sobolev: This is not a Russian picture. It was like that even in part one. There's nothing Russian in it . . . strange though it may seem, the only thing I feel is Russian about it is this twit, this cretin – Vladimir Staritsky. Ivan the Terrible is not Russian.[84]

Ivan Pyrev: I do not understand from this picture why the *boyars* are accused of being for foreigners, of being prepared to sell their Motherland to foreigners and so on. That's not apparent from the picture. On the contrary, judging from how Grozny and the *oprichniki* behave, how they are dressed, how they commit their deeds, the make-up they wear . . . the environment they live in, I could sooner charge Grozny and his *oprichniki* with selling out to foreigners, because they behave not like Russians, but like Jesuits of some kind . . . and Grozny is that grand inquisitor who heads this *oprichnina*. I acquit and stand fully on the side of these *boyars* who lose their heads, these bearded Russians, kind and good, because it is not shown why they are bad, I see nothing – no acts against the Russian State – against them. Thus I stand for the *boyars*, for Vladimir, because in him are the features of a real man, at least, flashes of this real man.[85] At the same time, there is nothing human, kind, good (in whatever century this is, but coming from the Russian people) in any of these people who follow Grozny, led by Malyuta . . . the Tsar looks here not like a progressive tsar, but only like a grand inquisitor who has surrounded himself with these strange young people who in the way they behave are like Fascists of the sixteenth century.[86]

Pyrev's last remark provoked laughter in the hall. Meanwhile, the mood amongst those discussing the picture was extremely gloomy. Everyone understood that it was not simply a question of the failure of Stalin's task or of the actual campaign to rehabilitate the Terrible Tsar. In essence, having 'revealed the method', Eisenstein blew up from within the supergenre of Soviet cinema: the historical film, constructed on its use of allusion, fulfilling important politico-ideological functions. (After *Ivan* there followed historical films almost exclusively about composers, writers and scientists, which could not solve the sorts of political problem that had been solved in films about tsars, popular leaders and military commanders.)

As we have seen, the conception of the Soviet historical film (both the 'people's' and the 'tsarist' series) was structurally unfinished and full of contradictions, which were uncovered literally in every new film. *Ivan the Terrible*, about which the author himself said that he was trying to show the 'contradictions', turned out to be the most uncontradictory of all of them. Everybody in essence understood what was clear even to Leonid Sobolev:

> Although Grozny swears he's doing everything in the name of the people, in the name of the future, in the name of an outlet in the Baltics, I see something different, that this man remains on the throne and wants to cut down his enemies.[87]

Whilst in other films the motives behind the behaviour of the characters and the social groups they represented were absolutely incomprehensible, and the political meaning of the struggle for power sheltered behind the flare of battle for a 'great cause', in *Ivan* the motives of the hero's behaviour were perfectly clear. Yes, Ivan constantly talks of a 'great cause', but it is clear that it is not this cause which occupies the Tsar, Eisenstein or the audience. Even how Ivan talks about it makes everything maximally clear. If Peter appeals for a life not to be spared for the sake of 'our beloved Fatherland', if Saakadze goes to senseless sacrifice for the sake of 'our beloved Georgia', then Ivan does everything 'for the sake of the great Russian kingdom'. Not for Russia (or Georgia) but for the kingdom (which is moreover not 'beloved' but 'great'). We will recall that the principle of temporalisation, on which the Stalinist historical narrative was constructed, can least of all endure such an absence of contradictoriness. It is called upon to hold together 'contradictory statements', without which the ideological system ceases being dialectically flexible; that is, it becomes politically dysfunctional. Thus, the simple glorification of the tsar, with the consequent elimination of any traces of class or revolutionary rhetoric, becomes in Stalinism politically senseless, if not dangerous.

And in fact, the officially posed problem of the production of *Ivan* was the basis of the 'historical progressiveness' of the absolute monarchy. Eisenstein brought the idea of absolutism to its logical conclusion. The film begins with Ivan's coronation and speech from the throne, where the new Tsar asserts the idea of power over time and history themselves: 'The second Rome has fallen, but the third, Moscow, stands, and there will be no fourth! And of that third Rome – that Muscovite power – the sole master I alone henceforth will be!' At the end of part three Ivan was to have proclaimed victory over space ('Over the seas we stand and will stand!'), thereby reaching a higher power – the realisation of a childhood dream. (In the unreleased prologue to the film showing Ivan's childhood, his nanny sings to him of 'the sea-blue ocean'.)

Between these points lies the transformation of Ivan through the key points of the plot, which the four coronations display in their own way.[88] The function of these is in no way only related to the plot; with each of them (although coronation is the very embodiment of legitimacy), Ivan's status changes fundamentally.

The first coronation, with which the film opens, transforms Ivan into the Tsar. Here power is given through an extra-social absolute. It is interesting that here Ivan, although he declares his aim to unite the country and discharge the *boyars* from power, finds himself in complete ignorance of the *boyars'* conspiracy, Kurbsky's treachery and the machinations of the European ambassadors. This ignorance stems from the fact that the Tsar is thus far still only a tsar. There is so far nothing personal (in other words, charisma) in him. Right in the interval between the first and second coronations Eisenstein brings together the Tsar and the people (who after the march to the Alexandrov monastery disappear completely from the film). As James Goodwin notes, '*Ivan the Terrible* attributes no revolutionary grandeur to the masses.'[89] At first they are a rebellious crowd (bursting into the Tsar's wedding), then a disciplined army obedient to Ivan (in the scenes of the capture of Kazan), and finally, a mass committed to the Tsar, flowing into Alexandrov monastery to entreat 'our dear father' to return to the throne. 'In both the battle and pilgrimage sequences the masses are spiritually – and dramatically – subordinate to the tsar.'[90] (In part two there are no mass scenes at all; none were planned for part three either.) Nevertheless, between the two coronations we are present at the dialogue of the crowd scenes – the first with a disorganised, turbulent, threatening mass, the last with the mass obediently stretched out in a living chain.

The second coronation (at the end of part one) turns Ivan into the people's tsar (leader). Throughout the course of the whole of part one Ivan, so it seems, consistently destroys the foundations of his legitimacy, based on tradition (eradicating the *boyars* and undermining the Patriarch's power) and legality (rejecting all established social institutions and setting up the *oprichnina*). Legitimacy of a higher order can be established only through charisma. Ivan comes to understand this at the tomb of Anastasya. He decides to go to Alexandrov monastery so as to return 'when the whole nation calls'. To Malyuta and Basmanov senior, who do not understand the profound essence of the transformation conceived by Ivan and think that he wants to return to Moscow 'as a conqueror', he replies:

> In that nation-wide call I will find unlimited power, I will accept the new anointing for a great and relentless deed . . . In that nation-wide call I will read the will of the Almighty, in my hand I will receive the avenging sword of the Lord, I will fulfil a great deed.

It is clear that here we are talking not simply about a political manoeuvre, but precisely about a new status and a new coronation – a new anointing. However, Ivan's transformation tells us less about the status of the tsar than about the status of 'the people'. As Žižek has shown, 'the people' exist in totalitarian reality only as a factor in the legitimisation of the leader.[91] (Therefore after the scene at Alexandrov, after the appeal 'Come back, dear father!', 'the people' become simply superfluous.) After the victory over Germany a similar approach to 'the people' was already described as 'Marxist'. Yurenev repeated the 'Marxist thesis' that 'the course of development of history depends on many chances, including the character of the people at the head of the movement':

> One can say audaciously: yes, the movement of the Russian people is expressed in the politics and image of Ivan IV, whose works 'are the conscious and free expression of this necessary and conscious movement' (Plekhanov). It is only a question of highlighting not 'the details of a sick personality' but the essence of the state activities of the hero. While artists have been occupied with these 'details', the image of Ivan was both a-historical and distorted and therefore, naturally, could not accommodate the image of the people. Soviet artists, armed with Marxist theory, are called upon to rehabilitate Grozny as the spokesman of the aspirations of his people in his time.[92]

Eisenstein demonstrates in part two a 'new Ivan', a popular tsar–leader. That is why, in his argument with Philip, Ivan says, 'On the will of the people I will lean!' That is why, in answer to Malyuta, who has suggested that the Tsar's power is supported by the *oprichnina*, Ivan replies: 'By the shoulders of the people I stand supported, by the power of the people I stand supported!' It is interesting that having received 'unlimited power' from the hands of the people, the people were substituted with the *oprichnina*. It is the *oprichniki* themselves who fulfil the function of the 'popular masses', which is not contradicted by Eisenstein's idea, written in his diary: Ivan 'raises the roots of social strata – to the *oprichnina*'.[93] What were the 'roots of social strata' for the director's class thinking? They were what Stalin himself called 'the dregs of society'.

What awaited the people themselves on Ivan's return to Moscow we are given to understand by the famous gigantic profile of Ivan, 'hanging over the procession of people like a black bird of prey'.[94]

The third coronation is carried out in the same cathedral as the first one took place and where Philip refuses to acknowledge and give his blessing to the Tsar. It is right here that Ivan uncovers the conspiracy, realising that Efrosinya lies at its centre. It is right here that, to all intents and purposes, he rejects the power of the church over him. It is right here that he not only refuses support for the *boyars*, but also declares his willingness to spill 'royal blood'. It is right here, in the 'Fiery Furnace' scene, that 'from the lips of a child' the name of the new Nebuchadnezzar is pronounced. It is right here that Ivan also takes his new name: 'Henceforth I will be that which you name me! I will be "the Terrible"!' Having destroyed every foundation of his own legitimacy, Ivan has left only one: charisma. But having substituted the people with the *oprichniki*, Eisenstein transforms him into the leader of the *oprichnina*. Here Ivan dies as a tsar. The first coronation is cancelled out. Now he is the leader, and in this capacity he is above ritual and can carnivalise it.

Of this kind is the fourth coronation – the mock coronation (with Vladimir Staritsky). Here Ivan is neither the people's nor the *boyars*' tsar, but the leader who is above ritual. In this final coronation it becomes clear that absolute power kills; in the murder of Vladimir Staritsky, the suicide of Ivan occurs. Both heroes – Ivan in childhood and Prince Vladimir – are endowed with similar features (not to mention the fact that Vladimir is a close relative of Ivan's). *Peter the First* is another subtext, where the murder of the 'feeble-minded' Tsarevich Alexei is given in a completely different context; the scene where Peter first accuses his son of betrayal concludes with Ekaterina's confession that she is pregnant, and part one of *Peter* ends with toasts to the new heir. The fact that Alexei and Ivan were played by one and the same actor meant that the scene of the murder of Vladimir was associated in mass consciousness with the famous image of the murder by both Ivan and Peter of their own sons, and constituted an important background for the perception of both pictures, reinforcing the parallelism of the plot lines linked with murder. This Ivan could pronounce straight to camera 'the tsar's right to amorality' in the monologue which so frightened Dovzhenko.

The paradox consists in the fact that with the strengthening of Ivan's absolute power his isolation also grows (until at the end of part three he was supposed to have been shown in complete solitude on the bank of the 'sea-blue ocean'), and with isolation, his powerlessness grows, leading in the final analysis to the failure of Ivan's 'great historical cause' itself. Thus the historical allusion creates not so much a projection of the 'historical achievements' of the Terrible Tsar as of the Time of Troubles which followed his reign, with Boris Godunov at its beginnings articulating ('via Pushkin') this tragic paradox. The theme of Godunov is opened up in the logic of the plot development, and then right on the threshold of the fourth coronation it declares itself most distinctly – in the scene of the *oprichniki*'s dance. As we know, in his unmade film about Pushkin, Eisenstein intended to turn Godunov's monologue into a 'nightmare in colour'.[95] The scene of 'buffoonery' and 'drunken debauchery' was just such a 'nightmare in colour'. The accuracy of the strike was emphasised by the reaction of the principal viewer. As we know, Stalin initially responded to part two with the words: 'It's not a film, it's some sort of nightmare!'

At the end of part two a total liberation occurs; Ivan frees himself from the 'bonds of tsarism'. He is no longer a tsar, but precisely a Party leader, controlling the punitive apparatus of the State. To all intents and purposes, he is a character of the first half of the twentieth century. Paradoxically, Soviet criticism was correct in its most daring 'Marxist' guess-work; Ivan the Terrible 'entered into uncompromising battle with the remnants of feudalism'.[96] In Eisenstein and Cherkasov's conversation with Stalin, Zhdanov and Molotov, the leitmotif of the leader's utterances was: there is no need to be afraid 'to tell the truth' – yes, there was terror! The main thing is that it has to be shown why it was necessary. This was the task of Soviet historicising art. Class logic was no longer capable of explaining anything. The logic of power was based on 'historical necessity'. Having realised this, the audience will also be liberated. This is the form catharsis takes here.

Eisenstein was a great master of the symbolisation of power. In the 1920s he created images which legitimised the Revolution, and which have been preserved forever in the history of world cinema. One of the most famous is the opening frames of *October*: 'Where *October* opens with the symbolic dismantling of tsardom as the masses dismember the Alexander III statue, *Ivan the Terrible* opens with the ceremony that constructs the tsar's image and his symbols of power,' Goodwin comments.[97] The main image is undoubtedly the Cap of Monomakh, which

> lives an independent life on the screen and almost becomes the hero of the film. The film begins with the coronation of the young Ivan, but the crown appears in close-up first. It, the sceptre and the power are given to someone outside the frame, and then again the crown appears on the screen, comfortably placed on someone's head. (Ivan is shot from behind.) And only after this does Ivan turn to the camera, presenting himself after the crown, in second place.
>
> The crown will also be more important than the head in the future: for example, in the mock crowning of Vladimir. The man on the screen who puts on the Cap of Monomakh loses his face and has no figure. The frame is cut along the lower edge of the crown and it rules the whole space alone, regardless of whose head it deigns to adorn.[98]

In the final scene of part two (after the murder of Vladimir), Malyuta goes up to the insane Efrosinya Staritskaya and neatly takes the crown out of her hands. Marianna Kireeva links this with Eisenstein's experience of working (right before he began work on Ivan) on the Bolshoi Theatre's production of Wagner's *The Valkyrie*. Like the ill-omened 'Ring of the Nibelungs', the crown 'possesses the same magnetically attractive power and in exactly the same way enslaves everyone who, as they mistakenly suppose, possesses it. It is as if it contains an ancient curse which nobody can master.'[99]

Undoubtedly, this emancipation of the Cap of Monomakh in Eisenstein was conceived as a metaphor, but it is referring, it seems, not to an ancient German epic, but to an image much closer to home: Pokrovsky's famous formula – 'trade capital roamed the land wearing the Cap of Monomakh'. Eisenstein endows this Marxist metaphor, rejected ten years previously, with a completely new meaning. The Cap of Monomakh possesses its own particular power, which is far mightier and more boundless than the 'trade capital' imagined by Pokrovsky. Absolutism again and again reproduces itself in Russian history, in effect enclosing it in a vicious circle of violence. This idea of repetition is intensified by the choice of object; the cap of Monomakh, used at coronations, is the incarnation of legitimacy through tradition and legality.

Here, however, history once again intervened; at the height of his power, after victory in the war, the problem of legitimacy through historical allusion lost its topicality for Stalin.[100] So in the same August days of 1946 when *Ivan the Terrible* was publicly condemned, Chiaureli's film *The Vow* was released, in which Stalin gained his legitimacy directly from the hands of the Soviet people – without any historical allusions whatever. However, it would have been impossible to present Stalin's 'direct coronation' in *The Vow* in 1946 without the historical films of the preceding decade.

But meanwhile, the dialectical triad was striving towards synthesis. The 'people's' series showed the popular leader, who was opposed by the *boyars* and the tsar; whilst it gave a positive image of 'the people', it did not give a positive image of power. The 'tsarist' series turned the tsar himself into a popular leader (or commander), opposed by the *boyars*. Meanwhile, as we have seen, both series contain serious ideological disjunctions. In synthesis there is always the danger of explosion.

In particular, this danger is present when such a delicate task is assigned to such an unpredictable artist as Eisenstein, who himself acknowledged his capacity 'at his own risk' for undertaking 'quixotic missions'.[101] It was sufficient to shift the conceptual bonds of the popular monarchy for the tsar, already shown as a free-floating romantic hero-leader, to be definitively emancipated. The already familiar solitude of the tsar-leader achieves its culmination in *Ivan the Terrible*. The people disappear. In essence, their function is given to the *oprichnina*, which makes the very idea of legitimacy irrelevant.

Meanwhile, the Soviet historical film strived for the heights from which it had to show that the most terrible figure of the Russian Middle Ages and his bloody 'historical cause' were 'progressive'. Hereby the bloodiest regime in 'the history of the Russian State' would also gain its legitimacy – Stalinism. As Eisenstein explained to Yuzovsky,

> I was told to make a picture not for the sake of the past, but for the sake of the future; it is not that today's epoch must explain yesterday's – what does that matter to us! – but that yesterday's can serve today's, serve with total devotion, or, if it comes to it, from fear as well, if your conscience is weak and you're that ceremonious! Understand?[102]

The Soviet Middle Ages, Stalinist feudalism, sought and found their substantiation in the 'authentic' Middle Ages. From this perspective the Soviet historical film resulted in an unexpected synthesis.

The tsar, turned into a national leader, had to ('in synthesis') be turned back into a popular tsar; to charismatic legitimacy were added traditional and legal legitimacy. Feudalism, already modernised into the ideal social organisation (in the manner of Soviet power) as a result of the 'dialectic reworking of history', was turned into . . . socialism, having received in its turn historical substantiation. The mirror of the Soviet historical film was arranged so that the past reflected the present, but not the other way round, so that the Middle Ages were reflected in the Stalinist present. Paradoxically, Eisenstein's explosion became the 'synthesis' of this historical dialectic, in the final analysis leading to the triumph of the 'law of the negation of the negation' abolished by Stalin and – to the 'historical truth'; it turned out that feudalism was fully suited to life, that absolutism was 'progressive', that terror was 'historically necessary', and that, consequently, the Middle Ages had not ended.

Stalinism had achieved, finally, an adequate historical context. Stalin read it correctly and for this reason banned the film, breaking the mirror. At odds with Karamzin in his assessment of Ivan the Terrible, he confirmed his rightness at least in the fact that in Russia 'the people's history belongs to the tsar.'

NOTES

1. *Istoriia Vsesoiuznoi Kommunisticheskoi partii (bolshevikov). Kratkii kurs*, Moscow: Gospolitizdat, 1938, p. 116. Translations are taken from *History of the Communist Party of the Soviet Union (Bolsheviks). Short Course*, Moscow: Foreign Languages Publishing House, 1939, p. 121.
2. *Kratkii kurs*, p. 105. (*Short Course*, p. 111.)
3. *Kratkii kurs*, p. 105. (*Short Course*, p. 110.)
4. Michel de Certeau, *The Writing of History*, New York: Columbia University Press, 1988, pp. 89, 92.
5. H. H. Gerth and C. Wright Mills (eds), *From Max Weber: Essays in Sociology*, New York: Oxford University Press, 1958, p. 78.
6. Mikhail Allenov, *Teksty o tekstakh*, Moscow: Novoe literaturnoe obozrenie, 2003, p. 55.
7. Ibid., p. 58.
8. De Certeau, *The Writing of History*, p. 3.
9. Slavoj Žižek, *The Sublime Object of Ideology*, London: Verso, 1997, p. 144.
10. Ibid., pp. 146–7.
11. R. Iurenev, *Sovetskii biograficheskii fil'm*, Moscow: Goskinoizdat, 1949, p. 225.
12. Ibid., p. 25.

13. S. Eizenshtein, *Izbrannye sochineniia v 6 tomakh*, 1970, Vol. 5, Moscow: Iskusstvo, p. 115.

14. Aleksei Surkov, 'Stranitsy geroicheskoi epopei', *Pravda*, 1942, 28 March, p. 4.

15. Terry Eagleton, *Ideology. An Introduction*, London: Verso, 1991, p. 5.

16. M. Serebrianskii, *Sovetskii istoricheskii roman*, Moscow: GIKhL, 1936, p. 53.

17. Viktor Shklovskii, 'Ob istoricheskom stsenarii'. In *Sovetskii istoricheskii fil'm*, Moscow: Goskinoizdat, 1939, p. 77.

18. Serebrianskii, *Sovetskii istoricheskii roman*, p. 69.

19. Ibid., p. 92.

20. See L. Mamatova, E. Khokhova, 'Ponizovaia vol'nitsa', *Russkii illiuzion*, Moscow: Materik, 2003, pp. 30–2; Iuri Tsivian (ed.), *Silent Witnesses: Russian Films 1908–1919*, London: BFI, 1989, pp. 56–8.

21. Kh. Khersonskii, 'Istoricheskaia tema v kino', *Iskusstvo kino*, 1938, No. 3, p. 43. Such criticism required a certain caution. Thus, the word 'river pirate' (*ushkuinik*) hides the meaning of this 'historical concept', which the *Tolkovyi slovar'* of those days explained in the following manner: 'a free person who, having entered a gang, sails around in boats and is involved in robbery'; that is, a 'robber'. See *Tolkovyi slovar' russkogo iazyka*, D. Ushakov (ed.), Vol. 4, Moscow, 1940, p. 1044.

22. Ibid., p. 44.

23. Viktor Shklovskii, 'Kakim byl Pugachev?'. In V. Shklovskii, *Za 60 let: Raboty o kino*, Moscow: Iskusstvo, 1985, p. 196.

24. Khersonskii, 'Istoricheskaia tema v kino', p. 42.

25. Ibid., p. 44.

26. Shklovskii, 'Kakim byl Pugachev?', p. 194.

27. Vsevolod Pudovkin, 'Khoroshii fil'm "Stepan Razin" '. In Vs. Pudovkin, *Sobranie sochinenii v 3 tomakh*, Vol. 2, Moscow: Iskusstvo, 1975, p. 206.

28. Ibid., p. 206.

29. Ibid., p. 207.

30. Shklovskii, 'Kakim byl Pugachev?', p. 195.

31. Serebrianskii, *Sovetskii istoricheskii roman*, pp. 59–60.

32. Ibid., p. 70.

33. A. Chapygin, *Razin Stepan*, Moscow: Zhurnal'no-gazetnoe ob'edinenie, 1936, p. 527.

34. Ibid., p. 530.

35. G. Chakhir'ian, 'Pugachev', *Iskusstvo kino*, 1937, No. 12, p. 34.

36. Marina Kuznetsova, 'Petr Pervyi', *Russkii illiuzion*, Moscow: Materik, 2003, p. 173.

37. V. Petrov, 'Idei i obrazy "Petra I" '. In *Sovetskii istoricheskii fil'm*, Moscow: Goskinoizdat, 1939, p. 31.

38. Aleksei Tolstoi, *Sobranie sochinenii v 13 tomakh*, Vol. 9, Moscow: GIKhL, 1952, p. 785.

39. 'Readers who would judge the film *Peter the First*, coming from the novel of the same name, according to how successful was the transfer to the screen of the contents of the literary work would be making a mistake . . . the picture and the book do not coincide in time: the action of the film involves a much later period than that which is depicted in the published parts of A. N. Tolstoy's novel.' A. Tolstoi, V. Petrov, 'Predislovie k fil'mu'. In *Peter I*, Moscow: Iskusstvo, 1937, p. 4.

40. R. Messer, 'Roman – p'esa – stsenarii – fil'm', *Iskusstvo kino*, 1938, No. 8, p. 55.

41. V. Shklovskii, 'Ob istoricheskom stsenarii'. In *Sovetskii istoricheskii fil'm*, Moscow: Goskinoizdat, 1939, p. 76.

42. G. Zel'dovich, 'Petr Pervyi', *Iskusstvo kino*, 1937, No. 8, p. 27.

43. L. Rovinskii, 'Petr Pervyi', *Pravda*, 26 July 1937, p. 4.

44. 'Kak ia rabotal nad rol'iu Petra (Beseda s artistom N. K. Simonovym)', *Komsomol'skaia Pravda*, 14 September 1937, p. 3.

45. Vs. Pudovkin, 'Vystuplenie na diskussii po fil'mu "Petr Pervyi" (2-aia seriia) v Moskovskom Dome kino 7 ianvaria 1939 g.'. In Vs. Pudovkin, *Sobranie sochinenii v 3 tomakh*, Vol. 3, Moscow: Iskusstvo, 1976, p. 178.

46. Vardan Bagdasarian, 'Obraz vraga v istoricheskikh kinolentakh 1930–1940-kh gg.'. In *Istoriia strany/Istoriia kino*, Moscow: Znak, 2004, p. 134.

47. Aleksei Tolstoi, *Sobranie sochinenii v 13 tomakh*, Vol. 13, Moscow: GIKhL, 1952, p. 539.

48. L. Gutman, 'Istoricheskii zhanr v zhivopisi i kino'. In *Sovetskii istoricheskii fil'm*, Moscow: Goskinoizdat, 1939, p. 97.

49. R. Iurenev, 'O Petre vedaite . . .', *Iskusstvo kino*, 1939, No. 2, p. 18.

50. G. Zel'dovich, 'Petr Pervyi', *Iskusstvo kino*, 1937, No. 8, p. 28.

51. *Ocherki istorii sovetskogo kino*, Vol. 2, Moscow: Iskusstvo, 1959, pp. 722–3.

52. Ibid., p. 722.

53. I. Manevich, *Narodnyi artist SSSR Mikhail Chiaureli*, Moscow: Goskinoizdat, 1953, p. 84.

54. Ibid., p. 87.

55. M. Geller, A. Nekrich, *Utopiia u vlasti*, Vol. 1, London: OPI, 1982, p. 316.

56. G. Mar'iamov, *Kremlevskii tsenzor. Stalin smotrit kino*, Moscow: Kinotsentr, 1992, p. 102.

57. D. Zaslavskii, 'Poema o velikom gruzinskom polkovodtse', *Pravda*, 13 September 1942, p. 4.

58. See Kevin Platt, David Brandenberger, 'Terribly Romantic, Terribly Progressive, or Terribly Tragic: Rehabilitating Ivan IV under I. V. Stalin', *Russian Review*, Vol. 58 (October 1999); James Goodwin, *Eisenstein, Cinema, and History*, Urbana and Chicago: University of Illinois Press, 1993; David Brandenberger, *National Bolshevism: Stalinist Mass Culture and the Formation of Modern Russian National Identity, 1931–1956*, Cambridge, MA: Harvard University Press, 2002; Maureen Perrie, *The Cult of Ivan the Terrible in Stalin's Russia*, Basingstoke: Palgrave, 2001; Bernd Uhlenbruch, 'The Annexation of History: Eisenstein and the Ivan Grozny Cult of the 1940s'. In Hans Gunther (ed.), *The Culture of the Stalin Period*, London: Macmillan, 1990.

59. See Kristin Thompson, *Eisenstein's Ivan the Terrible: A Neoformalist Analysis*, Princeton: Princeton University Press, 1981.

60. See Yuri Tsivian, *Ivan the Terrible*, London: BFI, 2002.

61. See Leonid Kozlov, 'Ten' Groznogo i Khudozhnik', *Kinovedcheskie zapiski*, 1992, No. 14; Naum Kleiman, 'Formula finala', *Kinovedcheskie zapiski*, 1998, No. 38; Joan Neuberger, *Ivan the Terrible*, London: I. B. Tauris, 2003.

62. P. Pavlenko, 'Georgii Saakadze', *Krasnaia zvezda*, 14 August 1943, p. 4.

63. Kevin Platt, David Brandenberger, 'Terribly Romantic, Terribly Progressive, or Terribly Tragic', p. 644.

64. Ibid., p. 653.

65. Even the greatest authority on Eisenstein in the USA, David Bordwell, suggests that '*Ivan the Terrible* offers virtually the only attempt in the period to create tragedy within Soviet Socialist Realist cinema'; David Bordwell, *The Cinema of Eisenstein*, Cambridge, MA: Harvard University Press, 1993, pp. 231–2.

66. 'Zasedanie khudozhestvennogo soveta pri Komitete po delam kinematografii. Prosmotr i obsuzhdenie vtoroi serii "Ivana Groznogo", 7 fevralia 1946'. In *Zhivye golosa kino*, Moscow: Belyi bereg, 1999, pp. 293–4. It is worth noting that none of his contemporaries talked in earnest about 'tragedy'. They all defined it in another way: the director Mikhail Romm as 'a courtly melodrama, not a tragedy' (p. 290); the actor Alexei Diky as 'a courtly melodrama' (p. 292); the playwright Vsevolod Vishnevsky as 'a courtly, gloomy thing' (Vs. Vishnevskii, 'Iz dnevnikov 1944–1948 gg.', *Kinovedcheskie zapiski*, 1998, No. 38, p. 67).

67. 'Zasedanie khudozhestvennogo soveta . . .', p. 285.

68. Platt, Brandenberger, p. 636.

69. Ibid., p. 654.
70. Bernd Uhlenbruch, 'The Annexation of History: Eisenstein and the Ivan Grozny Cult of the 1940s'. In Hans Gunther (ed.), *The Culture of the Stalin Period*, London: Macmillan, 1990, p. 278.
71. Iu. Iuzovskii, 'Eizenshtein!', *Kinovedcheskie zapiski*, Vol. 38, 1998, p. 62.
72. Vishnevskii, 'Iz dnevnikov', p. 62.
73. Uhlenbruch, 'The Annexation of History', p. 283.
74. Iurenev, *Sovetskii biograficheskii fil'm*, p. 150.
75. See Uhlenbruch, 'The Annexation of History', pp. 274–80.
76. Goodwin, *Eisenstein, Cinema, and History*, p. 191.
77. 'Zasedanie khudozhestvennogo soveta . . .', p. 283.
78. Perrie, *The Cult of Ivan the Terrible in Stalin's Russia*, p. 105.
79. 'Zasedanie khudozhestvennogo soveta . . .', p. 293.
80. See Kozlov, 'Ten' Groznogo i Khudozhnik'; Kleiman, 'Formula finala'.
81. Iuzovskii, 'Eizenshtein!', p. 42.
82. Igor' Mantsov, 'Priblizhaias' k vlasti', *Kinovedcheskie zapiski*, 1998, No. 38, pp. 32–3.
83. 'Zasedanie khudozhestvennogo soveta . . .', p. 291.
84. Ibid., p. 295.
85. Ironically, two years later, in 1948, Pavel Kadochnikov, having played Vladimir in *Ivan the Terrible*, played in the film *The Story of a Real Man* the main role of the 'real Soviet man', Alexey Meres'ev.
86. 'Zasedanie khudozhestvennogo soveta . . .', pp. 284–5.
87. Ibid., pp. 293–4.
88. See Goodwin, *Eisenstein, Cinema, and History*, pp. 191–5; Tsivian, *Ivan the Terrible*, pp. 9–11.
89. Goodwin, *Eisenstein, Cinema, and History*, p. 189.
90. Ibid., p. 190.
91. Žižek, *The Sublime Object of Ideology*, p. 147.
92. Iurenev, *Sovetskii biograficheskii fil'm*, p. 144.
93. *Ocherki istorii sovetskogo kino*, Vol. 2, Moscow: Iskusstvo, 1959, p. 705.
94. Marianna Kireeva, 'Ivan Groznyi', *Russkii illiuzion*, p. 245.
95. Goodwin, *Eisenstein, Cinema, and History*, p. 180.
96. *Ocherki istorii sovetskogo kino*, Vol. 2, p. 710.
97. Goodwin, *Eisenstein, Cinema, and History*, p. 201.
98. Marianna Kireeva, 'Ivan Groznyi'. In *Russkii illiuzion*, p. 248.
99. Ibid., p. 248.
100. As Uhlenbruch notes, 'After the victory over Hitler's Germany, the immediate past had much artistic material to offer. The system had legitimised itself internally and no longer needed historical parallels . . . The dilemma of history, into which the Stalin culture had manoeuvred itself during the years of foreign policy conflicts, becomes clear after the end of World War II. As seen from the chronology of events, Eisenstein's fight to save his Ivan Grozny is an outdated battle retreat. A true, vital interest was evident in the first part of the film, whose mistakes could be easily pardoned. The second part had to disappear into the archives, not only because of its mistakes, but also due to official indifference. The Stalin cult in the post-war period no longer needed a historical metaphor. In films such as *The Battle of Stalingrad* and *The Fall of Berlin*, Stalin himself appeared on the screen.

'After the victory over Hitler's Germany, the historical dualism could be abandoned in which Soviet history and its perfecter, Stalin, had positive prefigurations in the past history of Russia. The model of the early 1940s was discarded after 1945. If past history up to that point was to have been read as a result of prerequisites, which one could interpret "ex post" as prophecies of redemption – in the Old Testament too there were nearly redeemed persons – then Soviet culture found itself now, after 1945, in the state without history, focussing on the present and on the latest war events.' Bernd Uhlenbruch, 'The Annexation of History: Eisenstein and the Ivan Grozny Cult of the 1940s'. In Hans Gunther (ed.), *The Culture of the Stalin Period*, London: Macmillan, 1990, pp. 283–5.

As early as the 1960s, this idea was suggested by Isaac Deutscher: 'It was no longer good patriotic style to evoke the names of Kutuzov, Suvorov, Minin, and Pozharsky. It was no longer fashionable to glorify the great Tsars, Ivan the Terrible and Peter the Great, whom historians and writers had just treated with more reverence than discretion as Stalin's spiritual forebears . . . In part the new turn was probably a genuine reaction from the surfeit of wartime nationalism. In part, it may have been dictated by Stalin's personal considerations. In 1941–43 he could still be flattered by comparisons between himself and Peter the Great and take pride in analogies drawn between the two Fatherland wars of 1812 and 1941. Mounted on ancestral shoulders he gained in stature. As victor he has no need for all that. The Peters, the Kutuzovs, the Alexanders looked like pygmies in comparison with him.' Isaac Deutscher, *Stalin. A political biography*, 2nd edn, New York: Oxford University Press, 1966, pp. 562–3.

101. Kireeva, 'Ivan Groznyi', p. 244.
102. Iuzovskii, 'Eizenshtein!', p. 46.

2. HISTORY WITH BIOGRAPHY

In drawing rooms damask wallpaper,
Portraits of grandfathers on the walls . . .

Alexander Pushkin

SUVOROV'S GRANDSONS, CHAPAEV'S CHILDREN

Biography relates to the individual life in the same way that history relates to the social past; it transforms experience into material for narrative. But if in history such depersonalisation is not only permissible, but also inevitable (in the end history is significant in so far as it is supra-individual), then in biography it apparently contradicts the very nature of individualising discourse. The very notion of 'biography' involves a conflict between the life (bio-) and its description (-graphy). This conflict is traditionally removed by means of substituting the former with the latter; biographical discourse works more successfully, the less the personally lived experience remains in the text produced by it. This operation to seize and neutralise experience is directed above all at the destruction of alternative techniques of (life) writing (just as competing historical doctrines and descriptions of the same events of the past are directed not so much at establishing or debunking one historical fact or another, as at destroying the very alternative historical discourses). Biography is the arrest of the person, an operation to neutralise and instrumentalise his or her life experience (which only by having become a biography has pragmatic potential). The more politically topical a person, the more inevitable that person's 'biographical' isolation and arrest. Having been placed in biographical 'solitary confinement', the object passes through full de-realisation. The person literally pays with his or her own life in order to remain 'among the living' after death and function as a product of 'writing'.

The metagenre of Stalinist cinema was not the historical-revolutionary film (which reached its brief heyday in the mid-1930s) but precisely the biographical film. At the centre of these biographies there could be leaders of the revolution and tsars, figures in 'national liberation movements' and leaders of 'popular uprisings', writers and composers, scientists and military commanders. In the post-war years biographical film practically had a monopoly over the Soviet screen. Why did the Soviet historical film invariably turn into biography? Why did it in particular occupy the leading place among the genres of historical narrative? What, finally, is the nature and function of biography in the Stalinist political-aesthetic project?

To answer these questions we will turn to the most successful series of biographical films in Soviet cinema: films about military leaders (on the battlefield and in the navy). In contrast to the films about figures from the sciences, arts and culture, which took over after the war, this series began in 1938 with Eisenstein's film, *Alexander Nevsky*, which set out the new biographical canon. In contrast to the films about revolutionary and popular leaders which came out in the 1930s, this series flourished as much before the war (Pudovkin's *Minin and Pozharsky* (*Minin i Pozharskii*) in 1939, and *Suvorov* in 1940; Igor Savchenko's *Bogdan Khmelnitsky* in 1941) as it did during and after the war, right up to Stalin's very death (Vladimir Petrov's *Kutuzov* in 1944; Pudovkin's *Admiral Nakhimov* in 1945–6; Mikhail Romm's *Admiral Ushakov* and *The Ships Storm the Bastions* (*Korabli shturmuiut bastiony*) in 1953).

Military-biographical films have generally been viewed exclusively from the political-propaganda perspective; indeed, abrupt changes in (geo-)political priorities exerted the greatest influence on them. Anti-German rhetoric unexpectedly gave way to anti-Polish feeling (as a result of which the hugely successful *Alexander Nevsky* disappeared from cinemas and was substituted with *Minin and Pozharsky* and *Bogdan Khmelnitsky*), the rhetoric of 'war on enemy territory' gave way to the realities of defeat during the opening stages of the Great Patriotic War (thus *Suvorov* was replaced by *Kutuzov*), and yesterday's allies unexpectedly became enemies in the Cold War (here the naval commanders Nakhimov and Ushakov came to the rescue). It is obvious that in contrast to the 'tsarist' and 'people's' series, which had at their centre internal political agendas above all, geopolitics lay at the basis of the military series. (Stalinist cinema perceived the nineteenth century precisely according to these categories.) Siege mentality and 'conspiracy theory', deeply rooted in Russian political culture, brought about the heyday of this 'geopolitical' discourse. The military-biographical film became the sole forum for the visualisation of the geopolitical fantasies and phobias of Stalinism. Simultaneously, it is also the most suitable for analysis of the techniques of political manipulation through these fantasies and phobias.

It is worth bearing in mind that at the centre of this form of production stood two of the greatest artists of Soviet and world cinema – Sergei Eisenstein and Vsevolod Pudovkin. A good number of brilliant figures were attracted to it, from the former leader of the Formalists, Viktor Shklovsky, to the favourite Stalinist historian, the academician Evgeny Tarle, and the composer Alexander Prokofiev. Over the course of many – and very different! – years, the genre underwent a great deal of change, by no means only political, but precisely structural. In so far as these films in particular were directly bound up with (geo-)politics, their generic aspects have in general never been seriously discussed. Meanwhile, the truly political (and not the presently pragmatic) content of these pictures is impossible to understand without knowledge of their genre dynamics.

The history of the Soviet biographical film begins with a semi-fairytale figure, the half-military leader, half-saint, Alexander Nevsky. The film begins with a striking attempt to distil myth into history, and ends with the distillation of history into myth. It is not so much a question of the content of this mythology, transformed before one's eyes into a respectable historical narrative, as of the very mechanism of the outcome and functioning of these biographically visualised narratives. Their very presence in a social medium legitimises, promotes and makes easily assimilable the main biography – the biography of a leader. The biographical film is a true machine for the distillation of myth into history and history into myth. In their communicating vessels the political 'content' of Stalinism moves back and forth.

Before the release of *Alexander Nevsky*, the cult Soviet film was *Chapaev*, which laid the foundations of the tradition of mythologisation of historical biography (Pudovkin subsequently attempted to move in keeping with this tradition in *Suvorov* and in the first version of *Admiral Nakhimov*), at the basis of which was the individual distinctiveness of the person, his or her 'national character'. This tradition was definitively smashed by Eisenstein; in *Alexander Nevsky* he moved to the historicisation of myth, resurrecting the tradition of the epic cinema of the 1920s. Picked up in *Minin and Pozharsky* and *Bogdan Khmelnitsky*, and later reinforced in the second version of *Admiral Nakhimov* and in the films about Ushakov, this tradition, in the form in which it was reborn at the end of the 1930s, bore very little resemblance to Eisenstein's *Battleship Potemkin*, Pudovkin's *Storm over Asia* or Dovzhenko's *Arsenal*.

The history of the Soviet biographical film is the story of the non-meeting of film with biography. In Eisenstein's film, Alexander Nevsky is not so much an individual as a pure function of geopolitical myth, personified in the semi-fairytale prince of the thirteenth century. In *Minin and Pozharsky* and *Bogdan Khmelnitsky*, the characters are also functions of historical myth, but they are depersonalised functions. They are more like moving monuments, 'speaking statues'. In the foreground everywhere here is not so much the biography of the person as the historical events in which they are functioning. In *Suvorov* and *Kutuzov*, on the other hand, it is precisely the character of the military commander which is in the foreground. The characters are so vivid that, in the case of Suvorov, the events in which he participated are turned into a backdrop and lose any relevance from the point of view of the assessment of their 'historical progressiveness'. Finally, in the films about the naval commanders Nakhimov and Ushakov, the heroes are returned to the original condition of being functions of openly allusive political myth; they arrive from the opposite direction back at the point of departure – *Alexander Nevsky*. But this is not a simple return. Instead of the personification and historicisation of a semi-mythical character, here the depersonalisation of real historical figures is taking place; instead of the historicisation of myth, we have the historicisation of the present.

This dynamic of the genre was no more accidental than was the choice of characters for these films. Konstantin Simonov recalled that Stalin

> planned nothing as logically and systematically as future films, and this plan was linked with contemporary political aims, although the films he planned were almost always, if not always, historical . . . This can be traced through the figures he promoted in the cinema: Alexander Nevsky, Suvorov, Kutuzov, Ushakov, Nakhimov. It is significant moreover that at the height of the war, with the creation of the orders of Suvorov, Kutuzov, Ushakov and Nakhimov as decorations for military leaders, in first place were put not those who played a larger part in popular memory, Kutuzov and Nakhimov, but those who waged war and gained stunning victories on and beyond the borders of Russia.[1]

This reference to orders allows us to place these films in a somewhat unexpected context – the context of the history of Soviet phaleristics. The fact is that there is not a single Soviet decoration (and practically all of them were introduced during the war) for which there was not a corresponding film. And, equally, practically all the films about military and naval commanders correspond to decorations. The Orders of Suvorov, Kutuzov and Alexander Nevsky were introduced in July 1942 – the most critical point of the war. The Order of Bogdan Khmelnitsky was introduced after the victory at the Kursk Salient, on the eve of the liberation of Ukraine (in the second half of 1943). In November 1943 one of the most popular orders was brought in – the Order of Glory (awarded to around a million people during the war), which until the very publication of the decree was to have been called the Order of Bagration.[2] In the same year naval orders were introduced – the Ushakov and the Nakhimov. Among the projects for decorations during the war years which were never realised, there was the Order of Denis Davydov (for partisans), the Order of Nikolai Pirogov (for medical officers), and for civilians, the Orders of Mikhail Lomonosov, Chernyshevsky, Pavlov and Mendeleev. Thus all phaleristic projects were named. (The only exceptions were the Order of Victory and the Order of Glory, although the latter was also initially conceived as a named order, and the medals which were named after defended or liberated cities.)

It is worth noting that each order carried within it the imprint of its name. Thus the Order of Suvorov was conferred on military commanders for victories gained against a numerically superior enemy (corresponding to Suvorov's aphorism 'enemies are beaten with skill, not numbers'). And the Order of Kutuzov was given for good organisation of the withdrawal of large formations (retreat), inflicting a counter-attack on the enemy and pulling out to a new line with minimal losses. The Order of Alexander Nevsky, meanwhile, was awarded to commanders for showing initiative in the choice of a felicitous moment for a sudden, audacious and successful attack on the enemy, inflicting a major defeat with few losses among one's own forces. The plots of the films in this way turned out to be distinctive historical illustrations of the decorations. But the connection with the cinema was sometimes also absolutely direct.

Thus, in the course of work on the Order of Alexander Nevsky, it turned out that no contemporary portrait of the epic leader existed. And so the decoration used the profile of . . . Nikolai Cherkasov from Eisenstein's film.[3] And the idea for the Order of Bogdan Khmelnitsky came entirely from Alexander Dovzhenko.

During the war, when the decorations were introduced, the Soviet fighter had to be perceived as depicted in the famous caption by Samuil Marshak from a popular poster:

> We fight robustly,
> Chop off enemies' heads.
> Like Suvorov's grandsons,
> Chapaev's children!

For the few years of the heyday of the Soviet historical film at the end of the 1930s, 'Chapaev's children' were transformed into 'Suvorov's grandsons'. This concerted genealogical broadening resulted in the Soviet fighter of the war period turning out to be much closer to Suvorov than Chapaev. In his speech on the twenty-fourth anniversary of the October Revolution, 6 November 1941, Stalin touched on the theme of the 'national pride' of the representatives 'of the great Russian nation, the nation of Plekhanov and Lenin, Belinsky and Chernyshevsky, Pushkin and Tolstoy, Glinka and Tchaikovsky, Gorky and Chekhov, Sechenov and Pavlov, Repin and Surikov, Suvorov and Kutuzov!'[4] The following day in Red Square, in his parting address to the forces who were leaving in order to defend Moscow, Stalin concluded: 'Let the steadfast images of our great ancestors inspire you in this war: Alexander Nevsky, Dmitry Donskoi, Kuzma Minin, Dmitry Pozharsky, Alexander Suvorov, Mikhail Kutuzov.'[5] What is striking here is not only the selection of names of military commanders, as if it is directly cribbed from the thematic plan of Soviet cinema production and the orders which were introduced, but also the fact that in this selection there is not a single name which could be associated with the Soviet era. This is a completely pre-revolutionary heroic pantheon. The irony lies in the fact that in the run-up to the twenty-fifth anniversary of the Revolution (to which Stalin's speeches were dedicated), it turned out to be 'omitted', historically irrelevant. Thus yesterday's 'Chapaev's children' (literally: the generation that had played 'Chapaev' in the middle of the 1930s suffered the heaviest blow) now turned out to all intents and purposes to be Chapaev's grandsons, but children of Suvorov (who always addressed his soldiers with the words 'my children').

Soviet historicising art was resolving the goal of the unification of at least three mutually exclusive constructions: socialist ideology, national state and empire. The national State, being the product of the bourgeois revolution, contradicted socialist ideology and was incompatible with empire. Empire, in its turn, retaining the rudiments of feudalism, contradicted the very essence of the national State, not to mention socialist ideology. Finally, the latter (precisely as ideology!) was born as the means of destruction of State itself, and in its internationalism was directly opposed to both nationalism and imperialism. The goal of Soviet historicising art led to the harmonisation of these components and their legitimisation, condemning it to be notoriously ill defined, but at the same time endowing it with a dramatic quality and an internal plot-line. In it one thing contradicted another; the same people were 'people's heroes' and . . . 'oppressors of the people', they expressed 'national interests' and simultaneously . . . 'betrayed' them. They were 'Suvorov's grandsons' who participated in the rout of Pugachev and the suppression of the national struggle for liberation in Europe, and . . . 'children of Chapaev', the hero of the Civil War, in the course of which their victory was feted as both 'Pugachev's revolutionary cause' and a 'national liberation movement'.

We will attempt to understand the interconnections between these constructs through examination of the links of the historical genre to the biographical. In Soviet conditions, the historical film (like the novel) was conceived within the categories of the biographical genre; here, as one film critic of that time asserted, 'the features of the biography of the people are revealed in images of majestic power and beauty.'[6] The 'biography of the people' – of 'Suvorov's grandsons, Chapaev's children' – is an ideological harvest, stored in the seeds of the individual biographies of great commanders.

But what, strictly speaking, is there of biography in these films? As Grigory Vinokur noted, 'historical fact (the event and so on), in order to become biographical fact, must in one form or another be experienced by the given individual . . . by becoming an object of experience, historical fact gains biographical meaning.'[7] The sphere of experience coincides with the 'sphere of spiritual experience', and

> this is in fact that sphere of personal life in which we gain the right to speak of personal life as creation. The personal here is like an artist who models and mints his life in the form of experience from the material of surrounding reality. To experience something means to make a corresponding phenomenon an event in one's own personal life.[8]

In these films the characters experience nothing. They themselves have to become the object of experience. They themselves are the 'historical fact', its derivative and function; they are the medium through which this 'fact' manifests itself. Being deprived of subjectivity (that is, as they are not personalities but functions), they have neither biography nor spiritual experience. However, in order to be transformed into 'facts of the spiritual experience' of the viewer, they must for a start emancipate themselves. In other words, the aim is not for

Razin to be an individual, but for him to bring ideological information to the viewer (which can be achieved equally without individualisation). Ivan the Terrible became part of the viewer's experience, in so far as Eisenstein changed his aims, whilst Alexander Nevsky not only does not become an individual, but remains an ideological function according the very author's intention. He does not 'experience' the Battle on the Ice. The focus of the film is neither him nor the battle. As Eisenstein himself said, 'Our theme is patriotism.' The heroes and events are only functions of this 'theme'. These heroes have no personal life at all. They do not need one; it would only hinder them. Eisenstein's hero does not 'model his own life', but he is not a subject at all (and even less is he a subject of 'creation'!). He is himself 'the material of surrounding reality'.

Geopolitical Opera

Among Eisenstein's many pronouncements about *Alexander Nevsky*, the persistence with which the director emphasised the idea of the historically allegorical nature of the picture is striking. Eisenstein not only did not hide it (which all authors of historical genres usually do, speaking of their striving for 'historical truth'), but directly said that the Teutonic and Livonian Knights were ancestors of today's Fascists, who wanted to conquer the Slavs, that the bloody terror unleashed by them in no way differed from what was going on in present-day Europe, that the Teutons appeared as invincible then as today's Germany seemed now, but that just as it had proved possible to crush them then at Lake Chudskoe, so precisely would the Fascist army be crushed. The allegorical nature of his schema was turned by Eisenstein into an aesthetic principle. With this the director, in a paradoxical way, confirmed Pokrovsky's main thesis that history is politics projected on to the past.

The historical mask falls away right from the opening captions: 'It was the 13th century. The Teutonic and Livonian Knights had advanced from the West to Rus' . . . the German aggressors expected an easy victory over our people'. The 'Teutonic and Livonian Knights' – a reference that barely anybody in the audience understood – are immediately transformed into 'German aggressors', while the thirteenth-century inhabitants of Rus' become 'our people'. Corresponding to the propagandised pre-war doctrine (war will be waged on the enemy's territory), in *Alexander Nevsky* it is as if the very strategy for waging war is cribbed from the speeches of People's Commissar Voroshilov ('We shall fight on enemy ground!' Alexander declares to his troops. 'The dogs shall not set foot on Russian soil!'). What was the reason for the Russian victory at Lake Chudskoe? Eisenstein explains:

> The key here is not the icy surface of the lake, but its geographical location. The border of the Russian lands runs along the Eastern shore of the lake. The frozen surface of the lake in contrast to the Eastern shore is foreign, foreign soil. And the decisive rout of the interventionists in the

battle at Lake Chudskoe was in many ways determined precisely by this circumstance. The defeat itself of the Teutonic and Livonian Knights at Lake Chudskoe was an unexpected and staggering 'miracle'. Chroniclers sought an explanation for it in supernatural phenomena and in some sort of heavenly host which had supposedly taken part in the battle. But it was of course not a question of these dubious precursors of future aviation; the only miracle in the battle at Lake Chudskoe was the genius of the Russian people, who for the first time began to sense their national, people's might, their unity ... From their midst they promoted Alexander, a strategist and commander of genius. With him at their head they defended the motherland, crushed the perfidious enemy on foreign territory and did not allow them to defile with their invasion the soils of the native land. Thus it will be for all those who dare to encroach upon our great motherland now as well. If the might of the people's spirit was able to deal with the enemy thus, when the country was on its knees, in the fetters of the Tartar yoke, then the force will not be found which could shatter this country, which has now thrown off the chains of oppression, the country, which has become the socialist motherland, the country, which is being led to unprecedented victories by the greatest strategist in world history – Stalin.[9]

Thus Eisenstein rejects the mystical-miraculous explanation for the victory, substituting a military and strategic explanation (victory on foreign territory), a national and patriotic explanation (or more simply, nationalistic; the Russian victory is the result of the maturity of their national identity) and, finally, leadership (the charismatic leader Alexander, in whom Stalin's profile is clearly visible). Eisenstein would peddle the allusive nature of the material again and again. In the chronicles of those years he was 'struck most of all by the similarities with nowadays',[10] these people are

close, perceptible, a single language links them with us through the centuries, the sacred language of the work of the great people . . . These are the same people as us . . . They are kith and kin to the Soviet people with their love of the fatherland and hatred of the enemy.[11]

Not afraid of accusations of 'antihistoricism' or 'Pokrovskiism', Eisenstein readily politicised his film. In the article 'Patriotism is our theme,' he said that 'the one sole theme' of the film was 'the freedom-loving theme of national pride, the might of love towards the motherland, the theme of the patriotism of the Russian people', that he 'seized on this theme, hearing it almost as distinctly in the almost epic thirteenth century as we hear it in the hourly throb of the happy times of the Stalinist epoch'. He said that for him the events of the thirteenth century were indissoluble with events from today, when he read about the deaths at Guernica at the hands of the Fascists.

Thus, at the crossroads of three lines – the military-strategic, the national-patriotic and, finally, that of the leader – the image of Alexander arises not as an individual, but as a derivative great figure from the ideological functions at work in the film. The deep contradiction of Eisenstein's method and the image created in the film lies in the fact that biography strives towards uniqueness, while allegory strives towards typicality. Nikolai Cherkasov recalled how Eisenstein rejected all his suggestions for making the hero more psychologically alive. (The actor did not know how to play Nevsky, since the character was deprived of any individual features whatsoever.) Eisenstein needed a hero-monument: not a saint (Saint Alexander Nevsky left behind him exclusively hagiography), but not an individual either. He required a depersonalised hero. From the aggregate of iconographic signs grew the image of a leader. Stalin himself ordered the scene of the entrance of the victorious Alexander into Pskov to be the striking final scene of the film. In the course of correcting the screenplay, he crossed out the scene of Alexander's death, declaring: 'The screenplay ends here. With the triumphal entrance into Pskov. Such a good prince cannot die!'[12] Alexander Nevsky in this scene is not only a prince and a saint, but also the people's leader, entering liberated Pskov to the ringing of bells.

Mikhail Geller and Alexander Nekrich drew attention to the fact that Pyotr Pavlenko, writing simultaneously with the screenplay for the film a novel about the future war, *In the East* (*Na vostoke*), reconstructed in parallel a similar scene with Stalin. In the novel Stalin walks around Moscow on the night of the start of the war. It is expressed in the same words as the description of the triumphal entrance of Alexander into Pskov:

[T]he crowd cried and called: 'Stalin! Stalin! Stalin!' – and this was a call of glory and honour, it sounded like 'Forward!' In a moment of popular fury the crowd called their leader, and at two in the morning he went from the Kremlin to the Bolshoi Theatre to be together with Moscow . . . His calm figure, in a tightly fastened, simple overcoat, a cap with a soft peak, was so simple it brought a tear to the eye. There was nothing superfluous or accidental in him. Stalin's face was severe. He was walking, hurrying on, and frequently turning to the members of the Politburo and government surrounding him, saying something to them and showing his hand to the crowd of people.[13]

In *Alexander Nevsky* Eisenstein cut the path not from hagiography to biography, but from hagiography (which was changed in the sense that Alexander was deprived of any Christian features whatsoever and transformed into a real tribal leader) to allegory, omitting biography. Eisenstein did not even begin to simulate the genre; emphasising the allegorical nature of the film, he revealed the conditional character of his hero, depriving, in this way, his biography and personality of any relevance. Alexander Dovzhenko paid attention to this at the time. At a conference dedicated to historical film in 1940, he said that the allusive nature of historical pictures replaced the very historical material:

> In *Peter*, and in *Alexander Nevsky*, and in *Minin and Pozharsky*, and in *Bogdan Khmelnitsky* . . . there is a kind of obsequious desire to drag history closer to us and even to confuse the heroes' words with speeches of the leaders. It works out that Alexander Nevsky could really be appointed secretary to the Pskov regional Party committee, and Peter and Minin and Bogdan could also be something of the same kind.[14]

As leaders of all peoples they could in fact have boldly laid claim to the post of the General Secretary.

As David Bordwell noted of *Alexander Nevsky*, 'the film severs Russian nationalism from any religious roots . . . the church has relinquished its place to the secular leader.'[15] In this secular state religion is only the setting for daily routine. Judging by the architecture, the religion is Christian, but in effect these people are still heathens (or already 'atheists'). All Eisenstein scholars have focused on the absence of the Christian religion in the thirteenth-century Rus' depicted here.[16] Either Christianity has not yet taken root here or it has already disappeared into the past. This transformation of a Christian hagiographic narrative into a modernised leadership narrative of the twentieth century had important consequences for the biographical genre founded by Eisenstein. As Bernd Uhlenbruch observed,

> [T]he image of Alexander, his speech and behaviour testify to the ritualised presentation of a clan leader, who stands above daily life, deprived of any kind of personal connections, attuned only to his people, ready for self-sacrifice and demanding complete submission to himself.[17]

Uhlenbruch also notes the large number of not so much Christian as pagan allusions in the film;[18] the sun-hero Alexander takes on the roles of wise leader, warrior, matchmaker – the same functions fulfilled in Soviet mythology by the 'sun-Stalin' – military commander, leader, 'gatherer of lands', and often also matchmaker and substitute father.

Alexander's appearance in Novgorod is preceded by a speech by the local *voevoda*. The Novgorod merchants want to summon 'their' *voevoda*, Domash Tverdislavich, but he says he is not suited for such a task: 'Someone else is needed. One whose arm is stronger, whose mind is clearer. One famed throughout the whole world and known to the enemy. We need a leader, brothers – Prince Alexander, son of Yaroslav.' It is a matter precisely of a leader. As is well known, among the rejected variations of the film's title were *Rus'*, *Lord Novgorod* (*Gospodin Velikii Novgorod*) and *The Battle on the Ice* (*Ledovoe poboishche*),[19] but it was neither toponyms nor central events which gave their name to the film; the choice settled on the proper name, *Alexander Nevsky*, which focused attention on the hero, as is characteristic of the biographical genre.

The leadership aspect is connected to the distinctly nationalistic spirit of the film. The heyday of the historical-biographical film and novel accompanied the process of birth in the era of the terror of the Soviet nation. National identity, as if characteristic of the Russians in the thirteenth century, as it is presented in the film, arouses doubt even, as it seems, in the director himself. The theme of the unification of Rus' before the first – Western – threat sounds out from the very first frames, when in answer to the appeal to fight the Tartars, Alexander declares: 'The Mongols can wait. There's a more dangerous enemy than the Tartars. Closer to hand, more vicious. They will not be bought off with tributes. The Germans. Once we've crushed them, we can get down to the Tartars.' The Germans are more dangerous than the Tartars in that they threaten the very identity of the Russian nation. The fact that the latter exists, however, is apparent only to Alexander himself.

In the very first scene in Novgorod between the 'representatives of the people' and the merchants a skirmish occurs. At the call to prepare to repulse the Germans, one of the merchants declares: 'We will pay them off! We have too many goods anyway!':

> Olga: 'You would barter away the Russian land?'
> Merchant: 'Is there any such thing as the Russian land? Where have you seen it?'
> Anany (who turns out later to be a traitor): 'Each man for himself! Where you sleep, that's your motherland!'
> A wounded fighter: 'You're lying, dog!'
> Ignat (embodying the 'simple people'): 'For them, the rich folk, it's all the same – mother or stepmother – wherever there's a profit, that's their native soil. But we poor folk face certain death under the Germans.'

Judging from the phrase: 'Is there any such thing as the Russian land? Where have you seen it?', the very notion of the 'Russian land' is not fixed in any way. It is formed in the course of the picture, the main theme of which is 'patriotism'. In response to the words of the envoy from Novgorod who appeals to Alexander to defend the city – 'forgive our past offences, Yaroslavich. Stand up for Novgorod!' – the prince replies, 'I will stand up for the offence to the Russian lands!' Later, when he is in Novgorod, Alexander appeals: 'You are alone, Lord Novgorod. Rise up for your homeland, for your birth-mother. Rise up for the Russian cities. For Kiev, Vladimir, Ryazan. For your native fields, forests and rivers! For our great people!' It seems that Alexander lives in a special geopolitical space, with the 'homeland' and the 'great people'. In the film there is constant reference to the 'Russian land' (not the State, which did not yet exist!); the choir sounds out its refrain, 'Rise up, Russian people, defend our fair land . . . For native home, for Russian soil.' The refrain

'Russian people' and 'native home' fixes this as yet undefined geopolitical reality. At the centre of *Alexander Nevsky* there is a national myth, and this is why Alexander constantly appeals to Rus'; for him as a national, tribal leader, the 'Novgorod cause' does not exist, but there is a 'Russian' cause. *Alexander Nevsky* embodies the myth of the birth of the nation and of national consciousness. It is above all a nationalistic film (which cannot be said of *Ivan the Terrible*, a particularly statist film), and in this capacity has nothing in common with revolutionary history. (This first scene in Novgorod, from which we have already quoted, demonstrates the shift from class to national-patriotic conflict.)

To all intents and purposes, Alexander is a great figure derived from the arithmetical mean of these ideological calculations. Being a pure function, he cannot possess a biography. The very specific form within 'biography' of Alexander Nevsky (and to one extent or another of the whole biographical series of which it was the basis) sprung from the very artistic task which the director was resolving here. The main character was picked by Eisenstein deliberately; he was offered a choice between Alexander Nevsky and Ivan Susanin. Eisenstein settled on Alexander because practically no historical materials had been preserved from this time. 'Whatever you did would be correct, nobody could refute you,' he said to Mikhail Romm.[20] This freed him from dependence on 'expert consultants'. Such was the explanation of the director himself. There is also a contradictory explanation, confirming Eisenstein's initial conformism as he got down to work on the project. James Goodwin asserts:

> Eisenstein may have considered that the biographical subjects proposed to him represented a choice not only between two eras but between two movements in Soviet art as well. As a protagonist, Ivan Susanin belongs with the typical heroes of proletarian art like Marfa, who projects the masses' potential through exemplary action. In *Old and New* (*Staroe i novoe*) this heroism takes generative, open and spontaneous forms that shape history in terms of a promised future. The emphasis in socialist realism, on the other hand, is on legendary heroism mandated by State authority.[21]

It is worth remembering that, prior to *Alexander Nevsky*, Eisenstein had been condemned as a formalist and had in effect been denied the possibility of work in cinema. Therefore sober calculation in the hope of rehabilitation was a fully justified strategy (especially in 1938!).

Alexander Nevsky, the first large-scale, truly effective historical-biographical film about a military commander, was a roaring success. Whole classes of schoolchildren, pioneer groups, army detachments and factory brigades went to see it, as they had to *Chapaev* five years previously. *Alexander Nevsky* was a box-office hit, a rare occurrence, when a State-commissioned and sponsored patriotic film becomes a phenomenon of mass culture. This is a unique occurrence not only in the biography of Eisenstein himself (even his *Battleship Potemkin* was not a hit), but also in the history of the genre.

It is curious, however, that his most successful film turned out to be the most unsatisfactory for the director. In Eisenstein's many notes this dissatisfaction is explained sometimes by its straightforwardness, sometimes by its formal short-comings (insufficient rhythmicality, breakdowns of the montage, which seemed to him so patent that they were visible even to the man in the street). Nevertheless, it seems that behind all this is concealed Eisenstein's subconscious discontent at the unconcealed servility of the film (with *Alexander Nevsky* the director was after all rehabilitated, and Stalin called him 'a true Bolshevik'), which was expressed in its straightforwardly allegorical nature. It was so obvious that Eisenstein apparently decided to make it programmatic. It was just here that the internal discontent which led to the explosion of *Ivan the Terrible* matured – from the most opportunist film to the most dissident.[22]

Alexander Nevsky occupies a key place in the history of the Soviet historical-biographical film. On the level of iconography the hero of this film could be related to the 'tsarist' series. As with every film in this series, it is about a 'people's tsar' (in this case, a prince). The Slavophile idea of the 'people's monar-chy' is based on the unity of the leader and the people, on national unity and solidarity, and as such contradicts the class approach. Eisenstein derived the image of Alexander Nevsky from the image of Peter. The fact that 'the rearing steed under Alexander . . . is associated with Falconet's statue of Peter' had already attracted the attention of one critic at the end of the 1930s.[23] But this was not enough for Eisenstein, and thus he specifically explained that:

> [F]or good reason Peter, having completed centuries later the programme of the genius prophet of the thirteenth century, transferred precisely his remains to the place of the construction of the future Petersburg, as if identifying himself with the line which Prince Alexander Nevsky had conceived.[24]

On the other hand, the director transformed Alexander, a prince who had already been feted for his victory over the Swedes, almost into a poor peasant, living as a simple fisherman, which, as all the consultant historians pointed out, was a completely impossible distortion of 'historical truth' ('the exaggerated image of the prince as a "peasant", one of the "simple folk", at the time of his already celebrated great victory on the Neva over the Swedes, is historically untruthful'[25]). Nevertheless, Eisenstein took truly Bolshevik liberties with his treatment of non-existent history (and, as it turned out later, the risk was fully justified).

Thus *Alexander Nevsky* stands at the intersection of all the historical-biographical series – the 'people', the 'tsarist', and the 'military commanders.' If in *Alexander Nevsky* Eisenstein acts as the founder of the tradition of the Soviet biographical film, then in *Ivan the Terrible* he concludes the tsarist series. The director's interest in 'pure history' has been explained by scholars in various ways. Interesting here is the interpretation of him by Olga Yumasheva as shifting from 'collective consciousness' (*Strike, Battleship Potemkin, October*) to 'collective unconsciousness' (*Alexander Nevsky*).[26] An interpretation of this kind allows us to understand why the director turned to programmatic mythologism.

Eisenstein begins 'Patriotism is our theme', the key article to understanding *Alexander Nevsky*, with the strange, at first glance, opposition of the chronicle and the remnants of the material culture of that epoch. The chronicles speak of the 'saint' of the thirteenth century, with his 'bodily grandeur', his 'wisdom of Solomon', his 'strength of Samson', 'his voice like a trumpet' and so on. But what else remained of that epoch? 'Fragments of swords, one helmet and some chain-mail armour.' And here Eisenstein is repeating after the artist Surikov: 'I trusted in stones, not books.' How can this choice be explained? Surely by the fact that 'stones' are much easier to read than 'books'. You can 'read' into them anything you want (including a modified chronicle). Uhlenbruch states that Eisenstein in *Alexander Nevsky* came up against the same problem as Wagner (to a production of whose work he turned immediately after *Alexander Nevsky*): 'the impossibility of combining myth and history in the frame of a work of art'.[27]

Shklovsky notes that the nerve centre of the film lies right here, but he did not want to see a problem here, suggesting that 'in the epic there is truth. The historian must reveal it,' and swearing allegiance to Eisenstein ('I consider myself a foot-soldier, fighting at Potylikha in the summer on asphalt ice, and I stand under Sergei Eisenstein's banner, with a standard with quotations in my hands and in my heart, absolute belief in the rightness of the right for the new history'[28]). The 'new history', which Eisenstein was producing before the eyes, was the product of particular historical vision. In essence, Eisenstein is engaged in transforming myth into history by means of the cinema, thereby resolving Wagner's dilemma.

The historical figure, behind which the virtual mythological hero of Alexander Nevsky shone out, turned out to be a 'walking and talking monument'. The effect was the opposite of that in *Chapaev*, where the reverse operation was carried out – distilling history into myth. *Alexander Nevsky* is a conscious anti-*Chapaev*; if Chapaev is characterised by energy, humour, spontaneity, irascibility, passion, dynamism, then Eisenstein's prince is severe, static, reserved, distanced from those surrounding him, monumental. He is a character from an opera. The film heaped up the stylistic traditions of the genre; it was precisely to this 'horse-opera' (as Dovzhenko jokingly called the film) that the operatic nature of Soviet historical-biographical film, its deliberate theatricality, dated back. Was this not why Wagner strived to combine myth and history precisely in opera, which allows a solution to this political-aesthetic dilemma in an organic artistic genre?

Alexander Nevsky was called a poster-film, a slogan-film. These definitions came out of the absence of psychological nuances in the representation of the main character, who was closer to the clearly and accessibly portrayed hero of epic or fairytale. Of this in particular spoke the film's cameraman Eduard Tisse, admitting that he used 'the cinematographic device of a sculpturally pictorial construction of the frame'.[29] Pudovkin also spoke of this: 'The very 'tale' of the picture, if one can so express it, is, of course, the tale of a national epic.'[30] Straight after the film's release one critic wrote of the epic nature of the picture and its hero:

> An epos. Epic breadth, clarity, sharpness. Eisenstein's frame, flooded with sunlight, pellucid, capturing boundless space – everything in it is large-scale, voluminous, majestic – things, people, events. History appears here also only in broad brush-strokes, everything that is secondary is cast away . . . *Alexander Nevsky* is constructed like a *bylina*. Eisenstein sees epic images as large, integrated, carved out of a single piece, a single block, free from fragmented little features and psychological details . . . in turning to the epic pages of history, Eisenstein has found his strength. He shows people on another scale than others manage – precisely when they become *bogatyrs* . . . Neither antiquity, nor the past, nor the olden days are solely the property of the epos. Eisenstein was able to show it both in the Revolution of 1905 and in the great days of October. Nowadays *byliny* are formed about the life of the people today, about today's heroes, and the voice of the storyteller, creating a new epos, does not sound alien in Soviet poetry. More than at any time in history, our time is the time of the epos.[31]

In this 'epic nature of the present' the critic saw the reason for the allusive effectiveness of the picture. Historians would later talk of the film as a 'stylised heroic cheap print' (Maya Turovskaya[32]), and of the 'exaggerated' and 'extravagant simplicity' of the picture (David Bordwell[33]). The 'epic opera' with a geopolitical plot created for the screen by Eisenstein (and Prokofiev) resolved the central problem of reworking myth into history. (It is worth noting that *Alexander Nevsky* was released in the same year that the *Short Course* history of the party was published.) The paradigms of the Soviet historical-biographical film posed by this film demonstrated exceptional ideological effectiveness, stability and artistic cogency.

TALKING MONUMENTS

Yuri Olesha, in his novel *Envy*, introduced a new hero into Russian literature – the sausage-maker. Much has been written of the audacity of the writer and of the up till then unprecedented type of the hero. Meanwhile, in the pantheon of Russian heroes, there had already been a hero with just such a prosaic profession – the Novgorod butcher Kuzma Minin, who along with prince Dmitry Pozharsky, 'saved Russia from the Troubles'.

According to Pokrovsky, the Russian Time of Troubles, 1600–12, came down to a 'peasant war' against the *boyars*. The *boyars* were intriguing, betraying each other, State authority was weakened, foreign interventionists rushed into the country and the Poles installed a Pretender in the Kremlin, while at the same time supporting the peasant uprising. Class conflict was on hand and the Poles used it. However, after a decade of the Troubles, chaos, famine and ruin, a people's militia managed to be created and, having raised money, it expelled the Poles from Moscow. These actions were accomplished not, of course, by the peasantry, who were capable only of rebellion, but in no way of fighting the regular Polish troops. Minin and Pozharsky (whatever the motives for their actions) 'objectively' took on the role of suppressors of the peasant uprising. Their backing in the main by the ruling classes, who were more afraid of their own serfs than they were of the Poles, and gave money to the militia and effectively to a hired army, was explained by far from patriotic motives. Thus Pokrovsky viewed the matter.

In Stalinist historiography the Time of Troubles was transformed simply into a period of Polish occupation. There were no peasant rebellions (and those that did occur were directed against the Poles, not the masters). The 'people', accordingly, themselves gave the money. The only shortcoming of this picture was that it did not explain of what the Troubles, strictly speaking, consisted. According to this schema, the *boyars* wanted to suppress rebellion with the help of interventionists (to this end allowing the Polish troops into the Kremlin). However, the Russian people united, expelled the 'foreign predators' and routed the Polish forces outside Moscow. The conflict between the peasants and the *boyars* hindered the people's (national) unity before the face of the foreign interventionists. Therefore the rebellious peasants had to be removed from the new plot, the *boyars* displaced to the periphery (they participate only in the development of detective-story intrigues – conspiracies and treachery), and the 'people' promoted to the foreground, with their leaders Minin and Pozharsky, in their opposition to the Poles. Of class conflict nothing remained.

Pokrovsky's anti-autocratic school was accused of depicting the Pretender as a progressive figure, and Minin and Pozharsky as 'counter-revolutionary', of seeing a 'peasant revolution' in the Time of Troubles, and calling Minin and Pozharsky 'the organizers of the rout of the peasant revolution of 1612'. And although the Pretender really did support the peasant uprising, the fact that he was brought into the country by Poles and relied on a foreign army (to which the internationalist Pokrovsky was indifferent) made him completely unsuitable for the new interpretation of events. He not only was not a popular leader, but he also depended on 'the reactionary Polish aristocracy'. Minin and Pozharsky, on the other hand, in effect suppressed the Troubles, expelled the Poles from Moscow and were transformed into 'national heroes', unifiers. The Troubles were interpreted in Stalinist historiography, thus, as a simple weakening of statehood, bringing the 'people' themselves incalculable suffering – from foreign intervention to economic neglect. Class categories turned out to be completely inapplicable to the Time of Troubles, because the interpretation of the Troubles as a 'revolution' gave up no ideological capital. Interpreting it as a national-liberation movement was another matter entirely.

The events of the Troubles which lie at the base of Pudovkin's film, *Minin and Pozharsky*, were in political terms exceptionally obvious; this historical narrative (with, of course, the correct interpretation) speaks of the country collapsing, decaying and falling victim to foreign predators, when there is no strong authority and the State is weakened. The period between the tsars brought the country to the brink of destruction, before a new dynasty (the Romanovs) was born which could return to Russia its wholeness and greatness. It was brought to power by the 'people' themselves, having collected money for the 'people's militia' and expelled the Pretender and the Poles from the Kremlin. It is understandable why, in the very centre of Red Square in 1818 with the money of the great princes, a monument was erected to Minin and Pozharsky, unveiled in the presence of the entire royal family. It is also understandable why after the Revolution they wanted to destroy it; for the revolutionaries, in this story the hated 'people's monarchy' and 'Russian patriotism' merged.

In principle, it is also understandable why the author of the screenplay, Victor Shklovsky, undertook to write about the Time of Troubles in 1937. (His story 'Russians at the Beginning of the Seventeenth Century' (Russkie v nachale XVII veka) was published in the journal *Znamia* in 1938.) He knew himself, as a child and an active participant in the 'time of troubles' of the Russian Revolution, that to survive in Russia under a 'strong State' was in no way easier than in the epoch of the Troubles itself. It helped Shklovsky to arrange the ideological aspects of this new history without error, uniting the seemingly ununitable: a popular uprising with the love of the people for the princes, the treachery of the upper classes with their patriotism. In a word, Ilovaisky with Pokrovsky. The latter, also a child of the 'time of troubles', ended up being a participant by default in an argument that was being conducted – between the former leading formalist and the former leading 'vulgar sociologist'.

Shklovsky consciously constructed his screenplay as a counterbalance to Pokrovsky, accusing the latter of 'rejecting historical realism'.[34] The former formalist accused the former sociologist of 'suggesting that we should not analyze the past, but use it as a screen'.[35] Meanwhile, it was precisely Shklovsky who worked professionally on 'adaptations' of historical fantasies, which differed from Pokrovsky's schema only in that the absence of Marxist doctrine was compensated for by their greater 'historical realism' or, to be more precise, pragmatism.

Although Shklovsky also spoke of the fact that he was striving 'for the people not simply to be a backdrop to the picture, but its heroes', in the foreground of *Minin and Pozharsky* the idea of statehood was advanced: 'I wanted to show how the feeling of the unity of the State is created among the people, how the people are accustomed to fighting not only to defend their own gates. I wanted to show a change in the quality of patriotism.' He was referring to the 'patriotic' (that is, nationalistic) content of the 'historical lesson' which also appeared in *Alexander Nevsky*. In this light, the victory of the 'people' became the result of the triumph of a new national identity of the Russians which had been formed (which in fact in the seventeenth century was probably no greater than in the thirteenth[36]). The problem came down to the construction of the 'Russian people', consisting, in essence, of rebellious peasants, who had no sense of national identity; a small stratum of townsfolk and merchants, who 'identified' with their own interests much more than with the 'Russian people'; and, finally, *boyars* and servicemen, who had only just gone through the terror of the Terrible Tsar, and were least of all interested in the national identity of the rebellious peasant throngs, who had burned down their estates and homes, and were prepared to put anyone they pleased on the throne, if only to stop this never-ending 'Russian rebellion'.

Minin and Pozharsky had to appear before the viewer as leaders of the 'people's movement', promoted from below. The idea of a people's militia did not come from them. They were only at the head of a popular initiative (as 'the people', instead of rising up against their immediate oppressors, had unexpectedly risen up against the Poles, who – for their own reasons, of course – had supported their struggle in every way possible). Apropos of this Pudovkin wrote:

> The idea for organising a people's militia and collecting funds for it was born from below, it aroused a patriotic movement of all our peoples. Minin, a great patriot, an honourable, valiant citizen, imparted to this movement organisational forms . . . the fundamental acting power, the people, who raised Minin on high, which he himself did not expect, are the key to the interpretation of our theme.[37]

Pudovkin saw events in the projection of the *Short Course*, with a people's initiative, a 'patriotic movement', a leader who imparts 'organizational forms' and a grateful people, who raise the leader to 'unexpected heights'. To demonstrate this, a 'representative of the people', the runaway serf Roman (performed by Boris Chirkov, who had previously played the lead role in Grigory Kozintsev and Leonid Trauberg's trilogy about Maxim and had become in mass perception the embodiment of a Bolshevik), appears throughout the screenplay as a 'personification of the people, who seeks and creates a leader to stand at the head of a just deed'.[38] Minin and Pozharsky are represented in the film in the capacity of a single leader-commander, similar to Alexander Nevsky. 'Historical realism' coincided with the 'logic of the historical process'. As Shklovsky noted apropos of this, the past 'teaches us to understand how history creates leaders'.[39]

Relations between Shklovsky and Pudovkin were hostile. On one thing, perhaps, they did agree: the assertion of their method as . . . 'realistic'. What Shklovsky called 'historical realism' Pudovkin characterised in the following fashion: 'Here everything should be created by the imagination. You had to grow deep roots in this imaginary world, believe in it, feel free in it.' Pudovkin called this 'artistic truth'.[40] Correspondingly, the film opened with words in which the peasant uprisings and Troubles were . . . not even mentioned: 'For six years the Russian land has suffered under the yoke of interventionists.'

The reason for the all the misfortunes is fragmentation. 'If we could gather together all the Russian people . . .' Minin says dreamily, glancing at the ruin and hunger which prevail all around. Individualism and private property prevent unification. The merchants do not want unification. Trade in the Soviet historical film always acts as an opponent of patriotism. Just as the opponents of the fight against the enemies in *Alexander Nevsky* are the Novgorod merchants, so in *Minin and Pozharsky* the main obstacle on the path to a patriotic initiative is the Nizhny merchants. In contrast to the merchant who addresses the people with the words, 'Orthodox people! Defend Nizhny Novgorod!', Minin appeals:

> Citizens of Novgorod! Not for your town, not for Nizhny alone, but for the whole Russian State you must raise a militia! . . . The Poles have overcome us, nailed an iron yoke with iron nails around our neck, and we and our children will be serfs to Polish landowners, we will forget our motherland, we will forget our native tongue.

And then 'the people', who have led the 'Muscovite state' to 'Troubles' and disorder with their rebellions, suddenly manifest what Shklovsky called the 'feeling of the unity of the State'; that is, an unprecedented national maturity. They reply to Minin with the words, 'Could we really care about our own goods, and not the Russian soil?' In another scene 'the people' address the *voevody* with the words: 'The destruction of the entire State comes from your *boyars*' gang.' The support of 'the people' arouses Minin's reply: 'If everything is settled, we will force the merchants.' In reality, of course, everything happened the other way round; it was precisely with the merchants' money and in the interests of the '*boyars*' gang' that he managed to suppress 'the people'. The latter acts as a single social subject of the historical process, resembling a class. Marxist class is turned inside out, transforming into ethnic commonality. As a result, the leader of the social group is also transformed into a national leader.

This is why Minin and the head of the people's militia, Pozharsky, talk to 'the people' exclusively in cathedral squares and in front of the ranks. In no other space could 'the people' gather in the capacity of the subject of historical action. It is another matter for their enemies – the *boyars*, Poles and other traitors to the popular-national cause. Soviet historical films are full of traitors and spies (some very exotic ones appear in *Minin and Pozharsky* – from Portugal). Pudovkin himself asserted that during the Troubles 'treachery and betrayal became almost daily phenomena.'[41] The leader-commander, not being a representative of 'the people', differs from them in that he is not in a position to distinguish who is the enemy. Only the vigilance and decisiveness of the representative of the people allow him to see the true danger. In *Minin and Pozharsky*, the peasant Roman, the runaway serf of Prince Orlov, who turns out to be a traitor, at the end of the film finds and kills him. One critic wrote that this murder is 'an act of statehood, and Roman in it is higher than Pozharsky, who magnanimously forgives the secretly dispatched murderer'.[42] Similar scenes can be found in *Bogdan Khmelnitsky*, as well as in *Pugachev* and *Stepan Razin*.

Having cut his film from the template of *Alexander Nevsky* (the filming of *Minin and Pozharsky* even took place on the same sets and in the same studios where Eisenstein's film had just been shot, and in the crowd and battle scenes the same extras were hired who had taken part in *Alexander Nevsky*), Pudovkin, like Eisenstein, was dissatisfied with his first historical film. In so far as he always strived for a realistic style, he was unaccustomed to the historical environment, in which everything, from fake plates and knives to false beards, was artificial. In contrast to *Alexander Nevsky*, which was created in an emphatically conventional manner, in *Minin and Pozharsky* it is not the conventionality of it which is felt, but precisely the artificiality. This was for Pudovkin work on foreign territory, which the director could not assimilate. Pudovkin himself admitted this:

> In the wide scope of the events the living characters of the heroes became lost and indistinct. They turned out like chess pieces, with a name and a place in the game, but not a personality. What occurred was something like the direct opposite of *The End of St Petersburg* (*Konets Sankt-Peterburga*), where exactly the individual face of the hero and his particularly individual character made the generalisation real.[43]

'The abstract majesty of the legendary heroes has something in it of the monumental statues later dedicated to them. These characters appear in the midst of the set, uniting archaeological finds with the most elementary window-dressing and operatic qualities' – thus wrote even the most benevolent critic of the film.[44]

One could not have said the same of *Alexander Nevsky*, and not only because Minin and Pozharsky were somewhat luckier in terms of historical representation than Alexander. Martos's famous statue on Red Square, a model work of Russian classicism, depicts the liberator-unifiers at the moment of their dialogue with 'the people'. The appearance of the latter is easily reconstructed; in Pozharsky's majestic pose, in Minin's outstretched hand, we can read the nobility not only of these two great State figures, but also of their imagined 'interlocutors'. But Pudovkin's film went further, projecting the image of 'the people' in their leaders themselves. The actor Alexander Khanov, who played Minin in the film, spoke of the popular character of his hero. This was an 'ordinary Russian man', a 'people's leader, a tribune', 'the representative of the armed people, who have exchanged peaceful labour for a military cause'.[45] On the screen Minin moves slowly, his every movement emphatically theatrical, bowing from the waist to the people in the square, reaching out his hand in a monumental gesture, turning his body, as if he has stepped down from Martos's pedestal. Pozharsky only has a menacing gleam in his eyes, and constantly frowns and gives orders in a stern voice. He almost never moves independently at all. We see his motionless body, wounded in the convoy retreating from Moscow, or on a horse, slowly moving in front of the ranks. Khanov emphasised the conscious aim at monumentalism; characteristic of his hero are 'emotionalism, severity, majesty', the main points about him are 'heroism, national traits', a 'legendary nature', and the actor in particular spoke of his 'striving for an emotional interpretation of the image'.[46]

And here he is only following the director. 'Working on the images of Minin, Pozharsky and the peasant Roman,' Pudovkin wrote in his article 'A Film about the Great Russian People' (*Fil'm o velikom russkom narode*):

[W]e were not afraid that they would acquire a certain monumentalism, theatricality, animation. We did not want to supply them with an abundance of social features. That, perhaps, would have imparted more 'life' to the images, but would have inevitably deprived them of the charm which already surrounded their national legend.[47]

Pudovkin's biographer expressed the same idea thus: 'Concerned with the monumentalism of the images, Pudovkin was not afraid of theatricality. Along with this he decisively rejected all minor character traits and all possible superfluous social details.'[48] In socialist realist slang this was called 'an aversion to naturalism'. The latter would have destroyed the main point – the ideal correspondence of the heroes to their legendary, epic image, which was supposedly created by 'the people'. By the very same people who they saved . . . from themselves, and according to the film, liberated from the Poles.

The Polish theme occupies a central place in *Minin and Pozharsky*. It was precisely the Poles who in this historical production had to replace the Russian peasants, who were the initiators of the Troubles, having taken upon themselves the 'historical sin' of creating Russian misfortunes and weakening the State. The projection of an internal political drama on to an external enemy was all the more convincing as in autumn 1939, when *Minin and Pozharsky* was released, Poland had already been divided up and a vast part of its territory had been absorbed into the USSR. Thus the expulsion of the Poles from Russia at the beginning of the seventeenth century had to be considered a prelude to what was happening in 1939.

The present added to the film, drawing it closer to another anti-Polish film about a military commander – Igor Savchenko's *Bogdan Khmelnitsky*, which came out a year and a half later. Both of them are interesting in that it was not so much the biography of historical figures that became their central point, as the historical events themselves, in which the historical personality came into his own: for Minin and Pozharsky, the events of 1612, for Bogdan Khmelnitsky, those of 1648. The means of representation of the main character brought these two films together. The presence of the same enemy made a considerable contribution to this. *Minin and Pozharsky* and *Bogdan Khmelnitsky* are above all anti-Polish films; their very origins and reception are impossible to understand outside the context of the Molotov-von Ribbentrop pact and the rout of Poland in 1939.

As one cinema historian notes:

> [C]inematographers reconstructed the history of Russian-Polish relations exclusively as an epic of the confrontation of peoples hostile to one another, as an enumeration of national grievances and revenge for them. The blood ties of the Eastern Slavs were opposed to 'aristocratic' Poland. These films formed a negative image of Poland and the Poles in the viewer, justified the Soviet invasion of 1939 and introduced the idea that Poland was succumbing to historical retribution.[49]

But the films also had their own specific features, to which Vasily Tokarev draws attention. Characteristic of *Minin and Pozharsky* and *Bogdan Khmelnitsky* was their semantic opposition in the interpretation of class and national priorities in relation to one and the same event:

> The priority of the patriotic interpretation of the Troubles and the *Khmelnichina* in Soviet cinematography contrasted with the way that Soviet propagandists in 1939 made the national-liberational character of the Polish uprising of 1794 more prominent. Not the struggle for independence, but the class essence of the movement was brought to the forefront. The gentry-bourgeois character of the uprising effectively erased Suvorov's guilt.[50]

Soviet culture, which was ideologically required to take the side of Kosciusko and Pugachev, turned out to be on the side of Suvorov, who had crushed them. Poland proved to be the enemy, even when it was apparently defending the 'correct', in class terms, side in the Time of Troubles, and, on the contrary, those who suppressed the Troubles (which had, until very recently, been called a 'peasant uprising'), Minin and Pozharsky, turned out to be 'correct'. Poland turned out to be guilty before the Russian people, whatever the circumstances.

If this was a matter of national identity, then it was specifically Soviet identity, coinciding with Russian, in so far as Bogdan Khmelnitsky, acting against the Poles, was also effectively a Russian (even the Ukrainians themselves were already also integrated Russians, just speaking in some sort of Zaporozhye Cossack dialect), as un-Russian is un-Soviet. This coincidence of Soviet and Russian was defined by the structure of the Soviet empire. (After the war, as they joined the Soviet block, the Poles also became a 'fraternal people'.) And after all, if for Russians the Poles were not the main enemy (in Russian national demonology they ceded first place to the Germans, the French and even the Swedes), then for the Ukrainians they were historically the fundamental opponents, to whom Ukrainian identity was attached. Therefore when, following *Minin and Pozharsky*, *Bogdan Khmelnitsky* was released, many saw in it not only the development of the Polish theme (which occupied an enormous place in Soviet cinema in the pre-war years[51]), but also the fossilisation of the stylistic dominants discovered by Eisenstein.

The romanticisation of Bogdan Khmelnitsky had a long tradition. The leader of the Ukrainian Cossack forces, *hetman* Khmelnitsky, made a historic U-turn, uniting Ukraine with Russia. The monument in the central square of Kiev, in which the *hetman*, sitting on a horse, directs his mace to the North, towards Moscow, became not only a trademark for Kiev, but also the most famous representation of this historical figure, whose memory is imprinted, however, not only in stone, but also in the conception of the 'Khmelnichina'. The 'national-liberation movement of the Ukrainian people' ended not in independence, but in inclusion as part of Russia; it was accompanied not only by battles against the Poles and the destruction of all traces of 'Polish dominion', but also by slaughter, pillage and terrible pogroms against the Jews. The centre of the film – 1648, the year when Ukrainian forces were assembled, decisive battles took place against the Poles and the Polish army was routed, and relations were established with the Crimean khan – was the year of Khmelnitsky's effective accession in Ukraine.

Bogdan Khmelnitsky is not only a story of the history of a 'fraternal people'; it is also a Ukrainian national epic, and in this capacity the film relied on the tradition of Ukrainian poetic cinema and Ukrainian romantic literature already formed by that time. One critic wrote of the film as a 'brilliant model of cinema-epic in its new, realistic stage', and sought the origins of the cinema-epic genre not in the theatre, but in the novel and epic poem.[52] From his first appearance Bogdan Khmelnitsky is an epic hero submerged in thought. His figure is enormous, his movements slow, his speech expressive. He lives in the world of *bogatyrs* – theatrically dressed, hard-drinking, blaspheming, merry-making, anarchical Zaporozhye Cossacks. He is their wisdom, will and emotion; he is a heroic personification of this epic world.

The scenes in which Khmelnitsky acts are as if cribbed from the crowd scenes of Russian 'epic operas': the leader and the sea of people falling silent before him. Such stagings could have been taken from Rimsky-Korsakov's *The Maid of Pskov* (*Pskovitianka*) or *The Tsar's Bride* (*Tsarskaia nevesta*), Glinka's *A Life for the Tsar* (*Zhizn' za tsaria*), Mussorgsky's *Khovanshchina* or *Boris Godunov*, or Borodin's *Prince Igor* (*Kniaz' Igor'*). The Polish scenes in the film openly recall corresponding scenes in Mussorgsky's opera. Apropos of this, Yurenev wrote:

> It is a good thing that Savchenko was not afraid of the openly operatic nature of some of the Polish scenes. Splendid polonaises, religious rituals,

parades convey graphically the bombast and arrogant conceit of the Polish gentry. However, we feel that Savchenko was wrong in endowing only the Poles with civilisation. The Poles are even somewhat exaggerated in their cultural development; the Ukrainians sometimes look like heathens, endlessly drinking Ukrainian vodka and fighting 'with their fists'. He should have showed that the Ukrainian people also at that time had their national culture.[53]

This final reproach relates to the fact that the critic saw 'civilisation' only in polonaises, but did not notice it in the 'people's scenes', at the forefront of which stood Khmelnitsky.

It was not that Savchenko placed his hero on a buskin. He simply did not take him down from the pedestal. In so far as the 'epic hero has no need of careful psychological cultivation of his character',[54] his personal life is transformed into a type of epic melodrama (the Polish gentry send Khmelnitsky's wife, whom he loves, to poison him), whilst the metaphors jostle one another (thus the 'suffering of the Ukrainian people under the Polish yoke' is depicted to music by bandura players as if illustrating their terrible songs of 'a people in torment').

In the epic world of the film each of the heroes represents some group – Cossacks, Zaporozhtsy, peasants, Tartars, Polish gentry, 'State' Cossacks, traitors and so on, and only the *hetman* represents self-esteemed majesty. He is a military commander and simultaneously a people's leader, not of the people by birth but compensating for this with his permanent presence at the 'heart of the people':

> Bogdan acts as a people's leader. He is great in that the suffering of the people becomes his own suffering. Belonging to the affluent branch of the Cossacks, he rises above class prejudices and devotes himself to fulfilling the people's dreams of freedom ... Through the leader's mouth the people themselves are speaking here, indomitable in their hatred of the enemy and their striving for freedom.[55]

The means of expressing hatred 'through the leader's mouth' are themselves of particular interest. Khmelnitsky practically never speaks; instead, he declaims (the so-called 'artistic reading' popular in Stalinist times), and the richly intoned, emotional (more often irate) speech of the leader pours forth from the screen. Philippics and emotional cures are accompanied by theatrical gesticulations (excessive even on stage, not to mention on screen). The prose of the screenplay is transformed by Nikolai Mordvinov, who plays Khmelnitsky, into blank verse. Khmelnitsky three times repeats in anger, vigorously, as an incantation: 'From our vengeance the heavens will quake! Retribution to the Poles!' And in the background to this cry, the Cossacks go on their epic torment, raising bonfires, the Cossack cavalry storm Polish castles, the Poles fly down the stairs and walls of their fortresses, history is decided. Khmelnitsky's actions are like the actions of an enchanter or prophet; he raises his hand to the sky, rolls his eyes, flashes them threateningly, clenches his fists, cuts through the air with his mace – and there and then his actions are translated into the actions of the 'people's masses'.

The discovery in *Alexander Nevsky* of the means of representing the commander-leader, forging together with victory over the enemy the national identity of the people being led by him, proved to be exhausted, because the distillation of myth into history became impossible without a parallel distillation of history into myth. Eisenstein was working with pre-historic, almost fairytale material, having astutely rejected seventeenth-century stories; at the basis of *Alexander Nevsky* lay mythology awaiting historicisation. 'Historical realism' demanded quite a different level of psychologism and individualisation. Without them mythologised history petrified into a primitive epic form, which referred not so much to 'Marxist historiography' as to the original myth, which never, in the case of *Minin and Pozharsky* and *Bogdan Khmelnitsky*, underwent the anticipated transformation into 'historical truth'.

Decorations, and People to Boot

There was all of one year between *Minin and Pozharsky* and *Suvorov*. In this year Pudovkin created a film that was in practically every way the opposite of the monumental classicism of his first historical picture. If the distinguishing aspect of *Minin and Pozharsky* was the stasis of a monument, then *Suvorov* is dynamic; if in *Minin and Pozharsky* you do not see a single smiling face during the course of the whole film, and everything is permeated with supreme seriousness, then in *Suvorov* humour rules; if *Minin and Pozharsky* was criticised for its poor, static composition, then *Suvorov*, on the contrary, is distinguished by its dynamic composition and montage.

The film *Suvorov*, with a screenplay by Georgy Grebner, was to have been made by Mikhail Romm. (At first the screenplay was given to Pudovkin, but the then chief of cinematography, Semyon Dukelsky, decided to curtail historical subject matter and Pudovkin was obliged to turn it down.) In the personality of Suvorov, Romm was attracted by the genius of the commander and his eccentricity, in which the director saw his strategy for behaviour and survival in the Russian court. Romm planned to make the film in a genre he defined as 'heroic comedy'. With the arrival of a new head of cinematography, Ivan Bolshakov, the historical theme returned and Pudovkin demanded the screenplay back. Romm recalls:

> I. G. Bolshakov asked me: 'In what spirit are you intending to shoot *Suvorov*?' I replied, 'In heroic spirit, but it will be a comedy.' 'How can you have a comedy', I. G. Bolshakov asked, surprised, 'about a great commander?' And it was decided to return the screenplay to Pudovkin.

'You're not intending to make *Suvorov* as a comedy, are you?' Bolshakov asked Pudovkin. 'God forbid, I don't know how to make comedies at all,' replied Vsevolod Illarionovich. And he added, 'Unfortunately, I don't have a sense of humour.'[56]

Pudovkin turned out to be the most suitable candidate to realise the screenplay, which was cut by direct order of Stalin. Reading the screenplay, Stalin wrote detailed notes explaining how it should be presented on screen. The genius of Suvorov was in his strategy of attack and his tactics for evading the enemy (Suvorov's victories were most often of all sustained on his enemies' territory, in keeping with the pre-war aim of 'defeating the enemy on their own territory'), and in his ability to maintain discipline in the army, but the main thing was that the picture should overcome the stereotype of Suvorov the eccentric.

As Suvorov's eccentricities, which had become the subject of historical anecdotes, could not be ignored entirely, the filmmakers decided to use them for ideological aims, treating them as a type of subversive activity against the court and the etiquette of high-ranking officials, as 'an insult by the great commander to the courtly world that was alien to Suvorov'.[57] So Pudovkin barely had to caricature the Emperor Paul or Arakcheev. Suvorov did all the work to discredit them satirically with his 'eccentricities', which were presented by the director in the service of the struggle against tsarism.

Eccentricity and spontaneity in his behaviour, as well as 'national character', were the distinguishing features of Suvorov. The army was his family. He was their father and addressed his soldiers with the words: 'My children!' Pudovkin's Suvorov is a type of folkloric rogue. He is the embodiment of freedom, which comes to light not only in the unexpectedness and dynamics of his attacks. His final wave of the sabre, pointing in the direction of attack, is employed as a metaphor showing the way to ultimate freedom, as if leading the viewer to the future.

The palace at Gatchina is, on the other hand, a citadel of unfreedom: chequered parquet, motionless sentries, soldiers on drill on the parade ground, Prussian-style discipline. Paul is the embodiment of unfreedom. He says of himself that he created 'an Empire of great order'. Between the Tsar and the Field Marshal the following noteworthy dialogue occurs:

> Paul: My soldier is like an instrument, a spring for action with a bayonet or a sabre, an army of great balance and power.
> Suvorov: Mechanism . . . a spring . . . that means, a dummy! . . . A dummy, Your Majesty, and even with a bayonet or a sabre, he'll stay a dummy. With such an army not only I, a sinner, but anyone greater than me will not gain victories. I command people, Your Majesty, not springs!

Suvorov is free. He is more like a Decembrist than a tsarist field marshal and suppressor of popular rebellions; he writes freedom-loving verse and dreams of emancipating the serfs. (As one critic wrote, 'from Suvorov's lips the whole of progressive Russia, dissatisfied with the tsar, spoke.'[58]) His opponents are on the same line as him on the front: 'Suvorov's main enemies turned out to be those who gave him orders: the Emperor Paul and the "allied" Austrian command, limited, backward, and defending the backward principles of feudal Europe.'[59] The Slavophile Field Marshal is placed in opposition to the German court of Paul and the Prussian model of the army, of which the Emperor was an advocate. The Russian army, thanks precisely to his patriarchal nature ('one big family'), is presented as much more united and successful than the Prussian, in which all human connections were absent. Suvorov was not simply a commander, but effectively the leader of this 'people's army'. Just as in pre-revolutionary Russia class peace and national consent ruled (broken only by *boyar*-conspirators and cosmopolitan traitors in the court), in Suvorov's army nothing recalls its feudal, serf-based character.

In this united patriarchal family, alongside adoration of Suvorov the father, the horror of life-long military service fades. The myth of the monolithic Russian forces and the wholehearted love of the soldier (or sailor) for his father-commander were present in all films about military commanders. However, as materials of the discussions between screenwriters and consultant historians have shown, the latter were constantly pointing to the fact that in planning army actions, the factor of mass insubordination and desertion was always taken into account. This was a serf army, which screenwriters and directors refused to note. Thus, the consultants showed, there is in *Suvorov* a 'historically impossible' scene, in which Suvorov leads his troops through a dense forest, thereby shortening the route to the enemy and suddenly attacking them; such a manoeuvre would have been impossible 'because of the danger of mass desertion'.[60] Meanwhile, all the military leader films abound in such scenes; 'the people' cannot desert from 'their' army.

This army resembles the Soviet army, and Suvorov is transformed into a Chapaev of the seventeenth century. Thus occurred the final rejection of the model set out in *Alexander Nevsky*. At the centre of *Suvorov* was not 'patriotism' but personality. Pudovkin started from character and this remained his focus throughout. So much so that the very actions of Suvorov and his army proved to be irrelevant. Suvorov's campaigns are in no way linked to the 'defence of the Fatherland' – from the beginning of the film ('the Polish campaign') to its end ('the Italian campaign'). Thus at the centre of *Suvorov* lies not patriotism (as in Eisenstein) but personality. This is true in the literal sense. *Suvorov* is not so much a 'patriotic film' as a 'great-power film'; here they fight 'for the Fatherland' . . . in the Swiss Alps. *Suvorov* is above all an anti-Western film; all the commander's great victories take place beyond the borders of Russia. The viewer is given a graphic lesson about how the great Russian army with a commander-leader at its head is in a position to bring European states to their knees. Suvorov is as severe as Stalin; he is satisfied at how many enemy soldiers are killed on the battlefield ('That's right! A forest that has only been half cut down will grow again'). He is as shrewd as Stalin; from a changing facial expression he can recognise a French spy in his ranks.

As regards patriotism itself, here a split occurred through the opposition of Suvorov, embodying 'the people', to tsarism (the aims of pictures in the 'tsarist' series were quite different). In so far as the aim of the film was to show 'the superiority of the people in this battle against the backward tsarist government',[61] patriotism proved to be on the side of 'the people'. Tsarism, on the contrary, was anti-patriotic. This 'people's patriotism' is positioned as a direct precursor of 'Soviet patriotism' (the formula of which is 'great Russia minus tsarism'). Thus the real and only heir of true patriotism turns out to be the Soviet State.

On the other hand, as Shklovsky noted:

> Suvorov's tragedy was profound; he had in his hands a superior army, he was a great strategist, but his army had to fulfil politically backward ideas, it could not be an absolute victor. Therefore Suvorov had to win the battle but lose the campaign.[62]

It is worth noting, however, that at the centre of the film there were precisely battles that were won. (The question of the fate of the campaigns was not posed in the Soviet historical film. It was well known that Russia did not wage unjust wars; there were no conquerors in its history, only 'gatherers of Russian lands'.)

Suvorov, conforming to the Soviet military doctrine of those days, 'defeated his enemies on their territory':

> The enemy is slumbering, they're waiting for you in an open field. The enemy knows Suvorov is a hundred *versts* away. But we, with two or three *bogatyr*'s paces, will come down from steep mountains, out of dense forests, swoop like an eagle, like a bolt from the blue! Beat them, slaughter them, chop them down – don't let them come to their senses. On the flank, at the rear, at Russian bayonet point . . . And of course . . . Glory!

In these years films such as *Squadron No. 5* (*Eskadril'ia No. 5*) and *If War Comes Tomorrow* (*Esli zavtra voina*) were released, which assumed easy victory in a future war – a myth that was destroyed in the summer of 1941.

> In the pre-war period Stalin considered headlong attack and defeat of the enemy on their territory to be the only admissible means of fighting. And he considered Generalissimo Suvorov the most suitable figure who could function as an incarnation of this doctrine.[63]

Suvorov was the product of the geopolitical arrangements of 1940; the enemy was France (Hitler had just occupied Paris), the ally was Austria. The picture opens with victory over Poland (the conquered enemy). Of course, it was precisely Suvorov's 'Polish campaign' which was the most dubious from the ideological point of view (in essence, the rout of the Polish uprising). It is interesting that the positive depiction of the Polish campaign in *Suvorov* was defended by Soviet criticism as late as the 1980s, by returning the picture to the context of 1940:

> In the consciousness of the creator all Suvorov's military campaigns converged not so much with the campaigns of conquest of Russian tsarism, as with the people's struggle against foreign aggressors in the Time of Troubles, and in the eras of Alexander Nevsky and Peter the Great, and with the heroic defence of Sevastopol in the Crimean Campaign.[64]

In other words, the makers of the film were prisoners of the mythology which they themselves were promoting.

'We are seeking to make the people's past understandable in the light of the present, and the present in the light of the past,'[65] wrote Pudovkin. Correspondingly, not a word is said in the film about Suvorov's role in suppressing the Pugachev rebellion, but on the other hand his punitive expedition against the Poles is extolled, and the victories of Napoleon's army are explained exclusively by the treachery of the allies. Perhaps the only openly geopolitical passage in the film is the scene in which Suvorov speaks to Bagration about Napoleon:

> Oh, how he strides on, this boy! It's time to stop him, it's time! Or it'll be too late. You'll see where he's heading for. He's taken Italy. As for Austria . . . he doesn't even need to take it, it'll lie down under his feet itself. And then, where will the new blow fall? . . . Russia. But Europe advances in vain on Russia. It will find here fierce hatred, great valour, its own grave.

This passage gives a strong impression of how much the geopolitical imagery had been transformed. Until quite recently Napoleon had been seen as the bearer of a progressive political system and his attempt to introduce it to Russia was interpreted by Pokrovsky as wholly positive; very recently it had been a question of France, and not at all of 'Europe', which could not 'advance on Russia', since it 'lay under the foot' of Napoleon itself; very recently this hostile advance from Europe had been seen exclusively in terms of class categories ('Capitalist Europe wants to suffocate Soviet Russia'). Now it turned out that even 'progressive' Europe (at the time of Napoleon) was reactionary with respect to 'backward' Russia. The geopolitical categories of the end of the eighteenth century, with which Suvorov was reasoning, coincided with the categories operating in Stalinist culture.

But then the situation changed abruptly; attack (and even more so, 'victory on enemy territory') ceased to be a topical subject. On the contrary, now retreat demanded ideological grounds. Kutuzov came in as a substitute for Suvorov. The film about Kutuzov became one of the most important. Stalin demanded that the film be produced as quickly as possible, even before the end of the war.[66] The picture was entrusted to Vladimir Petrov. The main role in it was played by Aleksei Diky. Stalin liked the film so much that Petrov was later entrusted to make *The Battle of Stalingrad* (*Stalingradskaia bitva*), in which the role of Stalin, now 'the present-day strategist of genius', was played after the war by Diky.

Towards the end of the war, Kutuzov became much more important than Suvorov, Stalin applying Kutuzov's tactics of retreat to events in 1941–2. In the 'Open letter to Ramzin', Stalin directly appealed to the experience of 'our commander of genius Kutuzov, who ruined Napoleon and his army with the help of a well prepared counter-attack', for, according to Stalin, 'a well-organized counter-attack is a very interesting form of attack.' In his extensive military-historical commentaries Stalin thus avoided using the term 'retreat'. In this projection the catastrophe at the beginning of the war with a million victims and the slaughter of entire armies was only part of Stalin's brilliant strategic plan to lure the enemy deep into the country (right up to the Volga!) with the aim of then bringing about his 'ruin'. Such a striking exchange of personnel was apprehended by contemporaries with understanding. Shklovsky on this occasion noted: 'The times will accept the film *Kutuzov* and, examining it, will understand what the country was thinking about in those days, when the battle over the city on the Volga was only just entering into human consciousness.'[67]

The shrewd Shklovsky did not, however, notice the deeply traumatic impact of the change of images, from Suvorov to Kutuzov. He asserted that, when for political considerations of war-time the international aspect of the battle against Napoleon (the allies, Britain) was removed from the screenplay, it turned out that the conflict itself had disappeared:

> It is now awkward to show this. It was cut in the screenplay, but in the filmed episode Kutuzov and Alexander continue to quarrel and, it turns out, about nothing. Alexander, it turns out, wants to play safe, and this is foisted on Kutuzov, and there is no quarrel . . . We see only a very cunning man . . . It turns out that Kutuzov all the time simply employs cunning, and never fights. And Kutuzov, for whom it was worth making the picture, is in essence not there.[68]

Meanwhile, this was in no sense only a question of the political considerations of 1943–4; it was the fact that the very principle of the representation of the historical hero required emphasis on individuality and the study of character. The principle of *Alexander Nevsky*, in which in the capacity of historical metaphor completely conventional material was taken up, did not work. Here the personification of history was required. Therefore *Kutuzov* develops the theme less of the 'Patriotic War' than of a war between two personalities – Kutuzov and

Napoleon – and the conflict between the Field Marshal and the Tsar, mentioned by Shklovsky, fits in fully with the traditional opposition of the tsar (the court) and the military leader, who embodies wisdom, patriotism and the majesty of 'the people'. Corresponding to this Kutuzov, like Suvorov and, before him, Alexander Nevsky, demonstrates that strategic wisdom comes from the military commander, and it falls to the lot of the people to show tactical native wit. (In *Alexander Nevsky* the merchant Ignat tells the fairytale of the fox and the hare, which becomes a kind of metaphor for Alexander's action on Lake Chudskoe; something similar also happens in *Kutuzov*, when a simple soldier, finding French horseshoes without spikes, tells Kutuzov that the French horses will fall over on the ice and mud.)

Just as the Soviet viewer saw Stalin the strategist on the screen, occupied exclusively in scrutinising maps in his office and unhurriedly strolling along an endless table, so they saw Kutuzov always sitting at his desk writing something. For the whole of the Battle of Borodino Kutuzov sat over his maps and only after the fatal wounding of Bagration went into the field of battle. Sluggish, reasonable, corpulent and moving with difficulty, he was the complete opposite of Suvorov, who was always to be found in the midst of battle. It was as if he was engaged in a search for the hidden substance of what was going on. During the battle at Maloyaroslavets, Kutuzov, addressing his generals, says: 'You're seeking victories; I'm seeking the meaning in them.' What is the secret known to this old, tired man?

Above all this secret was defined as the 'spirit of the army'. Kutuzov's tactics are never shown in the film as retreat. On the contrary, Kutuzov emphasises that the battle has not been lost. (Thus, he says of the Battle of Borodino: 'The battle, if it hasn't been won, in any case hasn't been lost either.') More than that, he substantiates retreats in such a manner that they were not perceived as retreats. Thus, during the war council at Fili, he declares to his arguing generals: 'I am ordering a retreat. Russia is not Moscow alone. If we lose Moscow, but preserve the army, not all will be lost. If we lose the army, we will preserve neither Moscow nor Russia.' In this context, all the subsequent events can be seen as having been planned beforehand (and this is probably why we see Kutuzov always sitting over his maps). And indeed the retreat does not take place. Of the Battle of Borodino, Kutuzov says: 'We did not retreat at the will of the enemy, but of our own will. For the spirit of the Russian forces has not been overcome.' This was exactly how viewers had to look upon the history of war with the Germans before the Battle of Stalingrad. When a French envoy arrives at Kutuzov's headquarters with an offer to 'end this war', Kutuzov replies: 'We haven't even started yet. We've only made ready.' When the French have left Moscow, he says: 'Building up the army is complete. Now war begins!' Thus the 'retreating' part of the war should not be perceived as war (it is only the 'build-up'). War is victorious actions. Stalin needed this kind of picture, about which he wrote to the war historian Ramzin. It is striking that at the end of *Kutuzov*, the final word is given not to the hero-victor (as usually occurs in these films) but to . . . the defeated. Napoleon pronounces to the camera: 'Our main mistake was committed when we began this campaign to Russia.' Thereby it is as if he answers Alexander Nevsky, who warned everyone who 'comes to us with a sword' of their inevitable death.

These two military leaders are presented as psychologically completely opposite characters: the emotional, mobile, explosive Suvorov and the obese, reserved man of few words, Kutuzov. They were united by their emphatic psychologism and their unusual sensitivity. In many scenes their emotions are outwardly expressed. Suvorov goes into retirement, abandoning his army, with tears in his eyes; Kutuzov cannot keep his voice from trembling when he speaks of the need to evacuate Moscow. It is impossible to imagine even the smallest portion of this emotionalism in Alexander Nevsky; one cannot imagine Minin weeping or Bogdan Khmelnitsky's voice trembling. And although Suvorov and Kutuzov continued to remain as ideological functions, thanks to a change in the way they were represented, the ideological current flowed, finally, in the opposite direction; the historicisation of myth was turned into the mythologisation of history.

KILL THE VALET

Speaking of those who write about great people from the point of view of their petty human weaknesses and passions, Hegel once sarcastically observed that they were infected with 'a valet's psychology'. It was exactly of this sin that Pudovkin's third and final historical film, *Admiral Nakhimov*, was accused. In a crushing resolution by the Central Committee of the Party on 4 September 1946 about the feature film *A Great Life* (*Bol'shaia zhizn'*), Pudovkin was called 'an ignoramus' who had treated historical facts without the necessary seriousness and had shot a film with balls and dances about the personal life of Admiral Nakhimov rather than depicting historical events. In principle, the situation with Nakhimov was already fixed in 1940, when, as Pudovkin told the story, Stalin, after seeing Suvorov, said: 'You have made a good film about Alexander Vasilievich Suvorov, now a film needs making about the commander Suvorov.'[69]

It tuned out that after Suvorov further personalisation of historical characters was impossible. Indeed, in the first version of the film about Nakhimov, historical events were pushed into the background. In the foreground was Nakhimov 'in life', helping to settle the personal life of young Lieutenant Burunov, and much space is occupied by balls, duels and so on. In essence, the film was characterised in the Resolution with full justification as a film 'about balls and dances with episodes from the life of Nakhimov'. But as one critic, repeating the Resolution, pointed out, 'resolving the biographical image of a remarkable man can only be done by using the fundamental facts which constitute his biography, boldly handling significant historical events, and without deviating into trifling searches for amusing and original little episodes.'[70]

Pudovkin proved to be in an unexpected situation. In essence, he had shot 'the same' film for the third time – with a different story, transferred to a different time (17th – 18th – 19th centuries) and place (Moscow – Nizhny Novgorod – Moscow, Petersburg – Italy, the Black Sea), but with exactly the same ideological clichés. Pudovkin turned out to be a hostage of the very canon he had consolidated in his previous films.

One could suggest that Pudovkin was interested in Nakhimov's personality, particularly from the point of view of psychology. He wrote: 'When you address Nakhimov's biographical materials, the first impression they create is of an incredible life of service.' He had an unbelievably serious attitude towards his duty and in effect gave up everything of himself to it. He even, as Tarle observed, 'forgot to fall in love, forgot to marry';[71] 'he was naïve in his enormous love, and his punctiliousness in the fulfilment of his duty turned within him into something astonishingly moving.'[72] This distinctiveness is preserved in all the memoirs; everybody loved this apparently dry pedant, from sailors and officers to the inhabitants of Sevastopol. This is the enigma of individuality Pudovkin tried to solve in Nakhimov. He conscientiously reworked the film, bringing the historical Nakhimov to the foreground in the second version. A rare occurrence: according to the testimony of people who saw both versions (the first, savaged by the Resolution, was not preserved), the film only gained from its reworking. Pudovkin managed to achieve a synthesis, uniting the monumentality of *Minin and Pozharsky* with the dynamics of *Suvorov*. Nakhimov turned out simultaneously to be both a majestic figure and one who aroused warm sympathy.

These two sides of the personality of the hero reflect the usual, in historical-biographical films, clash of the military commander with the leader; simultaneously he is romantically raised above 'the masses' and is immersed in the 'people's element'. Pudovkin used here the method he had discovered when working on *Mother* (*Mat'*) of shooting from below. But if in *Mother* he used it for the infamous gendarme, who embodied the oppressive power of the tsarist regime, here he used it for Nakhimov himself. The view of the historical figure from below is fixed in the very first frames, as if the viewer finds himself at the pedestal of a monument: a storm at sea, enormous threatening rollers flooding the listing frigate, rolling across the deck. The sailors look above from below at the Admiral, awaiting salvation. Steadfastly and confidently he stands on the captain's bridge. Before the strength of his will the elements are calmed. The sailors cross themselves in terror. Nakhimov is absolutely calm and gives his commands in a normal voice. The storm has abated. The sailors look with relief and delight from the lower deck to the captain's bridge: 'Pavel Stepanovich has come to our aid!' An old sailor says to a novice: 'Do you know who you're looking at! Do you think that's a storm to him? The sea trembles before him.' Such is the 'great Nakhimov', in the eyes of sailors and viewers (an allegory reinforced at the beginning of the film with the depiction of the Order of Nakhimov, while at the end of the film not only the Order appears, but also Soviet warships furrowing the seas).

Reverence for a great historical personality required a particular type of 'background':

> The hero of the Crimean War [in *Admiral Nakhimov* – E. D.], like the hero of the glorious resistance to the foreign invaders of 1612 [in *Minin and Pozharsky* – E. D.], like Suvorov's soldier [in the film *Suvorov* – E. D.] is a simple Russian man in a soldier's uniform. The main character of Pudovkin's new film [*Admiral Nakhimov* – E. D.] is once more the heroic Russian people.[73]

In Minin and Pozharsky's 'army' (or, to be more precise, militia), the gentry and peasantry were united. It is not difficult to conclude that here there were more than a few 'class conflicts'. In Shklovsky and Pudovkin, as we have seen, there was not a single trace of this, in so far as the aim of the film was to show the patriotic unification of the nation against foreign invasion. In the face of common danger, class distinctions are completely cancelled out. Military commanders from the gentry are transformed entirely into 'progressive people of their time'. Their contribution to the nation almost automatically turns them into 'peasant democrats' – supporters of the 'advanced social order' and opponents of serfdom. This is true not only of *Suvorov*, but also of *Kutuzov* and *Admiral Nakhimov*.

Having been in the same place at the same time as the events shown in *Admiral Nakhimov*, Leo Tolstoy testified:

> In battle, when the influence of the commander should be greatest of all, the soldier hates him so much, sometimes even more than he does the enemy; for he sees the possibility of harming him. You can see how many Russian officers are killed by Russian bullets, how many are slightly injured and delivered into the hands of the enemy on purpose, you can see how the soldiers look at and talk to their officers before every battle: in their every movement, their every word the thought is obvious: 'I'm not afraid of you and I hate you.'[74]

Soviet cinema depicted the Russian army as monumental, strengthened by the courage of soldiers and officers, by mass heroism, patriotism, consciousness and discipline. This was the prototype of the Soviet army. The fact that this army was practically the fundamental part of the hated tsarist regime and the State machine destroyed by the revolution, that it was the instrument of its punitive politics, and the fundamental power in conducting the imperialist policy of the 'policeman of Europe' and was the guard of the 'prison of nations', that is, everything that was clear in revolutionary culture, could not even have been guessed at from watching the Stalinist screen. The social function of the tsarist army, like its social character, was located somewhere in another historical reality. In this tsarist army soldiers are not driven through the lines and beaten with rods, they are not mocked, the officers do not drink, play cards or steal. Here the commanders incessantly thank the soldiers for their bravery and love of the Fatherland, and have intimate conversations with them. In relying on the image of the 'accursed past', revolutionary culture had no need of that sort of army. National-patriotic Stalinist culture, on the other hand, needed legitimisation through 'the people' and found, in the capacity of 'the people'. . . the soldier. The ideal classless army proved to be a copy of that ideal classless society which was demonstrated in films from the 'people's' and 'tsarist' series.

Nakhimov was to be Pudovkin's final historical film. The history connected with its reworking showed that the biographical canon in Soviet cinema had definitively petrified. Meanwhile, the biographical chain had not been broken. Pudovkin himself considered his hero-naval commander as part of an endless chain of quasi-historical genesis. During discussions on the screenplay, Pudovkin formulated this aim thus:

> Nakhimov is the direct successor of the military-naval tradition, a trad-ition which was begun by Ushakov and Lazarev and then continued by Nakhimov. So far there is no theme of Nakhimov as the successor of the Russian military- naval tradition . . . for the outlay on *Nakhimov* to have a greater effect, this picture should act as a fulcrum for subsequent naval pictures. Screenplays on Ushakov and the others should be commissioned without delay. It would be good to show the old Ushakov with the young Lazarev, and the old Lazarev with the young Nakhimov.[75]

But as before, the composition of thematic plans for cinema production was defined by political considerations. As at the end of the war Kutuzov is the topical figure, embodying the idea of 'strategic retreat' as 'an interesting form of attack', Nakhimov in a strange way begins to resemble Kutuzov. When he speaks of scuttling the Black Sea fleet, he literally repeats what Kutuzov said about retreat: 'We have to retreat on to dry land, scuttle the boats and defend Sevastopol. Moscow burned, but Rus' did not perish because of that. And Moscow is still standing and will stand.' But this was 1945. In 1953 the active interventionist policy being pursued required a return to Suvorov and his stra-tegy of 'war on the enemy's territory'. In Mikhail Romm's two films, *Admiral Ushakov* and *The Ships Storm the Bastions*, the motif of this connection is insis-tently peddled. The director even brings Ushakov together with Suvorov so that the great naval commander can report to the great military commander: 'As far as possible I am creating on the sea what you are creating on dry land, Alexander Vasilievich.' The film was even conceived by Romm as a 'naval *Suvorov*'. This comparison with *Suvorov* clarifies the evolution of the historical-biographical genre in Soviet cinema.

Romm, who had at one point himself dreamed of making a production of *Suvorov*, deprived his Ushakov of any individual features, not even to mention his eccentricity, which was exactly characteristic of him. (It is sufficient to recall

Ushakov's nicknames: 'the bear', 'the bast-shoed nobleman', 'jet-black jacket'.) Romm's *Ushakov* is *Suvorov* after the 1946 resolution of the Central Committee. Deciding not to take any risks, Romm deprived Ushakov in one fell swoop of any kind of contradiction and doubt. If fairytale conventions came to the aid of *Alexander Nevsky*, *Bogdan Khmelnitsky* was helped by the screenplay and *Suvorov* by the legendary distinctiveness of the character and the work of the actor who played him, then nothing could save *Ushakov*. This hero 'appeared solid, like a monolith, and for that reason solemn and monumental. And, like every monument, cold and alienated from everything alive and individual.'[76] Critics were inclined to see the 'decline of the genre' in this. However, it is only a question of the transformation of the historical genre into the present; with the increase from film to film of topical geopolitical rhetoric, they were transformed from biographical into essentially political films of the Cold War (representing a special genre in post-war Stalinist cinema[77]).

Ushakov, depicted by Romm as the founder of the Black Sea fleet, like Suvorov, Kutuzov and Nakhimov, is fighting not so much enemies as talentless tsarist grandees, stupid regulations and dishonest 'allies', who dream of weakening Russia and betraying it. By depicting the enemy as being so stupid, Romm, always inclined to sharp political satire, over-egged the pudding; his Napoleon is no formidable conqueror, but an ordinary poseur. It is said of him only that he was defeated here and there, and that his generals and marshals were just looking for opportunities to be taken prisoner. Nelson is depicted as an intriguer and failure, who is in no way able to defeat Napoleon and is envious of the Russian victories. Against the background of these caricatured figures, who resembled characters from anti-American Cold War films, Ushakov looks even more monumental. Everybody else (as on the pedestal of a monument) plays the crowd. After viewing the film, Grigory Kozintsev wrote in his diary: '*Admiral Ushakov* . . . Turks, Tartars. Polevoi, Kukolnik. "How splendid, how beautiful!" Ushakov hates the Turks, obviously, because they all served in musical comedy.'[78] The same could be said of more than the Turks.

As is customary for a 'people's hero', Ushakov has intimate conversations with his sailors, works on ship-building as a carpenter with 'the people', spends all his salary and even sells his house in order to buy rations for the sailors, and incessantly thanks them for their 'feats of arms': 'Thank you, brother sailors. A huge Thank You for your work. Russia will not forget your feat. Thank you, my brothers.' (The Admiral's relationship with his sailors was so touchingly patriarchal that even the expert consultant on the film was obliged to admit that the film 'created an idyllic impression of life on ship.'[79]) Count Mordovtsev, a court intriguer who succeeds Potemkin and hates Ushakov, has a completely different view of 'the people'. He rudely upbraids Ushakov for his familiarity with the sailors: 'The officer alone has a voice. The boatswain has a horn. Sailors should be seen only as objects for the execution of commands. A sailor is dumb. Do you hear? Dumb!' This clash directly reproduces *Suvorov*, but in 1953 the situation differed greatly from that at the end of the 1930s. The situation had changed to the extent that at a Mosfilm conference calls were heard for the creation of 'the image of the mighty empress Catherine'.[80] It is interesting that the Tsarina's journey around the new Russian territories (Novorussia) was conveyed by frames of carriages quickly tearing along – 'stopping would have revealed a gap in the set design: there were no famous "Potemkin villages".'[81] Potemkin wanted to show Catherine that 'we are standing firmly on the Black Sea.' Catherine was satisfied: 'I can see with my own eyes; there is a fleet on the Black Sea.' The phrase 'I can see with my own eyes' during the famous journey through the Potemkin villages (which in the film had disappeared) sounds at the very least ambiguous.

'The people' were represented in the film by the gloomy Pugachev rebel, Tikhon, who has the nickname 'torn ear' (and who dies at the end, having raised the Russian flag on the captured bastion). On their first meeting, Ushakov shouts at the escaped convict, 'You're a trouble-maker and a mutineer,' but all the same he wins Tikhon over to construction of the fleet, telling him he understands him: 'I'm not a gentleman, Tikhon. I'm a sailor.' Ushakov's assistant persuades Tikhon: 'Stay with Ushakov, Tikhon. You won't be serving the masters. You'll be serving Russia.' The transformation from rebel to patriot which takes place in the film is a model for the transformation of 'the people'.

Romm's two films are constructed on the alternation of scenes of grandiose naval battles (fire, the thunder of cannons, ships colliding) and conversational episodes in luxuriously decorated palaces. It is right here that the spies' plans and threads of conspiracies are woven. Lady Hamilton sets Nelson against the Russians. The British (yesterday's allies in the coalition against Hitler) are again transformed into enemies. All the allies' actions lead to conspiracies; they bring the plague to Kherson and arrange an epidemic in the town, then burn down the shipyards where the Russian fleet is built. English scouts, spies and saboteurs organise the uprising of the Crimean Tartars and make an attempt on Ushakov's life.

The aim of the film was the historicisation of the geopolitical realities of postwar Europe. The main constructing principle was to prove that Britain had always been a treacherous ally. In *Ushakov* the Prime Minister's father instructs his son on the principle of British foreign policy:

> On this mortal planet there is but one sovereign of the seas – Britain. There has been no other, there is no other, and there will be no other. Understand this, my son. We cannot smother all the enemies of the British kingdom with our own hands. So let them smother each other themselves. While you follow this path, you will be a true English politician.

This principle was fulfilled by Britain in the eighteenth to nineteenth centuries. Prime Minister Pitt the Younger addresses the British ambassador to Turkey, Robert Ainslie:

Did you know that the Black Sea used to be called the Russian Sea – on all the old maps, including English ones? Russia cannot stand on its feet without this sea, it's as necessary to her as air, and having stepped on its shores, she will not turn back. You have let the genie out of the bottle, sir! . . . Strangle Russia, plug its throat. If England does not sweep away the Russians from the shores of the Black Sea today, tomorrow will be too late . . . Turkey has to declare war this year. Let the English dogs off the leash, Sir Ainslie!

This text, spoken to camera, is directed not so much at the British ambassador as at the viewer, as confirmation of Russia's rights to the Black Sea, which is admitted by its very opponents. Scenes of this type are executed in the style of a caricature by the Cold War official Soviet political caricaturists Kukryniksy and Boris Efimov, with the indispensable Anglo-Americans John Bull (and Uncle Sam) unleashing countless 'dogs' on the Soviet Union. The fact that the English spy-adventuress Lady Hamilton was played by Elena Kuzmina (who had only just played, in *The Secret Mission* (Sekretnaia missiia), the role of a Soviet intelligence officer upsetting British plans for cooperation with the Nazis) endowed the film with absolutely contemporary significance: 'A detective intrigue was stitched into the historical canvas, the role of the "allies", the English, united on the screen the past with the present, and *Admiral Ushakov* with *The Secret Mission*.'[82]

Besides the motif of the allies' treachery, central to the two films about Ushakov, an important role was played by the motif of the 'liberation of Europe'. Part two of the picture, *The Ships Storm the Bastions*, opens with a narrated text about the era of the Napoleonic wars in Europe; these were 'bloody expansionist wars'. (Suvorov says of him, 'I don't see a Jacobin in him but a despot,' and calls him 'the French Genghis Khan'.) Russia liberated Europe from 'Napoleon's invasion', and the people of Europe were only waiting for the arrival of the Russian liberators. All Napoleon himself did was retreat under the onslaught of the Russian army and navy. (It remained unclear how the only achievement of these invincible armies several years later came to be the 'non-defeat' at Borodino and the 'pursuit of the French' escaping from Moscow.) The English at this time were busy with intrigues and conspiracies against the Russians, and Nelson with his love affair with Lady Hamilton. The rest simply did not enter into the picture. The greatness of the Russian army and navy at the beginning of the nineteenth century was a direct projection of the new greatness of the Soviet Union after victory over Germany, 'liberating the whole of Europe'.

The European wars against Napoleon (with Russia's participation!) are treated as wars of liberation. Being a direct projection on to events in post-war Europe, the film about Ushakov turns out to be a film about the liberation by the Russians of Europe from the 'enslavers'. We learn that the populations of Greece and Italy 'rose up to fight against the French oppressors' and are boundlessly grateful to the Russians who returned them their freedom. 'We are not here as victors, but as defenders of the Greeks,' says Ushakov. The liberator of Corfu, he addresses the Greeks: 'Brothers of the faith, the blood of heroes has strengthened our brotherhood. Thus take from the hands of Russia this gift – your freedom.' The Russians are defenders of the Greeks from the brutality of the Turks, of the French prisoners from the brutality of the English, who kill unarmed 'republicans' (Nelson moreover personally leads the punitive operations). Ushakov refuses to kill prisoners: 'Where the Russian flag is flying there will be no death sentence!'

Although Ushakov battles against Napoleon in alliance with the English, throughout the film we see an extremely sympathetic attitude towards the French Republicans (Ushakov is himself a republican, writing a republican constitution for Greece), whilst the real enemy of Russia is the 'ally' Britain. The English are treacherous and cynical; Lord Hamilton organises revolts in the Russian rear, incites the Turks not to give the Russians provisions and the Austrians to accept the unilateral capitulation of the French, letting the latter loose on the Russian rear, and supplies the French squadrons with cannons, whilst Lady Hamilton is portrayed as a adventuress and spy, organising mutinies on ships and an attempt on the life of Ushakov.

The aim of the British is to direct Ushakov towards liberating Naples, leaving the Ionian Islands, which they want to control for themselves, seeing them as the key to the Balkans. 'Russia has become too strong for them' – thus Ushakov explains the treacherous actions of the English pseudo-allies. Turning to Nelson, he asks: 'How long will you be an enemy of your ally and an ally of your enemy?' The political content of the film was clear; this was exactly how Britain had behaved in the war that had only just ended. The anti-Turkish campaign was an important component in official foreign policy rhetoric in 1953. (In 1952 Turkey had joined NATO, which was particularly painful for the USSR to swallow, since it brought NATO right up to the Soviet borders.) Thus the first thing that the viewer learns is that 'the age-old Russian lands of the Black Sea coast are still under Turkish dominion. The Turks, incited by the English and French, are preparing for a new war against Russia.' Turkey is portrayed as a puppet of Britain (although the Turkish Sultan understands that the English are not to be believed: 'If English oaths could be smeared on cakes instead of honey, you'd be a rich man, my wise vizier'). The main threat to the Turks comes from Russia. 'Suvorov took Izmail. What next? Or are you going to wait until Ushakov starts firing on my palace from the Bosporus?' the Turkish Sultan cries in hysterics. (According to naval commander films, the Turkish navy was simply operated by the British.) Thus the words of the naval commander sound out at the climax of part one of Ushakov: 'There is no more Turkish navy. From now on the Russian navy is the master of the Black Sea.'

The film was made at the very height of the struggle against cosmopolitanism. Therefore all the elements of the post-war patriotic campaign are active in it. Thus the educated Potemkin calls the foreign ambassadors 'overseas monkeys', while the uneducated Ushakov, who does not speak French or know politesse, speaks of himself with pride: 'We are from Tambov.' So when Count Mordovtsev advises Ushakov to study the naval arts with Nelson, both Suvorov and Ushakov give this 'toady to foreigners' a patriotic rebuke:

> Suvorov: For how long will you call a crow in a foreign land a falcon, and an eagle at home a crow?
> Ushakov: Think about that and not tears but blood will pour from your eyes. We have Russian names. The Russian people gave us our language. The Russian people dresses us, gives us food and drink. The Russian people awarded us our ranks and titles. We will honour our wet-nurse!

This reverence for the wet-nurse also reveals itself through emphasis on the significance of Russia. Thus Ushakov's victory at Corfu is depicted as the crucial moment in the war against Napoleon: 'Our flag over Corfu can be seen by all of Europe!' These great-power fantasies seem particularly important when they come from the mouths of opponents. Thus, the British Prime Minister exclaims in horror: 'The Russian navy on the Black Sea! Well? It's the most terrible blow for England since the founding of Petersburg!' The degree to which such scenes are convincing for the viewer is directly proportional to their comedy value.

Behind all this one can see not so much the allusiveness of history as the total historicism of the present. The transformation of myth into history has become the mythologisation of history, only to turn out to be the total historicisation of the present. From long (ab)use the historical coulisses have been worn down to the extent that they have become completely transparent. Thus the historical costumes and powdered wigs of the characters ceased to conceal the present, but only had to impart to it a quasi-historical dimension. At the concluding stage of its reworking under Stalin, history becomes, as Pokrovsky asserted, 'politics projected on to the past'. But politics towards the end of the Stalinist epoch was definitively transformed into geopolitical fantasising. A conspiratorial view of the world endowed this fantasy with a plot and a particular kind of entertainment value and plausibility. The latter is especially important, as conspiratorial thinking needs plausibility, finding in dramatised 'reality' a confirmation of its own version of history, in which everything is shrouded in mystery and occurs 'behind the scenes' of the visible world. The aim of the narrative comes down to 'revealing the secret springs' of visible 'events', which only camouflage the 'true' events and therefore are fulfilled by 'historical meaning'.

We return to Vinokur's idea that 'the historical fact (the event and so on), in order to become biographical fact, must in one form or another be experienced by the given individual,' only 'by becoming an object of experience [does] historical fact [gain] biographical meaning.'[83] In a world where 'fact' is the product of hidden manipulation, where 'events' are concealed behind a secret, the conditions are absent for their being 'experienced', for the transformation of history into the 'spiritual experience' of the individual. Biography here cannot be constituted as a form of historical narrative. The history of this quasi-individual cannot be reduced to narrative. Quite the opposite: the historical-biographical narrative, constructed according to all the rules of Soviet ideological fantasy, engenders a kind of verbal and visual mannequin, who in rough-and-ready fashion gets up in historical costume, is provided with the personal features of real historical figures, and plays their role, understood as an ideological function. In itself the 'historical individual' and his or her life are deprived here of 'biographical meaning', as they are only the narrative 'embodiment' of transcendental demiurgic forces. It is not enough for these forces to be symbolised in the profiles on the decorations. Representation of their full value needs dramatisation, a plot.

History here fulfils a foundational function (like historical materialism, which is called upon only to substantiate the inevitability and correctness of the Soviet order), while the historical individual personifies history, which without an individual biography cannot be constituted as a narrative story. The consumer of screen action closes the circle, being not so much a viewer as an overseer of the virtual historical figure. In the waxworks of Russian history the viewer is the only living, acting person in a chain of ideological agents, and is positioned on the border of the history and present under construction. Thereby he or she does not allow the historical character (and with him history itself) definitively to slide into the present ('projected politics'). Like a border guard, the viewer holds them back in the flickering space of political imaginary and legitimising discourse, thus becoming an accomplice of the present.

NOTES

1. K. Simonov, *Glazami cheloveka moego pokoleniia*, Moscow: APN, 1988, pp. 189–90.
2. See V. A. Durov, *Nagrady Velikoi Otechestvennoi*, Moscow: Russkaia kniga, 1993, p. 46.
3. See Durov, *Nagrady Velikoi Otechestvennoi*, p. 36.
4. I. V. Stalin, '24 godovshchina Velikoi oktiabr'skoi sotsialisticheskoi revoliutsii. Doklad 6 noiabria 1941 goda,' Moscow, *Pravda*, 1941, p. 18.
5. I. V. Stalin, 'Rech' 7 noiabria 1941 g.'. In I. V. Stalin, *24 godovshchina Velikoi oktiabr'skoi sotsialisticheskoi revoliutsii*, pp. 30–1.
6. Kh. Khersonskii, 'Istoricheskaia tema v kino', *Iskusstvo kino*, 1938, No. 3, p. 42.
7. G. Vinokur, *Biografiia i kul'tura*, Moscow: GAKhN, 1927, p. 37.
8. Ibid., p. 39.
9. Sergei Eizenshtein, 'Aleksandr Nevskii'. In *Sovetskii istoricheskii fil'm: Sbornik statei*, Moscow: Goskinoizdat, 1939, p. 19.
10. Ibid., p. 20.
11. Ibid., p. 22.
12. Sergei Eizenshtein, *Izbrannye proizvedeniia v 6 tomakh*, Vol. 6, Moscow: Iskusstvo, 1971, p. 159.
13. Petr Pavlenko, *Na Vostoke*, Moscow, 1937, pp. 438–9. See Mikhail Geller, Aleksandr Nekrich, *Utopiia u vlasti*, Vol. 1, London: OPI, 1982, pp. 316–17.
14. *Iskusstvo kino*, 1964, No. 3, pp. 4–9.

15. David Bordwell, *The Cinema of Eisenstein*, Cambridge, MA: Harvard University Press, 1993, p. 212.
16. See Richard Taylor, *Film Propaganda: Soviet Russia and Nazi Germany*, London: I. B. Tauris, 1998, p. 90.
17. Bernd Uhlenbruch, 'Instsenirovka mifa: O fil'me S. Eizenshteina *Aleksandr Nevskii*'. In *Sovetskoe bogatstvo: Stat'i o kul'ture, literature i kino*, St Petersburg: Akademicheskii proekt, 2002, pp. 317–18.
18. James Goodwin also calls attention to this. James Goodwin, *Eisenstein, Cinema, and History*, Urbana and Chicago: University of Illinois Press, 1993, pp. 162–4.
19. See Richard Taylor, *Film Propaganda: Soviet Russia and Nazi Germany*, p. 88.
20. Mikhail Romm, *Besedy o kino*, Moscow: Iskusstvo, 1964, p. 89.
21. Goodwin, *Eisenstein, Cinema, and History*, p. 156.
22. This idea corresponds with Leonid Kozlov's work on the genesis of *Ivan the Terrible*: L. Kozlov, 'Ten' Groznogo i Khudozhnik', *Kinovedcheskie zapiski*, 1992, Issue 14.
23. L. Gutman, 'Istoricheskii zhanr v zhivopisi i kino'. In *Sovetskii istoricheskii fil'm*, p. 94.
24. Eizenshtein, '*Aleksandr Nevskii*', p. 23.
25. Khersonskii, 'Istoricheskaia tema v kino', p. 46. At the same time the screenplay was criticised for its unseemly depiction of the people. Thus, apropos of the scene of the fight in Novgorod, which subsequently was not put into the film, critic Khersonsky wrote: 'Yes, in Novgorod the *veche* often ended in a direct clash between the parties, with wide participation of the people. But is it worthy of a Soviet artist to reduce the political consciousness of the citizens of Novgorod to fisticuffs?' (ibid.).
26. Ol'ga Iumesheva, '*Aleksandr Nevskii* v kontekste evraziiskoi refleksii'. In *Istoriia kino/Istoriia strany*, Moscow: Znak, 2004, pp. 100–1.
27. Uhlenbruch, 'Instsenirovka mifa: O fil'me S. Eizenshteina *Aleksandr Nevskii*', p. 319.
28. V. Shklovskii, 'Ob istoricheskom stsenarii'. In *Sovetskii istoricheskii fil'm*, pp. 80, 81.
29. Eduard Tisse, 'Kak my gotovilis' k *Aleksandru Nevskomu*', *Iskusstvo kino*, 1938, No. 12, p. 8.
30. Vsevolod Pudovkin, '*Aleksandr Nevskii*', *Rabochaia Moskva*, 8 December 1938, p. 3.
31. I. Bachelis, 'Sergei Eizenshtein', *Izvestiia*, 11 February 1940, p. 4.
32. From Maya Turovskaya's lecture materials, delivered at Duke University, January–May 1993.
33. David Bordwell, *The Cinema of Eisenstein*, pp. 211, 221.
34. Shklovskii, 'Ob istoricheskom stsenarii', p. 74.
35. Ibid., p. 74.
36. As David Brandenberger has shown, national identity in Russia was very weak, even during the First World War. See David Brandenberger, *National Bolshevism: Stalinist Mass Culture and the Formation of Modern Russian Identity. 1931–1956*, Cambridge, MA: Harvard University Press, 2002.
37. Vsevolod Pudovkin, 'Fil'm o patriotisme i muzhestve velikogo naroda'. In Vs. Pudovkin, *Sobranie sochinenii v 3 tomakh*, Vol. 2, Moscow: Iskusstvo, 1975, p. 76.
38. A. Mar'iamov, *Narodnyi artist SSSR Vsevolod Pudovkin*, Moscow: Goskinoizdat, 1952, p. 209.
39. Viktor Shklovskii, 'Ob istoricheskom stsenarii'. In *Sovetskii istoricheskii fil'm*, pp. 82, 83.
40. Vsevolod Pudovkin, 'Fil'm o velikom russkom narode'. In Vsevolod Pudovkin, *Sobranie sochinenii v 3 tomakh*, Vol. 2, Moscow: Iskusstvo, 1975, p. 78.
41. Vsevolod Pudovkin, '*Minin i Pozharskii*'. In Vsevolod Pudovkin, *Sobranie sochinenii v 3 tomakh*, Vol. 2, p. 78.

42. Mar'iamov, *Narodnyi artist SSSR Vsevolod Pudovkin*, p. 209.
43. Pudovkin, *Sobranie sochinenii v 3 tomakh*, Vol. 2, p. 39.
44. A. Karaganov, *Vsevolod Pudovkin*, Moscow: Iskusstvo, 1983, p. 196.
45. A. Khanov, 'Obraz narodnogo geroia'. In *Sovetskii istoricheskii fil'm*, pp. 58, 60.
46. Ibid., p. 59.
47. Pudovkin, *Sobranie sochinenii v 3 tomakh*, Vol. 2, p. 79.
48. Mar'iamov, *Narodnyi artist SSSR Vsevolod Pudovkin*, p. 210.
49. Vasilii Tokarev, ' "Kará panam!": Pol'skaia tema v predvoennom kino (1939–1941 gg.)'. In *Istoriia kino/Istoriia strany*, Moscow: Znak, 2004, pp. 167–8.
50. Ibid., p. 162.
51. On *Minin and Pozharsky* and *Bogdan Khmelnitsky* in the context of the Polish theme, which arose in 1939–41 and practically took first place in Soviet cinema at that time, see Tokarev, ' "Kará panam!": Pol'skaia tema v predvoennom kino (1939–1941 gg.)', 2004.
52. R. Iurenev, 'Narodnaia epopeia', *Iskusstvo kino*, 1941, No. 4, p. 14.
53. Ibid., p. 14.
54. *Ocherki istorii sovetskogo kino*, Vol. 2, Moscow: Iskusstvo, 1959, p. 436.
55. Ibid., p. 432.
56. *Mastera sovetskogo kino. Dvadtsat' rezhisserskikh biografii*, Moscow: Iskusstvo, 1971, p. 251.
57. Mar'iamov, *Narodnyi artist SSSR Vsevolod Pudovkin*, p. 222.
58. I. Astakhov, 'Suvorov', *Novyi mir*, 1941, No. 3, p. 236.
59. Mar'iamov, *Narodnyi artist SSSR Vsevolod Pudovkin*, p. 225.
60. See Karaganov, *Vsevolod Pudovkin*, pp. 203–5.
61. Mar'iamov, *Narodnyi artist SSSR Vsevolod Pudovkin*, p. 249
62. Viktor Shklovskii, 'Fil'm o Suvorove'. In V. Shklovskii, *Za 60 let: Raboty o kino*, Moscow: Iskusstvo, 1985, p. 217.
63. Anatolii Latyshev, 'Suvorov: na vzgliad polkovodtsa', *Iskusstvo kino*, 1990, No. 5, p. 4.
64. E. Gromov, *Kinooperator Anatolii Golovnia*, Moscow: Iskusstvo, 1980, p. 136.
65. Cited by R. N. Iurenev, *Sovetskoe kinoiskusstvo tridtsatykh godov*, Moscow: VGIK, 1997, p. 56.
66. See G. Mar'iamov, *Kremlevskii tsenzor: Stalin smotrit kino*, Moscow: Kinotsentr, 1992, pp. 47–8.
67. V. Shklovskii, 'Kutuzov'. In Viktor Shklovskii, *Za 60 let: Raboty o kino*, p. 226.
68. 'Soveshchanie kinodramaturgov, pisatelei i kinorezhisserov, sozvannoe Komitetom po delam kinematografii pri SNK SSSR 14–16 iulia 1943 goda.' In *Zhivye golosa kino*, Moscow: Belyi bereg, 1999, p. 244.
69. Gromov, *Kinooperator Anatolii Golovnia*, p. 137.
70. R. Iurenev, *Sovetskii biograficheskii fil'm*, Moscow: Goskinoizdat, 1949, pp. 133–4.
71. E. Tarle, *Krymskaia voina*, Moscow: AN SSSR, 1944, Vol., p. 308.
72. Vsevolod Pudovkin, 'Kak mne predstavliaetsia obraz Nakhimova'. In Vs. Pudovkin, *Sobranie sochinenii v 3 tomakh*, Vol. 2, p. 88.
73. Mar'iamov, *Narodnyi artist SSSR Vsevolod Pudovkin*, p. 247.
74. Cited in Mar'iamov, *Narodnyi artist SSSR Vsevolod Pudovkin*, p. 247; Karaganov, *Vsevolod Pudovkin*, pp. 231–2.
75. Vs. Pudovkin, 'Vystuplenie na obsuzhdenii literaturnogo stsenariia *Admiral Nakhimov* Khudozhestvennym sovetom "Mosfil'ma" 4 fevralia 1944 g'. In Pudovkin, *Sobranie sochinenii v 3 tomakh*, Vol. 3, Moscow: Iskusstvo, 1976, p. 65.
76. K. M. Isaeva, *Istoriia sovetskogo kinoiskusstva v poslevoennoe desiatiletie*, Moscow: VGIK, 1992, p. 54.
77. See Maiia Turovskaia, 'Fil'my kholodnoi voiny', *Iskusstvo kino*, 1996, No. 6; Evgeny Dobrenko, 'Late Stalinist Cinema and the Cold War: An Equation Without Unknowns', *Modern Language Review*, 98:4 (October 2003).

78. G. Kozintsev, 'Chernoe, likhoe vremia . . .' Iz rabochikh tetradei, Moscow: Artist. Rezhisser. Teatr, 1994, p. 38.
79. Cited in Mark Zak, Mikhail Romm i traditsii sovetskoi kinorezhissury, Moscow: Iskusstvo, 1975, p. 177.
80. Ibid., p. 178.
81. Ibid., p. 178.
82. Ibid., p. 177.
83. Vinokur, Biografiia i kul'tura, p. 37.

3. RUSSIAN CLASSICS AND THE PAST IN ITS REVOLUTIONARY DEVELOPMENT

Scraps of a repertoire on an advertising column.

Boris Pasternak

Work which interprets the past 'in its revolutionary development' must, finally, be acknowledged as a legitimate part of socialist realism; Yakov Protazanov's film *Without a Dowry* (*Bespridannitsa*) is as much an 'exemplar of Stalinist art' as Ivan Pyrev's *The Swineherdess and the Shepherd* (*Svinarka i pastukh*). The 'problem of the classics' is reduced here only to the fact that at every turn it is the 'primary classic literary text' itself which impedes the work being attributed to that canon. It is difficult for us today to reconcile ourselves to the fact that we started out with Pushkin's (Gogol's, Chekhov's, Tolstoy's) texts, and ended up with . . . socialist realism. Yet the masters of Soviet cinema had no difficulty with this at all.

In 1938, Fridrikh Ermler wrote:

> What is socialist realism? I have thought endlessly about this, and this is how I have resolved it for myself. It seems to me that in everything we create – be it cinematography, or a tractor, the construction of a house, or a fashion salon – in everything, always and everywhere, the thought must exist: 'and communism'. Understand me, everything that we create is a movement, a step that leads to the greater goal toward which we are striving, in a word – 'communism'.
>
> And so it seems to me that if in the films we make, in every episode, every frame, every movement of every actor, every line of dialogue, that thought exists – 'and communism' – if that word is not taken as a cliché, a mere slogan, but is understood, deeply felt, stored away in the

brain and the heart, then I believe that this indeed will be socialist realism.[1]

All this applied, of course, not only to recent creations (tractors and fashion salons) but also to the reworking of the 'classical heritage', and the upshot was . . . Gogol and communism, Ostrovsky and communism, Chekhov and communism . . . As Grigory Roshal, one of the most passionate 'adapters' of Russian classics for the screen, stated in 1954:

> All creative potential should be mobilised for one purpose only: to inter-pret the original, its images and its emotions, from contemporary stand-points, from the standpoints of socialist realism. Does this mean we should always modernise these works, inserting our own thoughts and judgements into the mouths of the heroes or into the author's thoughts? I think not. When I speak of socialist realism, I am referring to it in the sense of a compass used to interpret a work, to reveal its deep-seated pro-gressive tendencies. Only authentic knowledge of Marxist-Leninist phi-losophy will enable us to gain a true understanding of the complex structures of major literary canvases.[2]

However, it was not a question of 'literary canvases' at all, in so far as the inter-minable debate between screen and book, which continued throughout the entire Soviet period (and was a favourite theme of the 'creative discussions' that flared up over just about every screen adaptation: 'No, that's not Pushkin!' 'Yes, that's Chekhov!' 'Does that look like Ostrovsky to you?') had, dare I suggest, nothing whatsoever to do with literature.

Adapting a classic for the screen has always involved working with the past in a particular way, 'from contemporary standpoints' (to use Roshal's phrase). And not only in the 1920s, when it was not Pushkin and Gogol who found their way on to the screen but . . . Pereverzev and his sociological interpretation of the classics; nor only under Stalin, when screen adaptations encompassed vir-tually the entire curriculum of classic texts taught in schools (as interpreted 'by Belinsky, Chernyshevsky and Dobrolyubov'); nor only during the Thaw, when above all the socio-psychological depths of the classics were revealed, which were grist to the mill for the reformers of the 1960s in their opposition to trite Stalinist schematics; and nor only during the Stagnation of the Brezhnev years, when the classics were being read as a sort of cinematic palimpsest, a compila-tion of allusions and socio-historical fantasies which were in a polemic with official doctrines. As regards the Stalinist era specifically, the issue is not just the 'distortion' of the classics to fit the Soviet historical model but also the literary provenance of the model itself. Literature has in no sense always played second fiddle to politics; frequently politics itself has been the fruit of literature.

The Russian Social Democrats, every last one of them, were 'members of the literati' (incidentally both Lenin and Stalin called themselves 'men of letters'). They assimilated the past, the great nineteenth century, which, for them, was drawing to a close and becoming part of history, through literature, about which they were really fairly knowledgeable (in the sense that they picked up the ready-made interpretations of the intelligentsia of the 1860s). Therefore, the schema of the past that was fixed in Stalinist culture was not only 'supported' by literature but, in many respects, emanated from it. History in this case had been colonised by literature. And hence the paradox: in the offerings of the Stalinist cinema, which were split more or less fifty-fifty into 'historical' films and 'biographical' accounts of historical figures and events, it is impossible to find a single film that really deals with the past. One could only see what daily life was like in the past (and not only that of the tsars, great military leaders, composers and scholars) in screen adaptations of the Russian classics.

However, this view of daily life in past times was not perceived as a product of the creative minds of Pushkin, Gogol or Chekhov. It was seen as the 'past per se', which the classic writers had merely shaped by adding a plot line. The writer 'grasps a fragment of life' and 'transforms' it ('realistically', it goes without saying). Then the director prevails over the writer in the process of adapting it for the screen and depersonifies life, disenchants it, so to speak. The reality on the screen has been purified, rendered as 'authentic' as it could possibly be. The coding of life by a classic writer and its decoding by an adept director guarantee that the screen event will not only be 'credible' but will 'live on through the ages'. Before us we have a process whereby reality is distilled into literature and then, through ideological interpretation in criticism, into film. This 'mythology cubed' is what the viewer 'took from the screen'.[3]

The complexity of this 'presentation' of history, which is transmuted into a complete synthesis of the arts, is connected to the very nature of the Stalinist political-aesthetic project. In April 1935, a conference of writers, composers, artists and film directors took place. It was presided over, it goes without saying, by Maxim Gorky – after all, literature traditionally reigned supreme on the Russian (Soviet) Parnassus. And what were the dreams of 'socialist realism's founding father'? The twentieth anniversary of the October Revolution (only two and a half years away!) 'demands results and we must provide them':

> Everything that has been made must be collected together in a single lump [kom], as it were, and if musicians, playwrights, poets – in general, literature and all the other arts – organised themselves, they could compose for the twentieth-anniversary celebrations, for example, a choral oratorio . . . a big production with great crowds of people, and good lyrics set to good music.[4]

It was precisely cinema that turned out to be in the position of providing this choral oratorio; the screen was the place for 'great literature', 'good lyrics' (and prose), playwriting and 'great crowds of people'. It is interesting that this lump – to use Gorky's elegant term – was needed not for its own sake but for the anniversary celebrations, as a historical marker. But history is more than just anniversary celebrations.

History is not just a narrative but an explanatory narrative. If history does not explain the past and does not draw logical conclusions about past (and current) events, it loses not only its social rationale but also its credibility. In 1992, Stanislav Govorukhin's film, *The Russia We Lost* (*Rossiia, kotoruiu my poteriali*), was released. The film became quite an event, although after five years of *glasnost'*, it was difficult to find anything that would surprise audiences. Even so, this monumental documentary film shocked a lot of people. (Unusually, it was shown at all the main cinemas, just like a feature film, and attracted huge audiences.) The montage of clips from pre-revolutionary newsreels, the shots of contemporary 'social ills', and Govorukhin's calm, reasonable narration were all intended to prove that pre-revolutionary Russia was a rich and thriving country that was constructing capitalism at full speed and would undoubtedly, by the end of the twentieth century, have 'caught up and overtaken' the West. The film conveyed this idea on all possible levels, and is extremely persuasive. The only question to ask that would not go away after the screening (and was similar to the one that crops up after reading Solzhenitsyn's *Red Wheel* (*Krasnoe koleso*) or any piece by a nationalistically inclined writer or journalist) is: If everything was so good why was there a revolution? Explanations along the lines of 'Bolsheviks in a sealed railroad car', 'non-Russian plotters' and so forth assume that the person asking the question is prepared to believe that a handful of people were in a position to create the greatest revolution in the twentieth century without the support of the masses (and the key phrase here is 'without the masses' – 'the people' – insofar as, if such support were forthcoming, it would have indicated that there was something wrong with the picture being presented and that all was not, in fact, 'harmonious' in pre-revolutionary Russia).

So history as a narrative for popular consumption is needed in so far as it explains things that are happening here and now, or simply legitimises them. It is precisely in this sense that we speak of history's 'credibility', credibility being a synonym of legitimacy in this instance. In his typology of the underpinnings of 'legitimate domination', Max Weber identified the first as 'the rational type of legitimate authority'. History is here seen as the underpinning and foundation of legitimacy; the legitimate is that which is logical, and the logical is that which proceeds from 'the most natural course of history'.[5] In this way history (and with it the classics) proves to be under the aegis of authority. The literary classics, unlike any other form of historical narrative – textbooks (which can easily be rewritten), documents (which can be forged), interpretations (which can be repeatedly revised), statistics (which are easily falsified) and so on – enjoy the status of unconditional authenticity, specifically by virtue of being pure fiction. This assertion holds particularly true for Russian and Soviet literocentric culture.

At the unveiling of the Pushkin monument in Moscow in 1880, Alexander Ostrovsky (of whom more later) said that the grief caused by the loss of the great poet was itself so great because it 'gave rise to an emptiness, a sense of mental bereavement; there is no one through whom to think, no one through whom to feel'.[6] In essence, literature is the organ of national thought and national feeling. This 'Russian specificity' overlays the cinema's own specificity. In its hundred-year debate with literature and the theatre, the cinema revealed not only its differences but also its connectedness, above all with literature.

And above all, vice versa, too. Boris Eikhenbaum stated that 'cinema opposes the culture of reading, and thereby also opposes literature itself', that the conditions of perception of the cinema run contrary to those of the reading process: 'from the object, from the collation of moving frames to their comprehension, their denomination, to the construction of the internal utterance'. Cinema 'takes what it needs' from literature, using it merely as a 'libretto for its screenplays'.[7] Vsevolod Pudovkin, on the other hand, insisted that:

> [T]he true motivating force in the art of Soviet cinema was those profoundly realistic traditions of Russian art and above all with Russian literature, so closely interlinked with the life of the people, that are inseparable from the great names of Pushkin, Belinsky, Turgenev, Tolstoy, Chekhov, and Gorky.

For its part, 'cinema, though directly engendered by the art of the theatre, departs from the dramatic genre and draws closer in its essence to the literary novel.'[8]

The kinship between cinema and the novel is perceptively explained by Susan Sontag:

> Like the novel, the cinema presents us with a view of an action which is absolutely under the control of the director (writer) at every moment. Our eye cannot wander about the screen, as it does about the stage. The camera is an absolute dictator. It shows us a face when we are to see a face and nothing else; a pair of clenched hands, a landscape, a speeding train, the facade of a building in the middle of a tête-à-tête, when and only when it wants us to see these things. When the camera moves we move, when it remains still we are still. In a similar way the novel presents a selection of the thoughts and descriptions which are relevant to the writer's conception, and we must follow these serially, as the author leads us; they are not spread out, as a background, for us to contemplate in the order we choose, as in painting or the theatre.[9]

The authoritarian nature of literature, which it shares with the cinema, placed these two art forms at the centre of the Stalinist *Gesamtkunstwerk*.

Without question, the fact that, in the 1930s, 'the cinematographic phase of cultural development gradually replaced the literary phase'[10] is one of the indicators of a cultural shift from an avant-garde elitist culture to a mass-appeal socialist realist culture. As a result of this change, the literary classics became known primarily through the cinema; audiences in the 1930s and 1940s would always think of Katerina as Alla Tarasova, Kabanikha as Varvara Massalitinova, Yudushka as Vladimir Gardin, Belikov as Nikolai Khmelev, and Zmeiukhina the midwife as Vera Maretskaya. When literary characters are given visual form in this way, mass consciousness is drawn into reshaping the source text – and the reader/viewer comes to think of the primary source no longer as the book but as the film. It is common knowledge that viewing anything in itself reduces the independence and individuality of the audience's perception. The literary source, finding it difficult to compete with its cinematic rival, slips into the background. As one critic of the 1930s quite rightly said, in a review of the screen adaptation of *The Golovlyov Family* (*Gospoda Golovlevy*): 'Just try re-reading *The Golovlyovs* after seeing the film and not only will you have Yudushka-Gardin before your eyes but also, as you read, his unforgettably expressive voice will ring in your ears.'[11]

To all intents and purposes, this is the point at which the classical literary text begins to disappear and is replaced by an alienating screen simulacrum. Thus adaptation for the screen is a process of alienation of the classics. The adapted work becomes an entirely Soviet artefact. Not only the literary source, but also 'historical reality' itself, familiar to the recipient from the book, turn out to be deprived of reference, whilst the consciousness of the viewer reproduces ready-made visual images of the past, now derived not from the book, but from the screen. And a strict logic governs those images.

Of the large number of screen adaptations of the Russian classics made during the Stalinist era, we shall focus on some of the most characteristic examples, which illustrate the basic strategies involved in converting a literary text into a visual historical narrative. In the course of this examination, we shall not only cover various types of images of the past that have been produced on the screen, but also analyse the techniques used with the original texts – the reshaping of plot into screenplay, the creation of new narrative constructions (the transformation of the image of the narrator), the 'dramatisation' of prose, the 'cinematisation' of dramatic works and so on.[12]

An adaptation for the screen is always an interpretation of the source text. Since there could be no interpretation in Stalinist culture, there could be no real adaptation either. In principle, an individual, unanticipated, original reading of a literary classic (or of anything else, for that matter) was out of the question; the screenwriter (or director) could not interpret anything. The only interpreter in Stalinist culture (and, accordingly, the only artist, designer and director as well) was Stalin himself, the master of the word. The process of screen adaptation here is boiled down to the reshaping of a source text in order to consolidate and give visual impact to an interpretation that critics have already canonised.

In this we have one explanation for cinema's attitude toward classical literature: that this kind of literature requires no interpretation. It coincides with what cinema says it is; Puskhin's *Captain's Daughter* (*Kapitanskaia dochka*) is, within Stalinist culture, on an equal footing with commentaries on it in school textbooks. And in this sense the classical corpus is integrated into socialist realism. Thus Ostrovsky's *The Storm* (*Groza*) is on an equal footing with the Dobrolyubov/Revyakin analysis of it taught in schools or with Vladimir Petrov's cinematic treatment of it, and, since the culture offers no other treatment and no classic can exist outside its interpretation, it could be said that this version of *The Storm* was the only version, and that as such it was a socialist realist text. (The same is true of any piece of classic Russian literature.) Similarly, within Stalinist culture no abstract *Dubrovsky* (with diverse interpretations) can exist; but there is a single *Dubrovsky*, as interpreted by critics and consolidated in school textbooks. This *Dubrovsky*, in all the fullness of its single possible interpretation, is a fully-fledged work of socialist realism.

But interpretation is not a constituent part of a literary text. Therefore, the transformation of a classic work into a piece of socialist realism demands a new kind of integration, of the text fused with its accepted interpretation. This is the cultural niche of screen adaptation in Stalinist culture; 'a classic adapted for the screen' is indeed a classic, but converted into socialist realism. What Eikhenbaum called 'the viewer's internal utterance' is, in the context of our discussion, the product of contemplation of the classics as presented by the Soviet cinema; 'the viewer's internal utterance' articulates the classic literary text as a work of Soviet culture.

How Iosif Vissarionovich Became Friends with Nikolai Vasilevich

Screen adaptations in the Stalin era were unique in that their goal was never to reproduce the literary source-text or the writer's artistic world, but to use the text solely with the aim of creating images of the past, to bring a visual perspective to bear on history. Cinema's aim in the 1930s was to demonstrate 'the idiocy and horror of Russian life', and for this purpose Gogol was indispensable.[13] Cinema turned to him with enthusiasm. Noteworthy among the pre-revolutionary adaptations of Gogol were Alexander Drankov's *Taras Bulba*, Alexander Khanzhonkov's *Dead Souls* (*Mertvye dushi*) and Yakov Protazanov's *May Night* (*Maiskaia noch'*). In the 1920s, in addition to the FEKS (Factory of Eccentric Actors) Group's famous *Overcoat* (*Shinel'*, 1926), it is worth mentioning the adaptations of *The Fair at Sorochinsk* (*Sorichinskaia iarmaka*, 1926) and *Cherevichki* (from *The Night Before Christmas* (*Noch' pered rozhdestvom*), 1928). Finally, the Stalinist era gave us the renowned film *The Marriage* (*Zhenit'ba*, 1937) by Erast Garin and Khesia Lokshina, new versions of *The Fair at Sorochinsk* (1939) and *May Night* (1940), *How Ivan Ivanovich Quarrelled with Ivan Nikiforovich* (*Povest' o tom, kak possorilsia Ivan Ivanovich s Ivanom Nikiforovichem*, 1941) and Vladimir Petrov's *The Government Inspector* (*Revizor*, 1952). From this embarrassment of riches, we have selected the adaptation of *How Ivan Ivanovich Quarrelled with Ivan Nikiforovich*. Kustov's film is interesting for being so unnoteworthy; it is one of those screen adaptations which does not have (like *The Overcoat*) a legendary history, to which no aura of scandal clings (as it does to *The Marriage*), and which was not a brilliant success (as was *The Wedding* (*Svad'ba*)).

The key element in Gogol's *Quarrel* is without question its language. In translating the content of this element into visual form, the director did not merely 'violate the integrity of Gogol's text' (which is the norm for any screen adaptation), but created an entirely new one. This is one of those films that Viktor Shklovsky called 'a breaking-and-entering screen adaptation'. The first to be doomed in the course of this operation is the narrator – the one who discusses his thoughts on the famous lambskin trim of Ivan Ivanovich's coat and many other wondrous things. In the film, the narrator's lines are divided up between the characters, converted into dialogue between the two Ivans and, finally, given . . . to Gogol himself. Jolting along in a *brichka* through Russia's trackless wastes telling his tale with a sombre face, Gogol is a sort of ghostly substitute for the absent narrator. In essence, this parcelling out of the narrator could be considered a sanitising procedure, since Gogol's narration is not lacking in clear signs of schizophrenia. Gogol's narrator is simultaneously a feather-brained gossip and a worldly sceptic, a pompous provincial and, finally, simply a spinner of yarns. (It is worth recalling the warning that comes with the story; in the very first sentence, we are told that the entire 'incident' is 'a complete fabrication'.) The film's writers simplified things for the viewer. For example, certain unnamed residents of Mirgorod tell us about the lambskin trim; textual interpolations inform us what 'a good man Ivan Ivanovich' is and that 'he is very fond of melons'; and all the 'sad' parts are conveyed to us by Gogol with his sombre face. In a word, the more people who tell the tale, the more credible the 'complete fabrication'.

The modification of the narrative structure of *The Quarrel* completely alters the chronology of the tale; Gogol's narrator is talking about events that happened in the distant past. The story opens with observations that 'Mirgorod is not what it was', that 'the puddle in the middle of town dried up long ago', that many of the participants in the 'incident' have since died, that the narrator last saw any of the characters five years previously; and that the 'incident' began twelve years before that. In the film, instead of a seventeen-year interval, it is suggested to the audience that the 'incident' is developing here and now, and ends with an encounter at a church between Gogol and the main characters. The new narrative structure causes a chronological dislocation that, in turn, causes a modification in the narration. If, as in Gogol's version, the events happened a very long time ago, all that remains is the telling – 'words, words, words'; if the events are developing here and now, as in the film, we are dealing not with words but with reality itself. And the screen is occupied with itself with a detailed painting of that 'reality'.

The first thing we see is livestock: pigs, turkeys, chickens, geese, goats . . . The screen grunts, quacks, squeaks, bleats and cackles. Amidst this incredible racket live the 'two unequalled friends'. As sound appears, colour disappears. For instance, in Gogol's story, the scene describing items being hung out to air in Ivan Nikoforovich's courtyard is very colourful; there is 'a blue padded Cossack jacket', 'a caftan of grass-green colour with brass buttons', 'a waistcoat trimmed with gold braid' and an ancient saddle, 'with a saddle-cloth that had once been scarlet in colour, with gold embroidery and copper disks'.

> [A]ll this mixed together created a . . . very diverting spectacle, while the sun's rays, glancing in places on a blue or green sleeve, a red cuff or a bit of gold brocade, or playing on a protruding sword-point, transformed it into something out of the ordinary, like those puppet-theatres that itinerant rogues take round the farms.

In a word, a picturesque scene. On screen, however, all we see is a pile of ancient rags, and the ill-starred rifle that so intrigues Ivan Ivanovich looks more like a pock-marked stick hung with tattered dusters.

Gogol's physical world has been completely transfigured. The sets are impossibly cluttered. Instead of broad panoramas we have before us ramshackle structures, crooked, straw-thatched hovels, broken fences and decrepit sheds, while instead of cosy yards with fruit trees, there are veritable rubbish dumps with chickens and ducks milling about. The interiors of the houses are even less cosy. In fact, they are not houses at all but dirty little huts, with dilapidated, broken furniture and peeling plaster, incredibly cramped and gloomy. In these dwellings live people who are constantly poking and shoving each other, dressed in what could be housecoats or some sort of civilian garb. One notable aspect of the screen population is the abundance of officials, clerks and civil servants of all stripes. They crowd about, always bent over or making snide remarks about one another. Their costumes are several sizes too small, fit way too tightly and are all splitting at the seams. And this freak show is the image we are given of Gogol's Russia. Its all-pervasive metaphor is impassable roads, mud and the famous Mirgorod puddle.

Gogol's world by its very nature does not lend itself to screen adaptation. The concretisation of this linguistic medium turns it into a banal sort of 'picture that painters love', to use Gogol's own words. The world of the transmuted Soviet Gogol – 'consuming in a blaze of satire everything vulgar and loathsome in [his] modern life' – is a different matter altogether. The screen adaptation of this Gogol offers entirely different results. From a sceptic, an occasionally cheerless moraliser or, entirely unacceptable as this might be, a religious thinker, the author is metamorphosed into . . . a positive hero. Gogol's endlessly quoted dictum that laughter is the positive hero of his comedy is taken quite literally (for instance, by giving us the narrator transformed into Gogol), and now we have 'Gogol' himself delivering his own narrator's lines.

Of course, 'Gogol the satirist' wrote satire and, in this respect, the classics proved to be a true treasure-house for Soviet cinema. At a time of 'satirophobia', when 'situational comedies', or what were known as 'lyrical comedies' (such as the musical comedies of Pyrev, Alexandrov and Yudin), were actually thought of as provocative, the pre-revolutionary classics were satire's last remaining bridgehead. Here one could vent all one's spleen at the past – and not only harmless spleen, but even spleen that might have some effect; this Russia, this land of idiots, nonentities, 'human lampoons', this country drowning in mud and idleness, this good-for-nothing Russia could not be grieved for. And the literary losses should be regretted even less. As Belinsky said, we feel 'a profound sense of melancholy' in parting company with Gogol's world. ('It's a tedious world, gentlemen!')[14] But in the Soviet film we are left thinking only about how obsolete this misappropriated world had become. And in that context, everything – melodrama, elegy, comedy, drama – begins to look like satire.

CHEKHOV IN A CASE

In modifying the genre of a text being adapted for the screen, the director comes face to face with an ideological challenge. In this single combat with the literary source, no one, as a rule, has ever come out the winner. Screen versions do not bear comparison with literature, not because cinema is incapable of creating works of equal value to literary classics, not because the visual image is one-dimensional and the screen's shallow 'reality' cannot recreate the profundity of the written word, but because the ideological task of screen adaptation itself presupposes that the work is read in one way and one way only, ideally from a school literature textbook.

In 1934, Alexander Ivanovsky adapted *The Golovlev Family*. The film, in all fairness, was actually called *Yudushka Golovlev*, because it centred on the monstrous Yudushka (played by Vladimir Gardin). In this film, the novel underwent a most extraordinary metamorphosis; in effect, instead of the novel, only Yudushka's storyline was adapted. In Saltykov-Shchedrin's novel, that plotline was, as one critic in the 1930s elegantly expressed it, 'rather weak', whereas, in the film, 'what had been diluted was now condensed'.[15] The work carried out on the text, while greatly simplifying it, distorted, however, neither the spirit of the novel nor the image of the main character (which is not to say that Yudushka was not generalised to the maximum extent, 'typified' and turned into a sinister representative of all Russia as a dark kingdom illuminated by not one single ray of light).[16]

When at the beginning of the 1950s the campaign against 'conflictlessness' in literature was in full swing, the slogan 'We need Gogols and Shchedrins!' was frequently proclaimed. The name of any classic author could have figured here, for they were all satirists (at least they were when wearing all their various hats) – not only Pushkin (for instance, Ivanovsky's *Dubrovsky* and Levin's *Journey to Arzrum* (*Puteshestvie v Arzrum*) in 1937), but also Lermontov, Turgenev and Tolstoy. And above all, of course, Chekhov. It is even difficult to understand why 'Gogols and Shchedrins' were included in that famous slogan and 'Chekhov(s)' were not. Isidor Annensky's 1939 screen version of Chekhov's *A Man in a Case* (*Chelovek v futliare*) can be examined as a translation of Chekhov into the language of Shchedrin.

A Man in a Case is the opening story of Chekhov's 'little trilogy', which also includes *Gooseberries* (*Kryzhovnik*) and *About Love* (*O liubvi*). The underlying theme of all three stories is loneliness, which finds its fullest expression in *A Man in a Case*. Indeed, the narrator Burkin sees Belikov, the unfortunate teacher of Greek, as an example of a person who is 'solitary by nature, who, like a hermit crab or a snail, tries to retreat into their shell'. Belikov's efforts to 'surround himself with a shell, to create for himself, so to speak, a case that would isolate him and protect him from external influences' are explained by the narrator by the fact that 'reality irritated him, frightened him, held him in a state of constant anxiety.' Although Burkin, who is both the narrator and also lived in the same house as Belikov, is portrayed in the story as a man with a critical attitude toward his milieu, that milieu itself – the life of a high-school teacher – is by no means cast in a satirical light. On the contrary, these people were 'all thoughtful folk, profoundly respectable, brought up on Turgenev and Shchedrin'.

The teacher Kovalenko and his sister Varenka are in no sense excluded from this provincial milieu. We are told that Varenka 'has a farmstead, and on that farmstead lives her mamma', that she is the daughter of a Councillor of State, that 'her life with her brother was not all that cheerful; all they ever did was squabble and call each other names', that she 'wanted a little corner of her own', and that if 'one took age into account . . . she was in no position to be choosy; it was time to marry whoever came along, even a teacher of Greek.' This is why Varenka 'started to treat our Belikov with distinct partiality', and 'out of sheer boredom' it was decided to marry them off. Of the brother we only know that he hated Belikov, that school bored him greatly, and that he said that he would 'go and live on the farm, catch crabs, and teach the locals'.

Annensky, the director and screenwriter of *A Man in a Case*, was accused of producing 'an inaccurate interpretation of the central image'. The critics unanimously agreed that:

> [I]n the film . . . the image of Belikov depresses with his significance. The penetrating eyes behind those dark spectacles gleam with intellect, his cautious movements speak not of cowardice but of internal strength; and all this, combined with a script which is supplemented with lines from other works by Chekhov, unexpectedly takes on a completely different, quite un-Chekhovian import. No longer a nonentity, a 'manikin' that

has brought the town low, but the powerful will of a malicious and cunning man.[17]

Not a pathetic little 'man in a case', who keeps the whole town in fear simply because he himself is scared of everything to the point of distraction, is scared to death, but a strong, gloomy man with pathological passions, with a malicious and energetic will – that is the Belikov we see before us on the screen, and he is more reminiscent of Dostoevsky than of Chekhov.[18]

In fact, all Annensky did was take the officially approved interpretation of Chekhov's story to the point of absurdity. He demonised Belikov and painted an improbably condensed picture of provincial society, as if he wanted to show a 'demon of darkness' in this 'dark kingdom' (a unique symbol of which is the fact that the screen Belikov never takes off his dark spectacles even in darkened rooms), typical of the satirical overstatement of screen adaptations. As Maya Turovskaya observed, Chekhov's prose is, by and large, 'graphically unrenderable':

> [It] dematerialises things, stringing them one after another in a phrase . . . Chekhov spent his entire life as a writer learning how to dematerialise details fit for newspaper exposés which had so tenaciously embedded themselves in his memory. But cinema employs all its technological might to return them to their original exposé-style materiality! What a strange paradox of art![19]

It is interesting that Gogol's prose is also 'graphically unrenderable', but for a different reason. The fantastic profusion of things that is created here is not material; these are verbal 'things' which cannot be 'embodied'. This situation, but 'precisely in reverse', is characteristic of Stalinist culture. Here, what is represented has no concrete referent and cannot in principle be 'embodied'; one cannot embody the excesses on the pediments of the Moscow subway or the Agricultural Exhibition; one cannot animate the stone heroes on Stalinist skyscrapers. These are pure 'screen adaptations' of the Stalinist word and of Soviet literature. But in the cases of Gogol and Chekhov, the 'paradox of art' in screen adaptation creates an entirely new reality by ignoring that which is specific to them. The physical world of Gogol on screen bears an astonishing resemblance to the physical world of Chekhov – the same piles of objects, the same interiors packed with broken things, the same darkened, cramped rooms. This reverse transformation of reality into a newspaper exposé defines the strategy of the screenwriters who worked on Chekhov's text.

First of all, Burkin's story was doled out to all the characters. Burkin on screen is turned into a drunk and a boor, and the teachers – 'thoughtful folk, profoundly respectable, brought up on Turgenev and Shchedrin' – are an absolute freak show: constantly drinking, playing cards, being rude to one another, trading insults with their wives, tugging each other's beards, gossiping and using foul language. But the Kovalenkos in the film, on the other hand, live in great harmony, never quarrelling but merely arguing, so Varenka's 'romance' with Belikov loses all motivation. It is impossible to understand why this woman, who has spent the entire film up to this point ridiculing him, suddenly decides to marry him (evidently out of sheer obstinacy, as Kovalenko hates Belikov; and, incidentally, the decision to marry them off is made so as to 'save the town from his watchful eye'). Furthermore, since Kovalenko is given the narrator's final monologue about freedom (to which is added the hero's irate invective, directed at the teachers, 'I see all your baseness and vileness' and so on) and is driven out of town (the scriptwriter's invention, of course), he becomes quite the revolutionary. Varenka, meanwhile, is a woman 'without a dowry' ('All you have by way of dowry is a guitar') and very nearly the sister of a revolutionary.

But the main point is that Chekhov's comic Belikov is mutated into a real monster who terrorises the town. His mannerisms are exaggerated. He seems to grope his way about, turning his whole body and literally boring into the people he is talking to with his eyes; his lines, half of which have been made up by the screenwriter, are perfect example of bureaucratese; we are told more than once that he is an informer and, because of this, 'enjoys the esteem of his superiors'; his loyalty goes as far as singing 'God save the tsar' on his deathbed, and declaring that 'they've permitted drama groups, soon they'll be permitting revolution' and that the Volga empties into the Caspian Sea. ('That's what loyalty means. Even when he's delirious he only says things that are permitted.') Chekhov's Belikov dies in silence.

It is worth noting that very soon after it appeared in print, Chekhov's *A Man in a Case* began to live a life of its own, becoming a common noun. Lenin, for instance, referred to it more than twenty times.[20] In fact, the screen Belikov (played by Stalin's favourite actor from the Moscow Arts Theatre, Nikolai Khmelev) is practically cribbed from a passage in one of Lenin's articles:

> Our reactionaries – including, of course, all the higher ranks of the bureaucracy – manifest good political instincts. So variously experienced are they in the struggle with the opposition, popular 'revolts', sectarians, uprisings, revolutionaries, that they are constantly 'on their guard' and understand much better than any naïve simpletons and 'honest hacks' autocracy's implacable attitude toward any kind of self-reliance, honesty, independence of convictions or pride in real knowledge. Having imbued themselves thoroughly with the spirit of servility and red tape that reigns throughout the hierarchy of Russian officialdom, they are suspicious of anyone who does not resemble Gogol's Akaky Akakevich or, to use a more contemporary comparison, the Man in a Case.[21]

Most surprising about this pronouncement is the jarring identification of Gogol's Akaky Akakevich with the 'Man in a Case'; in literary mythology,

Gogol's hero is a 'little man' who deserves our fellow-feeling, whereas Belikov, who 'keeps the whole town in fear', far from arousing fellow-feeling, is not worthy of even the slightest sympathy. According to Lenin, the 'Man in a Case' is more a symbol of the tsarist bureaucracy than the 'little man'. And the appearance of Akaky Akakevich here is no coincidence.

Akaky Akakevich Sinebriukhov – a Chekhovian Hero for Stalinist Times

Chekhov's skit, *The Wedding* (*Svad'ba*), was based on two short stories about particularly comic situations. The first, *A Marriage of Convenience* (*Brak po raschetu*), is about a scandal that erupts during a wedding because of a careless remark made by one of the guests, a telegraph operator, on the subject of the dowry. The story ends with the groom ripping open a feather bed and covering the entire street with feathers. The second, *A Wedding with a General* (*Svad'ba s generalom*), tells how a 'general' (in fact a retired naval officer) is paid to attend a wedding and proceeds to bore all the other guests to death with naval terminology no one understands. This story also ends in a scandal; the hostess gets sick of listening to the man and starts telling him off. At this point it is revealed that the 'general' never received his attendance fee. Five years later, Chekhov combined these two stories into *The Wedding*, removing the finale from *A Marriage of Convenience* so that the story ended with a scandal at the wedding feast. The comic situation itself of bombarding the dinner guests with naval terminology was, as recollections of people who knew Chekhov make clear, inspired by real events; Chekhov once purchased a number of rare old books at the Sukharev market, including a dictionary of naval terminology, which gave him the idea for a comic tale and then for a skit. To normal ears, the language used on board ship sounds so bizarre that in an appropriate narrative setting it can be used as a source of linguistic humour. In *The Wedding* this linguistic comedy is raised to another level. The 'general' turns out to be deaf; he bellows out his naval commands, not hearing what others are saying around the table or misinterpreting them. The scandal arises not only because it turns out the 'general' has not been paid for his 'visit', but also because is not even a general anyway. In the story, Revunov-Karaulov was a rear-admiral, whereas in the skit Chekhov demotes him to naval officer, second class. This alteration intensifies the comedy of the situation; the old man who, until a few moments ago, was terrorising the entire table, makes a rapid and mortified exit.

In short, Annensky based his *Wedding* – a film that differs sharply from the rest of the endless stream of Chekhov screen adaptations – on a purely vaudevillian skit. As Maya Turovskaya recalled it:

> This cinema vaudeville, with its incredible, almost improbable richness of individual artistry (I can remember no film with a more star-studded cast), which was, moreover, released during the difficult war years (1944), was

such an explosion of thespian talent, such a concentration of the funny and the gifted, that no expert investigation of its Chekhovian *bona fides* could undermine its authority. Through it, Chekhov did his bit for the war effort, both at the front and in the rear; it was fate's gift to a time when joy was hard to come by . . . The authority of *The Wedding* as a screen adaptation of Chekhov, in my recollection at least, has never been challenged.[22]

But by 1964, Rostislav Yurenev, whilst sharing Turovskaya's high opinion of the acting, was commenting on the film's 'bland, expressionless direction', the lack of taste, and the fact that the 'melancholy significance inherent in this vaudevillian piece was not fully conveyed'.[23]

This 'melancholy significance' was clear to film critics of the Stalinist era; *The Wedding*, for all the excellence of its component parts, was not an integral work of art. In spite of its Chekhovian text, it was not a Chekhovian film. The satirical denunciation of small-minded, lower middle-class, pre-revolutionary Russia, exposing its spiritual philistinism, its lack of respect for human dignity – this was the essence of Chekhov's idea in *The Wedding*. Its laconic expression, unusually well-defined composition and concise characterisations all for Chekhov served to further the author's satirical intent. But when *The Wedding's* ideological compass was lost during its transfer to the screen, the satirical edge so characteristic of Chekhov was also lost. This cruel, coarse, lower middle-class crowd cannot see that the wedding party has been the scene of a crime against humanity, in which an honourable old man was swindled and insulted. Chekhov was ridiculing vulgarity, bourgeois tastelessness, brash and ill-mannered stupidity, spiritual mediocrity . . . No matter how funny the characters in Chekhov's satirical works might be, they also carry something dreadful around with them; their denseness, insolence and self-satisfaction are offensive, their company morbidly depressing, leaving one wishing to escape the stifling, noisy, tiresome atmosphere that surrounds them. None of this comes across from the majority of the characters in the film version of *The Wedding*.[24]

This film, meanwhile, has everything: humour, satire, tastelessness and a brilliant cast. But these elements fail to come together to the extent that they frequently cancel each other out. For example, the vaudeville does not limit itself to the theme of 'a crime against humanity', but some of the 'general's' lines in Chekhov are turned into entire scenes, accompanied by 'heartrending music', and a comic episode develops into the true culmination of the 'little man's' humiliation. The motif of the 'little man', such a favourite of Soviet critics, turns up everywhere – even in a vaudeville skit; even a 'general' could be awarded that honourable title. But after all, the critics of the early 1950s were right; the theme simply did not come off here. Annensky had altered the skit's textual 'framework'. The film opens with a purely comic scene – 'Daddy and the Groom' (*Zhenikh i papen'ka*) – in which the groom declares himself an escaped convict and lunatic, simply in order to avoid marriage, and ends with the finale from *A Marriage of Convenience*, in which the groom rips open the feather bed. The 'crime against humanity' is lost amid all these shenanigans. And, more important, the actors help to bury it, too. The roles Chekhov wrote – played in the film by Erast Garin, Zoya Fedorova, Aleksei Gribov, Faina Ranevskaya, Sergei Martinson, Vera Maretskaya, Osip Abdulov, Mikhail Yanshin and Lev Sverdlin, the entire set of the best comic actors of the period – in no way fit into the frame of reference that the screenwriter of *The Wedding* had created.

Contemporary critics could hardly avoid noticing the weakness of the frame of reference before the adapted text. This is why Maretskaya fared so badly in the role of the midwife Zmeiukhina:

> Maretskaya lives a full-blooded life on the screen. She is attractive, human, and . . . not funny. What we have here is apparently a mischievous woman saying stupid things just for a laugh, but we cannot believe she has no words, feelings, thoughts of her own. Maretskaya neither shows us clearly Zmeiukhina's ugly character traits, nor makes us see how ridiculous they are.[25]

A dogged determination to turn any piece of nineteenth-century literature into satire was the norm in Stalinist culture; as before the Revolution writers were using the method of 'critical realism', everything written at that time had, in one way or another, to be a 'critique of the existing order'. As a result of ideological pressures, a change of genres came about. Comedy was forced out and replaced with either satire or melodrama. In this respect, a comment made by Vsevolod Pudovkin in a review of Vladimir Petrov's *Jubilee* (*Iubilei*) (also based on Chekhov and also released in 1944) is both astute and typical: 'The material ceases to work as comedy and shifts to drama.'[26] Retaining the original genre of the source text proved to be virtually impossible as a result of pressures exerted by a frame of reference that was not even innate to the literature being adapted.

This frame of reference is traditionally dubbed 'vulgar sociology'. However, it is more aesthetic than sociological; events in 'classic literature' certainly do not develop as an audience not equipped with a 'Marxist-Leninist worldview' (or, in simpler terms, rose-coloured Soviet glasses) might expect. It is not a matter of whether readers find something funny or are moved to tears by it, but of the need for them to have a conscious attitude towards their own reaction. For example, it is important for the reader to understand thoroughly the 'profound social criticism' apparently contained in the source text. This requires a cultural shock, a degree of alienation. Turning the reader into a viewer and adapting the literary text for the screen are the most reliable ways of keeping the recipient's feelings under rational control. Laughter 'for its own sake' is an unconscious act with no ideological content; it has no social function. When there is no 'ray of light in the dark kingdom' (which is the case in the majority of Russian classics, given that the ray of light had to be social, not, for instance, merely moral or, even worse, religious), it remains only to invent one, in the form of an ephemeral narrator (such as 'Gogol' in Kustov's film) or to use the model of Gogol's *Overcoat*, out of which, it was asserted, the whole critical direction of Russian literature emanated. Here both satire and the little man were ready to hand, 'rising up in protest' (albeit a 'timid and unconscious' kind of protest). Akaky Akakevich became 'the Hero of Our Times'.

The Wedding was written in the language of a little man of the late nineteenth century. As Aplombov puts it:

> I am not some Spinoza, to go about twisting my legs like pretzels. I am a man of substance and character . . . I found out today that your tickets have been pawned. Pardon me, *maman*, but only cheats behave like that. I'm not doing this out of egoisticism [sic] – I don't need your tickets – but out of principle. I won't allow myself to be swindled by anybody. I have made your daughter a happy woman, and if you don't give me the tickets today, I'll have her for breakfast. I am a decent man!

Aplombov/Garin goes on in this vein throughout the whole of *The Wedding*. And this is Martinson, as Yat, the telegraph operator:

> That such a cruel creature, if I may be allowed to so express myself to you, should have such a marvellous, marvellous voice! With such a voice, if you will pardon the expression, you shouldn't be a midwife, but should give concerts, sing at public gatherings!

Viewers in 1944 would have no difficulty recognising the characters played by Garin and Martinson. They are satirical characters taken from popular musical comedies set in the Soviet pre-war years, such as *A Musical Story* (*Muzykal'naia istoriia*, 1940), in which Tarakanov, played by Garin, expresses himself in the same love-struck language as Aplombov, and *Anton Ivanovich Gets Angry* (*Anton Ivanovich serditsia*, 1941), in which the composer Kerosinov, played by Martinson, is a 'greasy boor' just like the telegraph operator Yat. The language was also quite familiar to the pre-1946 Soviet reading public and film audiences. It is the language of Mr Sinebriukhov, Zoshchenko's character, who also proved himself to be one of Russian literature's 'little men'. This nondescript character – very familiar, very funny, but also fraught with 'ideological baggage' – became not only an unanticipated outcome of screen adaptations, occupying a space somewhere between Gogol and Zoshchenko, but also a Soviet cultural icon with all the right credentials.

As Turovskaya subtly observed in connection with screen adaptations of Chekhov, 'the authority of a screen adaptation – including those based on Chekhov – in the context of its own times, is linked not only to the writer's reputation but also to completely different social functions which it fulfils unintentionally.'[27] *The Wedding* also fulfilled an 'unintended function', and not only in satisfying the audience's hunger for real comedy. It also had an aesthetic function; the film showed that screen adaptations have their limits. After a certain point, the pressure exerted by the frame of reference begins to wane, punctured either by the multivalency of the literary text or by the actors themselves. One way or another, the outcome of such screen adaptation is unpredictable.

It is a curious fact that all film critics and historians who talk about Annensky's adaptations of Chekhov mention the brilliant casts he usually managed to assemble for his pictures but invariably complain about the weak direction. And this 'weakness' can be taken quite literally; finding himself in the role of 'tamer' of Chekhov's texts, Annensky rarely coped well with the author's obstinacy and, more often than not, was 'thrown out of the saddle' like an inexperienced horseman. A pathetic teacher was transmogrified on screen into some sort of mythical monster, vagrants became revolutionaries, a character from Zoshchenko became Gogol's little man. And it was exactly this unpredictability that totalising Stalinist culture could not, in all fairness, accept.

Ostrovsky's Dowry

Three screen adaptations of Ostrovsky's works – Protazanov's *Without a Dowry* (*Bespridannitsa*, 1937), and Petrov's *The Storm* (*Groza*, 1943) and *More Sinned against than Sinning* (*Bez viny vinovatye*, 1945) – serve as graphic examples, on the other hand, of the organised and consistent conversion of literature into Soviet historical narrative. The melodramatic conflict in *Without a Dowry* becomes a class conflict, and the melodrama itself is played out as a tragedy, complete with a 'little man', a 'dark kingdom' and a 'social protest'. In *The Storm* the polarisation leads directly to the alteration not only of the author's design, but even of the personalities of the main characters, many of whom resemble Ostrovsky's heroes in name only. By means of 'satirical hyperbole' and straightforward textual substitutions, the entire population of *The Storm* is transformed into a 'dark kingdom,' Katerina becomes practically a revolutionary, and the drama is turned into heroic style. Finally, in *More Sinned against than Sinning*, the heroine becomes a 'simple Soviet mother', and the film, about a reunion with an abandoned child, released immediately after the war, was perceived as an optimistic picture of contemporary life.

Adapting a work for the screen is a particularly responsible ideological act. Audiences are presented not just with a 'picture of the past', but also with condensed blocks of meaning, while the director ventures into the dangerous zone of 'interpretation'; that is, he does something which is in essence forbidden. Indeed, it only needs a shift of accent in the interpretation of, for instance, *Without a Dowry*, for the themes of 'social protest' and the 'little man' to disappear, and instead of Protazanov's *Without a Dowry* we have Eldar Ryazanov's *A Cruel Romance* (*Zhestokii romans*, 1984). Screen adaptation operates not only through pictures but also (and no less significantly) through concepts; the screen gives these concepts visual expression, filling them with 'concrete content'. The viewer sees something that could not be found in the original literary source before it was reworked for the screen – a 'dark kingdom', a 'class struggle', a 'little man'. These are the models for constructing the past, stock concepts:

> The mass audience had to be fed a 'rational' diet. Almost all the dishes tasted the same, as they had been prepared to a single recipe by various cooks tackling a single problem – how to turn different ingredients of varying quality into a square meal fit for the Stalinist 'cultural' cafeteria.[28]

In his analysis of 1930s screen adaptations, Evgeny Levin drew attention to the fact that they reflected the ambivalence of viewers' attitudes towards the past. On the one hand, they brought the audience abruptly face to face with the past, which, for a Soviet citizen in the 1930s, was 'a time during which painful, shared recollections were directly experienced as a biography of yesterday'. On the other hand, the distance between past and present, minimal when viewed from one angle, is maximal when viewed from another. Removing that distance both enables and is consistent with the utmost active psychological contact between the audience in the auditorium and the events on the screen. Alongside this an opposite tendency thrusts viewers away from the world on the screen, destroying their personal, intimate contact with it and substituting it with communal contact. Close contact is also damaged by the fact that screen adaptations of the classics create a world of misappropriated people – one-dimensional, primitive in comparison to the original, impoverished from the psychological point of view, deprived of individuality and uniqueness.[29]

It is impossible to empathise with this world, but that was never the aim. Moreover, aside from the effect of repulsion and attraction, the cinematic world also has a specifically aesthetic dimension. This is engendered not at 'time close to hand' but from contact between the audience of today and the screen. This applies most aptly of all to Protazanov's *Without a Dowry*, a film even today considered 'unquestionably the most tasteful screen adaptation of a Russian classic of all those released during the 1930s and 1940s'.[30] Protazanov was himself a living classic, who began his career in the cinema in 1907, had made about eighty films by 1917, and had an enormous amount of experience in adapting Russian classics for the silent screen. Viewing his film today is a recherché experience. It now seems to have a split personality, being both a reanimated psychodrama à la Bauer about life in high society and also a thoroughly Soviet 'picture of the past'. The world of silent films – with its affected femmes fatales biting their lips and wringing their hands, and middle-aged male romantic leads in evening dress with their pocket watches, cigars and whiskers – is reorganised along fully Soviet lines. It is as if the characters from a pre-revolutionary film had taken over a Soviet screenplay.

However, converting Ostrovsky into a Soviet writer was no easy matter. His own ideological 'dowry' was dubious. A durable 'realist' and an indisputable expert on the merchants, minor nobility and lower middle class, and, of course, of the theatrical milieu of Moscow and the provinces, Ostrovsky created a world in which, after one has been immersed in it for a certain length of time, it becomes hard to breathe, and from which, like Katerina, one longs to 'break free'. The one thing missing from these masterfully polished plays is a voice from the world outside; they lack not only authorial commentary, but also the external voice, even one built into the action, of a hero who somehow manages to break out of the milieu being presented. Yet creating such a counterpoint is essential, as without it there is no 'dark kingdom', nor, of course, any rays of light within it. However, if in the case of Gogol, Tolstoy and Chekhov, the heroes are provided with the traits (and text) they lack by the narrator, with Ostrovsky the material to do this is quite simply not there.

It would appear that Protazanov wrung from *Without a Dowry* everything that could possibly be extracted for a 'tasteful screen adaptation'. Thus he worked hard to amplify the play's social significance by piling the film up with endless 'contrasts', presented in scenes that interrupt the flow and exist only to create a sense of 'social antithesis'. But Ostrovsky's play is constructed above all on psychological conflict. Without question, Larisa Ogudalova (played by Nina Alisova) stands out in the film, if not as a rebel then at least as a distraught heroine, and Karandyshev is selected to play the part of the little man, while in the play not only does no one ever 'revolt' against the 'mercenary world of the Paratovs, the Knurovs and the Vozhevatovs'; on the contrary, everyone, from the serving girl at the inn to the heroine herself, passionately desires to be part of it. It hardly matters that between the various characters in the play traditional melodramatic relationships of love, sympathy, antipathy and hatred are played out; the film also has a seducer, a victim and a vengeful murderer. What in Ostrovsky's play is psychologically multivalent is one-dimensional in Protazanov's film. The usual merchants, quite sweet people in their own way, actually support the Ogudalovs – Knurov and Vozhevatov, the loving mother, and the imperiously expansive Paratov, who himself acknowledges that he is 'not innately mercenary' (an 'ideal man', as Larisa calls him) – all these characters are transformed in the film into scoundrels. Knurov and Vozhevatov are debauched cynics, Paratov is a shameless seducer and mother Ogudalov is a procuress, plain and simple. In all this 'dark kingdom' only two characters stand out – Karandyshev and Larisa.

Karandyshev is perhaps the only character in Ostrovsky who is portrayed with unconcealable revulsion. With his cheap rugs, his Yaroslavl wines with French labels, his 'carriage' that is on the point of falling to pieces, and his unsatisfied 'self-esteem', about which he himself talks incessantly, this pathetic precursor of Smerdyakov is probably the most worthless creature in Ostrovsky's world. Meanwhile, in the film Karandyshev lives a sort of double life. On the one hand, he is despised by everyone; on the other, he has to act as at least a rough approximation of a 'little man'. (Accordingly, his 'revolt' must be if not morally then at least psychologically justified.) Karandyshev in the film is so physically repulsive that, even with the removal from the screenplay of almost all his negative characteristics (in the play, Vozhevatov talks about his envious nature, and Larisa says that, far from loving him, she does not even respect him, and so on), he cannot meet the ideological type of the 'little man' assigned to him. Unable to cope with this duality, he gets stuck between pillar and post, and his unwed bride is stuck with him.

Larisa is unquestionably part of the Vozhevatov/Knurov/Paratov world. One is a childhood friend and she is in love with another of them. Yet Ostrovsky's unhappy Larisa – and lovers in this play are always unhappy – displays the persistence of a 'professional fiancée', in the way she pressurises Paratov. But in the film we have before us a suffering woman, endlessly wringing her hands, moving about uncertainly and ready at any moment to fall into a swoon. Larisa's constant state of excitement is supposed to demonstrate her 'other-worldliness', her conflict with the 'dark kingdom' to which she apparently does not belong, but the finale, when Larisa realises that she is just another piece of merchandise, is presented in the film as a deathbed revelation of certain class-based truths. The famous chains in which the heroine dies supposedly complete the development of the ideological schema; in this society, marriage is a financial transaction and women are the merchandise.

The film retains traces of the director's attempts to turn Karandyshev into a little man and Larisa into a ray of light in the dark kingdom, which leaves the two main characters somewhat lacking in legitimacy. Inconsistency is the natural outcome of this 'tasteful screen adaptation'. After this, Protazanov stopped trying to 'trample over' Ostrovsky and, whenever the play failed to fit into the framework of the screenplay, the director capitulated. What the audience was supposed to get from the screen was not simply 'pictures', but a ready-made version of the past, already fitted into familiar concepts and frameworks. But all Protazanov succeeded in creating was a 'dark kingdom'. The side-effect of the simplification of psychological characteristics was the mutation of drama into melodrama.

However, the melodramatic tendencies for which Protazanov was reproached by critics were actually a real discovery for the director; through melodrama the wholesale assimilation of ideological clichés becomes much easier. It was perhaps not the most reliable means of showing the viewer the 'dark kingdom' of the past (in 1937, when *Without a Dowry* was released), but to make up for that, it was certainly the most hygienic. Such, we must suppose, is the politico-aesthetic equivalent of a 'tasteful screen adaptation'. When we speak of social hygiene, we mean the 'healthy mass taste' to which Anatoly Lunacharsky appealed in his famous article, 'What Kind of Melodrama Do We Need?' (Kakaia nam nuzhna melodrama?). He claimed that it was precisely melodrama that opposed the 'morbid aestheticism' of cultural elites, that it was 'superior to other dramatic genres': superior to realistic drama in that it is free of naturalism and psychologism; indisputably superior to symbolic drama in that it does not 'play' with the viewer; superior even to tragedy in that the latter 'is guilty of a certain pomposity and . . . literariness'. Melodrama, on the other hand, reveals

> a great power which contributes to the growth of life in its struggle with whatever is harmful to life . . . a life-enhancing struggle . . . revealed through the light it throws on staggering situations which arouse anger and compassion in simple souls capable of feeling infinite anger and compassion to the point of tears.

Lunacharsky supposed that 'the mass of the people' loved melodrama because its 'forms [are] healthy and handsome, its gait full of strength and purpose, its voice clear and enchanting'.[31] It is hard not to recognise in this the 'healthy art' of socialist realism.

Bringing Dobrolyubov to the Screen

Ostrovsky was not enough for Protazanov; he filled his film with Tchaikovsky's music and cinematic versions of paintings. It opens with a shot of a spring landscape that might have been copied from Alexei Savrasov's *The Rooks Have Arrived* (*Grachi prileteli*), then we have scene of a wedding in a church which literally reproduces Vasily Pukirev's *Unequal Marriage* (*Neravnyi brak*), and the Volga boatmen who play a not insignificant role in the film are apparently cribbed from Repin's famous painting. These visual images did not distract the audience but rather helped yoke the visual impressions together in the viewer's mind in a single spectacle of the past. If Protazanov, for whom *Without a Dowry* tuned out to be his last serious cinematic achievement, laid his emphasis on paintings, then Vladimir Petrov, for whom *The Storm* became his first major work in the cinema, accentuated concepts. And if Ostrovsky was not enough for Protazanov, then Petrov found him too much. In fact, one could say he did not need Ostrovsky at all; what Petrov brought to the screen was actually Alexander Dobrolyubov's two famous articles on *The Storm*: 'The Dark Kingdom' (*Temnoe tsarstvo*) and 'A Ray of Light in the Dark Kingdom' (*Luch sveta v temnom tsarstve*). The status of these critical articles was undoubtedly a great deal higher in Stalinist culture than that of Ostrovsky's plays. Petrov, unlike Protazanov, was not aiming at a 'tasteful adaptation'; as Andrei Platonov wrote, 'work that creates great things cannot be done with squeamish hands.'[32]

Alla Tarasova, who played the heroine in *The Storm*, wrote of the task facing the director:

> In those days, it was quite popular to interpret the image of Katerina as a representative, perhaps, of the 'dark kingdom' itself, and in no essential

way differentiated from it. But I was more inclined toward Dobrolyubov's view of Katerina as 'a ray of light in the dark kingdom'. I certainly could not have played a woman who was just distraught for no apparent reason. I had to play and tried to play her as a downtrodden Russian woman making frantic attempts to liberate herself and perishing under the burden of her own tragic destiny. That way the heroine's death could be seen as the inspiring culmination of her irrepressible attempts to protest, to free herself from the oppressive atmosphere of her family and society, from the Rus' of merchants and serfs.[33]

Petrov paid particular attention to creating that 'atmosphere'. In Tarasova's words, he:

> understood very well and said more than once that . . . the heart of [Katerina's] tragedy, the rage and power of her impulsive action depends . . . in large part on the atmosphere created in the picture, on the sharpness of the contrast. And he was extraordinarily insistent in creating the stifling, oppressive atmosphere of that 'dark kingdom'.[34]

The entire dramatic ethos of the play is subordinated to the creation of the 'dark kingdom'. In scene after scene, the director introduces interior shots of a church, which always give a sharp sense of contrast between the service and the mercenary conversations of the congregation, then shots of violent altercations, and finally the wedding at the Kabanov house:

> This scene is saturated with savage debauchery. For five minutes we watch a celebration of the most bestial instincts of the riotously drunken crowd: Kudryash throws dishes on to the floor; Dikoi roars like an animal, clowns about, makes frenzied faces, pours vodka all over himself, and finally collapses in a drunken stupor. Fat, porcine women gobble their food, drink, and howl at the happy couple to kiss. An inebriated woman lolls in the doorway. This swinish herd escorts the bride and groom to the bedroom that has been made up for them, screaming vulgar instructions behind them . . . The guests keep up the commotion, more and more of them pass out, dead drunk. Vodka is doused on the heads of the fallen.[35]

Petrov was taken to task by critics on the grounds that scenes such as these 'recreate not so much the socio-historical essence of the merchant milieu as the biological'. Still, the visual approaches which had become standard in screen adaptation – coarse faces, glossy with sweat and grease, vacant, smirking, drunken, hostile, appearing one after another in an endlessly long panning shot – did actually give us a 'socio-historical essence' via biology (not to say, of zoology). It was the most reliable means of conveying the ideological schema of 'the animal debauchery and savage morals of the merchant class'. Those faces, those drunken orgies were much more effective than any number of words. Petrov was so caught up in creating his 'dark kingdom' that he consigned all the play's characters to it.

The power of the 'dark kingdom', it goes without saying, lay not in the fact that the entire town of Kalinov was turned into a freak show into which Katerina flies like a miracle from another world; the point should have been that people of all kinds – including good, kind, loving and intelligent people – are powerless in the face of society's unwritten laws. The basic conflict in *The Storm* is not, of course, social (in terms of class, the play's population is fairly homogenous) but rather familial and generational. At one extreme we have the 'elders' (Kabanikha and Dikoi), and at the other the 'youngsters' (Tikhon, Varvara, Boris, Kudryash and, of course, Katerina).

Ostrovsky did not short-change any of them in terms of human sentiments and attractive qualities. Even the despotic Kabanikha, the very embodiment of the 'dark kingdom', may squabble with her daughter, but she does let her out of the house; she may be stern with her daughter-in-law, but she tells her and her son, 'I am no stranger to you; my heart aches for you', and she leaves them alone together when the parting ceremony is over. But in the film, Kabanikha (played by Varvara Massalitinova), with her unremittingly stern facial expressions, her heavy step, her sharp voice and her coarseness, is despotism absolutely personified. Yet if in the case of Kabanikha we are simply talking of a simplification of her character (which is not uncommon and is sometimes inevitable in an adaptation); in the case of all the other characters the director unceremoniously overturns Ostrovsky's design. The incredible metamorphosis inflicted on all the characters without exception turned Petrov's film into a veritable handbook on committing 'a breaking-and-entering screen adaptation'.

Tikhon, Katerina's husband, was endowed by Ostrovsky with enormous significance, because any notable reduction in his role would have the same effect on Katerina herself. She has married a man who may be feeble, weak-willed, timid, drunken and firmly under his mother's thumb, but is also sincere and kind, sympathetic to the sorrows of others, and loving and respectful of his wife, for whom he feels sorry. Petrov's Tikhon, however, is a dullard, indifferent to whatever anyone else is going through, as greasy as all the other 'tradesmen'. He feasts with prostitutes in Moscow, whips his wife in a state of total frenzy, and threatens to kill her 'like a dog'. And Tikhon's final act of 'rebellion', when he screams at his mother over Katerina's body, 'You have destroyed her! You! You!', is omitted entirely by the director.

Varvara and Kudryash in the film are also 'children of the dark kingdom' and direct descendents of Kabanikha and Dikoi. Ostrovsky's Varvara has an independent mind, is compassionate towards Katerina, casts a critical eye on herself, despises her brother's lack of will, is in constant conflict with her mother, and yet – unlike Katerina – she is cynical, sneaky, adept at lying, coarse and rather too easygoing. But in the film, Varvara's character is:

a variation on three qualities: the humdrum desires of a body that is running to fat and languishing in inactivity, boredom and laziness. The rendezvous between Varvara and Kudryash are primitive and lustful, without the slightest intimation of even elementary decency, and are interpreted in a manner that is entirely alien to Ostrovsky's intent.[36]

Kudryash, a cynic and a boor, is at the same time a practical, decisive, independent man, not lacking in self-esteem, and quite capable not only of snubbing 'the masters of life' but even of threatening them; in the film he becomes a debauched, greasy, vulgar tradesman. It is typical that in Ostrovsky Kudryash sings folk songs, whereas in the film he sings vulgar 'cruel romances'.

Another failure is Boris, with whom Katerina is in love. From an intelligent and kind, if somewhat dependent man in the play, he is transformed into an indifferent scoundrel, who rejects the woman who loves him.

The Storm, which became the exemplar of screen adaptations of the 1930s, creates a peculiar impression. The action unfolding on the screen thematically resembles Ostrovsky's play, the characters have the same names and speak more or less the same lines as in the play, but they are endowed with characteristics diametrically opposed to those Ostrovsky gave them. Paradoxically, the critics reproached Petrov for not showing, for instance, that Dikoi 'senses the frailty of his power' and that Kabanikha 'fears the approaching storm'.[37] Meanwhile, these representatives of 'a Russia that is on its way out', far from being weakened by the younger generation, are on the contrary strengthened by it and had nothing to fear. In the screen adaptations of the 1930s the official doctrine-myth was given a visual form and thus firmly established in mass consciousness. The mechanism of mythology was accurately described by Roland Barthes:

> A myth is a word that has been purloined and then restored. But the restored word is not the same word that was purloined; in the process of restoration, it is not replaced exactly where it was before. And this petty theft, this bit of sharp practice are responsible for the immutability of the mythical word.[38]

Indeed, in Stalinist cinema, the Russian classics are not where they were before. Of course, the cinema does not 'purloin' literature simply in order to 'replace' it 'where it was before', but that is not the sense of 'sharp practice' here; on the contrary, 'distortion' simply serves as evidence of the polyvalency of the classics. Stalinist cinema is unique in that the very word 'distortion' comes to mean 'an accurate reading'; if Dobrolyubov's articles represent the only 'correct' reading of the plays, then their adaptation for the screen will guarantee a correct reading of Ostrovsky himself. (The very status of adaptations suggests that an 'incorrect' reading could never appear on screen, as *The Marriage* demonstrates.)

In place of complex familial and intergenerational conflict, Petrov's *The Storm* offers up the familiar heroic/romantic conflict. To the extent that the 'dark kingdom' grows ever more gloomy, the 'ray' – Katerina – glows all the brighter:

> Always alone, the whole meaning of her existence is to challenge the darkness, to unmask the autocratic, patriarchal world of Dikoi and Kabaknikha, while the death of the heroine in an unequal struggle presages the imminent victory of a new day. In this respect – in her life-affirming death for the common cause of freedom from oppression – Katerina is typologically akin to Nilovna [the heroine of Maxim Gorky's *Mother* – E. D.], not just to Larisa Ogudalova, and even more so to Timosh in *The Arsenal*, Vasily in *Earth* (*Zemlia*), and the Vasilev brothers' *Chapaev*.[39]

She had to be played in the film as exactly such a character from the socialist realist canon by Alla Tarasova, who, as we may recall, described Katerina's suicide as the 'inspiring culmination' of her unsuccessful protest. Critics agreed with her: 'Katerina's suicide is an expression of protest, an act of rebellion against the vulpine laws of merchant life.'[40] They were really talking about the conversion of Ostrovsky's drama into a familiar socialist realist genre: optimistic tragedy.

To achieve this, Katerina had to be transformed, if not into a female commissar then at least into material for 'reforging'; she had to become a Soviet heroine. Her dialogues and monologues were carefully sifted and cut; everything in them that might hint at Katerina's deep religious faith – her stories of prayers, dreams, golden cathedrals, unseen voices, magical gardens, cooing doves, edenic trees and hills . . . 'and the scent of cypress' – was consistently excised.

The only scent in the air in this film is that of the coming storm. A play of opposites constantly intrudes: the open expanses of the Volga versus the enclosed atmosphere of Kabanikha's house, with its fences, bolts, massive oak gates with enormous heavy locks and . . . a caged canary in the window – Katerina as a prisoner. But the melodrama breaks through all these heroic/romantic trappings; the heroics do not 'raise' Ostrovsky's drama to the level of tragedy, but rather reduce it to the level of melodrama. And this is above all thanks to Tarasova, in whose interpretation Katerina becomes a sublime, suffering woman going forward to her certain death, her actions indicative of both martyrdom and a lost cause. Everything works to this end: 'her passionate and spirited voice, her eyes brimming over with horror – halting, unblinking, wide open like a mad woman, her nervous movements, her limp, helpless gestures'.[41]

Just as Annensky created out of a pathetic teacher of Greek a veritable embodiment of social evil, so Petrov tried to make the suffering heroine of a psychological family drama into a lodestone of goodness – not even just a 'ray of light' but the sun itself. And the result is a loss of integrity. As one critic wrote in the 1930s:

In this film, Katerina is interpreted from the social perspective. And, from this perspective, the film condenses those traits which characterise her not only as 'a ray of light in a dark kingdom' but also as a refined ideological product of that kingdom. Katerina, according to the film, is a convict who has come to believe in the legality of her sentence yet lacks the strength to endure it. Katerina carries within herself, in her most profound beliefs, the same stick with which the strong beat the weak in the dark kingdom.[42]

'Carrying within herself a stick', as this critic so elegantly put it, in those days meant that she does not mutate into a female commissar. 'There is no shaft of light in this film, no emotional resolution looking forward positively into the future.'[43]

But how could that positive look forward into the future be created? Criticism offered the most radical of advice:

Here there could have been only one way of looking forward – denigrating this entire dark kingdom without exception [this critic found that Petrov had not 'denigrated' Kudryash and Varvara sufficiently – E. D.] and inspiring in viewers at the end the kind of feeling that cries out to be expressed in words like 'to hell with you, dark kingdom!' Greater emphasis on the ambivalence of Katerina's character would also have allowed us to look forward; even if only for a few moments the viewer could have had the chance to perceive that Katerina had the potential to rebel against the dark kingdom, could have momentarily united with her in that protest, so as to derive from these up-beat and decisive moments an impression of compassion, of judicious anger on behalf of Katerina, and of intensified enmity toward the dark kingdom.[44]

That is what they meant by 'looking forward'. And Ostrovsky, of course, had nothing to do with it.

MORE SINNED AGAINST THAN SINNING OR, THE GOOD LIFE IS NO CRIME

Stalinist culture is characterised not only by its aestheticisation, but also by its totalising historicisation of reality. If cinema in the first half of the 1930s concentrated on the present, the focus shifted in the second half of the decade to Party history. The historical-revolutionary film became the supreme genre. After the war, when biographical films moved to the foreground, the viewer was immersed even further into history. Films about 'contemporary life' became very much the exception in the post-war years; the few that could possibly be so categorised were screen adaptations of works awarded the Stalin Prize – Semyon Babaevsky's *Cavalier of the Gold Star* (*Kavaler Zolotoi Zvezdy*), Vasily Azhaev's *Far from Moscow* (*Daleko ot Moskvy*) and Galina Nikolaeva's *Harvest* (*Zhatva*). Since these biographical films focused on great military commanders and leading figures in the sciences and arts from the past, the baggage they came with was also significantly revised. Satire became inappropriate, and with it everything which even remotely recalled Russia as it used to be also disappeared. A large part of the action now took place in palaces; and with this change in the characters' 'social make-up', their clothes and external appearance also altered. Instead of filthy little hovels, palatial parquet floors appeared; and the magnificence of the films' sets, the sumptuousness of their costumes, were all the more apparent due to the introduction of colour. Comparing images of Russia's past in pre- and post-war Soviet films, we could come to the conclusion that two different countries were being depicted. All this equally applies to post-war adaptations of Russian classics; they depict a completely different image of Russia's past than that represented in the cinema before the war. Good examples of this are Petrov's adaptations of Ostrovsky's play *More Sinned against than Sinning* (1945) and Gogol's *The Government Inspector* (1952), and Annensky's film based on Chekhov's story, *Anna on the Neck* (*Anna na shee*, 1954).

These films must be viewed in the context of the post-war Stalinist empire: Moscow high-rises, luxurious apartments in new buildings on Gorky Street, the splendours of post-war Moscow subway stations, buildings with granite facades, the abundance depicted in those hefty post-war Soviet novels . . . The luxury of pre-revolutionary Russia in biographical films and adaptations of the classics made during the post-war decade – reflections of Pyrev's *Kuban Cossacks* (Kubanskie kazaki) – constituted a 'representation of "a good life" still beyond the reach of the majority of people', 'the affluent Stalinist style' and 'an embodiment of the bourgeois ideal'.[45] At the same time, the mythologising of the country's past no longer accentuated the backwardness of tsarist Russia and the negative aspects of Russian life, which had predominated before the war. The concept of Russian imperial grandeur, the worthy heir of which was the Soviet Union, victor in World War II, moved to centre-stage.

This reflects a thorough-going revision not only of ideological priorities, but also of the very strategies used to portray power; victory in the war brought Russian history of the first half of the twentieth century full circle. Having been born out of the defeats inflicted in World War I, the new power structures to all intents and purposes suffered from the trauma of illegitimacy until after the victories of World War II. And, as we have seen, the image of Russia's past in Soviet cinema during the 1930s was designed precisely to confirm the legitimacy of the Revolution and the new power structure. After victory the nation was shaped by ideas that differed fundamentally from those of pre-war times. Post-war culture was qualitatively different from the culture of the 1930s. It reflected the intent of a power structure no longer in need of confirmation of its own legitimacy. Victory had vanquished the Revolution. The very question of legitimacy dropped away. The time of justifying the power structure (historical-revolutionary films, showing the pre-revolutionary past as the run-up to inevitable revolution) had passed; the issue was now that of the legitimacy of the inheritance (biographical films showing Russia's glorious past). This is the backdrop for the new face of Russian history.

In this respect, *More Sinned against than Sinning* is, in every sense of the word, a highly indicative adaptation. The film did not just depict a 'good life' that was almost entirely out of the audience's reach. Ostrovsky's play is supported by two themes: the contrast between the nobility of Kruchinina's talents as an actress and the talentless vulgarity of provincial townspeople; and the tragedy of a mother who has lost her child. The first theme is completely erased from the film because the provincial town is replaced on screen by the 'good life'. Instead of 'passably furnished' rooms in a provincial hotel (in the play, someone comments that Kruchinina is living in a 'dirty room in an unsavoury hotel') we have an opulent drawing room with a grand piano, luxurious armchairs and carpets. The ladies' dressing room at the theatre with as Ostrovsky tells us, 'the wallpaper torn in some places and peeling in others . . . a threadbare armchair and a motley collection of furniture', becomes something like a boudoir. Instead of a provincial playhouse we see a many-tiered gilded theatre fit for a capital, with spectacular variety performances in the evenings and elegant ballerinas standing in the wings. In place of the patron Dudukin's *dacha*, where, in the garden, under the old lime trees, the final act unfolds, we are shown a ornate palace, the venue for an enormous ball, a banquet, an opulent, heaving table . . . The sets in this film by Petrov were subjected to no less radical metamorphoses than those suffered by the characters of *The Storm* previously.

Seven years later, Petrov's pre-revolutionary Russia became yet more ornate; even the provincial town in *The Government Inspector* would look positively decorous in his 1952 screen adaptation, while the governor's house is turned practically into a palace with its glazed verandas, abundance of light, space and parquet shining like mirrors. And things have disappeared from Gogol's 'nasty little town' as well: the old fence, the forty cartloads of every kind of rubbish, the offices with pigs wandering about them, and the hospital where the patients get better 'like flies'. In fact, the town in *The Government Inspector* is deserted. It bears no resemblance at all to the Gogolian world seen on screen only a decade previously, in *How Ivan Ivanovich Quarrelled with Ivan Nikiforovich*.

Let us return, however, to Ostrovsky's *More Sinned against than Sinning*. Had it been necessary to rename this film, it could (in the spirit of Ostrovsky's own tendency to use Russian maxims in the titles of his plays) have been called *The Good Life Is No Crime*. But we should bear in mind that 'the good life' is only the product of a shift in viewpoint and it was not on this that the production's success or failure depended.

The main issue, of course, is genre. In his discussion of the film, Pudovkin called the choice of the play for adaptation 'off-centre', as it was based on 'a melodrama of not particularly high content', and 'the melodramatic tenor, the melodrama itself comes crawling out of the screenplay as if it belongs there. The perspective is displaced . . . A moribund theme appears in the screenplay which for Ostrovsky was only a crutch.'[46] Meanwhile, it was not simply the case that audiences after the war years were yearning for melodramas. *More Sinned against than Sinning* was released in 1945. Tarasova later recalled:

> After a screening, I always receive flowers and letters, letters addressed to Kruchinina. But they are different from the ones I used to receive back then, after the film was first released. Back then, a lot of the letters were from young frontline soldiers. This is a passage from one of them: 'But now a few words about myself. I was seventeen when I went to the front, and after that the Nazi-German invaders took our village and what happened to my parents I have no idea. But yesterday we saw the film with you playing the Mother and it didn't matter in the slightest that it all happened before the Revolution, I still believed it would all turn out like that and I, too, was bound to find my mother . . .' Some of them are signed: 'Your Neznamov.' And here is another letter: 'Today I saw you and in your face I saw the face and the soul of the great Russian mothers. I watched your *More Sinned against than Sinning*. People who for four years have seen nothing but weapons and enemies saw their own mothers today' (from Z. I. Palei, dated 5 December 1945).[47]

Tarasova went on:

> So many Neznamovs wrote to tell me that one day they too would perhaps find their mothers. These letters were written after the war. I would even get letters from detention centres; people who seemed to have lost all faith in life and justice would see *More Sinned against than Sinning* and feel hope once again.[48]

The film did its job. For the first time, audiences identified with the events taking place on screen; rather than distancing them from the Russia of the nineteenth century, it drew them in. The audience was oblivious to the temporal gap: 'And it didn't matter in the slightest that it all happened before the Revolution.' It was as though the Revolution had never happened.

Contemporary critics wrote that Kruchinina's function was 'to be a ray of light in the dim, grey existence of the old Russian provinces'[49] and, out of sheer inertia, rebuked the director for making his production short on 'dimness and greyness', even if its great splendour made up for it. The critics were in a new situation; they did not know how to interpret this new 'old Russia'. It was clear, however, who Kruchinina/Tarasova was:

> We, the audience, take away in our hearts the sublime, noble image of an actress and a woman defending the poetry and purity of her soul as she resists the filth and vulgarity of the bourgeois world . . . Our Soviet reality every day, every hour shapes characters unprecedented in their beauty and

their spiritual strength, who are growing and ripening in the struggle for communism.[50]

In effect, Tarasova was playing a Soviet heroine in a nineteenth-century setting. Thus the 'struggle for the classics' came full circle.

Generally speaking, there is no such thing as a ready-made 'classical heritage'. Every culture has to create one for itself. Socialist realism worked on the creation of a 'classic corpus' painstakingly and persistently – selecting, pursuing, polishing it, giving it a new face. It worked equally painstakingly and persistently at creating an image of the past; in the end the classics are a 'mirror of the Russian Revolution'. The higher the status of the classics (and in the Stalin era it became absolute), the more authority they were accorded as 'eyewitness testimonies'. However, the classics only became a 'mirror' by being processed for the screen – and not only a mirror, but also a justification and a substantiation of the revolution. And it was this that made the reworking of the classics worthwhile. But history, as Lenin often said, is 'a stern taskmistress'. Today, when the lights go up in the cinema, that 'mirror' up there on the screen now reveals what was really reflected in it. It proved to be not so much a mirror as a delusion of the Revolution.

NOTES

1. Fridrikh Ermler, *Dokumenty. Stat'i. Vospominaniia*, Leningrad: Iskusstvo, 1974, p. 140.
2. Grigorii Roshal', *Kinolenta zhizni*, Moscow: Iskusstvo, 1974, p. 94.
3. It is worth noting that this relates not only to the cinema. The status of 'literary illustrations' in Stalinist culture was in general also extremely high: 'It is significant that in the twentieth century, book illustrating nowhere achieved such wide dissemination and gained such an honored place as in the art of socialist realism. Illustrations of the classics and of Soviet writers were awarded Stalin prizes, and their creators (D. Shmarinov, E. Kibrik, Kukryniksy and others) occupied first place in the artistic establishment alongside court painters' (I. Golomshtok, 'Sotsrealizm i izobrazitel'noe iskusstvo'. In H. Guenther, E. Dobrenko (eds), *Sotsrealisticheskii kanon*, St Petersburg: Akademicheskii proekt, 2000, p. 138).
4. Maksim Gor'kii, *Sobranie sochinenii v 30 tomakh*, Vol. 27, Moscow: GIKhL, 1953, pp. 435–6.
5. Max Weber, *Economy and Society*, New York: Bedminster, 1968, pp. 214–16.
6. A. N. Ostrovskii, *Polnoe sobranie sochinenii*, Vol. 13, Moscow: GIKhL, 1952, p. 165.
7. Boris Eikhenbaum, 'Literatura i kino'. In B. Eikhenbaum, *Literatura. Teoriia. Kritika. Polemika*, Leningrad: Priboi, 1927, pp. 300, 297, 301, 298.
8. Vsevolod Pudovkin, 'Rabota aktera v kino i sistema Stanislavskogo'. In *Voprosy masterstva v sovetskom kinoiskusstve*, Moscow: Goskinoizdat, 1952, pp. 79, 83.
9. Susan Sontag, *Against Interpretation and Other Essays*, New York: Dell, 1966, pp. 243–4.
10. N. Khrenov, 'Dialog kino i literatury v kontekste protivorechii razvitiia kul'tury 30–40-kh godov'. In *Ekrannye iskusstva i literatura. Zvukovoe kino*, Moscow: Nauka, 1994, p. 166.

11. V. Goffenshefer, 'Restravatorstvo ili tvorchestvo? (Klassiki i kino)', *Literaturnyi kritik*, 1934, No. 4, p. 162.
12. Adaptation for the screen (including of the classics) was the subject of numerous discussions and, in particular, several books in the Soviet era. See, for example, A. Vartanov, *Obrazy literatury v grafike i kino*, Moscow: Izdatel'stvo Akademii Nauk SSR, 1961; M. Kuznetsov, *Geroi nashikh fil'mov*, Moscow: Izkusstvo, 1965; N. Gomitskaia (ed.), *Literatura i kino*, Moscow, Leningrad: Prosveshchenie, 1965; I. Manevich, *Kino i literatura*, Moscow: Iskusstvo, 1966; U. Gural'nik, *Russkaia literatura i sovetskoe kino*, Moscow: Nauka, 1968; *Fil'm sporit s knigoi*, Moscow: Iskusstvo, 1973 and so on. These discussions reached a climax in the 1960s when, as so many more films were being made, there was an increase not only in the relative number of film adaptations but also – with cinema's rediscovery of the classics – in the serious attention being given for the first time to the issues surrounding the screenwriter's interpretation of the classics. The adaptations of the 1930s and 1940s were viewed in a predominantly negative light, and, since Stalin-era adaptations in effect involved no fresh approaches to the classics, they did not attract any particular interest. The discussions followed a well-worn pattern; new productions were compared to films of the 1920s and the Stalinist era was traditionally 'overlooked'.
13. For a view of Gogol as a Stalinist cultural icon, see Stephen Moeller-Sally, *Gogol's Afterlife: The Evolution of a Classic in Imperial and Soviet Russia*, Evanston, IL: Northwestern University Press, 2002.
14. One of the best-known quotations from *The Quarrel*, which was entirely omitted from the film.
15. I. F. Popov, *Problemy sovetskoi kinodramaturgii*, Moscow, 1939, p. 104.
16. We note in passing that by the mid-1930s the image of Yudushka had acquired an entirely stable political connotation. Trotsky was called 'Yudushka' everywhere, so the on-screen demonisation of Yudushka could have been calculated to achieve some very immediate political aims.
17. L. Pogozheva, 'Ekranizatsiia literaturnykh proizvedenii klassiki'. In *Ocherki istorii sovetskogo kino*, Vol. 2, Moscow, 1959, pp. 470–1.
18. R. Iurenev, *Sovetskaia kinokomediia*, Moscow: Nauka, 1964, p. 297.
19. M. Turovskaia, 'Ob ekranizatsii Chekhova. Predvaritel'nye zametki', *Kinovedcheskie zapiski*, No. 5, 1990, p. 36.
20. See V. I. Lenin, *Polnoe sobranie sochinenii*, Additional reference volume, Part 2, Moscow: Politizdat, 1970, p. 602.
21. V. I. Lenin, *Polnoe sobranie sochinenii*, Vol. 5, Moscow: Politizdat, 1963, p. 327.
22. Turovskaia, 'Ob ekranizatsii Chekhova', p. 33.
23. Iurenev, *Sovetskaia kinokomediia*, p. 373.
24. S. Dudina, *Narodnaia artistka SSSR Vera Petrovna Maretskaia*, Moscow: Goskinoizdat, 1953, p. 48.
25. Ibid., p. 49.
26. Vsevolod Pudovkin, *Sobranie sochinenii v 3 tomakh*, Vol. 3. Moscow: Iskusstvo, 1976, p. 96.
27. Turovskaia, 'Ob ekranizatsii Chekhova', p. 39.
28. Evgeny Levin, 'Ekranizatsiia: Istorizm, Mifologiia, Mifografiia (K tipologii obshchestvennogo soznaniia i khudozhestvennogo myshleniia)'. In *Ekrannye iskusstva i literatura: Zvukovoe kino*, Moscow: Nauka, 1994, p. 91.
29. Ibid., pp. 82–3.
30. Ibid., p. 79.
31. A. V. Lunacharskii, *Sobranie sochinenii v 8 tomakh*, Vol. 2, Moscow, 1964, pp. 214–15.
32. A. Platonov, 'Fabrika literatury', *Oktiabr'*, 1991, No. 10, p. 198.
33. *Alla Konstantinova Tarasova: Dokumenty i vospominaniia*, Moscow: Iskusstvo, 1978, p. 154.

34. Ibid.
35. F. Zhurko, 'O printsipakh ekranizatsii dramaturgii A. N. Ostrovskogo.' In 'Trudy Vsesoiuznogo gosudarstvennogo instituta kinematografii', Issue 10. *Kino i literatura*, Moscow, 1974, p. 55.
36. Ibid., p. 60.
37. Ibid., pp. 56, 57.
38. Roland Barthes, *Izbrannye raboty. Semiotika. Poetika*, Moscow: Progress, 1994, p. 91.
39. Levin, 'Ekranizatsiia', pp. 78–9.
40. N. Kalitin, *Narodnaia artistka SSSR Alla Konstantinovna Tarasova*, Moscow: Goskinoizdat, 1951, p. 7.
41. Zhurko, 'O printsipakh ekranizatsii dramaturgii A. N. Ostrovskogo', p. 65.
42. Popov, *Problemy sovetskoi kinodramaturgii*, p. 111.
43. Ibid.
44. Ibid., p. 112.
45. Turovskaia, 'Ob ekranizatsii Chekhova', p. 34.
46. Pudovkin, *Sobranie sochinenii v 3 tomakh*, pp. 100, 101.
47. *Alla Konstantinovna Tarasova: Dokumenty i vospominaniia*, p. 159.
48. Ibid., p. 87.
49. Kalitin, *Narodnaia artistka SSSR Alla Konstantinovna Tarasova*, p. 25.
50. Ibid., pp. 30, 31.

4. (AUTOBIO/BIO/HAGIO)GRAPHY: PESHKOV – GORKY – DONSKOI

Every past is in itself a plot.

Boris Eikhenbaum

A genre, whether literary or not, is nothing other than the codification of discursive properties.

Tzvetan Todorov, *Genres in Discourse*

When he was visiting America in 1906, Gorky decided definitively to 'undertake an autobiography'.[1] The idea had occurred to him earlier, in 1893, but he only began to write it almost two decades later, in 1912, and finished work on it ten years after that. Thus was born the autobiographical trilogy, a central work in Gorky's creative biography, and one with which every person in Soviet Russia was familiar from childhood (it became part of the school curriculum for nine- and ten-year-olds). In 1938–9, another two decades later, the director Mark Donskoi put Gorky on the screen when he made his film trilogy, a work which would prove to be profoundly influential for world cinematography.

We are speaking here, however, not so much of different kinds of art, as of different genres: autobiography, biography and hagiography. If we 'reduce' these words to their component parts, we easily reach a common denominator; it is always a question of '-graphy' – that is, representation, description. The differences between the genres are differences between strategies of 'description'. The change is in their fundamental meaning, as well as in their conditions and functions.

In connection with this, Grigory Vinokur's idea, formulated in his 1926 book *Biography and Culture (Biografiia i kul'tura)*, attracts our attention. The author of an (autobio/bio/hagio)graphy has to deal with the continually elusive subject of 'graphy'. This is related to both the genre and the object of the representation ('graphy') itself. It is undoubtedly the case that genre processes are, strictly speaking, inter-genre processes. Thus, the instance in question – the relationships between Alyosha Peshkov, Maxim Gorky and Mark Donskoi – can only be described in categories of aphasia of genre, agraphia. The very fact that the strategy of Gorky/autobiographer led him to create a biography of a certain Alyosha Peshkov who really existed, while the film trilogy created by Mark Donskoi transformed the life of the character described by Gorky into a saint's life (biography into hagiography) compels one to think that the 'purity' of biographical genres is entirely conventional.

This also explains why the 'subject matter' of representation in biographical genres is destined to be perpetually elusive. Meanwhile, both the subject and the object of the narration are 'subject matter'. At the heart of any kind of historicisation lies the strategy of distilling the past into a story ('graphy'). The need itself for historicisation in the era of 'revolutionary creativity' was enormous.

One should take into account the fact that the first two parts of Gorky's trilogy were created in the 'era of reaction' after the first Russian Revolution, and the third part after the October Revolution; finally, Mark Donskoi's film trilogy was created in the new, post-revolutionary era, the era of the Stalinist Revolution and the Great Terror. 'Social demand' had, of course, been changing as well, each time selecting its genres for bio-mythology. The general cultural situation remained unchanged, as Osip Mandelshtam sensed acutely: 'we have entered a zone of powerful social movements, of organised mass movements, and the individual's stock in history is falling,' as a result of which people found themselves

> cast out of their own biographies, like balls out of billiard pockets, and the laws of their actions, like the collision of balls on a billiard table, are guided by a single principle: the angle of reflection is equal to the angle of incidence.[2]

It was precisely the 'person without a biography', the person outside history (and biography is history), who turned out to be not only the main character, but also the main 'consumer' and 'transformer' of the biographical genres. The search for genre forms was in this sense a search for the 'angle of incidence'.

BETWEEN AUTOBIOGRAPHY AND BIOGRAPHY: 'THE I' AS 'OTHER'

'Maxim Gorky is equal to Aleksei Maximovich Peshkov, a person who to a large degree related his own biography. Gorky is the subject-matter of his own books. Gorky's books are a single continuous novel, without a plot, about a traveller who had many encounters.' Thus Viktor Shklovsky began his expressively titled 1925 essay 'About Peshkov/Gorky'. The essay was later published in his book, *Successes and Defeats of Maxim Gorky* (*Udachi i porazheniia Maksima Gor'kogo*).[3] This was one of the books for which Shklovsky was never forgiven, even in the era when Gorky had already ceased to be Peshkov, having while still alive been transformed into the 'chief writer of the Soviet lands', 'assembler of literary forces', 'founder', 'forefather', 'patriarch', 'inspiration', 'storm petrel' and 'standard-bearer'. In this capacity he had neither 'successes' nor 'defeats', only victories (or, occasionally, 'mistakes due to hesitation').

Gorky was distinguished by a constant need to describe himself. One could say that he spent his entire life writing his autobiography. Of course, this involves not only his strictly autobiographical texts, but his work as a whole as well. The most intensive period of work on his autobiography coincides with the most crisis-ridden period of the writer's life. From 1912 to 1925, autobiographical works occupy a central place in his creative output.[4] This is also what allowed Shklovsky to say that Gorky was always 'relating his own biography'. But having 'turned up' at the centre of Gorky's biography, the autobiographical works confirmed Shklovsky's insight; autobiography is the central event of Gorky's creative work. Gorky's Other is always to a significant degree himself. Gorky only wrote about what he knew; thus in his aesthetics a decisive place is given over to 'knowledge of life'. To all intents and purposes, all of Gorky's characters, all those Chelkashes and Konovalovs, Dostigaevs and Bulychovs, Gordeevs and Kozhemiakins, Zheleznovs and inhabitants of Okurov, Artamonovs and Samgins, inhabitants of doss-houses and underground workers – all of this motley, pitiless, turmoil-filled, clamorously 'philosophical' world of Gorky's – are only the recollections of 'childhood, boyhood and youth'. Autobiography also explains Gorky's Proletkult fantasies – those of a man who felt acutely the inadequacy of his own culture, and who knew the difficulty of making one's way out of the depths – and his active role in 'assembling literary forces' and the 'literary legacy', his aid to the intelligentsia and 'autodidacts', and his hostility to the Russian village. Autobiography explains a great deal. We would not be mistaken if we said that it explains everything.

But in exactly the same way that autobiography explains Gorky's art and his social position, it must in itself be explained as a phenomenon of Gorky's 'artistic prose'; just as the Other is always part of Gorky's 'I', so his 'I' is always to a large extent his 'Other'. In a period of crisis, Gorky began to write differently. Autobiography is the result of this difference: no more, but no less either.

In autobiography – here and subsequently we are referring to Gorky's trilogy *Childhood* (*Detstvo*), *My Apprenticeship* (*V liudiakh*) and *My Universities* (*Moi universitety*) – Gorky's very 'method' of writing, finally, is focused. Autobiography proves that Gorky possessed a staggering memory. This is the basis of Gorky's 'realism'. But being 'protestant' by nature (a most significant self-characterisation in *My Universities*: 'Very early on I understood that a person is created by his resistance to his environment'[5]), Gorky proved to be one of the most brilliant mythologists of the 'era of wars and revolutions'. As we know, it was precisely from this mixture of 'total realism' and 'revolutionary romanticism' that socialist realism was born, at the roots of which stood Gorky.

Gorky's autobiographical trilogy had its precursors in Russian literature. Among them, the most famous are the autobiographical works of Sergei

Aksakov, Leo Tolstoy, Nikolai Garin-Mikhailovsky and Vladimir Korolenko – two-part works, trilogies and tetralogies.[6] By placing at the centre of the narrative a child through whose perception the world surrounding him is revealed, the authors of course resolved their own biographical, artistic and ideological problems. If Marxist criticism explained this type of 'centripetal force' in the autobiographical works of the nineteenth century as the egocentrism of the 'bourgeois novel', then formalist criticism on the contrary saw in this a 'rejection of romantic clichés, in the spheres of both style and genre.'[7] As opposed to Marxist criticism, the formalists were trying to explain the very nature of biography (as evidenced by the above-mentioned *Biography and Culture* by Grigory Vinokur) and of autobiography (here one should mention above all Boris Eikhenbaum's *The Young Tolstoy* (*Molodoi Tolstoi*)) as genres. By comparing Tolstoy's diaries with different variants of his *Childhood* (*Detstvo*), Eikhenbaum demonstrated that the author had been working chiefly on 'problems of description, not narration, and problems of style rather than those of composition or genre'.[8] The most essential thing that Tolstoy developed for all his later works was his optics, which Eikhenbaum calls 'generalisation', in which the author is 'not a narrator who connects himself in any way with his main characters, but rather a bystander, a perspicacious observer and even experimenter . . . he watches and passes judgment.'[9] As a result, the 'personality of the hero is a direct combination born out of self-observation and the diaries; this is not a "type", nor even a personality, but rather a vehicle of generalisation, through whose use Tolstoy motivates the detail of the descriptions.'[10] Eikhenbaum came to the conclusion that the idea for an autobiographical 'novel' occurred to Tolstoy 'not out of a desire to represent the psychological development of a particular personality with its typical and individual peculiarities, but rather out of a need for "generalisation", along abstract lines.'[11] His work on an autobiography became the 'arena' in which Tolstoy discovered the synthesis he sought of 'generalisation' ('general ideas') and of 'detail' ('dialectic of the soul'). 'Monologism' is a constant in autobiography. But the 'objectivity' of narration (via the hero) remained just as constant in Russian tradition. Gorky made this constant a variable. While traditionally the subject of the narrative in his 'childhood, teenage years and youth' was to be found in the foreground in autobiography, even being the object of the author's description, now the subject not only disappeared from the foreground, but itself was transformed into a function, to use Eikhenbaum's words, 'motivating the detail of the descriptions'.

Gorky's contemporaries, however, could not appreciate his 'innovation'. '*Childhood*', Mikhail Prishvin wrote to Gorky in 1915, 'is a very good book, but still it is only half of what is needed: there is not enough of the child Peshkov himself in it.'[12] Prishvin had been educated in the tradition: in Tolstoy, Aksakov and Garin-Mikhailovsky, the distance between the child and the narrator is very clearly defined. Gorky does not simply 'erode' this distance, but almost completely 'replaces' the child. Accordingly, even Alyosha Peshkov's 'jobs'

(Prishvin was writing about *Childhood*, but in the stories of *My Apprenticeship* we see Alyosha as a 'boy' in a shoe-store, a draftsman's student, a dishwasher on a steamer, a salesperson in an icon shop, a student in an icon studio, a *kvas*-deliverer, a stevedore at a port, a watchman at the railroad and so on) are only grounds for creating 'morality sketches', constant new portraits, which ultimately combine into that very 'epic image of Russia, of the life of the Russian people' so beloved by Soviet criticism, which emphasised the 'authenticity of the picture':

> One cannot but be amazed by the striking clarity of the writer's recollections. He saw everything he had experienced so clearly through the veil of the past that the reader does not doubt for even a second the absolute authenticity of what is represented.[13]

This 'accuracy' meanwhile, presented an, in principle, new dimension for the autobiographical genre in Russian literature. At the heart of Gorky's autobiography lies a specifically anti-autobiographical principle. This relates to Gorky's anti-Rousseauism. Gorky's attitude towards Rousseau was formed in a complex way (it is sufficient to look at Gorky's *Confession* (*Ispoved'*) to see the influence Rousseau exerted on Gorky) until it converged into an open polemic in Gorky's *Story of a Young Man* (*Istoriia molodogo cheloveka*), in which Gorky spoke out against individualism, against the idea of 'genius which needs no experience', against the 'independence' of the individual from class influences and from the conditions of his era, against the cult of 'social isolation', and against the idea of an 'exceptional personality' as such. Gorky now styled Rousseau 'the most talented apostle of individualism'.[14] All of this could not but be manifested in Gorky's trilogy; in autobiography the 'auto-' was called into doubt.

Soviet criticism explained Gorky's move beyond the boundaries of the genre's tradition as the 'social direction of Gorky's work as a proletarian artist':

> A social proletarian direction burst open the narrow framework of the typical 'family' and 'psychological' genres of the literature of the nobility and bourgeoisie (the story of childhood days), and filled it with a broader content, inserting 'recollections of childhood' into the picture of a detailed portrayal of social life with all its contradictions.[15]

'Autobiography' is in fact only 'inserted into the picture', serving as no more than the plot of Gorky's narrative. Characterisations such as 'He was able to transform a short autobiographical tale of a child's life, poor in events and clear impressions, into an amazing, socially significant picture of one of the eras of Russian historical life'[16] seem like faint praise for an autobiography. It would be more correct to say that Gorky had written a biography, in his usual way, like the biographies of the Artamonovs, Gordeevs or

Konovalovs. The aim of describing 'not myself' is absolutely distinct in Gorky's autobiography:

> A dense, variegated, and inexpressibly strange life began and flew past with frightening speed. It comes back to me like a cruel fairytale, well told by a kind but torturously truthful genius. And now, when I bring the past to life, I myself find it at times difficult to believe that everything was precisely the way it was, and I want to argue with much of it, reject it; the dark life of the 'ignorant tribe' is too abundant with cruelty. But truth is higher than pity, and after all I'm not telling the story of myself, but rather of that close, oppressive circle of terrifying impressions in which the simple Russian man lived, and indeed still lives even to this day.[17]

There are numerous such 'lyrical digressions' in the text; 'I'm not telling the story of myself' is a structural principle of Gorky's narrative 'of himself'.

One is easily convinced that Gorky was writing 'artistic prose', even though he was asserting that he was writing an autobiography, if one compares *Childhood* with the 1893 sketch 'An account of the facts and thoughts from whose interaction the best parts of my heart withered [otsokhli]'. When Gorky undertook to write an autobiography, he did not have this sketch at hand, but the coincidences in the episodes, observations and even individual expressions speak not only of a striking memory, but even more of the extent to which Gorky 'fictionalised' the story of his life. To take just one example: the most memorable image of *Childhood* is that of the grandmother. Her poeticisation in *Childhood* delighted Gorky's contemporaries, as did her 'wonderful' fairytales and the atmosphere of familial warmth surrounding her. But in the 'account', Gorky said his grandmother's fairytales frightened him, and more than once mentioned the fact that 'Grandmother drinks', that she 'was often drunk'.

In Gorky's 'autobiography' the descriptiveness, 'prettiness' and depth of detail are striking. There is no need to say that Gorky 'recollected' things which he undoubtedly could not have remembered. A child of three or four could not have remembered what adults had said, what they looked like or what they were thinking about. This is all, without doubt, invented. Just one example of this kind of 'recollections': *My Apprenticeship* opens with a description of Alyosha working as a 'boy' in a shoe-store. The author retells in detail what the shop assistant and owner said, adding that 'I didn't like the things they were saying, I didn't understand most of the words, and it sometimes seemed that these people were speaking a foreign language.'[18] It goes without saying that, years later, this language did not seem 'foreign' to Gorky; but to remember for one's entire life an unknown language, the unfamiliar words heard in childhood, is indeed impossible. What, then, is the status of the descriptions and conversations found here?[19] Gorky was not 'recollecting' a child's sensations; he was creating them, and only in this sense perhaps was Gorky located within the lines of the tradition of the autobiographical genre. The strategy of creating a 'cruel fairytale' leads us to the question of the very nature of the autobiographical genre.

In *Biography and Culture*, Grigory Vinokur insists that one 'must look for the greatest true-to-life and genuine qualities in the style. It is precisely here that we find all that is most authentic and truthful in personal life.'[20] It was a question of 'style of behaviour'. But Vinokur also observed here that 'any reflection, even the slightest, upon one's own behaviour, is outright stylisation.'[21] In other words, autobiography, which is indeed a 'reflection on one's own behaviour', is by definition stylisation. True, Vinokur did try to escape from this kind of categorical approach when he explained that:

> [A] character who stylises his own behaviour merges with the image and ideal which constantly stands before his inner perspective to such a degree that he ceases to perceive the boundary between the actual and the ideal, the true and the fictional. At this point he takes that which only appears to be canon and prescription to be factual and true to life. Thus arise fictional biographies, in the creation of which the greatest share of participation falls directly to the hero himself. In this kind of fictional biography, it is not the facts themselves which are fictional, but only the expressive atmosphere which they convey. It is not a person's life as such that is created here, only its style.[22]

But in so far as 'style', according to Vinokur, is the basis of biography, the latter's 'fictional nature' by no means diminishes the fact that the 'facts' are preserved. Yet artistic 'autobiography', according to Vinokur, proves to be absolutely impossible. A 'poem' cannot

> serve as reliable material by which to judge the factual content of a person's life . . . A personality with experiences as a subject, and a poetic theme as a subject, are things which are simply not capable of being compared . . . these are different subjects, different meanings, different areas of spiritual culture.[23]

'From a biographer's perspective,' Vinokur concludes, 'a poem is not so much a specific phenomenon of culture as a sort of authorial act, a form of behaviour.'[24] And although nowhere in his book does Vinokur talk about autobiography, his constructs are completely applicable to the genre of interest to us. Autobiography is first and foremost an 'authorial act' and 'form of behaviour', just as is any 'poem'.

None the less, Gorky did not remotely regard his trilogy as a 'poem', advising his biographers to check the facts of his scholarly biography against these stories.

Soviet criticism spoke tirelessly of the fact that Gorky had created 'completed artistic images' in his 'autobiography'. And without a doubt, justly so.

It would be naive in the extreme to explain the course of the narrative solely as the workings of memory, mechanically reproducing the life impressions experienced in their own time. The trilogy has its own construction which is no less strict and planned-out than in Dickens's *David Copperfield*, with its cleverly woven plot. But the selection and composition of images are not influenced by the need for romantic intrigue, but by problems of a different, epic idea; each new character arising from Gorky's pen represents the boundary of a certain larger whole, of an epic image of Russia and the life of the Russian people . . . Gorky's trilogy itself is not simply biography; rather it is a work of art with its own 'plot', particular content and its own problematics.[25]

Since in his autobiography Gorky valued 'instructiveness' above all, it is clear that the Other was advancing in the foreground. It is significant that the book by Gorky's chief biographer, Ilya Gruzdev, published in the biographical series organised by Gorky himself, *The Lives of Remarkable People* (*Zhizn' zamechatel'nykh liudei*), contains the assertion:

He is presenting neither a biography, nor a confession, nor a portrait in his tales. He has written a history of which he was a witness. It is not his fate which is at the centre of the tale, but the history of the Russian people as it was reflected in the fate of his family and the people he encountered.[26]

Such assertions are, of course, extreme. Gorky's trilogy is precisely a biography. One could say that the 'stylising' impulse (in the sense with which Vinokur endowed it) destines autobiography to be transformed into a 'work of art with its own "plot", its peculiar content, and its own problematics'. Composition of the real biography of Alyosha Peshkov was replaced by Gorky with a new 'constructedness'. The author's unconditional aim of creating a 'broad epic picture of Russian life' presupposed a diachronicisation and selection of the most essential scenes in a characterological and typological sense. But the child's consciousness functions in a fundamentally different way; it is synchronic, discrete and has no strategy of selectivity. On the contrary, the child's 'selectivity' is spontaneous and is, of course, far from the demands of characterisation and typologisation, as even the author admits: 'Life persistently and rudely erased its best inscriptions from my soul, maliciously replacing them with some kind of unnecessary nonsense.'[27]

The central hero of Gorky's trilogy is not, of course, 'I' but precisely 'the Other' for the author, a character who in principle differs little from the majority of Gorky's other characters. The trilogy was so easy to integrate into the corpus of 'the classics of socialist realism' because it read like a socialist realist *Bildungsroman*. The fact that Gorky himself, the 'founder of socialist realism' and the 'forefather of Soviet literature', became this kind of hero should not lead us astray. This is a different myth, the myth of Gorky (of which we will yet have occasion to speak in connection with Donskoi's film trilogy). But meanwhile Gorky's trilogy opened an endless gallery of the 'coming into being' of the heroes of Soviet literature for every ten-year-old Soviet child. There is no basis therefore for taking Soviet criticism to task for 'overstatement': 'Pavel Korchagin is the direct descendant of Aleksei Peshkov. Carrying forth the best traditions of Gorky, Soviet writers are successfully developing this genre, showing the history of the shaping of the people of our times.'[28]

The transformation of autobiography into biography, into *Bildungsroman*, had a fundamental significance for socialist realism.[29] At the heart of this lies the process of exteriorisation of 'the self', the transformation of 'I' into 'the Other'. One might say that Gorky's 'autobiography' is the biography of the Other, written from Gorky's perspective. The space of this text is, to use Bakhtin's term, 'unreachable' [*vnenakhodimo*]; it is not simply that it does not correspond to either Gorky or Alyosha Peshkov, it is also indivisible between them. This is neither a story about the self, nor a story completely about the Other. It is an attempt to make the Other out of oneself: the peculiar inner side of Gorky's life-creation [*zhiznetvorchestvo*]. Gorky's optics were so unusual that they could not but be re-reflected in socialist realist art.

BETWEEN BIOGRAPHY AND HAGIOGRAPHY: 'THE OTHER' AS 'I'

Impossibility is an absolute concept. Gorky's trilogy is in this sense a sort of limit of the aphasia of genre; a text 'about the self' becomes the story of 'the Other' ('after all I'm not telling the story of myself'). The second life of Gorky's text in Stalinist culture, Mark Donskoi's film trilogy, forces us to doubt such an obvious truth. My 'autobiography' (even if it is 'not about me') cannot be written by the Other. The autobiography of the Other cannot be adapted to the screen without a cardinal change of the optics (in other words, without a change of genre). The screen adaptation of the autobiography of the Other is – by definition – the biography of the Other.

Consequently, it is not the premise of the author of the original text (in this case, Gorky) which comes to the foreground, but rather that of the director, Mark Donskoi. If in his trilogy Gorky had written Alyosha Peshkov into his own monologue, now not only Alyosha but also Gorky himself are written into a new sphere of 'graphy'. Donskoi's trilogy demonstrates the effect of 'multi-monologism' in art. Amplified into the temperament and style of Donskoi, monologism does not simply 'double'; the change takes place not in arithmetic but in geometric progression. We are transported into a new genre-space.

Nurtured by hagiography as a form of genre and style, biography took centuries to develop. The breakdown of this form occurred with the secularisation of literature. In the Soviet era, literature underwent a process of re-secularisation for a new ideology. Accordingly, the 'genre-memory' of hagiography was also resurrected.[30] The operation of this memory gave birth in Soviet literature to certain patterns, the norms of which comprised the distinctive features of the socialist realist canon.[31] In film, the reflection of the 'operation of memory' is not so clearly visible, perhaps because the language of the cinema itself was shaped much more recently. Here a borrowing of literary forms, their 'cinematisation', takes place. But since the 'grafting' of the genre is not a simple translation from the language of one form of art to that of another, one should not speak so much of the potentiality of devices of genre and style, as of their novelty and diversity.

In *The Human Being in the Literature of Ancient Rus'* (*Chelovek v literature Drevnei Rusi*), Dmitry Likhachev introduced the concept of 'genre styles' and suggested in particular that the 'hagiographic style' be distinguished from hagiography as a literary genre.[32] The 'hagiographic style', according to Likhachev, is characterised by:

> accumulation of synonyms, tautological and pleonastic combinations, neologisms and epithets, with their rhythmical organisation of language, creating an impression of the infinity of feelings. All of this is intended to impress on the reader the grandiose and significant quality of the events, and to create an impression of their ineffability through the human word. Concrete meanings are erased in these combinations and accumulations of words, and expression and dynamics move to the foreground. The word becomes non-concrete, 'unweighable'.[33]

This characterisation of the 'hagiographic style' would be applicable to Donskoi if we were attempting to characterise his style in contrast to something else. What is striking in Donskoi's films is the amazing concreteness and materiality of the world, the 'weighability', if not to say 'heaviness' of the texture. Everything which can be described as Donskoi's 'style' is diametrically opposed to 'hagiographic style'. 'Early neorealism' fed on this. (The most prominent French and Italian neorealist directors, who discovered a fundamentally new stylistics and principles of vision in the trilogy, and in his films *Rainbow* (*Raduga*) and *The Unconquered* (*Nepokorennye*), subsequently spoke of Donskoi's influence.) But Donskoi's world is also striking for its 'accumulation of words', and for its advancement of 'expression and dynamics to the fore-ground'. Precisely from the combination of these features the striking 'expressive overload' of his films is born, as well as their 'romanticism' and 'poeticism'. The hybrid of 'cruel realism' and 'revolutionary romanticism' is Gorky's style, which he tried to cultivate in Soviet literature, supposing that socialist realism would allow the synthesis of both these principles. And Gorky, by Donskoi's own admission, remained the latter's teacher in art throughout his life.

Donskoi's paradox is the combination of the uncombinable: 'anti-hagiographic style' with the 'hagiographic genre'. Donskoi's films are indeed hagiographies – the Gorky trilogy, *How the Steel Was Tempered* (*Kak zakalialas' stal'*), *The Rainbow*, *The Village Schoolmistress* (*Sel'skaia uchitel'nitsa*), *Mother* (*Mat'*), *Foma Gordeev* and the two-part film about Lenin's mother, *A Mother's Heart* (*Serdtse materi*) and *A Mother's Loyalty* (*Vernost' materi*) – everywhere here there are events lasting a lifetime; the coming into being of the heroes; their maturation and service to an ideal; their faith and heroic deeds; and ultimately, their 'posthumous miracles'.

It is obvious that the 'anti-hagiographic hagiography' was based on a 'deconstruction' of the existing model of the genre. Speaking of the hagiographic genre, Likhachev noted a curious split within the object of idealisation between the personal and social roles. A hagiography idealises, but according to Likhachev this is:

> not an idealisation of a person; this is idealisation of his social position, of the place he occupies in the hierarchy of feudal society. A person is good chiefly when he suits his social position or when this suitability is ascribed to him (more often the latter).[34]

This principle corresponded ideally to Gorky's method of 'typologisation'. Practically every character in Gorky's trilogy is definitely typologised; of each one it is possible to say which social type (merchant, tramp, deacon, student and so on) they represent. The same applies to the main character as well. His story has an ending well known to the reader. Gorky as the author of the trilogy was a well-known figure in literature (which could not have been said of Leo Tolstoy when he appeared before the reader in his autobiography); Alexei Peshkov was typologically fixed for the reader by the writer Maxim Gorky. He was a 'representative of the working man', making him (as far as hagiography is concerned) an extra-generic figure, since the 'working man' was situated 'beyond the feudal social ladder, and consequently, beyond the ladder of feudal ideals as well'.[35]

Thus the genre was yet to be created. But there was already a matrix for it.

> All the psychological conditions with which hagiographic literature so generously endows a person [writes Likhachev] are only exterior layers upon the basic, uncomplicated inner essence of the person, be it good or evil, and determined by the decision of the person himself to start out on one path or another. All the psychological conditions are, as it were, clothing which can be either discarded or adopted.[36]

It is precisely here that the boundary delineating Gorky's biography from Donskoi's hagiography lies, since all of Donskoi's characters are absolutely monosemantic in precisely their 'inner essence'. Gorky, in transforming himself and the people around him into characters of his own biography, preserved their 'looseness' (sometimes bordering on 'Dostoevskianism') and their tendency to development. But Donskoi's characters do not develop in the slightest. At work here is that ever-deductive mechanism of the hagiography: 'subjugation of true-life phenomena to a single normative ideal'.[37] The ideal of a 'new saintliness' was just such an ideal in Donskoi's era.

Critics noted the 'insipid performance' of the young actors (Lyarsky in the first two parts of the trilogy and Valbert in the third); they are 'equally devoid of individuality, stiff and constrained, as if the responsibility of the task – playing the future great writer – fettered them in advance, deprived them of naturalness and simplicity'.[38] None the less, the 'absence of individuality' in Alyosha Peshkov comes, as has already been said, from Gorky's text, in which the author-biographer is endowed with individuality in his appraisals, judgements or vicious invectives. The actors found themselves in a fundamentally new genre situation. They were in fact playing the 'future great writer' (accordingly, the first film of the trilogy is not called *Childhood*, but rather *Gorky's Childhood*), which Donskoi emphasised even in his 'frames'. Each part begins with a title screen upon which it is not Gorky that is portrayed, but rather the engraving of him which was very familiar from the 1930–50 gift editions of his books. Furthermore, each part begins with the dedication 'In memory of the great Russian writer Alexei Maximovich Gorky,' and is framed at the beginning and end of the film with an epigraph, a quotation from Gorky (and at the bottom of the text is the familiar flourish of Gorky's signature). Within this framework, Alexei Lyarsky, who plays Alyosha Peshkov, is transformed into just that Soviet Pioneer whom Soviet cinema from the 1930s to the 1950s portrayed.

Critics were inclined to explain the ascents at the end, these true paroxysms of 'revolutionary romanticism' in Donskoi's films, as an attempt to 'open up' the film, to 'broaden its physical and emotional horizon', or as a means of 'finding a way out from this black hell into harmony, hope, a new ascent, as emphasised by the striking lyricism and the musicality of the theme'. This was how the French film critic Albert Cervoni, author of a book about Donskoi, characterised the ending of *Gorky's Childhood*.[39]

Donskoi 'elevated' and 'literaricised' Gorky's text on all levels, restaging life into hagiography. It is worth remembering that the 'life of Gorky' itself, with which Gorky acquainted the reader, had already in its turn been 'literaricised' (as compared to Gorky's 'Account of the facts and thoughts from whose interaction the best parts of my heart withered'). This process can be described in just the same way that the process of interaction between literary and extra-literary factors in the creation of a hagiography is described. ' "Unbookish" redactions of hagiographies', Likhachev comments, 'witnesses' notes about them [i.e. the subjects of the 'lives' – E. D.], are replaced by bookish redactions of hagiographies.'[40] Moreover the 'original redactions of the works are as a rule less literary, less "bookish" than subsequent ones. The textual history of individual works shows as the text moves forward, that the work strengthens its literariness.'[41] This is how matters stand with the 'hagiographisation' of original 'true accounts'. The same trajectory is found in the texts under examination here.

When the canon of the hagiographic genre is discussed, what is usually meant is the author of the hagiography's observance of a strict plot scheme, which is composed from a selection of obligatory episodes: a demand to make a sacrifice to pagan gods, which the Christian refuses to do; a 'debate about faith' between a pagan, an authority figure and a Christian; a description of torture, hyperbolised to the point of incredibility, during which the tortured individual remains unharmed and only affirms his faith more strongly; the miraculous healing of the martyr, if he is thrown into prison; and finally, execution by 'beheading' and posthumous miracles. The saint must also come from honest parents, manifest from childhood an aptitude for learning, early heroic deeds and piety, and so on.[42] This kind of plot-scheme was only present in Gorky's narrative in potential. A whole series of modifications of the source was necessary in order to draw this scheme out of its latent condition. It was precisely in this direction that Donskoi was working.

First of all, it was necessary for the director to combine Gorky's uncoordinated texts into a single one. Gorky's trilogy is a text which dissociates. Moreover, it is not just a matter of each part individually, but also of the internal lack of coherence of the different fragments within the parts themselves, which frequently consist of uncoordinated genre portraits. Quotations from Gorky's texts become Donskoi's principal 'clamps' for the plot of the biography. Gorky's *Childhood* opens with an epigraph/introduction: 'In bringing the past to life, I myself find it hard to believe that everything was just like this', and closes with the famous call 'To life! To life!', which rings out as a prelude to the film *My Apprenticeship* and as a challenge to broaden the picture of reality. The second film closes with Gorky's maxim about 'the other life', where the challenge to struggle with the 'life' of the present 'for the sake of the other life – a beautiful, bold, honest life' sounds. The film *My Universities*, where the pictures of 'leaden abominations' acquire an almost suffocating significance, opens with Gorky's aphorism, 'Truth is higher than pity', and closes with a promise of 'posthumous miracles': 'I go forth to be burned and to illuminate life.' Such is the strategy of the staging of the source.

The next aspect is the selection of material, which is aimed at making Gorky's variegated picture monochromatic. The selected scenes are built up into a new, clearly hagiographic plot, by means of staging 'ideological blocks'. If we were to enumerate everything which did not make it into the film, the director's strategy of 'distilling' Gorky's life from one generic canon into another would become utterly clear. As examples, Alyosha no longer keeps birds in cages nor trains them, Tsyganok no longer steals at the market, and the grandmother does not drink.

> By intermingling on an individual level differing aspects of one and the same character, with the aim of highlighting their dominant features with no ambiguity, Donskoi sharply separates 'good' from 'evil' on the social plane and even intensively accentuates their opposition, so that these characters somewhat resemble the bright angels and dark demons of certain medieval paintings,

wrote French film critic André Devalles of Donskoi, observing that, as a result of the director's transformations, Gorky's text 'is shrunk and simplified'.[43]

Thus Gorky's picture is rendered flat and the voluminousness of his images disappears. It is as if the plot flows backwards. With Gorky it was centrifugal, spilling out into portraits and genre sketches; with Donskoi, it becomes centripetal. The result of this kind of centring is that the 'picture of growth' is transformed into a 'picture of struggle'. Here Donskoi resorts to radical changes in Gorky's plot, and no longer selects so much as introduces. For example, in *Childhood*, Alyosha makes friends with the children of the neighbouring colonel, with absolutely no distinction of the 'social contrasts' of the street (even though he collects rags from the scrap-heap, he continues to go to school). In *Gorky's Childhood*, however, the street is polarised; the well-dressed children throw stones at a beggar, but absolute ragamuffins defend Alyosha when he takes the beggar's part, and they become his best friends (the 'friendly band'). The 'Good Deed' neighbour is in the film similar to Gorky's character perhaps only in nickname. Donskoi transforms him into a revolutionary and conspirator who makes bombs. Whereas in Gorky the police show up at the grandfather's house for an old lodger who has robbed churches, with Donskoi they come for this 'alien in his native land'. It is, of course, explained that he is 'a mutineer against the Tsar'. And a few scenes later we see him fettered in leg-irons, leaving for penal servitude and bequeathing the lessons of revolutionary morality to Alyosha: 'Don't obey the evil order, and don't hide behind another's conscience.'

The image of penal servitude is transformed by Donskoi into a recurrent motif of the whole trilogy. A martyr, according to the canon, must undergo imprisonment. And Donskoi creates this. There are convicts in each film. Moreover, Donskoi always combines this image with everyday life, which in no way differs from penal servitude. One and the same device at the beginning and end of the films attracts our attention; each begins with a picture of 'leaden abominations'. Thus the first shots in *Gorky's Childhood* are a tableau of Ilya Repin's 'Barge Haulers on the Volga'; *My Universities* opens with the famous panorama of Marusovka. The endings are, conversely, passionately declamatory throughout. In *Gorky's Childhood* we see Alyosha going off into a field to meet 'the people' (in Gorky's work, the boy does not 'go off' anywhere; his grandfather brings him to work in the store); the film of *My Apprenticeship* closes with Alyosha sailing away to Kazan on the Volga, its waters rolling into eternity, and with the grandmother's touching parting words; *My Universities* comes to a definitive close with boundless watery expanses and the image of Gorky as storm petrel: 'Shout, Mankind!' Convicts and gendarmes are invariably located between 'leaden abominations' and 'revolutionary romanticism'. Donskoi's plot develops on the field of battle between 'tsarism and the people', which constitutes an indisputable modernisation of Gorky's trilogy, as if read through his novel *Mother* (which was adapted for the screen by Donskoi two decades later).

Let us turn to the central film in the trilogy, *My Apprenticeship*. Donskoi constructed a completely new plot out of Gorky's reminiscences. The film is distinctly divided into three parts: life in the draftsman's house, work on the steamer, and finally, work in the icon-painter's studio. The film opens with 'Queen Margo', and with her the theme of books is introduced. Following the scenes in the 'queen's' drawing-room comes the confession scene, which Donskoi arranges grotesquely (whereas Gorky describes it in ironic tones). The confession (both the speeches of the confessor and those of the penitent) resounds throughout the church, and the priest only whispers when speaking of 'forbidden books'. Immediately following this scene we see Alyosha walking down a street and looking through windows, where certain young people are in fact reading these 'forbidden books'. Pushkin's lines resound: 'While we burn with freedom, while our hearts live for honour, my friend, we will consecrate the beautiful impulses of the soul to the fatherland.' One of the people behind the windows, listening to a book being read, sinks into hysterics. Straight after this there is the scene at Alyosha's lodgings, where his masters are trying to make him understand the harm in books. The explanations are interrupted by the news of the Tsar's murder and the phrase which hangs in the air: 'It's them, those readers.'

The theme of books is central in Gorky's work. These novels resound passionately with hymns to the book; Gorky says of himself that he was 'Baptised by the Holy Spirit of honest and wise books'.[44] For the hagiography created by Donskoi, this motif is undoubtedly important. But books in Donskoi's work are exclusively revolutionary. The next stage of the Gorky biography after life in the draftsman's house is his work as dishwasher on the steamer and his friendship with Smury. The whole of this second part of the film moves in constant contrast; Donskoi portrays the sailing steamer in parallel with the prisoners' barge passing alongside. All of the action on the steamer, from beginning to end, develops as if within a 'frame'; with the unseeing eyes of its barred windows, the prisoners' barge watches everything that takes place. And the following takes place: Alyosha reads *Taras Bulba*. He reads: 'Could we really find anywhere in the world such a force that would exceed Russian might?!' The camera moves to the window of the cabin. Beyond the window is the prisoners' barge with the barred windows. 'We couldn't!' Smury replies.

The central event of the third part of the film, which portrays Alyosha's job in the icon-painter's studio, is the reading of Lermontov's *The Demon*. This book is also defined as 'forbidden'. The fundamental opposition in this part, 'church/anti-church', reaches its culmination in the dancing scene at the celebration of Alyosha's thirteenth birthday. He is given a present – an 'icon' of . . . the Demon. In Donskoi's treatment, Alyosha never tires of repeating, 'I won't submit!' and 'I won't put up with it!' This part of Gorky's text is as if read through the play *The Lower Depths* (*Na Dne*), its central motifs: 'Truth is higher than pity', 'I am rebellious!' (As a demonstration of the latter thesis, Alyosha in Donskoi's film thrashes the owner of the icon shop.) The scene of

Alyosha's birthday is set up by Donskoi in heroic tones. People tell the future founder of Soviet literature that he is 'kin to all the people', and that he 'doesn't face things from the side, but straight-on. Keep facing them that way!' Alyosha, proud and rebellious, heeds and accepts this 'precept'. Gorky describes this scene thus:

> He was speaking in a boring way, the studio was making fun of him, [and] I was standing there with an icon in my hands, very touched and confused, not knowing what I should do. Finally, Kapendiukhin, annoyed, shouted at the orator, 'Would you stop reading this burial service?! Look, his ears have even gone blue!'[45]

Thus, by logically arranging the scenes of Gorky's story, Donskoi creates a new plot. In *My Universities* plot construction operates differently, based on contrast. For example, a work scene – the unloading of the sinking barge at night in the rain – closes with the maxim, 'The people craved labour.' This is immediately followed by the scene with the bakery owner about the worth of the working man, which alternates with the scene of the populist students' debate about the 'poetry of labour'. Alexei pronounces angry words here: 'My faith is tanned into my back.' But for the director this kind of contrasting juncture of scenes proves insufficient. Donskoi also constructs a visual image of 'ideological priorities'. Outside the window (as usual) are State convicts. The viewer sees this through the window. Then the camera position changes and we see the people looking out of the window; the first at the window is Alexei, behind him is a Marxist, and beyond the Marxist, in the distance, is a populist. Afterwards – before our very eyes – there is the scene of 'revolution in the bakery'. Alexei has already become a leader.

However, in portraying the 'debate about faith', Donskoi refuses to introduce collisions into the film which would lead the hero to attempt suicide. According to Gorky's text, the decision to commit suicide was the result of disenchantment with 'the people', who did not want to 'rise to the struggle', and not only made peace with their persecutors, but even participated in the thrashing of the 'fighters for the people's cause'. Donskoi changes the motivation; the decision to commit suicide is explained purely by narrative-textual 'titles' projected on the screen, from which the viewer learns that the 'motives' for the student strike 'were unclear' to Alexei. The 'image of the people' remains unblemished. 'Simple people' are not shown participating in pro-government demonstrations, but on the other hand, we see their arrival at the hospital to visit the stricken leader, their precept 'Gather up the words!' and Alexei's 'moral healing' (although it is true that in Donskoi's work, it is not clear, from what). The cover of *History of an Illness* in the doctor's hands is transformed into the cover of the dossier in the gendarme's hands, who reads therein that Alexei Peshkov is a mutineer and revolutionary whose actions are 'aimed at overthrowing the existing order'.

But the revolutionary, meanwhile, travels 'throughout Rus'' with his staff, 'gathers up words', becomes an adult and, transformed before our very eyes into the 'storm petrel', is about to take flight.

'BEHEADING,' OR LEADEN ROMANTICISM

Thus we see the 'rejection of one's earlier faith' ('I won't take it!,' 'Truth is higher than pity'); the 'debate about [new] faith' (in *My Universities*); the 'description of torture, hyperbolised to the point of incredibility, during which the tortured individual remains unharmed and only affirms his faith more strongly' (Donskoi's realism); 'imprisonment' (the recurrent motif of all three films); the 'miraculous healing of the martyr' (Alexei's healing in the finale of the trilogy); and the 'posthumous miracles' (promised in the finale of each film). There is no need to mention that our hero 'manifests from childhood an aptitude for learning', performs 'early heroic deeds' and demonstrates 'piety'.

As far as 'beheading' goes, this was arranged after Gorky's death. The 'Gorky myth', at the heart of which lies Donskoi's trilogy, was exactly that point after which the 'posthumous miracles' began. Did Gorky himself foresee such a posthumous fate? He was in too close contact with the authorities (both with Lenin and with Stalin); he too well understood how things stood in reality, and went through 'universities' that were too cruel, not to understand what kind of game he was playing in.

Gorky was involved personally with Donskoi's films. There are two pieces of reliable evidence for this. The first belongs to Donskoi, who during an encounter with Gorky 'some time around 1936' shared with him his intent to bring the trilogy to the screen. He remembered Gorky's answer 'for [his] entire life': 'It's not good to build a monument to a person during his lifetime!'[46] The monument was not in fact raised 'during his lifetime', but construction was already underway by then. Why were the films produced only after Gorky's death? It was not, of course, because Gorky thought this was 'not good'. (He was powerless before the 'Gorky myth'.) Circumstances beyond his control were at work here. The other evidence, that of Varvara Massalitinova, sheds light on these. The actress had, as early as the 1920s, dreamed of playing the role of the grandmother in a film, and had put the question to Gorky: 'What do you think about my trying to play the role of the grandmother in a film of your *Childhood*?' After some reflection, Gorky replied 'Go ahead!' Massalitinova's meeting with Gorky took place in 1928, in Moscow, after his return from Italy. She recalled how:

> Discussion of a film came up more than once, but each time was put off for one reason or another.
>
> In the summer of 1937, when I was vacationing in Abramtsevo, [some people] from the Soiuzdetfilm studio approached me with a suggestion of playing the grandmother. To my question about why the production of

the film was always being put off (nine years had passed since I had met with Gorky), I got an unexpected answer. It turns out that the image of Kabanikha, which I had played in a film (*The Storm*), did not, in the producers' opinion, allow them to offer me a directly opposite role. They were afraid of internal contradictions, which they said I was sure to come up against in the job. But for me as an actress, these doubts did not exist; I think every genuine artist must sustain a thesis and an antithesis in his work.[47]

The 'producers' of whom Massalitinova speaks were far from showing such touching concern for the actress; myth-making has its own logic, and the iconography of socialist realism can equally well include a Massalitinova-Kabanikha and a Massalitinova-grandmother. These are non-coinciding (the four-year gap was not sustained in vain), diametrically opposed images of the past, or to use Massalitinova's words, a 'thesis' and 'antithesis'; but none the less they are from one and the same past, the third quarter of the nineteenth century. This period in Soviet historical mythology has two stable characteristics: the 'dark kingdom' and the 'protest against leaden abominations'. In so far as the grandmother in Gorky is an incarnation of the 'old faith' (pity), but 'truth is higher than pity,' we still face the task of understanding what we observed above; for the hagiographic scheme, dissolved in Gorky's autobiography, to come to light in Donskoi's films, it was not so much a transformation of the 'story of a life' that was required, as a transformation of the genre itself. But the productivity of genre conflict is conditioned by the non-correspondence of the 'hagiographic genre' with the 'anti-hagiographic style'. But the very significance of the 'style' discovered by Donskoi goes far beyond the narrowly ideological aims of the 1930s.

Among the numerous responses to Gorky's *Childhood* was that of Fyodor Sologub:

> You read it and get annoyed. Involuntarily, you recall the sweet-smelling childhood of Leo Tolstoy. By contrast. Such a mean, rough childhood. They fight, they beat each other up, they flog people in every instalment. [*Childhood* was published in instalments in the newspaper *The Russian Word* (*Russkoe slovo*) – E. D.] A kind of absolute sadism, completely inexplicable psychologically. We do not see what kind of spiritual force moves people to commit abominations. But the fabric of the story is still so sturdy that you involuntarily follow it. You keep waiting for the light of creative art to shine forth into the dark souls of these dark people, and we would understand why.[48]

Soviet critics took Sologub to task for (being, of course, a 'decadent') allegedly failing to see either the grandmother or Tsyganok in *Childhood*. Meanwhile, Sologub was doubtful of the very perspective of Gorky's autobiography; when the grandmother and Tsyganok disappear from the narrative, Gorky's world stands forth in all its lack of divine grace. Gorky, as if foreseeing such a reaction to *Childhood*, observed in the first part of the trilogy that:

> In recalling these leaden abominations of savage Russian life, I sometimes ask myself if it is worth speaking of it. And, with renewed conviction, I answer myself that it is worth it; for this is the tenacious, foul truth, and it has not to this day breathed its last. This is that truth which must be known to its very roots, so that it can be torn by the roots out of one's memory, out of the soul of man, out of all this painful and disgraceful life of ours.
>
> And there is another, more positive reason compelling me to depict these abominations. Although they are repulsive, although they suffocate us, crushing the majority of beautiful souls to death, the Russian man is nevertheless so healthy and young in his soul that he tries to and will overcome them.[49]

Characteristic here is the rupture between the plane of representation ('cruel truth', 'leaden abominations') and the plane of expression ('optimism, faith in the people' and 'revolutionary romanticism'). Sologub refused to read this rupture. Gorky was to repeat the same tirade in *My Apprenticeship*, strengthening it with sarcasm, as if in direct reply to Sologub:

> Why do I tell of these abominations? Why, so you could know, dear sirs, that this is not over, not passed! You like invented terrors, horrors prettily told, what is terrible in a fantastic way troubles you pleasantly. But I know what is truly terrible, horrible in an everyday way, and I have the undeniable right to trouble you unpleasantly with stories about it, so that you remember how you live and what you live in.
>
> It is a foul and nasty life that we all live, and that is the fact of the matter! I love people greatly and would not want to torment anyone, but one must not be sentimental and one must not hide the terrible truth in the flowery little words of a pretty lie. To life, to life! We must dissolve into it everything there is of the good and human in our hearts and minds.[50]

With a surprising sensitivity, Donskoi maintains and reproduces this bipolarity of Gorky's 'method', and truly maintains a 'fidelity to the essence of the original'.[51] It is a combination of 'leaden abominations', 'faith in mankind' and 'revolutionary romanticism'. Accordingly, we will call this 'method' leaden romanticism.

In his autobiography Donskoi recalled that, arriving at the Lenfilm studios in the 1920s, he began production on a short experimental film, *The Fop* (*Pizhon*). The experiment consisted of professional actors playing out their roles right on Nevsky Prospect, with passers-by who suspected nothing and all the film equipment hidden. The experiment (a film 'like the flow of life') did not succeed; on two days in a row actors were beaten up by passers-by.

> Later [Donskoi recalled], when the enthusiasm for 'the flow of life' had passed, I began to understand that it is necessary to relate this 'trueness to life' in artistic works, and that subject to knowledge of life, the penetration of the regulated flow into the 'flow of life' becomes the artistic truth of life.[52]

One could say that the 'regulated flow' for Donskoi is not simply a universal law of art. Here the rules of his realism are formed.

'Mark Donskoi's trilogy was a unique work in the cinematography of the 1930s', writes the Soviet film historian Khaniutin.

> Perhaps not in a single other film did the screen raise to such cruel, merciless truth the depiction of Russian pre-revolutionary life . . . The director, following the writer, places 'truth higher than pity'. He mercilessly reveals the dull, meaningless, suffering existence, the pitiful envy, the patent malice of Russia's inhabitants.[53]

In this sense, Donskoi's trilogy joins the long list of 'adaptations of the classics' of the 1930s, in which the recent past of Russian life was presented to viewers in its most terrifying aspect.

'Donskoi's realism' cannot be understood outside the context of the aim which these 'adaptations' fulfilled in the 1930s. Revealing the 'general purpose, defining both the fundamentally ideological-political schema and the culturological orientation of the adaptations', E. Levin defines the character and meaning of the works that were being put on the screen thus:

> The distance between the past and the present is artificially truncated, history is deprived of length and depth, not to mention the distinctive features of different periods; they were all the same, like twins, in all past times one and the same thing happened – the class struggle, scientifically realised, being realised, or – in times long before the October Revolution – not realised by their participants. The adaptations repeated in one voice: remember, all this was not long ago at all, and in the 1930s, actually on cinema screens, and not only there, psychological time prevailed over chronological time – the time of direct experience of the combined burdensome past as the biography of yesterday's events. October liberated the country from it, but in order to evaluate its abundance, it is necessary over and over again to recognise oneself in Katerina, Larisa, Efimov the musician, to be horrified by the closeness of one's own destruction, the inevitability of yesterday, which passed by like a terrible dream which visits one every night.

In the background of this 'black yesterday', the 'bright tomorrow' of socialism was all the more attractive, while the 'burdens of the present' found justification and meaning. Here we come up against the basic paradox of the screen adaptations of the 1930s; the mechanism for modernising the past could be called 'modernisation in reverse', in so far as pre-revolutionary reality looks here like the 'absolute past'. 'Epicisation' was also an expression of actuality, the world of the past which turned out after the revolution to be 'pre-historic'. In this form, Levin writes, it is presented to the viewer as:

> a perfectly static, immobile world. There is no kind of internal movement in it, no noticeable signs of development, it is as if it has ossified, to be destroyed from within. In these films we almost never find authentic historical time, the depth and breadth of life's real content; their time is the typological, conditional calendar of the struggle between light and darkness, local correlations and so on and so forth – only signs of a given social life, external indicator-characteristics, signals for the identification of the time of the action at its primary source – in a word, marking.[54]

The world of 'leaden abominations', so expressively painted by Donskoi, was also filled with just such a type of 'marking'. This is, however, only the functional aspect of 'Donskoi's realism'. The director himself discovered a means of 'marking' 'terrible reality'. Aesthetic aims changed in 1930s, but the methods founded by Donskoi remained.

> Most often of all it seems that the world of *Gorky's Childhood* was passed through the prism of the vision of a myopic person or a mole. Nowhere does Donskoi allow himself to break out into fresh air. He confines us together with Alyosha in a crowded, overstrained space.[55]

This space of 'Donskoi's realism', which proved to be such a strong influence on post-war European cinematography, especially Italian neorealism, is formed from fully defined visual solutions, which are always strongly characterologically concentrated.

This is evident, above all, in the defined characteristics of the portraits. Thus, on the screen we see all the time people who have not brushed their dirty, dishevelled hair (it seems that nobody here apart from the grandmother ever brushes their hair) – a constant characteristic of the portraits of all the heroes, as are their flabby, sleepy faces, hollow cheeks, dull eyes, rotten teeth and dirty hands with broken fingers. All these portrait details were 'registered' by Donskoi and picked out.

It is also apparent in the definite style of their clothing. People here go about in unimaginable rags. Of course, Gorky talks of the poverty in which Alyosha himself and those around him live, but Donskoi reinforces its signs from film to film in such a way that, already by the time of *My Universities*, the main characters go around in shirts, coats and shoes, more than a quarter of whose fabric is taken up with holes. Since here there is not even a hint of anyone ever taking off these clothes or washing them, it is often even impossible to say definitively what the characters are wearing. These 'clothes' could be more accurately described as filthy, greasy rags.

We also see it in the specifics of the sets. The action is always played out in semi-darkness, either in basements or sheds, with overhanging ceilings and floors which differ little from dirty streets, on which stand either old trunks or bedsteads, on which, instead of mattresses, there lie heaps of filthy rags. If there is furniture, it is more like debris – a chair missing a leg here, a wobbly table there. Amidst all this splendour there are always dirty pots with remains of food, basins full of washing up, buckets. This space, both in the composition and quality of the signs which fall within one's field of vision, and in the details of their description, strongly recall Pliushkin's house from Gogol's *Dead Souls*. And if everything here is not covered with cobwebs, it is only because there are people everywhere. People, however, do not live here, but creep about. They lie around on piles of rags and, without fail fight, or in the best case, curse. We can observe the same set in *Childhood*, at the grandfather's house, on the ship on which Alyosha serves in *My Apprenticeship* and in the Marusovka lodging houses, which become 'Universities' for the hero . . .

It is also present, finally, in certain 'landscape solutions'. Usually in the trilogy attention is drawn to the role of the countryside, in particular the Volga. If the river is a 'poetic' image linked with the 'romantic' side of Gorky-Donskoi's style, then the urban landscape is the chief space of 'leaden abominations'. The street in Donskoi is a special image. It, like the majority of other visual images, is anti-aesthetic. We are always in some sort of outskirts of the town, with rickety streetlamps, broken fences, broken-up roadways and unpaved sidewalks with all sorts of potholes, huge puddles and an unbelievable amount of dust. Drunks loll about in the filth and dust. On Donskoi's streets there are almost no clean clothes or normal people going about their business. It is a sort of panopticon; here cripples and the destitute pass by, drunks roam about, children run along barefoot (in rags from childhood). Children throw stones at the poor, janitors beat drunks over the head with stones, innkeepers drive out cripples like mangy dogs and so on. But the main thing on the streets is, of course, houses. They, it seems, grew up from the earth and stand forever crooked. Moreover, the camera usually moves at basement and ground floor level, so that the facades are almost never visible. This links the streets with the yards, rendering the facades transparent. In Donskoi's work the yard is no different from the street. The facade is seen as if in cross-section. The absence of the vertical aspect of the facade is compensated for by the 'panoramic' nature of the yard. Donskoi's yards are constructed like 'microscopic sections' of society. The entrance – the space between the street and the yard – is Donskoi's favourite space. His streets and yards – and that means entrances – have peeling plaster, cornices broken into pieces, stains on cracked walls, puddles of slops, broken staircases and balconies which look as though they are on the point of collapse. And against this background, an insane student is yelling about 'the greatness of the human spirit'. . .

'Today, when you watch the beginning of the film *My Universities*,' Khaniutin writes, '[with its] panorama through the windows of Marusovka (slop buckets, a husband beating his wife, a deacon with a hangover, a barrel-organ in a gateway), it seems as though it was produced after the films of early neorealism.'[56]

This was not, however, 'neorealism', but socialist realism, although the situation of a man 'cast out of his own biography' is similar. Socialist realism began the attempt to overcome the rupture between man and his biography only by means of a narrative-genre solution to the 'problem of the fate of the individual in history'. Mandelshtam connected the fate of the novel with this problem. His prognosis was inauspicious: 'The subsequent fate of the novel will be none other than the history of the breakdown of biography as a form of personal existence, and even more than breakdown – the catastrophic death of biography.' Mandelshtam ascertained the 'powerlessness of psychological motives when faced by real forces', and concluded: 'The contemporary novel has suddenly lost both its plot, that is, the individual who acts in the time belonging to the plot, and its psychology, since it [the plot] no longer gives a reason for any actions.'[57]

The fates of Alyosha Peshkov, Gorky's books and Donskoi's films demonstrate that in the age of a 'flood in history' (to use Mandelshtam's words), the individual maintains his or her freedom. Life overflows the banks of genre. Depending little on genre and narrative strategies (means of 'graphy'), it separates itself, as it were, from 'framing' time and outgrows the urgent cultural and ideological aims. It sets forth into novelistic 'great time', the time of history.

And this is where our encounter with it awaits us.

NOTES

1. Maksim Gor'kii, *Sobranie sochinenii v 30 tomakh*, Vol. 13, Moscow: GIKhL, 1951, p. 641.
2. Osip Mandel'shtam, 'Konets romana', *Sochineniia v 2 tomakh*, Vol. 2, Moscow: Khudozhestvennaia literatura, 1990, pp. 203–4.
3. Viktor Shklovskii, *Udachi i porazheniia Maksima Gor'kogo*, Gomel', 1926, p. 9.
4. See Andrew Barratt, 'Maksim Gorky's Autobiographical Trilogy: The Lure of Myth and the Power of Fact', *Journal of the Australasian Universities Language and Literature Association*, No. 80 (November 1993).
5. M. Gor'kii, *Moi universitety. Sobranie sochinenii v 16 tomakh*, Vol. 9, Moscow: Ogonek, 1979, p. 308.
6. On the mythology of childhood in Russian literature, see Andrew Wachtel, *The Battle for Childhood: Creation of a Russian Myth*, Stanford, CA: Stanford University Press, 1990.
7. Boris Eikhenbaum, *Molodoi Tolstoi*, Petersburg, Berlin: Izd. I. Grzhebina, 1922, p. 58.
8. Ibid.

9. Ibid., p. 59.
10. Ibid., p. 60.
11. Ibid., p. 72.
12. *Gor'kii i sovetskie pisateli. Neizdannaia perepiska. Literaturnoe nasledstvo*, Vol. 70, Moscow: Izd. AN SSSR, 1963, p. 323.
13. S. Rybak, *U istokov lichnosti: Mir detstva v izobrazhenii A. M. Gor'kogo*, Kishinev: Lumina, 1970, p. 183.
14. M. Gor'kii, *Sobranie sochinenii v 30 tomakh*, Vol. 26, p. 161.
15. V. Desnitskii, *A. M. Gor'kii: Ocherk zhizni i tvorchestva*, Moscow: GIKhL, 1959, p. 333.
16. Ibid., p. 338.
17. M. Gor'kii, *Detstvo. Sobranie sochinenii v 16 tomakh*, Vol. 8, Moscow: Ogonek, 1979, p. 214.
18. M. Gor'kii, *V liudiakh. Sobranie sochinenii v 16 tomakh*, Vol. 9, Moscow: Ogonek, 1979, p. 6.
19. Characteristically, it is only at the end of *My Apprenticeship* that the author informs us that Alyosha has turned thirteen. Until this point in the text, there has been no indication of the age of the child.
20. G. Vinokur, *Biografiia i kul'tura*, Moscow: GAKhN, p. 49.
21. Ibid., p. 51.
22. Ibid., p. 53.
23. Ibid., pp. 53, 76.
24. Ibid., p. 78.
25. E. B. Tager, *Tvorchestvo Gor'kogo sovetskoi epokhi*, Moscow: Nauka, 1964, pp. 44, 64. See also S. Kastorskii, *Gor'kii-khudozhnik: Ocherki*, Moscow, Leningrad: GIKhL, 1963, pp. 100–3.
26. Ilya Gruzdev, *Gor'kii*, Moscow: Molodaia gvardiia, 1958, p. 212.
27. Ibid., p. 235.
28. A. Miasnikov, *M. Gor'kii. Ocherki tvorchestva*, Moscow: GIKhL, 1953, p. 405.
29. On the socialist realist *Bildungsroman* see Hans Günther, 'Education and Conversion: The Road to the New Man in the Totalitarian Bildungsroman'. In Hans Günther (ed.), *The Culture of the Stalin Period*, London: McMillan, 1990; Katerina Clark, *The Soviet Novel: History as Ritual*, Chicago, IL: University of Chicago Press, 1981. It is worth mentioning that the genre diffusion of autobiography which occurred under Gorky's influence went far beyond the confines of Gorky's work. With characteristic energy, Gorky undertook to extend his own experiment. Alongside two enormous cultural projects of the 1930s, the series *The Lives of Remarkable People* and *History of a 19th Century Young Man* (*Istoriia molodogo cheloveka XIX stoletiia*), Gorky was tirelessly engaged in publicising autobiographies. With his counsel, and often with his immediate help, were created Ivan Volnov's *Tale of the Days of My Life* (*Povest' o dniakh moei zhizni*), Semyon Podyachev's *My Life* (*Moia zhizn'*), Alexei Chapygin's *My Life* (*Zhizn' moia*), Fyodor Gladkov's autobiographical trilogy, Fyodor Shaliapin's *Pages of My Life* (*Stranitsy moei zhizni*) and so on. See in particular M. F. Pakhomova, *Avtobiograficheskie povesti F. V. Gladkova i traditsii M. Gor'kogo*, Moscow, Leningrad: Nauka, 1966.
30. On the significance of hagiographical canon in new Russian literature and in the forms of its development, see Margaret Ziolkowski, *Hagiography and Modern Russian Literature*, Princeton, NJ: Princeton University Press, 1988.
31. See Hans Günther, *Der sozialistische Übermensch: Maksim Gor'kij und der sowjetische Heldenmythos*, Stuttgart, Weimar: J. B. Metzler, 1993; and Katerina Clark, *The Soviet Novel: History as Ritual*, Chicago, IL: University of Chicago Press, 1981.
32. Dmitry Likhachev, *Chelovek v literature Drevnei Rusi*, Moscow: Nauka, 1970, p. 128.

33. Ibid., p. 76.
34. Ibid., p. 26.
35. Ibid., p. 29.
36. Ibid., p. 73.
37. Ibid., p. 104.
38. Iu. Khaniutin, 'S distantsii vremeni'. In *Mark Donskoi*, Moscow: Iskusstvo, 1973, p. 53.
39. Al'ber Servoni, 'Gor'kii snova i navsegda'. In *Mark Donskoi*, p. 64. See also Albert Cervoni, *Marc Donskoy*, Paris: Seghers, 1966.
40. Likhachev, *Chelovek v literature Drevnei Rusi*, pp. 131–2.
41. Ibid., p. 132.
42. See *Istoki russkoi belletristiki: Vozniknovenie zhanrov siuzhetnogo povestvovaniia v drevnerusskoi literaure*, Leningrad: Nauka, 1970, pp. 67–8.
43. André Devalles, 'Esetika dobra'. In *Mark Donskoi*, pp. 211, 214.
44. Gor'kii, *V liudiakh*, p. 296.
45. Ibid., p. 227.
46. Mark Donskoi, 'O sebe i o svoem vremeni'. In *Mark Donskoi*, p. 20.
47. Varvara Massalitinova, 'Na s'emkakh *Detstva*'. In *Mark Donskoi*, pp. 226–7.
48. Quoted in Desnitskii, *A. M. Gor'kii: Ocherki zhizni i tvorchestva*, p. 351.
49. Gor'kii, *Detstvo*, p. 376.
50. Gor'kii, *V liudiakh*, pp. 298–9.
51. Khaniutin, 'S distantsii vremeni', p. 51.
52. Donskoi, *O sebe i svoem prizvanii*, p. 17.
53. Khaniutin, 'S distantsii vremeni', p. 49.
54. E. Levin, 'Ekranizatsiia: Istorizm, mifografiia, mifologiia (K tipologii obshchestvennogo soznaniia i khudozhestvennogo myshleniia)'. In *Ekrannye iskusstva i literatura: Zvukovoe kino*, Moscow: Nauka, 1994, p. 82.
55. Al'ber Servoni, 'Gor'kii snova i navsegda'. In *Mark Donskoi*, p. 64.
56. Ibid., pp. 50–1.
57. O. Mandel'shtam, *Slovo i kul'tura*, Moscow: Sovetskii pisatel, 1987, pp. 74–5.

5. THREE MOTHERS: PUDOVKIN – DONSKOI – PANFILOV

There's no honour in secret business.

Maxim Gorky, *Mother*

A Timely Book/Untimely Thoughts (Gorky-Dostoevsky: 1906)

Maxim Gorky's novel *Mother* (*Mat'*) must be read exclusively in the academy edition of his collected works. Moreover, one should start at the end – with the extensive commentaries, where, in great detail, in close-set brevier over almost a hundred pages, practically every reference to the novel from letters and memoirs is reprinted. The greater part of these letters are from Gorky himself. They contain assessments of the novel over various years. Almost all of them range from negative to death-dealing. There is practically nothing positive or even semi-positive. Gorky was a writer who knew his own worth; with the years his self-esteem (like the status of Gorky himself) only grew, until it reached truly fantastic proportions. But all the same, his assessment (to be more precise, self-assessment) of the novel did not change over the years. He must have been firmly convinced of the novel's absolute failure to have judged it in this way:

> I wrote *Mother* in the summer of 1906 in America, without any materials; that's why it turned out so badly.

> *Mother* is a truly awful book, written as an agitational work after 1906, when I was 'quick-tempered and irritable'. I would suggest that – to a certain extent – although it achieved its aims, that still does not make it any better than it is.

> It is not the done thing for a writer to foist his opinions on the reader, but all the same allow me to say to you that *Mother* is one of my least successful books.

I think that the book is not one of my successes. It's chaotic, lacking internal harmony, put together with obvious negligence and without the necessary respect for style. If I had to write a critique on Gorky, it would be the most vicious and merciless.

Mother is an unsuccessful thing, not only outwardly, as it's long, boring and carelessly written, but the main thing is it's not democratic enough.

The longer I go on, the more I dislike *Mother*.[1]

Let us consider what is in essence a startling fact. Gorky is talking about a book which occupies an extremely special place in Soviet literature, the book which was declared the first work of socialist realism, and which became not simply canonical, but protocanonical; strictly speaking, the socialist realist canon begins with *Mother*. And here we have the creator of this novel, the 'founder of socialist realism' himself, not pulling any punches and abusing it in foul language.

Every child in the Soviet territories knew this book and therefore one can say that it is an inalienable part of the collective memory of many generations of Soviet people. Lenin's characterisation of it as a 'timely book' was the subject of constant jokes. Everybody knew the book, but at the same time it remained unread, as Gorky himself remained unread. Meanwhile, it is an amazingly jolly book. Its characters are always jesting, apparently playing about ('Happily, as if boasting of childish pranks, Sofia began to tell mother about her revolutionary work . . . Mother listened to her tales, laughing and looking at her tenderly'[2]). There are no serious relationships or passions in the novel – everything is apparently done for fun. It is a merry sort of underground. Here there are no serious enemies, and it is almost incomprehensible why it is, strictly speaking, underground – nobody is even apparently in hiding. Revolutionary activities are described as jolly escapades which pull the wool over the eyes of stupid detectives. It is unclear why the latter do not find the revolutionaries – probably because they are only pretending to look and are not serious. Here, to use Nilovna's words, 'everybody is ours.' Here things are good for everyone everywhere (even in prison). They all speak warmly about one another: 'It's good to be with you!'; 'You're a good chap!'; 'What a good chap you are!'; 'Do you know how good it is to be with you?'; 'How kind you are' . . . Every dialogue (and this novel is made up of dialogues) is packed with such utterances. The characters are apparently ashamed of their roles and their words. They are always, it would seem, somehow embarrassed – by improbable sentimentality and excessive emotion.

This novel is – undoubtedly – a counter-*Devils* (*Besy*), given the obsessive ideological hostility of Gorky towards Dostoevsky, and given the manifest impossibility of 'overcoming' Dostoevsky. As a counterbalance to the revolutionaries' world in Dostoevsky – a world of treachery, murder, dishonour and provocation – in Gorky, the world in which the revolutionaries move is a world of goodness. This goodness and falsity stunned contemporary criticism:

> The endless virtue of Gorky's heroes and heroines depresses the reader. There is no life in the novel, but instead something is performed in front of you that is not quite a rite, and not quite a mass. There is much grandeur, a great deal of incense, a lot of anointing oil, and moreover both the grandeur and the oil are somehow special, social-democratic. But the reader is not in the least put at ease by this. And, wearied by the excessive length of the service, he not without pleasure abandons the stifling temple, so as to commune anew with the vanities of the world, to feel again the joy of its rich variety and complexity of experience.[3]

> *Mother* serves as a clear illustration of the false-sentimental period in the writer's work . . . he paints a picture of a joyous idyll of contemporary relations arising out of the foundations of the workers' movement, and paints it in the sort of colours which you come across on popular cheap prints, but which are not generally to be found on the palate of a true artist. Such sugar-coating, such an attempt to fit the tone to the characters, such neglect of spiritual processes and delights before the lovey-doveyness of the relationships, we have not until now been forced to read in the works of Mr Gorky . . . what has been written up to now only shows how a great talent can be broken by the aspiration to master not what corresponds to his mood, but the task suggested by the times.[4]

So, a 'timely book'. But nevertheless there is in it an eternal, extra-temporal (and therefore always 'untimely') idea. After all, the most prohibited idea for Soviet consciousness – 'Dostoevskiism' – relates to the novel. It is interesting that in a novel about revolutionaries there are no 'non-Russians'. Vasily Lvov-Rogachevsky openly wondered at this in his letter to Gorky: 'Why amongst such a mass of revolutionaries have you not depicted a single Jewish revolutionary? They really played an enormous role in the movement.' No, he did not 'depict' them. He had written a 'Russian revolutionary novel'. Gorky did not convey any 'Dostoevskiism', any 'baseness' to anyone. (We will recall that in his article on 'Karamazovism', he defined both that and 'Dostoevskiism' as a whole as 'a generalisation of the negative signs and attributes of the Russian national character'[5].) There is in the novel, undoubtedly, a scene 'from Dostoevsky' – the murder of Isai (a traitor in the factory). This is not a 'frenzied murder' (which would have been understandable), and although it is not planned, it is premeditated. Introducing into the novel the motif of such a murder, Gorky links Dostoevskiism to his least sympathetic character, Rybin ('a peasant, and that means a slave',[6] in Gorky's own words). There is an astonishing scene in the novel. Rybin asks the revolutionaries for some 'literature', and announces that when the gendarmes appear, he will 'palm' the proclamations and pamphlets off on to the schoolteacher, so that she will be arrested ('why should I pity the gentry!'). Pavel is indignant at the 'dishonesty' of such an act. Rybin answers him reasonably, as a peasant: 'your thinking's too green, brother! There's no honour in secret business.'[7] These final words could stand as the epigraph to the history of the 'revolutionary movement'.

The artificiality of style, the unconvincing nature of the speech and behaviour of the characters were only derived from the impossibility of coping with the loftiness of the task. Gorky is so unconvincing in *Mother* because he wanted to prove the unprovable: that 'secret business' and 'honour' were compatible. In essence, this is indeed a novel about the honour and worthiness of revolutionaries – this is why they declaim, this is why they live a totally 'unsecret life'. Did Gorky know what a really secret life was – the murky life of 'underground people'? He knew very well and depicted it with genius, on quite another artistic level than in *Mother*. Only in his stories did he enter into a polemic with Dostoevsky and turn all his 'devils' – the characters of *Karamora*, *The Tale of a Hero* (*Rasskaz o geroe*), *The Life of a Useless Man* (*Zhizn' nenuzhnogo cheloveka*), *The Old Man* (*Starik*), right up to *The Life of Klim Samgin* (*Zhizn' Klima Samgina*) – into . . . counter-revolutionaries: detectives, spies, provocateurs. It was they, according to Gorky, who were the real 'devils'. And so, in *Mother*, the revolutionaries were turned into 'anti-devils'; but then in other, definitely more convincing works by Gorky, the counter-revolutionaries (also 'secret people') are turned into real 'devils' à la Dostoevsky. It turned out that the world of Dostoevsky, the world of devilry, was transferred in Gorky to the opposite social pole.

Gorky refused to see revolutionaries as 'superfluous people'; on the contrary, the 'superfluous people' for him were the counter-revolutionaries. He turned them into 'grand inquisitors', he sees in them black 'Karamazovism', he makes them (and not the revolutionaries, who are without exception happy people full of integrity) unhappy, spiteful, 'underground people', real 'enemies of life' (as Gorky considered Dostoevsky himself). It is precisely reactionary (and not revolutionary) ideas which, according to Gorky, corrode the personality; people decay (even physically, as with one of the heroes of *The Life of a Useless Man*), and moral putrefaction infects everything around. They (and not the revolutionaries) are blackguards, the lumpenproletariat, human garbage; they are the real villains, people with obvious criminal tendencies, sadists and scum, misanthropes, not even hiding this from themselves ('I'll kick the bucket soon', cries the 'decaying' hero of *The Life of a Useless Man*. 'I've got no one to be afraid of, I'm alien to life – I live in hate of good people.'[8]). These people are finished. Being near them is not without its dangers in any respect.

The astonishing thing is that both were right: Dostoevsky in his depiction of revolutionaries; Gorky in his depiction of 'counter-revolutionaries'. Gorky was 'incorrect' only in *Mother*, where for the first time he experimented with the direct recoding of Dostoevsky. It turned out badly, artistically unconvincingly; the 'forbidden people' (from both sides!) could be only 'underground' people. The twentieth century proved this in terrible fashion. The Gulag became a kind of materialisation of the subconscious of Dostoevsky's 'underground people', when they came out from underground; Auschwitz became the materialisation of the subconscious of the reactionaries when they came into power. Dostoevsky's rightness, understood by Gorky, cost him dear; he had to stop depicting revolutionaries. After this (*Mother* served as a good lesson), Gorky decided to depict reality not as a counterbalance to Dostoevsky, but exactly according to Dostoevsky – only changing the object of representation.

The Life of a Useless Man was written straight after *Mother* as a counterbalance, a counterpoint. (They have practically nothing in common.) It is as if the author decided this time to show the 'reverse side' of *Mother* – those who turned up on the other side of the barricades in the first Russian Revolution. It proved to be pure 'Dostoevskiism', something completely opposite to *Mother*. But was it really the opposite? In a letter to Alexander Amfiteatrov, Gorky described how one spy read *The Life of a Useless Man*: 'We Russians, he says, are by nature traitors! Revolutionaries serve as spies, spies work in the ranks of revolutionaries – is it really possible?' 'I would suggest that in this he's right – it's impossible', Gorky concluded.[9] But, as it turned out, something else was impossible as well: 'It is impossible', responding to *Karamora*, Alexander Voronsky asserted in the pages of *Pravda* in 1926, 'it is impossible to write so ambiguously about provocateurs, impossible, especially here in Russia.'[10] In what did the ambiguity and 'untimeliness' of Gorky's idea consist? Was this 'ambiguity' expressed, as always in Gorky, by the most 'inappropriate' character and in the most 'inappropriate' situation – in the detective's conversation with his prostitute lover?

'You catch them, catch them, and they won't die out!' she said lazily.
The detective grinned and replied importantly:
'You don't understand politics, that's why you talk rubbish, my dear! We don't want at all to destroy these people completely – they're like sparks for us and they have to show us where exactly the fire is starting . . . It's a very subtle game.'[11]

Analysing this 'subtle game' seven decades later, Michel Foucault came to the conclusion that power only creates an illusion of the struggle against criminality. In effect, it actually creates a secret criminal army in the reserve of the secret police, and precisely through this army controls the whole of society. In other words, whilst asserting legality, power creates forms of antilegality (criminal and political) directed by it, through which total control over society is realised. Incidentally, from this perspective revolutionaries turn out to be provocateurs against their will, in so far as they are the very same 'sparks' which illuminate the entire 'underground' for the authorities. Be that as it may, the world of 'forbidden people' is united; the State (and even more so, the police state) cannot exist without dissidence and 'revolutionaries', whilst 'political criminals' and the secret police are a single organism.

Having agreed – evidently even against his own will – that 'there's no honour in secret business' (and it was this in particular which determined his hostility to the revolution which took place in Russia in 1917; *Untimely Thoughts* (*Nesvoevremennye mysli*) can easily be read as a rebellion against the victory of 'Dostoevskiism' – amongst the 'people' and the 'revolutionaries'[12]), Gorky wrote no more novels about revolutionaries. *Mother* remained a monument to Gorky's aesthetic mistake (aesthetic par excellence, since his ideological opposition to Dostoevsky only grew). It is significant that precisely this novel ended up being the foundation of socialist realism. Yuri Tynianov wrote: 'Every deformity, every "error", every "anomaly" of normative poetics is – potentially – a new principle of construction.'[13] And, we would add, perhaps more than one. *Mother* began to live a life of its own, separate from the author: the life of a political and cultural myth.

The Film: An Untimely Book/Timely Thoughts (Gorky-Pudovkin: 1926)

The mythology of *Mother* gained the fullest possible development in Soviet culture. This entirely constructed myth not only condensed the fundamental problematics of Soviet culture – the heroisation of the revolution, the victory of political consciousness over unconsciousness, the history of 'reforging' and 'ideological growth'. Its uniqueness consists in its 'transhistoricism' – in the fact that this 'artefact' (the novel and its screening) is unified and multifaceted; through its 'screening', the novel itself passed through all the stages of 'reforging' and 'ideological growth'. It is worth remembering that there were at least several Soviet cultures; the epoch of the 1920s differed enormously from the epoch of the 1950s, which in its turn differed from that of the 1980s. These milestones, so to speak, marked out the different political, ideological and aesthetic stages of Soviet history. *Mother* was reflected in each of these mirrors.

The motives which led Gorky to get down to work on his 'timely book' are well known. Let us think, however, about why twenty years later (and then thirty years after that, and then another thirty . . .) it was still in demand. In his review of Pudovkin's film, Shklovsky declared that 'revolution in the USSR is now the most cultured client.'[14] From this assertion it follows that the Revolution (read: the new authorities) was alone in a position to oppose the commercialisation of art. We will recall that the true flowering of propaganda art and, in particular, cinema, was connected precisely with the period of the New Economic Policy (NEP). But it was not only utilitarian-propaganda projects that arose out of the influence, unique in its intensity and power, of the mythologisation of the Revolution in the second half of the 1920s, in the period when not only a new leader, but also a new system of power were being formed in the country. *Strike, Battleship Potemkin, October, Mother, The End of*

St Petersburg, Storm Over Asia, The Arsenal . . . the revolutionary uprising had to be represented, finally, as history. This historicisation turned the Revolution into an allusion, deprived of its place in the present. The contribution of 'revolutionary cinema' to the cause of turning the Revolution into history towards the end of the 1920s was enormous. At the beginning of the 1920s the Revolution was still perceived as spontaneously continuing in the eyes of contemporaries, but by the beginning of the next decade it had already been turned into the complete past and historical myth. Here we have the most important ideological and socio-psychological premises of the Stalinist dictatorship.[15]

Pudovkin, conforming fully to avant-garde aesthetics, saw his task as 'collecting around the theme powerful visual cinematographic images'.[16] Revolutionary art is constructed on symbols; the metaphors and symbols of Eisenstein, Pudovkin and Dovzhenko entered all the textbooks. The symbol, in its turn, is based on a process of concentration. Here little is 'shown' and even less is 'said', demanding a great deal of work from the viewer. This strategy is diametrically opposed to that of Gorky's novel. One reviewer of those years wrote that the film 'does not have the usual "far-fetched" ideology, here the whole atmosphere is full of irresistibly convincing ideas.'[17] One could say that to the extent that the picture does not have a 'far-fetched ideology' and that it is concentrated on the idea, it contains nothing of the novel, which consists entirely of 'far-fetched ideology'. Pudovkin was very cautious when he spoke of the film's links with the novel:

> We wanted, if one can express it like this, to feed on the novel in our artistic work on the creation of screenplays and pictures . . . We wanted to go into the novel, to live in it, to breathe its air, to drive blood saturated with its atmosphere through our veins.[18]

Fortunately, Pudovkin did not manage to become saturated with the atmosphere of the novel; that is why he creates a picture of genius which is in explicit conflict with the aesthetics of Gorky's novel.

Pudovkin expressed his aesthetic credo at the time of working on *Mother* with absolute clarity: 'As the actor is only one of the elements in the frame, only a subsidiary moment in the montage phrase; in relation to him the absolute dictatorship of the director's eye must be realised in full.'[19] It was exactly 'Pudovkin's eye' that Mikhail Romm later admired:

> Where did he find these people, how did he manage to convey without a single word whole chapters of Gorky's story in a single glance, a single turn, where does this authenticity come from, how did he sense the air of the revolutionary workers' underground?[20]

Here, it is quite likely, there is even an unconscious aberration; 'Gorky's story' in general did not convey the atmosphere of the 'revolutionary workers' underground'. M. F. Andreeva recalled that at the same fifth congress of the Russian Social Democratic Workers' Party, at which Lenin spoke to Gorky about his book, it was quite energetically discussed in the breaks, but the worker-delegates thought that in it 'everything was depicted more elegantly than in life.'[21] It is worth remembering, however, that 'life' and the book generally had a complex relationship in Gorky. Thus, one of the most improbable points in the book, Pavel's speech to the court – a kind of mixture of *The Communist Manifesto* with 'Song of the Stormy Petrel' – was 'reality'. The prototype of Pavel Vlasov, the worker Pyotr Zalomov, really did give a speech at the trial of the Sormovo demonstrators which was edited by . . . Gorky. As we have already stated, the 'distortion' of reality in the novel was the result of the aesthetic experiment aimed at overcoming Dostoevsky, and in this sense was fully conscious, although also fatal for the book.

The fact that the question of literary origins is raised here is not at all accidental; criticism said in chorus that Pudovkin's film was 'pure cinema'. The contribution of Pudovkin, as 'adaptor', was regarded above all else as him having triumphed in the struggle with hateful 'literature' on its own territory. (Not even Eisenstein made that contribution.) Shklovsky perceived in Pudovkin's film 'the gradual displacement of everyday situations by purely formal elements', so that in the end this initially 'prosaic' cinema becomes 'poetic'. '*Mother* is a peculiar centaur . . . the film begins in prose with persuasive captions which climb up the frame in quite a poor fashion, and ends with purely formal verse'; according to Shklovsky, 'plotless cinema is cinema in verse.'[22] In the 1920s Shklovsky simply did not yet know what constituted 'prosaic cinema', one of whose active participants, incidentally, he was himself to become in the epoch of socialist realism. It is cinema which has begun to talk and has simultaneously grown dumb; by turning to voice, it is deprived of the true language of film. Further discussion of this lies ahead.

For now we will turn our attention to another aspect of the problem. When plotlessness was in fashion, the screenwriter Natan Zarkhi, adapting Gorky's novel, was considered a 'plot man'; when plot came into fashion, Zarkhi began to be seen as a 'non-plotter'. This failure to adapt to the 'mainstream', this 'lack of timeliness' exposes an important peculiarity of Zarkhi's work; in the 1920s he said something important to his contemporaries about the cinema of tomorrow, while in the Stalinist epoch his approach to his material was too reminiscent of the past, of the avant-garde, revolutionary face of Soviet art.

Zarkhi said that he thought up the image of the mother, 'roughly speaking, in direct opposition to Gorky's image of the mother', in so far as Gorky's mother was 'from the very beginning a conscious woman'. That is why, Zarkhi said, the only thing the mother does in the first half of the screenplay is strive to save her family. As she is downtrodden and unconscious, catastrophe is inevitable. The motif of the 'unwilling traitor' becomes the critical moment.[23] Thus is born a conflict which is absent in Gorky; both mother and son begin their journey to the heights 'from a lower point than in the story'.[24] The father is placed on an even lower level, being transformed into a member of the pre-revolutionary anti-semitic organization, the Black Hundreds. The motif of the double murder (of the revolutionary and the Black Hundred, Mikhail Vlasov) appears in the film, imparting to the picture the features of a psychological drama, which in the end is transformed into tragedy.

And after all, as one critic asserted, a film becomes a social drama because its directors are interested not in the individual, but in typically recurring, socially significant features, as a result of which the film fits entirely within the general flow of the 'monumental, epic cinema of the twenties'. It seems the question is neither of orientation towards the typical, nor of interest in 'the recurring nature of the behaviour and motives of the actions of the characters, which enables them to represent the masses',[25] but precisely the fact that Gorky's story, in which elements of 'revolutionary romanticism' are intricately interwoven with melodrama, logically turns into a tragedy. We shall recall here that Zarkhi was not alone. The director also conceived of the film as a tragedy; Pudovkin would subsequently recall that the stimulus for the work was a picture which arose in the director's imagination of the corpse of a woman who had been torn to pieces by gendarmes on a railway station platform. Everything, as we can see, began from the ending – from the scene, which does not take place in the novel, of the death of Nilovna.

The author of the literary 'source' had given very little basis for such displacements in the plot. One critic, in raptures over the new engine of the plot which had been invented – 'the motif of the mother's tragic guilt', wrote:

> Nilovna, as created by Gorky, was fully prepared to commit treachery, if she thought it would save her son and deliver him from the negative influence of his friends. Treachery, based on a tragic misunderstanding, is not in conflict with the logic of the mother's character.[26]

The 'logic of the character', however, little occupied the author of the screenplay.

Pudovkin recalled 'Zarkhi's law', which the latter repeated many times: 'You can sometimes speak passionately about the simple, but always speak simply about the passionate.' 'For me', wrote Pudovkin, 'this law signified the greatest sensation of internal, versatile balance in the whole organism of the work of art; it signified a subtle sense of proportions, without which true culture does not exist.'[27] This is precisely what is completely missing from Gorky's text – subtlety and a sense of proportions. True, years later, Zarkhi would say to Nikolai Yezuitov, Pudovkin's biographer, that the end of the picture now seemed to him incorrect; the mother had to die, but the son should have remained alive in order to go forward to 1917 with the banner in his hands. Then the ornamental ending of the picture would not have been necessary.[28] The hero would have had to go on for a long time.

Lunacharsky was convinced: 'The bitter, tragic end of the film should not under any circumstances be exchanged for some sort of triumphant fanfare.

Our present revolution itself is the triumphant fanfare.'[29] Did the People's Commissar of Enlightenment notice that, even in the extensive literature on the film, for some reason nobody paid attention to an astonishing detail: in the final frame above the Kremlin's Palace of Soviets there is flying not simply a red flag, but exactly the same flag with the hole by the pole – the flag which the mother was carrying during the demonstration. This ideological ornamentalism was not simply another metaphor, but the product of a new social task and a new historical perspective.

> From the great *Mother* [said Pudovkin] a small child appeared – a new plot. Being deeply related along internal lines, this small child began to grow separately from the mother, like the essence daughterhood, repeating all her features but, in essence, in a completely new sense.[30]

But the film became a masterpiece because the adaptation of the plot was only part of the reworking of the whole 'artistic method' of the novel. In official Soviet culture, Gorky's *Mother* retained the status of the 'great *Mother*', but 'by the Hamburg rating' the 'great *Mother*' turned out to be in fact Pudovkin's film. Does this not explain the silence with which Gorky, having so loudly and publicly abused his novel, met the film?

It is worth noting that, just as the novel *Mother* was declared the first work of socialist realism, so Pudovkin's film was later also declared 'the first swallow of Soviet cinema': 'The Soviet feature film usually begins its genealogy precisely with *Mother*.'[31] The word 'usually' sounds awkward here – because it was not with Pudovkin, of course, but with Eisenstein, that Soviet cinema begins its 'genealogy'. Pudovkin, however, fitted better into the role of the 'founder' of socialist realism in the cinema, in so far as socialist realism needed a plot, a 'story of growth', and 'reforging' (precisely what Pudovkin brought to the screen via Gorky's novel); in so far, further, as Pudovkin was 'the first film director to place the actor at the centre of the film, to be concerned with the actor's ensemble'; in so far as even the 'unusual foreshortening' was in *Mother* the result not of 'formalistic trickery' (as in Eisenstein), but was 'justified by artistic necessity'; in so far, finally, as 'the new, complex devices of montage, applied for the first time in this film, were not for Pudovkin an end in themselves'.[32]

In a word, in the Stalinist epoch Pudovkin's film was consciously transferred into the socialist realist canon. The film was then criticised for the fact that it did not fit into this canon: for example, 'the tragedy, at times intensified by the naturalistic details in the scenes of the deaths of the metal worker Vlasov, his son Pavel and Nilovna, is alien to the ideological meaning of the work',[33] or the obvious 'formalistic trickery' contradicts 'artistic necessity' – the famous policeman who, according to the director's own admission, he 'used to good effect', just as Eisenstein 'used' the battleship. Here a socialist realist critic who was irreconcilable with formalism asserted that:

[I]t is precisely in the treatment of the figure of the policeman that not the best but on the contrary the weakest sides of the film are apparent. This character did not have to appear to be monumental; his monumentalism destroyed historical truth.[34]

Zarkhi's screenplay aroused even greater indignation: 'the incomplete mastery of the socialist realist method [in 1926! – E. D.] . . . is manifested in the fact that the screenwriter turned into excessive melodrama certain points of a stead-fast and severe book.'[35] But most of all the critics' dissatisfaction was mani-fested in the assessment of the reworking in the screenplay of the new role of Vlasov's father. Soviet criticism in 1952, at the high of the Stalinist anti-semitic campaign, could not forgive Natan Zarkhi for the fact that in ' "developing" the motif of the steel worker Vlasov's backwardness', he had turned him into a participant in the pogroms, as a member of the 'Black Hundreds':

> Gorky's Mikhail Vlasov was not, of course, a revolutionary, nor could he have become one. But the strength of internal protest [?!] alive within him, made him just as far from the 'Black Hundreds'. He is not by nature a bad man at all [?!]; he had gone wild from the terrible conditions of life. For all that Vlasov even tried in his own way to defend the dignity of man [?!], the reason for his alienation is precisely in this [?!]. The Russian worker-Black Hundred is in general an extremely atypical phenomenon [we must suppose that it was not Russians at all who joined the 'Union of the Russian People' – E. D.] . . . Therefore the interpretation given by Zarkhi is far more superficial than that contained in the book [a constant motif in the characterisation of Mikhail Vlasov in Gorky's book was that of the 'man-beast' – E. D.]. By turning the outline of the plot into melodrama, the author tried to oversimplify it.[36]

We have undertaken such a detailed re-examination of Pudovkin's film within Stalinist culture in order to clarify fully why the more time passed, the less *Mother* conformed to the principles of socialist realism. It was creating its own type of ideological and aesthetic niche, for a new, radical adaptation.

THE ADAPTATION: A TIMELY BOOK/TIMELY THOUGHTS (GORKY-DONSKOI: 1955)

The closer an adaptation to the literary original, the fewer its chances of success. The success of Pudovkin's film lay in the fact that it was not an adap-tation at all. Strictly speaking, an adaptation of *Mother* was accomplished half a century after the novel was first published, and three decades after Pudovkin's film – by Mark Donskoi.

A cultural niche for it had long been prepared. The time was not simply ripe for an adaptation – it was overripe. And for that reason it was a flop. Donskoi was three years too late. Had his film come out not in 1955, but in 1952, it could have anticipated quite a different reception. Donskoi's film was the first and only true adaptation of Gorky's story. The novel was understood precisely as being entirely 'timely' (which in Stalinist culture signified 'classical', and for that reason a museum-piece). All possible 'untimely thoughts' relating to its problematics were removed, except that the film itself turned out exactly at that time to be amazingly untimely.

In principle, its release was not accidental; readaptations of the classics at this time came out one after the other. In 1958 Vladimir Kaplunovsky filmed *The Captain's Daughter*, with a screenplay by the same Nikolai Kovarsky who refashioned *Mother* for Donskoi (readapting the 1928 version of *The Captain's Daughter*, titled *The Sergeant of the Guards* (*Gvardii serzhant*) by Yuri Tarich, with a screenplay by Viktor Shklovsky); the following year Alexei Batalov filmed *The Overcoat* (*Shinel'*) with a screenplay by Leonid Solovyov (as if in answer to Grigory Kozintsev and Leonid Trauberg's *Overcoat* of 1926, with Yuri Tynianov's screenplay); in 1961 a new adaptation of *The Cossacks* (*Kazaki*) was completed (director Vasily Pronin, screenplay Shklovsky), which 'replaced' Vladimir Barsky's *Cossacks* of 1928 with a screenplay by the same Shklovsky, and so on. Donskoi's *Mother* only opened this series. But it also, in a strange way, closed it; aesthetically Donskoi's film is a classic product of mature socialist realism in its post-war form, and should have been be positioned in the history of the cinema somewhere between *The Tale of the Siberian Lands* (*Skazanie o Zemle Sibirskoi*) and *Unforgettable 1919* (*Nezabyvaemyi 1919*). Yet it turned out that it was released only on the eve of 1956, when the stock of revolutionary cinema had risen sharply, and the stock, conventionally speaking, of Chiaureli and Pyrev was low. The fate of the two films by Pudovkin and Donskoi was quite unusual; one became the triumph of the great Pudovkin, the other the failure of the great Donskoi. But it is not the fate of these films which occupies us here. It is more important to see the aesthetic and social reasons and contexts for these 'victories' and 'defeats'.

Donskoi's picture was torn to pieces. If it had come out three years earlier, the reproaches which critics rained down on Donskoi would simply not have entered their minds. In essence, they tore the film apart because it was socialist realism. Let us listen to a benevolent (!) critic:

> Strange to say, the film lacks humour, and its characters have no slyness or mischief, it is monochrome, at times even ascetic . . . If there is no variety of nuances in the film, then Gorky's aphoristic, apt, rich speech, like proverbs, is also in places concealed. The text sounds 'neutral' . . . You also meet in the film individual displays of bad taste, sentimentality, which feel like alien impregnations in the general steadfast structure of the film.[37]

Unbenevolent criticism was much harsher. 'It was difficult for Zarkhi to write *Mother* after Gorky, but then he created a good screenplay from a novel of genius, having changed a great deal in it', wrote Shklovsky. 'It was easy for Kovarsky to write *Mother* after Gorky; he created a copy of the novel, but simultaneously everything was prepared by this screenplay for the reels to turn out to be mediocre.'[38] In fact, Pudovkin turned the novel (which was far from a work of genius, as Shklovsky himself understood) into a tragedy (which it was not at all – in it neither the son nor the mother dies), creating an emotionally and ideologically infectious film. Donskoi created a narrative-illustration, returning everything to the level of everyday life. Trying to repeat (and more-over surpass) Pudovkin and his earlier self, he followed Gorky's novel exactly as it is. Zarkhi overcame Gorky mainly because he 'reduced' its revolutionar-ies, who never shut up, thus uncovering the story: 'Father' – 'Mother' – 'Son'. The underground disappeared, and with it, the endless 'tea-drinking' with political conversations and 'emotions'. It was this 'socialist-realist' garrulous moralising underground that Donskoi reconstructed on the screen. The direc-tor followed Gorky out of habit, and the failure of the adaptation was guaran-teed by the quality of the book. It was not only a question of the 1956 'Thaw', as a result of which all socialist-realist 'artistic production' began to melt, like Pudovkin's ice on the river. Pudovkin tried to import into the novel 'timely' thoughts for his own time. He needed the novel like a cause, and this is why he and Zarkhi handled Gorky's text, which was so 'untimely' for them, so freely.

Donskoi was another matter. He was organically incapable of a similar treat-ment of Gorky. As Maya Turovskaya observed, in Donskoi's films there was 'a different emotion than that in the pictures of the Big Three, which were showing an immediately revolutionary breaking and alteration of conscious-ness. Mark Donskoi, having discovered Gorky, turned to deeper sources of the break that had occurred.' It was precisely thanks to Gorky that Donskoi:

> also discovered that variegated, wandering Rus' that is rising like yeast, which he himself found partly in his searches for his profession, place and meaning of life. It was opened up to Donskoi via Gorky and via Dostoevsky, whom he never filmed, but whom he apprehended thanks to the very same Gorky, confessionally and discursively.[39]

This is very true, but in relation above all to Donskoi's work on Gorky's auto-biographical trilogy.

In *Mother* fidelity to Gorky fatally undermined the director. The film was in colour, but Gorky's world in Donskoi's film was, strange though it may seem, lacking in the very colour for which the black-and-white trilogy had been notable. Life here had 'fermented' and already 'turned sour' – as if everything were already over. Pudovkin had had to pull events forward to the realisation of the aims of the mother and son – the flag the mother is carrying when she dies fluttered above the Kremlin twenty years later. Donskoi, on the other hand, had constantly, so to speak, to drag time backwards, to stylise 'the past', create it.

Pudovkin was one of those by whose efforts in the 1920s the Revolution was transformed into history. It ceased to be current; the era of the 'heirs' was thereby opened up. By the efforts of those same artists in the 1930s the Revolution was transformed definitively into epic. In the 1950s, there was a constant need for this museumised history to be revived – not at all for the legitimisation of power (which the regime no longer needed after the Great Terror and the victory in the Great Patriotic War), but for its demonstration.

Socialist realism needed exactly Gorky's 'bad' novel, with its moralising, its artificial 'spirit', its 'pathos', its melodrama, its psychological unreliability and indigestible 'revolutionary romanticism'. Socialist realism needed this operatic novel, where the heroes do not speak, but orate, pronouncing emotional 'arias' on the theme of the 'struggle for the rights of the working class'. Corresponding precisely to this were the blatant kitsch of Donskoi's landscapes, with their wild combination of fiery summer lightning, toxic-red sunsets and ultramarine skies; the interiors packed with objects, full of rubbish, with chests of drawers, some sort of little coloured nets, heavy curtains and table cloths; the inclusion of a voice-over by the narrator straight from the novel, in which the unpronounceable is pronounced – the emotional monologues about the great word 'comrade' or 'the people's disgraceful rags' and so on; the visual solution of the living bas-relief of the mother at the beginning, and her return to bas-relief at the end of the film – a bas-relief which could have adorned Gorkovskaya station on the Moscow metro (Donskoi found a radical solution to the end of Gorky's novel; his mother does not die, but is turned to stone, transformed into a monument to herself); the appearance of the participants in this production – clean workers in bleached and ironed shirts and neat jackets, the lady-revolutionaries all noble maidens in dresses with lace collars, singing 'Hostile Whirlwinds' (*Vikhri vrazhdebnye*) (in scenes like these Donskoi's revolutionaries are transformed into heroes of Sergei Gerasimov's *Young Guard*); the sentimentality, as a result of which the actors do now know how to behave in many scenes, being required endlessly first to kiss one another, then almost to play the fool in front of the camera, then to bow like peasants from the waist (and moreover more than once) – in a word, to act in a way that is not only psychologically unconvincing, but even inexplicable for grown-ups.

The fact is, however, that in reality Gorky's novel is just the same. Critics wanted Donskoi to 'embellish' it, something the director was organically incapable of doing. He was simply unable to repeat the success of his trilogy; in terms of quality, Gorky's *Mother* was as poor in comparison with his autobiography as Donskoi's adaptation was compared to his trilogy.

Donskoi's depiction of the revolutionaries is a particular theme. Their 'dangerous activity' is shown in the film exactly as it is in the novel – merrily and lightly. Instructive in this regard is the scene in which Nilovna distributes leaflets at the factory, where the theme of the 'clever revolutionaries/idiot detectives' achieves its full development. Here Donskoi's film continues the tradition of *Lenin in October* (*Lenin v Oktiabre*) and *Maxim's Youth* (*Iunost' Maksima*).

The revolutionaries are visible from miles away. Everything they do is distinguished by their astonishing lack of professionalism; they have darting eyes and take risks by doing strange things in plain view: for example, for some reason they hand each other leaflets in the street, although this could quite easily have been done at home. All this absurdity follows from the trivialisation of the depiction of the Revolution which occurred in the 1930s – with its indispensable closed, half-dark rooms in which the revolutionaries meet. In these lodgings it was usually smoky, but in Donskoi everything here too is sterile, and dirt – patently hyperbolised – appears only where it is necessary to show the 'hopeless life of the people'.

The 'secret agent' is also a special type. Like the revolutionaries, the agents are also visible from miles away, as if the task of both was not to conceal themselves but on the contrary to make themselves as noticeable as possible. Traditionally, they are depicted in Soviet cinema as if in 'uniforms' (one cannot understand why they in general do not just wear policemen's uniforms) – that is, the invariable bowler hat, small moustache, short jacket, walking stick, darting, cunning eyes . . . Such characters are more like provincial actors in operettas than people serving the State security services. All this traditional iconography of revolutionaries and 'secret agents' in Soviet cinema was part of the general strategy of turning the Revolution into banality, and was aimed at reducing the fundamental participants in the revolutionary struggle to the status of familiar figures out of central casting, in so far as in the historical-revolutionary film (and Donskoi's *Mother* was one such) everything usually led to the leader, with the revolutionaries being left the role of 'foot soldiers' ('ardent', 'selflessly committed', sharp-witted and resourceful) to whom only the 'little demons' going under the name of 'secret agents' can correspond. In essence, this is a set of heroes for another Soviet genre – 'stories from the pioneers' campfire'.

Donskoi had shown himself to be a master of such 'stories' already in his Gorky trilogy, although in *Mother* he also had to settle the cultural problem which Pudovkin's film undoubtedly raised. For instance, if in Pudovkin-Zarkhi the turning point in the consciousness of the mother is accented, linked with the motif of the 'unwilling traitor', then this is ultimately registered in her cry to her son after the trial: 'Forgive me, Pashka!' In Donskoi, on the other hand the turning point is emphasised in the behaviour not of Nilovna, but of Pavel, transferred to the beginning of the film and also expressed in a cry: 'Oh, forgive me, mother!' and . . . the drifting of ice. One could bring in more than a few examples like this – much in his adaptation is constructed in direct polemic with Pudovkin's film.

Speaking of the characters, the eyes, the 'non-material landscape' in Pudovkin, the cameraman Anatoly Golovnya (half a century later!) wrote: 'I thought the most successful filming devices in *Mother* were the "portraits" (in close-up) and the graphic solution to the actors' scenes';[40] and further, the landscapes, which he called 'landscapes of feeling, not of nature; frames were chosen in which material specificity would be absent, concentrating the attention of the viewer on them . . . The photographic treatment of these land-scapes removed their naturalness.'[41] This 'lack of materiality' of the frame strikes in *Mother* even now. It was quite another matter with Donskoi – here we have frames overfilled with life, where not just faces but the figures of people themselves are lost, and landscape is done on the level of an almost Pyrevian kitsch. Gorky's 'aesthetic mistake' became, just as Tynianov had predicted, 'a new principle of construction' – the foundation of socialist realist style.

In world cinema Donskoi's films have been defined in various ways: as 'film-poems', 'dramatic elegies' or 'film-metaphors'. His 'method' has been defined as 'neo-romanticism', 'passionate lyricism' or 'transcendental realism'. . . . This final oxymoronic definition probably characterises most accurately the 'mature socialist realism' of late Donskoi. This truly is the realism of what is incom-prehensible and outside experience. His references are in the sphere of ideo-logical 'higher conceptions'. What was being reflected here was not, of course, 'a lie', but a visually constructed ideology; one has to teach Soviet history according to these 'visible' constructions of reality, which alter reality itself. Ideology, as Sergei Tretyakov once noted, is not in the 'material', but in the form. From this he came to the conclusion which was refuted by new Soviet art: 'Village girls from Arkhipovo will not become members of women's sections just because a caption tells you so.'[42] In the 1920s, when cinema was only just learning to make new 'captions', few thought that, having learnt to 'forge cap-tions' and having mastered 'new principles of construction', it would be possi-ble not only to turn 'village girls from Arkhipovo' into 'members of women's sections', but to forge banknotes of even higher value: the history of the Revolution. It truly is not only a question of the material alone . . .

There's no Honour in Secret Business: Untimely Books/Untimely Thoughts (Gorky-Panfilov: 1989)

As it turned out, Tretyakov was completely wrong; ideology is in the 'material' as well. Gleb Panfilov altered Gorky's story until it was unrecognisable, uniting at least three works in one plot (*Mother*, *The Life of a Useless Man* and *Karamora*), and what is more with the greatest subtlety, expressing not so much Gorky's spirit as the unresolved questions Gorky raised, but which were drowned out by this spirit. Here was, undoubtedly, a serious aesthetic and ide-ological argument with the great director-opponents Pudovkin and Donskoi. However, Panfilov had on his side Gorky and Dostoevsky, great allies in their understanding of the underground. They finally met – all five.

Gorky was tormented by Dostoevsky's 'accursed questions' and could not resolve them, and for that reason always turned out to be 'untimely'; and he demands accordingly an 'untimely' reading. Gorky, as Alexander Troshin noted during a discussion of Gleb Panfilov's *Mother*, 'was evading them, running away from them, concealing himself, deceiving himself, pulling upwards . . . the romantic-revolutionary idea, while they, these secret heterodoxies, were breaking their way through on to the page'. Hence in Panfilov there are 'no innocent people and no guilty ones, no "us" and no "enemies". Everyone here is seen as participants in a tragic theatre. Not a moralist, but an artist, Panfilov resolved Gorky's "untimely" contradiction; he left it open for all times.'[43]

Seeing in Panfilov's film 'the tragedy of the integrity of man', 'the tragedy of thought', 'the tragedy of feeling', 'the tragic element of existence', Troshin wrote: 'Panfilov's film, if it "returns" something to us, then it is only one thing: the feeling of the tragic, a tragic (and therefore, truly mature) vision of the world, history and the self within them.'[44] Why 'of the tragic'? Participants in the discussion of the film answered this question – here there are no 'enemies': 'Each has his own rightness. Both the Tsar and Lenin. And it is impossible to choose, because having chosen, you immediately become narrowly Party-minded people. That for me is the dry residue of the film.'[45] Meanwhile, here there is still no 'dry residue'. Lenin, the Tsar, the Governor, Pavel – all are right. But they are right in their own way, each in 'his own' rightness; yet as it turned out, before the face of history, tragically, fatally, they are all wrong. That is the 'dry residue'.

In the course of their discussion of the film, the critics spoke truly about the next romantic attempt to break the 'thousand-year paradigm' of Russian history being doomed. Of what does this 'paradigm' consist? The problem was very precisely formulated by I. Germanova:

> Social circumstances broke people in two, so that some went to the Revolution and others into the secret police. Social circumstances did not offer normal variations. There were just the two poles of illegal existence: some were illegal revolutionaries, others illegal in their investigations. Everything was secret.[46]

The age-old problem of Russian history: the acute shortage of a centrist-orientated part of the ruling class. The 'conservatives' in its masses turn out to be reactionaries and obscurantists, relying on pure force (such in the film are the people in the court room, who after Pavel's speech cry in one voice: 'Shoot them!', 'To Siberia!'). This engendered at the opposite pole the most radical, revolutionary protest. And so on, in a vicious circle. Reformism simply could not develop with the millstones of Russian history. From this the police state in Russia always gained, and on this it was constructed; thus it was never able to become either liberal or democratic. (As Herzen had noted long before, 'the state took up position in Russia as an occupying army.') Panfilov's film is about this. As regards the 'legality' of which Germanova spoke, this too, as the twentieth century showed, is not a question of 'democratism', but is again a product of violence. (The Bolshevik dictatorship was no less 'violently legitimate' than serfdom.) 'Legitimacy' was provided by the Tsar who never understand anything, and as always by the 'silent people', a powerful image of whom is given in one of the most tragic scenes in the film – the scene of the demonstration: the complete indifference of the crowd, the total lack of understanding, the silence of the grave, the songs and slogans being yelled out by the demonstrators drowned out in the deathly quiet – it is as if they are rebounding off the onlookers. A handful of people stand between the awesome silent crowd and the authorities. What could be more contemporary in the conversation about Russian history than the horror of these historical acoustics, in whose emptiness the voice of the thinking individual is doomed to remain unanswered?

All the reviews spoke of the 'untimeliness' of Panfilov's film, but only a few saw in it 'an attempt to construct *Mother* not as a "contemporary book" . . . but as timeless: that is, integrating itself into all periods of Russian history'.[47] Gorky possessed not only the voice of a great writer, but also a rare historical ear. His *Untimely Thoughts* turned out to be just as timely; in 1917–18 nothing could have been more urgent than these. This is why he was so fascinating to read again and again (which does not prevent us considering him one of the most unread Russian writers of the twentieth century). Many turned to him, each for their own reasons. Pudovkin created a propaganda film which would inflame; Donskoi made an 'adaptation of a classic', which would turn the past into a museum; as for Panfilov, he, according to Leonid Kozlov's observation, 'created a truly historical film, fully based on historical consciousness and historical understanding'.[48]

Panfilov's film can also, however, easily be read as a historical allusion; the end of the 1980s was the next skid of the revolutionary wheel, the threshold of the next 'tsarist manifesto'. Nor did the director hide this topical-political layer. It is no accident that among the slogans which Pavel and his friends shout out, we have, for instance, 'Long live democracy and *glasnost*',' as if taken now from the last meeting of the radical supporters of Gorbachev's reforms; and it was no accident that Vasily Kurochkin's 1866 verse about the fact that 'the era of *glasnost*' has begun', and one was permitted to say 'one times one equals one' was interpolated into the film. This is neither a superficial reading of the film and nor simply one possible reading. This contemporary-timely plan was important to the director. This background clarifies something fundamental; in his rejection of the idea of transforming into devils both the revolutionaries and the spies, Panfilov enters into a polemic not just with Pudovkin and Donskoi, but also with Gorky and Dostoevsky.

To all intents and purposes, *The Devils* was the first Russian 'historical-revolutionary novel'. Translating Dostoevsky's critique of revolutionism into a critique of the reactionary-conservative police state, Gorky attributed Nechaevism to the gendarmes themselves. Panfilov, on the other hand, takes only one, bright side of the Russian Revolution, knowing, of course, very well that there was a lot of Nechaevism in it – even the *Short Course* could not hide this. We will note in passing that precisely in the Sormovo story with Pyotr Zalomov described by Gorky there was everything – including the murder by revolutionaries of a provocateur 'in the little wood'. In the film, as a parallel to this motif, we are given the scene in which Rybin offers Pavel a revolver, which the latter refuses, saying that 'we' do not need it; in Pudovkin-Zarkhi, Pavel not only does not refuse it, but he also hides the weapon, which becomes the reason for his arrest.

So, by looking on the bright side of the Revolution, Panfilov succeeds in an apparently unwinnable game, which before him had defeated Gorky and Donskoi. His *Mother* is, in a surprising fashion, an improvement on Gorky. Panfilov did what Gorky failed to do (and which Donskoi did not attempt); he compelled the viewer to believe in the events taking place. Much in the film works towards this. For example, the characters are in an overt manner brought closer to the experience of the contemporary viewer; from speech to costumes and interiors, everything is modernised. These are contemporary people who no longer go around in rags, who do not eat gruel, but use forks and eat mouth-watering-looking cakes, who live neither in ramshackle hovels nor in single rooms with one bed, but in quite spacious apartments (which, incidentally, workers of more recent times might have envied, huddled together as they were in communal apartments or, later, in Khrushchev's 'low-rise blocks'). It is amusing to observe how from film to film – from Pudovkin to Donskoi, and from him to Panfilov – the 'welfare of the working people grows'. Whence came this 'steady growth'? From the aesthetic and ideological goals, of course.

Why does Panfilov insert the scene of the work in the factory, with its expressive monotony, dominated by fiery-red, hellish colours? The director here was taking a conscious risk, giving this familiar workshop, so to speak, a fragment from another reality – from *The Big Family* (*Bol'shaia sem'ia*) or *Spring on Zarechnaia Street* (*Vesna na Zarechnoi ulitse*). And do not be mistaken: this workshop, in which workers spent 10–12 hours a day, this hard physical labour depicts not at all that with which it was traditionally – from the 1930s – associated, but explains something very important about the origins of the Russian Revolution. Simultaneously, Panfilov with striking subtlety reproduces official Russia – its comfortlessness, its uninhabitability, the impossibility of living. Where this Russia appears – with its terrible peeling walls, heavy metal doors, dirt, slush under foot, soldiers' loutishness – the terrible ordinariness of violence is concentrated; it is, it seems, in the very air of the State. It makes one feel terrified for human beings.

It is now usual to say that Andrei Platonov introduced the theme of orphanhood into Soviet literature – his heroes are nearly always orphans. Meanwhile, the theme if not of complete orphanhood, then more precisely of fatherlessness was introduced into Russian literature of the twentieth century by Gorky. (It was also, let us not forget, an enormous theme in Dostoevsky.) Not only in *Mother*, but also to a somewhat greater extent in *The Life of a Useless Man*, not even to mention Gorky's autobiographical trilogy, the story of childhood occupies an enormous place. It is no accident that a quarter of the film is taken up with the portrayal of the childhood of the heroes of *Mother* and *The Life of a Useless Man*, while the cry of the youthful Pavel, 'I want my daddy!' so to speak completes the process of growing up, and becomes the detonator for the suicidal explosion-initiation and the harsh reality of adulthood. This motif of the replay of childhood in adulthood is logically played out in the film. Pavel's cry 'Down with the Tsar!' during the demonstration even reproduces something altogether childish: 'Down with the Tsar and down with the Tsarina!' in the empty workshop. Through the slaughter of the child Panfilov finds an explanation for the turning point – something which we find neither in Gorky nor in his earlier interpreters. It was only possible to make the novel realistic by finding motifs which would cement its development. Realism is above all motivation.

Speaking of realism, let us mention that Panfilov's film emphasises a biological aspect that was in Gorky latent and bashful. This is the opposition in the children, emphasised from the beginning, of the healthy and the sickly, crippled and wounded, who have a complex for their entire lives. One could suggest that it is precisely from here that the underground develops. But Gorky, and with him Panfilov, go further; biology, it turns out, explains nothing. Thus from the healthy child, Yakov Somov-Karamora, something even more terrible grows than from his sickly brother, Evsei Klimkov. The film intentionally includes a great deal of sexuality, which, undoubtedly, comes from Gorky, although it is not in the plot. Thus the seduction of the thirteen-year-old Pavel in the film reproduces the seduction of the adolescent Evsei Klimkov from *The Life of a Useless Man*, which, in its turn, goes back to Dostoevsky.

In all this the general strategy of the director is perceptible: to make the novel psychologically authentic, to improve on Gorky. Thus, all the dialogues and speeches of the characters are sifted, altered, shortened, and where there are no direct changes, authenticity is achieved by the work of the actors and their intonation, and by the camerawork. It is as if Panfilov demonstratively reproduced almost all of the most unsuccessful scenes of the novel and Donskoi's film, but now they are strikingly psychologically authentic, convincing and carefully constructed so as to remove all traces of emotionalism. Characteristic in this sense is the scene of the meeting in the prison, the conversation of the mother and son in the presence of a third person – the jailor. Pudovkin placed here his infamous soldiers – one drowsy from unrestrained drunkenness and sleep, the other drowning a cockroach in a saucer. Donskoi makes the mother quarrel with the jailor. But in Panfilov everything is constructed so that these three are turned in such a way that the jailor can see Pavel, but not his mother, who uses signs to show Pavel what she needs to tell him. This purely cinematographic solution to the scene is reinforced by an amazing device of Panfilov's; time and again a 'fourth' appears on the screen – an eye at the spyhole, following all three. The image of the prison is complete. At the same time Panfilov rejects a series of textbook scenes. Thus in the film we do not see scenes of the mother distributing leaflets at the factory; instead of this we are given the scene of her symbolic departure into the darkness of the workshop (the tragic 'departure into revolution'). The novel's culminating trial scene is also removed; we are given in effect only Pavel's reshaped speech, in which remains not a trace of the novel's moralising.

Nevertheless, this is not a translation of emotionalism into everyday life. The film retains an amazing sense of poetry. Its imagery is created by an astonishing use of visual quotations. It is strange that no one who has written about the film has paid attention to the fact that Panfilov reconstructs on the screen (in overt polemic with Pudovkin and Donskoi) Kustodievan landscapes: the unchanging picture of an astonishingly beautiful winter, repeated many times – from the same symbolic series as the endlessly resounding romance, about which it was noted that 'this is the hero of the film . . . romance is the disguise of a gathering, but in fact this is its content . . . Life itself becomes a disguise . . . The normal takes the form of a disguise.'[49]

But why did Panfilov undertake to depict precisely the bright side of the Revolution? Why did he reject following the truth of the author of *The Devils*, or of *Mother, The Life of a Useless Man* and *Karamora*? He bound provocateurs and revolutionaries together in a single plot-bundle, but refused to move any further in this direction. Having rejected the stamp of the historical-revolutionary film (his spies no longer go round in bowler hats, their eyes do not dart – on the contrary, they speak cleverly and coherently), Panfilov stopped on the threshold of *The Devils* (going in this direction meant betraying Gorky and creating a 'timely' pamphlet); he stopped on the threshold of *Mother* (adapting *Mother* in the form in which Gorky had created it meant reshooting Donskoi's film). But he also stopped on the threshold of *The Life of a Useless Man* and *Karamora*. In particular, *Karamora*.

The fact was that in *Karamora* Gorky made a great discovery and glanced, finally, into the depths into which nobody after him dared glance, and for well-known reasons were unable to. In *Karamora* it was not just a question of the revolutionary becoming a provocateur, but of Gorky discovering a new, terrible and real type. It was precisely this type who later defeated the Vlasovs, about which Gorky can hardly even have thought, when he wrote *Karamora* at the beginning of the 1920s. Panfilov was another matter, knowing how everything ended: Pavel, his trial, his doomed sacred faith. This is why the director, in so carefully reproducing individual scenes from the novel, threw out almost all of its second half: precisely where (with her move into the city) the mother finds herself in the real revolutionary underground, in the midst of 'professional revolutionaries', and carries out their work. To portray this truthfully, while remaining on the bright side of the Revolution, was impossible: 'there's no honour in secret business.' It is because of this that in a film about revolutionaries Panfilov depicts them with such caution – workers, people on courses, students – but only in passing shows the real revolutionary-doctor, whispering into the mother's ear at the museum, just like a devil, that she has to take leaflets to the factory in order to save her son.

Panfilov, finally, added the words 'Outlawed People' to the title, but for some reason only to the title of part one, while part two remained without a title. Therefore the title 'Outlawed People' can be seen as a subtitle of the whole film. And in fact, everyone here turned out to be 'outlawed' – revolutionaries, gendarmes, provocateurs, Lenin, the Governor, the Tsar . . . In a situation where 'the people are silent', there is no legitimacy, it comes down to pure violence, and the question of power is decided 'by revolutionary means', any outcome to this situation will be 'legitimised' 'by the silent people'. This, of course, is not just a problem for the characters in the film or figures from Russian history, but is the problem of Russian political culture itself – that same 'thousand-year paradigm'.

Thus we come to yet another finale of all this story. It is interesting that nearly all the interpreters and dramatisers of *Mother* have made attempts on Nilovna's life. (Perhaps for this reason the real mother, Anna Kirillovna Zalomova, died in 1938 at the age of 90.) Of course, each had his own reasons for the mother's 'murder': reasons of aesthetics and, more narrowly, of genre. The end of Panfilov's film – the slaughtered mother lying in a pool of blood at the station – is indeed the culmination of the cycle; finally, the scene with which Pudovkin's project began and which he simply never shot, was adapted. The unexpected finale of Panfilov's film is no more realistic than Donskoi's, where everything occurs to conform to the ideological socialist-realist task; the mother petrifies into a monument.

In almost all interpretations of the novel, either mother and son both perish, or they both remain alive. But in Panfilov, the mother perishes, while the son remains among the living. The mother dies in the most unconvincing fashion. Her death in front of everybody's eyes at the hands of Yakov Somov is an impossible murder. The mother could not die like this. Her murder is as unreal (symbolic) as the concluding scene of the film is unreal (symbolic) – with the living mother. Both endings say the same thing: nothing should any longer restrain Pavel; the mother dying thus should 'untie' his hands, again bringing together the provocateur and the revolutionary. One of them must die now. A new cycle of violence has already begun. For this reason the dying mother's question to her killer, 'How will you live after this, Yakov?' has already been answered. He will not live; he, Yakov, in Gorky as well, is not long for this world. He is already a vampire. It is no accident that precisely in this scene at the station we have before us two pieces of Gorky; the very brother betrayed by a provocateur (from *The Life of a Useless Man*) himself becomes a provocateur (from *Karamora*), a fact which is consolidated in the most 'Dostoevskian' scene in the film – the scene of Somov's recruitment, in the same room where he killed, and with the same pen which he used at gunpoint to force his provocateur-brother to sign his own death sentence. That is why, in this 'black man' who kills the mother at the end of the film, it is already difficult to recognise Yakov Somov.

A pool of blood. Prisoners are led to a carriage through the very door through which the murdered mother has just been taken away. Pavel sees her from a window. He calls (and these are the final words in the picture): 'Mum! . . . Mother!' She turns round and silently leaves along an ice-bound river. Thus we again return to Pudovkin; instead of the celebrated victoriously exultant drifting of ice, we have the deathly, icy silence of the mother, without a hint of a thaw; everything is bound in ice. This pessimistic finale reflects the tragic element of the fate not only of the mother, but also of the son. For that reason also absent here are the celebrated final words of the mother, repeated always and everywhere: 'They cannot kill a resurrected soul!' No, nothing here can rise again, although 'everything is ahead', and the 'time of action' is 1901. (It is no accident that we are reminded of this by the caption at the beginning of each part.) 'Ahead' lies the terrible twentieth century.

We must admit that Lenin's definition, 'a timely book', was at that point, at the beginning of the century, the truest characteristic of Gorky's unsuccessful novel. But what is amazing is the recurring interest in the novel and its life in the theatre (from Brecht to Lyubimov), as well as in the cinema, where each of the three adaptations of the novel has struck us with its staggering 'timeliness', which consists not only (and in the larger scheme of things, not so much) in the involvement of the artistic work in 'contemporaneity', as in the ability to reflect this contemporaneity itself (and through it, Time) in art. Through the three *Mothers* one can study the history of Soviet culture and Soviet historical consciousness. The bad novel has not died, but has turned out to be claimed many times; its timeliness has endured for a whole century. What else could the author have desired for this, as it turned out, great book? Though it may not be the most timely of great works, it is undoubtedly the greatest of the timely.

NOTES

1. Maksim Gor'kii, *Polnoe sobranie sochinenii v 25 tomakh*, Vol. 8, Moscow: Nauka, 1970, pp. 474–84.
2. Ibid., pp. 185–6.
3. Ibid., p. 491.
4. Ibid., p. 488.
5. Maksim Gor'kii, *Polnoe sobranie sochinenii v 30 tomakh*, Vol. 24, Moscow: Nauka, 1953, p. 155.
6. Gor'kii, *Polnoe sobranie sochinenii v 25 tomakh*, p. 478.
7. Ibid., p. 134.
8. Ibid., Vol. 9, p. 168.
9. Ibid., p. 530.
10. Ibid., Vol. 17, p. 616.
11. Ibid., Vol. 9, p. 65.
12. On this see Robert Jackson, *Dostoevsky's Underground Man in Russian Literature*, The Hague: Mouton, 1958, pp. 127–46.
13. Iu. Tynianov, *Poetika. Istoriia literatury. Kino*, Moscow: Nauka, 1977, p. 263.
14. *Mat': Sbornik*, Moscow: Iskusstvo, 1975, p. 209.
15. On the mythologisation of October in the first decade following the Revolution, see Frederick C. Corney, *Telling October: Memory and the Making of the Bolshevik Revolution*, Ithaca, NY: Cornell University Press, 2004.
16. Vsevolod, Pudovkin, *Sobranie sochinenii v 3 tomakh*, Vol. 2, Moscow: Iskusstvo, 1975, p. 49.
17. *Mat': Sbornik*, p. 214.
18. Vsevolod Pudovkin, *Izbrannye stat'i*, Moscow: Iskusstvo, 1955, p. 309.
19. *Mat': Sbornik*, p. 234.

20. Mikhail Romm, *Besedy o kino*, Moscow: Iksusstvo, 1964, p. 28.
21. Gor'kii, *Polnoe sobranie sochinenii*, Vol. 8, p. 479.
22. Viktor Shklovskii, 'Poeziia i proza kinematografii (1928)'. In V. Shklovskii, *Za 40 let*, Moscow: Iskusstvo, 1965, pp. 98–9.
23. *Kak my rabotaem nad kinostsenariem*, Moscow: Kinofotoizdat, 1936, p. 85.
24. A. Karganov, *Vsevolod Pudovkin*, Moscow: Iksusstvo, 1983, p. 53.
25. Ibid., p. 55.
26. A. Vartanov, *Obrazy literatury v grafike i kino*, Moscow: Izdatel'stvo Akademii Nauk SSR, 1961, p. 154.
27. *Mat': Sbornik*, p. 185.
28. Ibid., p. 228.
29. Ibid., p. 227.
30. A. Mariamov, *Narodnyi artist SSSR Vsevolod Pudovkin*, Moscow: Goskinoizdat, 1952, p. 74.
31. Ibid., pp. 75, 77.
32. Ibid., p. 85.
33. Ibid.
34. Ibid.
35. Ibid.
36. Ibid.
37. Z. Vladimirova, 'Dushu voskresshuiu – ne ub'iut!'. In *Mark Donskoi: Sbornik*, Moscow: Iskusstvo, 1973, pp. 127–8.
38. V. Shklovskii, 'Ne dumaite, chto instsenirovka – spasenie.' *Oktiabr'*, 1958, No. 10, p. 149.
39. Maia Turovskaia, 'Mark Donskoi v dvoinom svete', *Kinovedcheskie zapiski*, Issue 13, 1992, p. 49.
40. A. Golovnia, *Ekran – moia palitra*, Moscow: Soiuz kinematografistov SSSR, 1971, p. 11.
41. A. Golovnia, *Svet v iskusstve operatora*, Moscow: Goskinofotoizdat, 1945, p. 122.
42. See *Novyi LEF*, 1928, No. 1, p. 3.
43. See '*Mat*' Gleba Panfilova. Opyt kollektivnoi interpretatsii', *Kinovedcheskie zapiski*, No. 9, 1991, pp. 72, 74, 79.
44. Ibid., p. 64.
45. Ibid., p. 62.
46. Ibid., p. 60.
47. Ibid., p. 65.
48. Ibid., p. 61.
49. Ibid., pp. 60–1.

6. SHOTS FROM UNDERGROUND: DIALECTICS OF CONSPIRATORIAL IMAGINATION

Cinema is an illusion, but it dictates its laws to life.

Joseph Stalin (1924)[1]

We should create a film . . . which would not mimic life or catch it off guard because life is not a petty thief, but would train it like a young puppy.

Viktor Shklovsky (1928)[2]

THE HISTORICAL-PARTY FILM: POLITICAL PARANOIA AND THE UNPREDICTABLE PAST

The first successful Soviet experiment in cinema sound-recording was a chronicle of the Promparty trial.[3] Stalinisation of Soviet cinematography coincided with the appearance of talking pictures. As Oksana Bulgakowa notes,

> The model of the 'Soviet film' achieves its total expression at the very moment when cinema becomes the medium not of another art (a traditional and therefore an impaired solution), but of another reality, and above all of 'another' history. The uniqueness of Soviet monumental films is defined not just by their rejection of tried and tested narrative structures. Cinema inherits the mantle of the chronicler, which is merely a modification of its general interpretation as a 'medium'.
>
> The same subject is developed in parallel in different art-forms: the novel, plays, opera, ballet, pictures, sculpture and film. Or rather, one subject is hit upon, elaborated, supplemented by new details in different films, depicted as a somewhat fictitious time and space, which is however

defined ever more precisely with each new work. Practically every leading Soviet film director produced a history of the October uprising. Beginning with Eisenstein's *October*, this story was dramatised every decade for the new anniversary from a pre-prepared selection of firmly established components, frequently in several films at once. The years 1937–8 saw the creation of the first such group of films: Mikhail Romm's *Lenin in October* (*Lenin v Oktiabre*), Mikhail Chiaureli's *Great Dawn* (*Velikoe zarevo*), Grigorii Kozintsev and Leonid Trauberg's *The Vyborg Side* (*Vyborgskaia storona*), and Sergei Yutkevich's *Man with a Rifle* (*Chelovek c ruzh'em*). These films focus on the same episodes, and therefore the reappearance of fictitious heroes from one film to another was possible (Maxim [from Kozintsev's and Trauberg's trilogy – E. D.] also appears in 1938 in *The Great Citizen* (*Velikii grazhdanin*) as a familiar emissary from the Central Committee), as is the transference of episodes from one film to another, as happened on Stalin's orders with the scene of the dissolution of the Constituent Assembly, which was imported from Yutkevich's screenplay into Kozintsev and Trauberg's film . . .

Certain scenes become canonical and are replayed over and over again; Romm reproduces Eisenstein's composition of the storming of the Winter Palace (a striking *mise en scène* which had nothing to do with the actual movements of detachments of workers), while Yutkevich in the much later *Stories about Lenin* (*Rasskazy o Lenine*) simply cuts to this scene as a black and white 'documentary' quotation in a colour film. If *The Vyborg Side* develops in detail the story of the ransacking of the Winter Palace's wine cellars, presented as a preconceived provocation, then *Man with a Rifle* focuses on the seizure of Gatchina. There are also strange divergences; Romm has Lenin save the worker Vasily, rather than Eino Rakhya, a real fellow-traveller, admittedly repressed by that time. In Chiaureli, Stalin takes on this role personally.

This maniacal refinement of the fictitious history of the October Revolution works towards the establishment of historical myth. Stalin's opponents, sentenced in the trials of 1937, are represented in the films as enemies of the people, even in 1917. Lenin is present in order to enable Stalin to act. In the first of Romm's two films about Lenin, Stalin saves Lenin in his refuge on the Finnish Gulf from Kamenev and Zinoviev. (The latter accompanied him there.) In the second Stalin (not Trotsky) wins the Civil War and saves Russia from famine, sending bread to the centre from the Volga while Lenin is recovering from the attempt on his life, organised with Bukharin's participation.

These films represent the beginning of the unique 'commemorative acts', reproducing the Revolution anew every decade and in the process introducing ever newer corrections to history. History moreover, the independent creation of the cinema, is established as an endlessly variable present, while cinematography becomes a veritable collective work, stepping outside the bounds of a single work. All the films are created as if by collective effort.[4]

Meanwhile, Stalinist cinema aesthetics in all seriousness thought out the problem of 'realism' of the new history being engendered before our eyes. Thus it was asserted that all this was 'historical truth'. ('The picture *Lenin in October* is distinguished by its supreme historical specificity; every fact, every detail is carefully adjusted from the point of view of its historical authenticity,'[5] while in the trilogy about Maxim, 'Maxim-Chirkov appears to be transferred from the pages of historical chronicles on to cinema screens as a living, authentically existing figure in our Revolution.'[6]) At the same time, appealing to that 'reality', the 'reflection' of which supposedly appeared in one film or another, critics claimed the cinema image as a self-referential reality.

> Kartashov's phrase-mongering, posing, hysterical frivolity and tendency to descend into panic at the first sign of difficulty, Borovsky's careerism, insane ambition and lust for power – surely these are the typical features of the whole rank of representatives of all kinds of anti-Soviet blocs and centres, which figured in our recent trials?

the critic Kovarsky asked rhetorically in connection with the film *The Great Citizen*.[7] In actual fact, it was not the film that 'truthfully reflected' the people who figured in the Moscow trials, but rather the reverse; the scenarios of the show trials were invented by Stalin – the same great director who personally oversaw the screenplay of *The Great Citizen*. One could say that the film becomes a kind of appendix to the court transcripts, the most important material witness, filed as 'evidence'.

On the other hand, the historical revolutionary films themselves appear to be not only the product of 'reflection', but also of 'prognosis'. 'Reflecting' that to which they themselves are bearing witness, these films become screen adaptations of Stalin's paranoid fantasies: 'In exposing the true circumstances of the attempt on Lenin's life', wrote a reviewer of *Lenin in 1918 (Lenin v 1918 godu)*,

> the film goes considerably further than many works published up to now. Relying on a huge amount of historical material, in particular on materials from the recent trials of the enemies of the people, the makers of the film have drawn a historically truthful picture of how all the forces of counter-revolution united into a single force, directing the villainous hand of the criminal Kaplan. It truthfully showed the abominable double-dealing of the despicable conspirators, the Trotskyites-Bukharinites, who participated in the plot against Lenin's life.[8]

There is no question that at the basis of the great historical-revolutionary narrative lay the *Short Course*, which by the time of its publication to all intents and purposes fixed the already settled official version of the history of the Revolution. We are dealing here with a grandiose project of literary screen adaptation. Like a classic literary text, the *Short Course* had to be read independently, the reader had to be one on one with the Stalinist Word; in a break with the whole of Bolshevik tradition, this book was not to be discussed in reading circles (even under the guidance of propagandists!). Stalin insisted on independent work with the text. During the meeting of the Central Committee on the occasion of the publication of the *Short Course*, he interrupted one of the presentations with the response: 'Now we must bring in uniformity through print, and we need fewer readers' circles',[9] and to the observation of one of the speakers that 'all the same, people who will be studying individually need help, consultation', Stalin replied irritably, 'Leave them in peace!'[10]

But was the leader really so 'patently afraid that propagandists, who knew the history of the Communist Party from old textbooks now doomed to destruction, would bring chaos to the study of the past according to the "uniform textbook"',[11] as today's historians assert? It was a question, it seems, not so much of 'knowledge' as of the magic of acquaintanceship; being the chief prototext of Stalinism, the *Short Course* was subject not to discussion, but to direct 'embodiment in images' – be that in a novel, film or picture. In each case this was a very individual dialogue between the reader/viewer and the text. And this one-to-one meeting was a prerequisite for 'the study of the history of the Party'. 'Uniformity' and collective 'knowledge' were the sum of individual meetings with the Stalinist narrative, and this is why it was so effective and assimilable.

Film criticism of the Stalin era fully recognised the birth of a new cinematic style and a new generic canon when it asserted that the line which included *Battleship Potemkin* and *The End of Saint Petersburg*, at the centre of which lay 'collective mass psychology, which is developed against a backdrop of historic events',[12] ended with Efim Dzigan's film, *We are from Kronstadt* (*My iz Kronshtadta*, 1936). The new line began with *Chapaev* and reached its conclusion with Romm's two films about Lenin. This was the line of the 'historical chronicle', in which, in the words of the same critic from the 1930s, 'a real process of learning from Shakespeare' took place, and at the same time 'original Soviet dramatic arts were created, growing out of attempts to disclose the images of the leaders.'[13] Dark Shakespearian historical chronicles – a world of conspiracies and murders – proved to be an adequate generic peg on which to hang Soviet cinema.

This cinema was, of course, not only the product of defined repressive techniques (from total control over film production and censorship to terror directed against individuals), but was also part of a global political-aesthetic project, and in this capacity it must be understood in the context of the worldwide experiment of totalitarian ideology and practice. Western totalitarianism used cinema as one of the most effective means of propaganda: that is, as the product of the contemporary market society side by side with advertisements (such, strictly speaking, was early Soviet revolutionary cinema as well). Propaganda (including political propaganda) gravitates in contemporary culture not to the text, but to the visual image. Stalinist cinema, on the other hand, gravitated towards the word and speech.[14] But this is not remotely a question of traditional Soviet 'technological backwardness'; Soviet culture was a culture of the word par excellence.

These films were not called 'talkies' by accident; in 'historical-revolutionary' ('historical-Party') films characters are forever delivering orations, enthusiastically polemicising and arguing until they are hoarse. But, as Lilya Mamatova observed:

> One should not think that the distinctly expressed ideas of the orators and disputants are conclusively confirmed or rejected. This verbal abundance conceals an extreme poverty of content, and moreover not only moral and philosophical, but also strictly political content. We never learn anything instructive about what the programmes were or whose interests the Mensheviks, SRs [Socialist Revolutionaries – E. D.], anarchists, cadets, monarchists we are being shown expressed . . . Suspicious individuals of mixed social origins, designated by Alexei Kapler's screenplay [this refers to Romm's two films about Lenin, *Lenin in October* (1937) and *Lenin in 1918* (1939) – E. D.] as 'characters of the Menshevik-SR type' exchange incoherent responses and fraternise with 'a group of Russian capitalists'. For years Trotskyite-Zinovievites meet in secret dens to present each other with poisonous glances and dark hints, trying all the time to hide the nervous trembling of their anaemic hands. [in Fridrikh Ermler's *The Great Citizen* (1937, 1939) – E. D.][15]

But the same could be said of the Bolsheviks as well. In Grigory Kozintsev and Leonid Trauberg's trilogy about Maxim, *Maxim's Youth (Iunost' Maksima,* 1934), *Maxim's Return (Vozvrashchenie Maksima,* 1937) and *The Vyborg Side* (1938–9), pages of the *Short Course* rise up before the viewer. In Romm's two films a stream of October quotations by Lenin, familiar from school, is released on the viewer. In *The Great Citizen* the endless party discussions of the 1920s are resurrected (in part one) and then quotations by Stalin on mass labour enthusiasm (in part two). Words here mean everything – and precisely nothing. The 'arrangement of forces' is so obvious that, even if the sound suddenly disappeared, everything would still be clear without the words. What, then, do the heroes say, and what is the status of the word in these films?

One can definitely assert that the 'historical-revolutionary film' was not simply a visual 'superstructure' built over a verbal ideology, but was the true domain of the Soviet political imagination – not only where it was revealed, but also through which it was articulated and to a significant extent formulated.

Totalitarian society is based on a conspiratorial view of the world, in so far as this view ideally responds to the demand to camouflage the real social links and political interests of the powerful elite with explanations based on ideological postulates and historical myths. The conspiratorial picture of the world easily takes the place of the real social picture, dehistoricises it and renders it historically flat, because history and social links in it are exchanged for conspiracy, explained not only as the source of world evil, but bringing order and logic into the world. This consciousness – precisely by virtue of its total narcissism – does not know the Other. (There is no place here, for instance, for opponents or rivals, but only enemies liable to destruction.) All attempts to construct the Other within this consciousness and this picture of the world inevitably turn into self-referentiality 'in reverse'; the Other is always the starting-point for constructing one's own identity. In other words, the Other turns out to be a projection of one's own paranoia. In this sense the 'historical-revolutionary film' is the ideal screen for reading the Soviet political mentality.

On the other hand, the Bolshevik Revolution (and Stalinism certainly) was only one particular instance of the traditionalistic reaction to modernisation, the global clash in the twentieth century of the complex of liberal Enlightenment ideas of the New Age with the conservative 'collectivist' utopia, which proposed a combination of industrial-technological progress with the preservation of archaics. Traditionalism and antimodernism are the true domain of conspiratorial thinking. Modernisation in this mindset is always erosion, decay, the product of planned, end-directed activity and, in the final analysis, an act of sabotage. For the paranoid, traditionalistic consciousness, reality is a constructed system, a machine in which there is no place for unconscious motives, accidents or unpremeditated acts. Everything 'bad' inevitably turns out here to be part of a conspiracy.

Robert Tucker, the author of probably the most insightful and accurate biography of Stalin, asserted that the Moscow show trials (which made up the 'background' for the historical-revolutionary film):

> were basically a one-man show of which Stalin himself was organizer, chief producer, and stage manager as well as an appreciative spectator from the darkened room at the rear of the Hall of Columns, where the trials were held. Vyshinsky spoke for the prosecution, but we must understand that he spoke with the voice of Stalin.[16]

Stalin – this, to use Molotov's words, 'greatest conspirator'[17] – is interesting here, however, not so much in all these hypostases, but rather in his only, it seems, impossible capacity – that of an actor: that is, of the very accused. In the final analysis, in these productions it was above all he himself who was acting, disclosing himself in endless self-projections, recorded in the speeches of various people (including, with hindsight, via the transcripts of these trials which were corrected by him). The magic of conspiratorial thinking consists in its mirror-like nature: the magic of conspiratorial discourse, in tautology. 'History as conspiracy' – so Tucker called his work, in which he described Stalin's paranoid character (a textbook example – alongside Hitler or Pol Pot – of the influence of mania on politics[18]).

Paranoia feeds not on ideas, which give birth to critical thinking, but on 'facts', which the paranoiac manufactures, constructing a reality which corresponds to his or her own logic. In this logocentric world everything is subordinated to a totalising system, based on the selection of facts, each of which is seen as testimony, a piece of evidence. The production of 'facts' is an entire industry for the paranoid personality or society. The picture of the world created here, although one-dimensional ('good' and 'evil' are fixed and invariable; chance does not exist, and so on), is (by definition) plot-driven; conspiracy is the plot. It is a space that is simultaneously centrifugal and centripetal; in it everything revolves around the paranoiac. On the one hand, it is a space deprived of an irrational dimension (in this 'chance-less' world, rationalism and the belief that deception is concealed behind every conflict, that everything is disguised, dominate); on the other, it is a space of total suspicion and fear, which is open to the unconscious.

The paranoid picture of the world, like any totalising system, is a veritable factory for a new reality. In the witty comment of Robert Robbins and Jerrold Post, the paranoiac 'meets reality halfway'.[19] One could say that the paranoiac half-creates this reality (in so far as the real world is somewhat less organised and subject to someone's will and logic than it appears to the paranoiac). This is the true domain of political fantasising. The paranoiac's world is based on insecurity and uncertainty. From this arises the urgent need to externalise it; the paranoiac 'transforms an intolerable internal threat into a more manageable external threat', constantly producing a war scenario or threats of invasion from within.

Alluding to the long history of the existence of secret societies and circles in Russia and the tradition of conspiracies in Russian history (it was not unique, but without it one cannot understand the terrorist nature of the Stalinist regime[20]), to the fact that in Russia a traditional conviction has long existed to the effect that practically every ruler's death was due to murder or that he was not dead but still alive, or that, on the ideological level (among the Slavophiles in particular), the West was weaving constant intrigues and conspiracies against Russia, Robbins and Post assert that:

> Stalin found a well-primed canvas on which to paint his paranoid delusions. The tsarist state nurtured a society in which beliefs in conspiracy and victimization were pervasive. In fact Russian events often were caused by conspiracies, and this led to the paranoid belief that conspiracy always created policy,[21]

and was the organising and moving force in history. This political culture which took shape long ago in many ways also defines the post-Soviet view of the world and history.

Seeing conspiracy in everything, the paranoiac himself becomes a conspirator. But the picture resulting from this tendency towards conspiracy is not simply a caricature of the real world. It is full of magic and mystery. (Everything is 'invisible' and 'concealed', secret links are hiding in everything, anything 'visible' is not worth believing.) This methodology of grasping the secret reasons and concealed sources of events reflects in a caricatured fashion the Bolsheviks' appropriation of Marx, whose merit lay in the fact that he was considered to have 'revealed the roots of the previously unseen mechanisms of exploitation in capitalism'. In essence, the Bolsheviks' very conception of the masses and their control were based on the idea of conspiracy.[22] This idea, which apart from anything else relies on the 'legitimizing myth',[23] is essential for the creation of the image of the enemy, for the demonisation of the repressed social group. The Bolsheviks had conspiracy in the blood; they began (in 1917) and ended (in 1991) with conspiracy and coup.

It is amusing that the makers of both the trilogy about Maxim and *The Great Citizen* appeal to the same phrase by Lenin (from his work *What is to be Done?*): 'We are moving forward with a very small group, up a steep and difficult path, having firmly taken each others' hands. We are surrounded on all sides by enemies.'[24] Ermler said that during filming he constantly returned to this idea of Lenin's.[25] Kozintsev asserted that, 'we shot the best episodes of *Maxim's Youth* from the feeling of the words about the "very small group".'[26] The traumatics of power, with their origins in the very history of Bolshevism, were born from the everyday contact of the 'professional underground revolutionaries' exclusively with the repressive side of the state. One of the founders of the repressive system of the new state, Felix Dzerzhinsky, who spent long years in tsarist prisons, expressed this very accurately in his prison notebooks:

> What oppresses most of all, what the prisoner cannot be reconciled to, is the secrecy of this building, the secrecy of life within it, this regime, which it directed towards each of the prisoners knowing only about themselves, and even then not all of them, but as few as possible. And the prisoners fight passionately to tear down the screen of this secrecy.[27]

There is a feeling of enclosedness and isolation. (Conspiratorial thinking always strives for isolation – national, religious or State; evil, on the other hand, is 'international' – international Zionism, the international church, world revolution, the international financial system, international political and economic links, globalisation and so on.) Isolation is the artificially created birthplace of threats, in Slavoj Žižek's words, 'the empty space of power'. It needs not so much filling, as the constant simulation of fullness. The historicisation of the Revolution, the peak of which was reached in the second half of the 1930s, when the problem of the legitimacy of the regime, occupied at that time with the destruction of those who made the Revolution, had become particularly acute, became the most effective form of simulation under Stalinism. (After the war the historical-revolutionary film lost its position; the Great Victory that had just been achieved became the centre of identity.) From the large number of historical-revolutionary films I have chosen three of the most striking pictures, representing its different subgenres: the 'biographical' film (the trilogy about Maxim), the film about the leader (Romm's two-part film) and the so-called 'publicistic film' (Ermler's two-parter). The order in which they will be examined is connected not so much with their chronology (they were released practically simultaneously) as with the logic of how they reflect the transformation of the image of the revolutionary into the image of the counter-revolutionary. At the centre of the trilogy about Maxim lies the revolutionary underground, which is opposed by external forces (the tsarist regime). Romm's films about Lenin concern the transformation of the revolutionary underground into revolutionary power. (Accordingly, the image of counter-revolution changes from the secret police in *Lenin in October* to internal conspiracy in *Lenin in 1918*.) Finally, in *The Great Citizen* former revolutionaries are transformed into underground counter-revolutionaries – 'enemies of the people' – spies and saboteurs. We have here the full cycle of the ideological utilisation of the product of political paranoia. It is interesting, above all, on the level of the construction of a new political imagination via the externalisation and projection of Stalinist fantasies.

This, in its turn, engenders a profound generic (and not only thematic and superficial) link between the pictures. In the Maxim trilogy, the directors of which were attempting to create, in their own words, a 'magnificent prose of the underground', the positive construction of the revolutionary's image dominates, corresponding to the genre of the biographical novel. In place of 'objective prose' comes the drama of the dualised 'I' (leader/enemy of the revolution) in Romm's Lenin films. And, finally, in *The Great Citizen*, traumatic externalisation (the transformation of the 'I' into the 'Other') achieves the highest degree of 'subjectivity', an almost psychoanalytic lyricism. The epos, drama and lyric of the Revolution, visualised, articulated and uttered by the leading figures of Soviet art, allow us to see in the 'empty space of power' the triumph of the Stalinist *Gesamtkunstwerk*.

'Magnificent Prose of the Underground': Kozintsev and Trauberg's 'Trilogy about Maxim'

With the completion of the Stalinist Revolution, after the paroxysms of collectivisation and industrialisation, the authorities, having definitively found a new face, needed a representation of its historical rootedness. The problem of a new identity became central, requiring a positively constructed image of the revolutionary – the new regime needed a prototype. Soviet cinema, under the leadership of Boris Shumyatsky, 'decisively turned its face to the mass of viewers'. In place of the intellectual montage and avant-garde experimentalism of the revolutionary era, 'cinema for the millions' comes in; *The Road to Life*

(*Putevka v zhizn'*), *Counterplan* (*Vstrechnyi*), *Chapaev*, *Jolly Fellows* (*Veselye rebiata*) and *Maxim's Youth* are film-manifestoes of the new 'people's aesthetic'.

Viewers appreciated it immediately. Kozintsev recalled of the first showings of *Maxim's Youth*:

> The hall, and this was clear at the very first screenings, shared our thoughts and feelings. What had happened? Simply that it was no longer 'us' and 'the viewers'. Time brought together two reels, the film and life, and from now on they moved synchronically. The man on the screen thought and felt like the people in the hall, the kinsfolk of the hero were sitting in the cinema. Everyone felt at home. How could they not be agitated, when the police tracked down their kith, one of their own, and dragged them off to prison, how could they not sympathise, when he wanted to leave the world of secret agents and security services, phrase-mongers and bureaucrats? And this man behaved on the screen in such a human way, he did not strike poses, did not speechify, did not campaign and without all that people understood him.[28]

Mass success, which had become the criterion for ideological effectiveness, could not, of course, take place without success at the very top. We know little about Stalin's renowned film screenings, but one of them – fortunately, precisely *Maxim's Youth* – has entered the annals. This is in part thanks to Mikhail Kalinin's famous phrase, 'When we made the revolution, we did not play guitars', and in part because, in the tense silence which ensued at the end of the screening, one of the directors (Kozintsev said it was Trauberg, Trauberg that it was Kozintsev) fainted, after which Stalin banned directors from his screenings. Kozintsev's recollections of how Stalin behaved during the screening of *Maxim's Youth* have, however, been preserved:

> It is not just the characters conducting dialogues among themselves, but the man in the hall who is implicated in the action, guided by the people on the screen. The underground man Polivanov mingled with the crowd at the workers' demonstration.
>
> 'What for? Where are you going? He wants to destroy the organisation . . . What's the hurry?!' he lectured the shadow on the screen.
>
> Indeed, today it was easy for Natasha to turn a lesson at the workers' evening class into an opportunity for agitation.
>
> 'Well done!' rang out his voice from the hall. 'That's how you should work! You're a good teacher, comrade Natasha!'
>
> But then when, after the exposure of the organisation, she went into decline and made a clumsy proclamation, her past service was immediately forgotten.
>
> 'Idiot! . . .,' came an indignant voice. 'Couldn't she think up anything cleverer! . . . You need a head on your shoulders, comrade Natasha!'

And only Maxim, assessing the text of the proclamation in the same way and getting down to business himself, assuaged his anger.

Thus it went on for the whole film.[29]

In these dialogues with 'shadows on the screen' Stalin is interesting, above all, as a 'viewer from the masses', as 'kith', 'a man in the street', interpreting the film on the level of a whodunit. Stalin accepted Maxim, although the director feared the leader's anger, not without good reason.

The film had a long and difficult history. Its idea was related to 1929, when the directors, in Kozintsev's words, 'decided to produce a film going against the already established tradition of showing the Revolution in a completely sympathetic light'.[30] For three years the screenplay travelled round the 'highest levels of the authorities', acquiring more and more new comments, and demands for more and more new reworkings. Even before it had been made, the film had powerful enemies (Commissar of Enlightenment Andrei Bubnov) and friends (Alexei Stetsky, head of the Culture and Propaganda section of the Central Committee, and the cinematographers' chief, Boris Shumyatsky). 'Old Bolsheviks' wrote reviews of it, finding in it a great many failings and distortions. The authors endlessly (and right up to the last minute) rewrote the screenplay.[31] But all the same the chief thing remained in the picture – the biography of 'professional revolutionary', with emphasis on the word 'professional', in which, as Kozintsev wrote:

> Nothing external was even slightly animated, not to speak of emotion – there was no trace of it . . . a beautiful woman in a Phrygian cap with a red banner in her hands – Delacroix's symbol of the barricades – could not appear with people who looked like that. Against the forces of the old world, against its cruelty, its blunt power, its brutality, a quiet man of incredible patience and self-possession came into battle . . . In this man's appearance there was nothing heroic . . . So-called monumentalism, the genre of the epopee, emotionalism, symbolic heroes – all this has become alien. You could look for pathos in the opposite direction, in the 'lowered tone' of the story, as Trauberg characterised it at that time.[32]

The screenplay was born from documents from the Bolshevik underground – Party archives, and from the archives of the *okhrana* and police administration. The initial screenplay was all clashes, motives and stories corresponding to the most severe taste of the Factory of the Eccentric Actor (FEKS) group: 'the screenplay and the film mix up revolutionary speeches, failures, arrests, fantastically audacious escapes, trips abroad and a return to the underground, unbelievable meetings and legendary duels with the *okhrana*.'[33] In a word, the exemplary art of conspiracy. From hundreds of prototypes at least two are well known. These are Maxim Litvinov, who travelled from a remote settlement to become a People's Commissar (the name Maxim came from him) and Boris Shumyatsky, repressed in 1938, the godfather of the film, a former legendary professional revolutionary who became the prototype of Polivanov.

When Kozintsev wrote of the 'magnificent prose of the underground', free from exaltation, posing and romantic sacrifices, he in effect established a change in the stylistics of the 'revolutionary hero'. The heroic aesthetics of the Populists and SRs were above all poetry. In the memoirs of the old Bolsheviks Kozintsev discovered precisely the prose of the revolutionary conspiracy, which was constructed on a rejection of the Populists' and SRs' 'hysterical revolutionism, impatience, exaltation, cult of individual heroic deeds'.[34] Later Trauberg told the story of how in 1933, preparing for work on the trilogy by reading the memoirs of the old Bolsheviks, he and Kozintsev discovered for themselves the complete disparity of what they had read from the 'usual depiction' of 'revolutionary heroism':

> We are reading the memoirs of the underground men, book after book (about a hundred). The shock! Heroes – but no heroics (not to be confused with heroism). If it had just been one or two . . . but it was almost all of them.[35]

It was not a question of dehistoricising the Revolution, but just of aesthetics. Kozintsev records what is almost an anecdote. A Bolshevik and an SR were arrested at the same time. To the gendarme's question, 'Who are you?', the SR immediately struck a pose and said: 'I am a member of the Socialist Revolutionary party, fighting to overthrow autocracy.' When the Bolshevik was asked, he replied, 'I am a poor office clerk; this is the first time I've heard anything about this.' That night the office clerk escaped from prison, while the SR stayed there. 'There arose', Kozintsev concluded the story, 'these great prosaics, linked with remarkable humour and great orientation. There arose a wonderful and complex image of people who were calm and happy in the consciousness of the strength of their task.'[36] Such was the new, post-FEKS hero – a cunning 'prosaist', a gambler, an eccentric, an artistic personality, but now also a Bolshevik.

The prototype of the new power – the 'professional revolutionary' – proved to be above all an underground man, a conspirator, and in historical perspective, a Chekist. 'Professional' in Kozintsev's formulation meant: 'A conspirator above all. A revolutionary who has not mastered the art of conspiracy would disappear not in a few days, but in a few hours, because the system of police provocation had been brought to virtual perfection.'[37]

Kozintsev's hero, Maxim, is irrepressible and cunning, finding a way out of every difficult situation. The revolutionary underground is a cynical counterbalance to emotionalism, which is in general contraindicated by the underground. (Thus the emotionalism of the Mensheviks is ridiculed in *Maxim's Return*, as are Kartashov's emotional speeches in *The Great Citizen*.) The sphere of public politics, on the other hand, is packed with emotion (Maxim in

The Vyborg Side, Shakhov in *The Great Citizen*). But this emotionalism in the public sphere is created by yesterday's underground, cynical Bolshevik conspirators. All the pathos of *The Great Citizen* would be directed at the displacement of this memory of the Bolsheviks' underground past. The appearance of Maxim neatly dressed in a jumper in *The Great Citizen* was the appearance not of a rebel of yesteryear, but of a party functionary. To the extent that the 'jolly people of the underground' were transformed in *The Great Citizen* into regular emotional characters, the underground itself was filled with infernal villainy.

The paradox lay in the fact that the 'jolly prose of the underground' in *Maxim's Youth* was created in the far from jolly era of *The Great Citizen*, and the 'jolly people of the underground' did not want to recognise their previous selves. Kozintsev even later could not understand why the screenplay was criticised:

> The first version of the screenplay (*The Bolshevik*) was scattered to the four winds. I reread the reviews that had been kept: neither a history of the party nor an image of a Bolshevik; why show the era of reaction (gloom, defeat)? Events should be transferred to the era of development; show the battle of the party on two fronts – against the liquidators (who called for limitation by legal means) and rejectionists (who demanded the boycott of the Duma and would only work in the underground).
>
> Alas, among the most savage of our critics there turned out to be some whose memoirs had fascinated us and roused us to get down to work on this film. For some unknown, strange reason, the 'jolly, strong, mischievous people' (Drabkina) wanted us to make a boring film about them. But what could we do? The demands were insistent. We had no choice but to settle down to making these alterations. However, no matter how we tried, Maxim did not want to fight either the liquidators or the rejectionists.[38]

The fact was that yesterday's 'mischief-makers' but today's 'savage critics' had already found themselves completely within a pre-prepared myth, which described their actions a quarter of a century previously. It was not only that their former jolliness, strength and mischievousness were not honoured in the stagnant Stalinist 'historical party sciences'. These qualities were dangerous; indeed, the repressions of the Great Terror rained down above all on the heads of these same memoirists who inspired the directors to produce the trilogy. (A revealing feature: in 1935, when *Maxim's Youth* was released, the Society of Old Bolsheviks was closed down.) The mischief-makers of bygone times wanted to see themselves depicted in totally safe, if boring categories. Maxim in *Maxim's Youth* and *The Great Citizen* is a direct reflection of the change that had taken place. At the beginning of the 1930s, when the trilogy was first conceived, Maxim was still a cheerful fellow and a mischief-maker; in the years of the Great Terror, when *The Great Citizen* was made, not a trace of that cheerfulness remains. In Maxim's eyes the former 'cunning and mischievousness' of the revolutionary-conspirator have definitively been replaced by the suspicious, mocking squint of the Chekist.

So, earlier the path to revolution was depicted tragically. (It is sufficient to recall Pudovkin's *Mother*, or the nameless main character from *The End of St Petersburg*.) But here we have a bright path, vivacious, with humour, songs and happiness. The plot is built at the intersection of revolutionary chronicle and historical epic. But the milieu and reality are depicted in too much detail and the main character is too dynamic, light-hearted, jolly and open for an epic. On the other hand, all three parts of the film construct the image of Maxim on the principle of the camera zooming in; at first we see an immature youth (*Maxim's Youth*), then an experienced revolutionary (*Maxim's Return*), and finally, an agent for the state (*The Vyborg Side*). Thus the trilogy can to some extent be related to both stylistic dominants.

And although romanticism was not to the directors' liking (Kozintsev suggested that the Revolution should have travelled to Russia 'third class'[39]), nor did realism suit them. As Oksana Bulgakowa observed, 'the mechanisms [from FEKS practice] of the entertaining genre, with a simplified structure, were used in the fable about Maxim . . . In the twenties these signs were aestheticised; in the thirties they were ideologised.'[40] Continuing that idea, Maya Turovskaya asserted that in the cinema of the 1930s:

> [G]enre as the art of entertainment was pushed to the edge of the cinematic process. But on the other hand ideology was dressed in the garb of genre and this imposition of generic structures on the material of reality was constituted as 'socialist realism'.[41]

From this comes the rejection of both the conventional adventure story and the storyless montage technique of revolutionary cinema, and the discovery of the prototype in the genre of the biographical novel. Barbara Leaming traced in detail all the points on the abrupt transfer from one aesthetic to the other. If FEKS emphasised conflict and rupture, then now Kozintsev and Trauberg 'aspire[d] to embody an ideology of totality'; if, for FEKS, interest in movement and gesture was characteristic, then now directors focused on faces; if, for FEKS, rhythm was important, then now theme and character were central for directors.[42]

The aesthetic strategies of FEKS were a trivialisation of tradition, of the academism. Their favourite term was 'boulevardisation'. In the trilogy the directors effectively boulevardised Bolshevik history, but in fact the boulevardisation of Bolshevism occurred in the *Short Course*, while Bolshevism itself, in its turn, was a boulevardisation of Marxism. The FEKS actors were propagandists for the 'lower genres', but could one find a 'lower genre' of historical narrative than the *Short Course*? Nor did the directors hide their sources: 'We imagined the history of the party in the era of reaction adapted for the screen,' said Kozintsev in 1937:

> What should there be in this textbook? The rout of the old generation of revolutionaries: strikes, demonstrations, the crushing of demonstrations by the police, the Bolsheviks' studies in prison, illegal pre-revolutionary May day meetings outside the town. And these are the basic episodes of our picture. You will find them in any book on the history of the Party, in any story of that time. Our 'attractions' were not made up. They were there in the material.[43]

Only a little time was to pass until that 'material' would appear before yesterday's viewer in the engraved formulae of the *Short Course*.

This occurred towards the end of the 1930s. But in the first half of the decade the tendency towards 'simplification' was a response to a new aesthetic programme.

> It was not only that the characters were life-like – that is, they came to the screen from life-but they also came into life from the screen and were taken as kin . . . And it was not that in the twenties the cinema was experimental, but in the thirties returned to simplicity and clarity. In the first decade (to be more precise, the first five years), the viewers influenced the cinema, and then the cinema returned to the viewers what it had taken from them,

Kozintsev wrote later,[44] having in mind the cinematic context in which the trilogy was born – the Vasilevs' *Chapaev*, Boris Barnet's *The Outskirts* (*Okraina*), Zarkhi and Kheifits's *Deputy from the Baltics* (*Deputat Baltiki*), Sergei Gerasimov's *The Teacher* (*Uchitel'*) and Raizman's *The Last Night* (*Posledniaia noch'*).

In other words, the 'masses' of early revolutionary cinema, of the era of *Battleship Potemkin*, *Strike*, *Storm over Asia* and *The Arsenal*, were no longer needed. What was needed was a hero from the people and for the people. This also led to hostility towards the academy, particularly towards the Moscow Arts Theatre (MKhAT): 'We have springing up in art now a sort of universal MKhAT,' Kozintsev grieved. 'What is being done in cinematography now is MKhAT of not quite the first rank, taken at second hand.' The director did indeed seek a new acting aesthetic for the creation of his 'people's hero':

> The whole genre and style of acting in *Youth* and *Return* arose . . . from daily life in the workers' suburbs, from the romance of the outskirts, from an accordion that is sometimes lyrical, sometimes mischievous. We were looking for a burning realism. We were looking for a ringing form of acting.[45]

He pointed without constraint to the genres that were close to him:

> [U]ndisguised melodrama, undisguised vaudeville, farce and so on, not to
> speak of variety, on which a whole range of methods is constructed. The
> whole stylistics of acting, without cancelling out the seriousness of the
> theme, the requirement and truthfulness of motivation, came from the folk
> arts of the lower genres of theatre.[46]

It was not, however, only a question of FEKS aesthetics, but also of the fact
that Kozintsev and Trauberg could neither construct a film on the model of
'detectives' adventures', nor imitate folklore (although they preserved the orientation towards 'popular narrative' even in the titles). They did not like
realism and its templates that had been developed for reasons that were not so
much aesthetic as, so to speak, moral-ideological:

> [F]eigned realism was even less to our liking than the romantic pathos of
> silent films. 'Entertainment' and 'warmth' seemed to us words that
> destroyed the integrity of Soviet cinematography. We could hear some-
> thing shifty, cunningly fixed up for both politics and the box office, in
> these ever more frequently expanding definitions. In the fight against that
> style *Maxim's Youth* was conceived at the very beginning of the 1930s.[47]

It turned out, however, that the trilogy was a true incarnation of that style, and
the directors successfully 'fixed up both politics and the box office'.

'Entertainment' came out of the detective story plot, while the plot itself came
from conspiracy as the fundamental work of the 'professional revolutionary',
with the underground as the sphere of his existence. The directors did not want
to admit this. Kozintsev wrote:

> We soon realised that all the previous experience of so-called 'revolutionary-
> adventure' pictures, such as *Little Red Devils* (*Krasnye d'iavoliata*), *The
> Traitor* (*Predatel'*), *The Happy Canary* (*Veselaia kanareika*) and others,
> could not help us at all in terms of dramaturgy, direction or acting.
>
> All these enigmatic provocateurs, effective escapes from prison, secrets
> of the underground and other such romantic fluff not only do not come
> from the material of the revolutionary movement, but distort it, turning
> the images of the Bolsheviks into something like heroes out of an adven-
> ture novel.[48]

Kozintsev named the sources from which the 'strict truth of the revolutionary
underground' was derived: 'books by Lenin and Stalin, old proclamations, revolutionary memoirs, photographs in the Museum of the Revolution'.[49]

The Museum of the Revolution is not mentioned by accident. The feeling of
being in a museum was almost tangible in this picture. The emigrant writer and

critic, Georgy Adamovich, expressed it very precisely but in his own way, writing of his impressions of the premiere of *Maxim's Youth* in Paris. He came out of the cinema almost depressed – 'In the film it was impossible to breathe.' He summed up his feeling in one word – 'carrion' – whilst 'the most characteristic feature of the film' he named 'the absence of any movement – internal or external'.[50] In essence, what Adamovich was describing is history already transformed into a museum exhibit, which no kind of 'entertainment' could save.

Kozintsev and Trauberg, meanwhile, were fully aware of the problem they faced when they wrote in connection with *Maxim's Return*:

> The difficulties of the production, showing the history of the Party, were obvious to everyone. Here two dangers existed. Firstly, it was easy, having subordinated the material to the existing traditions of dramatic cinema, to create a normal adventure film, with escapes from prison, enigmatic provocateurs and solid props falsely understood as 'cinematography'. The second danger facing us was a mechanistic dramatisation of episodes from a textbook on Party history.[51]

In fact, the directors fell into both traps. If previous adventure films (such as *Little Red Devils*, to which Kozintsev loved to refer) had been shot with ideological flavouring, then now, with the creation of the first historical-revolutionary (historical-Party) film of the Stalinist era, a true genre revolution took place; this was, above all, an ideologically correct textbook, flavoured with 'cinematographic qualities', not the reverse, as before.

Aesthetics and ideology found each other. Trauberg wrote of the '"domestication" of the emotional history of the underground' in the trilogy, and linked this with the device of estrangement: 'It is probably not worth calling these films an illustration of the device of "estrangement", but without paying attention to this concept we would hardly have thought up our work.'[52] (This device of domestication through 'the story of bloody battles with the help throughout of everyday things', Trauberg pointed out, was used in *Chapaev*.[53]) But the mischievous hero was needed by the directors not only because he allowed them to 'estrange' the revolution, and not only because the roguish hero demystified the revolutionary myth, but also because it was their task to 'demonstrate the era'. This era was until that time no less mythologised than the revolutionary era; it was called the 'era of reaction' – frightening, gloomy and suffocating. A hero was needed who would make the era digestible: 'We were afraid that the era of reaction would arouse a feeling of heavy depression, and that the viewer would leave the cinema with a heavy heart. And we tried to place the hero in opposition to the era: that is, to give the viewer a hero who could pull along the theme through this terrible era.'[54]

In the first versions of the screenplay the 'era of reaction' overwhelmed the Bolshevik hero, Polivanov. The gloomy, crushing atmosphere recalled the FEKS versions of *The Overcoat* and *The Club of the Great Deed* (SVD). The prologue for the screenplay of *The Bolshevik* (as it was then called) looked like this: Petersburg on New Year's Eve, drunken revelry, Polivanov walking round secret rendezvous that had been discovered by the secret police. (Someone has been arrested, someone has rejected the struggle, someone has become a provocateur.) At the end of the prologue a detective says to the arrested Polivanov, 'I'll tell you straight, there's nothing for you to fight for – the Party organisation in Petersburg has been destroyed.' The journal, *Sovetskoe kino* (*Soviet Cinema*), reacted to the publication of the prologue thus: 'The circle of despair of the reactionary period is enclosed. The movement, which had hardly flared up, has again gone out. The prologue breaks off, leaving, it seems, no threads for the continuation of the action.'[55]

And although, after many years of wandering through the higher offices, this screenplay was in the end banned in Moscow by the commission of the Central Committee, the problem of the 'era of reaction' did not disappear:

> 'When we worked properly on the period of reaction we saw that we were threatened by a great danger – depressing the viewer. When you burrow around in archive materials from the era of reaction, you see such a huge amount of treachery, terror and blood that showing all of it would cause depression, but without it there is no era of reaction,' Kozintsev said after a showing of the film at the Leningrad cinema club.[56]

As a result the directors decided to 'make an optimistic picture of the period of reaction'. Thus there appeared 'the Till Eulenspiegel of Russian capitalism of the beginning of the twentieth century'.[57] (Incidentally, Boris Chirkov, who played the main role, was discovered in the Leningrad TIuZ (Theatre of the Young Viewer) playing 'Till Eulenspiegel'.) Trauberg directly admitted that 'cinema art in the image of Maxim found its Till Eulenspiegel, its Colas Breugnon . . . the main thing was the authentic popular origin of Maxim.'[58] Kozintsev was also very proud of the popular origins of Maxim; he was ecstatic when someone called *Maxim's Youth* 'a picture of coarse effects'.[59]

One should be fully aware that from the start aesthetics were dictated not so much by ideology as by the internal impossibility for the FEKS movement of continuing the experiment, in the first place; of working on the ready-made official canon, in the second place; and of making a film according to the laws of mass cinematography of that time, in the third place. The latter circumstance is particularly important, in so far as the viewer's horizon of expectation advanced defined demands, even in such an ideologically charged genre as the historical-revolutionary film: 'A wide prescription existed for the historical-revolutionary pictures,' Kozintsev said. 'These were detective dramas with escapes from prison, romantic melodramas with enigmatic students, etc.' Kozintsev called all this 'old rubbish'.[60] The aim was to create a film which was simultaneously watchable, ideologically correct and worthy from the aesthetic point of view. (The directors were not prepared to sacrifice either their reputation as recherché artists or elevated professional status.)

It was in this context that they approached *Maxim's Youth*. The main thing that brought the hero closer to the viewer was the absolute coincidence of the personality and the historical role:

> The idea of *Maxim's Youth* [Kozintsev wrote] was just that nothing was there 'for ideology's sake'. And everything was there only for that. The essence of the film consisted of the fact that this fellow inevitably had to become a revolutionary. He was endowed with the best features of a Petersburg worker: wit and humour, an innate sense of justice, loyalty to his comrades, sincerity and decisiveness, courage and patience. He could not reconcile himself to arbitrary rule and the absence of rights. There could be no life for him without the Revolution. And the Revolution turned out to need him: both his love of cunning jokes and of his favourite boulevard song, 'The blue sphere is spinning.' There was not the least need for him to be restructured, to change landmarks, to acknowledge his mistakes (the usual motifs of the dramatic arts in those years). And he became a propagandist not because clever and knowledgeable people gave him the correct books; the need to give other people spiritual nourishment was in his nature. The human character and the image of the revolutionary did not exist separately. There was simply Maxim and that was all.[61]

In contrast to Shakhov, the main character in *The Great Citizen*, Maxim develops, although to all intents and purposes, like Shakhov, he also remains unchanged. There always remains some sort of unchanging sediment of his character, which allows the hero to act even rashly, intuitively (whether because of his youth, as in *Maxim's Youth*, or unconsciously, as in the second part of *The Great Citizen*), but nevertheless always to act correctly:

> [Maxim] enters the Bolshevik underground naturally and simply, because it is his milieu, because his class instincts, even if as yet unconscious, drive him there. He does not resist the events which draw him into revolutionary activity; he quickly finds his place, responding to his character, his personal preferences and his class psychology. Therefore the content of *Youth* is what happens to Maxim and not what happens within Maxim. His psychology is not laid bare before the viewer.[62]

Rationalism turns into total irrationality; Maxim simply does everything by inspiration – so correct are his character, preferences and psychology. (Something similar would happen in *The Great Citizen* with Shakhov, who also 'by inspiration' would not only ascertain but also defeat the enemy.)

Maxim's Youth is dedicated to the birth of such a hero, and before us we have, so to speak, two layers of reality: one sacred (with emotional appeals and party debates, secret rendezvous, underground printing presses, dreadful prison cells, pursuits, disguises and passwords) which corresponds to the detective narrative (as, for example, the prologue to the film is constructed); the other profane (with accordions, guitars and drinking dens), corresponding to the 'penny-dreadful' narrative (the simple speech of the characters, the subtitles, in fairytale style). These two realities are united in the image of the main protagonist, who towards the end of the first part is transformed into a 'Petersburg Bolshevik', resolutely moving from the profane space to the sacred. In essence, in the course of the film the hero undergoes a process of initiation: the working lad is transformed into a conscious revolutionary as a result of the death of his friend Dyoma (and in many ways, thanks to it).

At the basis of the stylistics of each of these semantic constructions lay a ready-made canon. In 1934 this canon could only be Gorky's. The narrative structure of Gorky's autobiographical trilogy, the influence of which the directors mentioned themselves, and the Maxim trilogy, are directly linked. (Thus the narrative of the hero's life is maximally close in the film to colloquial style; this is particularly evident in title frames such as 'Three comrades lived in St Petersburg by Narvskaya gate', 'Maxim ends up at "university"', 'And Maxim began to live between heaven and earth', and so on.) Meanwhile, Gorky created not only the canon of the Soviet *Bildungsroman*, but also the narrative of the underground (from *Mother* to *The Life of a Useless Man* and *Karamora*). And he indeed criticised the directors for their incorrect depiction of the Bolshevik underground: 'In the picture *Maxim's Youth* the author-director – I don't know who – not having sufficient notion of underground work, committed more than a few factual errors.'[63] One could, however, suggest that it was not factual errors, but precisely stylistic confusion which aroused Gorky's displeasure. If *Maxim's Youth* is, in Gorky's words, 'the history of hero's growth', then his biography should be located universally in the sacred space. (The Gorkian narrative always – beginning with his early romantic works and ending with *Klim Samgin* – strove towards stylistic and generic purity.) The diversity of the FEKS stylistic collage (which later, with the 'growth of the hero's consciousness', disappears from the trilogy) could not be to his taste; Gorky's world was, as we have seen, simultaneously both clearer and more stylistically homogenous.

What makes *Maxim's Youth* such an interesting film is its direct use of the detective story for strictly stylistic ends. Enemies (policemen, spies, secret agents, masters and factory owners) fill the film, guaranteeing it a detective story atmosphere, all the more so as the underground is transformed into the most important (sacred) part of reality, whilst, on the other hand, everything visible (profane) turns out to be only a disguise, like the deliberate simple-mindedness of the hero, his constant habit of singing songs, which turn out to be passwords, and so on. This 'disguised reality', besides everything else, fulfils an important ideological function; *Maxim's Youth* depicts the period 1910–11, the most difficult years for the Bolsheviks, the period of the 'Stolypin reaction', when 'the Party worked deep underground.' Such was the official version, which took shape long before the *Short Course*. In fact, the Party had simply fallen apart. (Its leaders were in emigration, exile or prison, its cells had been uncovered, there were large numbers of provocateurs in their ranks, and so on.) In other words, this historical reality itself needed 'disguising' and recoding, which the directors of *Maxim's Youth* also did, not so much fearing 'making the viewer depressed' with the gloom of reaction, as needing the underground as a crucible to temper the protagonist of the Soviet *Bildungsroman*.

In *Maxim's Return* the *Bildungsroman* is transformed into the novel of ordeal – with an unchanged hero, who has now only changed Party jobs. In this necessity of 'creating a hero with ready-made characteristics', Kozintsev saw more than a few difficulties. Meanwhile, the logic of transforming a proletarian into a professional revolutionary dictated things in its own way:

> He is no longer a worker groping for the truth, but a professional revolutionary, a professional Bolshevik. He has behind him prison, absolute understanding of the class struggle, understanding of what exploitation is. He has a great teacher behind him – the older generation of the Bolshevik Party, he has exile behind him – the revolutionary's university. Therefore there is no room for him to change. He can only grow.

But there also turns out to be nowhere for the hero to grow – 'the time intervals are very small'.[64] It remains only to present new facets of the hero in every new scene.

What are these facets? 'A conspirator above all.'[65] In essence, conspiracy is the basic quality of the 'returning' Maxim. The mask of the simple-hearted joker from the workers' suburb is definitively detached from him, and he needs it only for conspiracy. Certain critics said that they had not noticed the change taking place in the hero. For them he remained 'a wonderful fellow, lightly and confidently travelling the difficult road of the revolutionary struggle'.[66] 'Chirkov's characteristic cunning', admired by others, in no way prevented one from noticing the use of total disguise in the picture: 'The ability to show the actions of the hero as lively and natural characterises even the very manner of Maxim's disguises, when they are needed for revolutionary work.'[67] The transformation of 'the story of Till Eulenspiegel from the Narvskaya gates neighbourhood' into the story of an underground revolutionary is only in part explained by ideological requirements (showing the political struggle, caricatured images of representatives of the non-Bolshevik parties, and so on). In essence, the trilogy about Maxim is the story of the transformation of Till Eulenspiegel into a Chekist. Thrift and experience are the main qualities of Maxim in *Return*. The hero's 'charm' cracked, which the first reviewers could not help but notice:

> From frame to frame the duality of this character unfolds, the broadness of the tactical methods he uses, the ease with which he masters new tasks.

In order to act with honour in so many different circumstances, in order to find the correct means of conducting the struggle in each of them, Maxim has above all to be able to talk to different people in different ways, to impress different people, to use the human qualities given to him by nature with strength and sincere conviction, with the authentic purity of his revolutionary conscience. Only these qualities could truly raise up his image, make him ready to fulfil new party missions.[68]

And the 'missions' pour forth one after the other. In *Maxim's Return* the plot revolves around strikes organised by the Bolsheviks on the eve of the First World War; for their refusal to fulfil their military orders, the workers at the Nevsky factory are sacked. Comrade Fyodor – Maxim's party name – 'throws' himself into organising the strike. For this job he needs only a guitar with a ringing sound and secret rendezvous address – a drinking den with a billiard room. The surname which the directors finally give Maxim in part two is a telling one – Lisitsyn.[69] The image of the simple Russian worker from *Maxim's Youth* takes on the guise of the professional Bolshevik. In effect, in *Return*, Maxim only plays the role of the earlier Maxim. His spontaneity is only a means of conspiracy, concealing his new image – as a quirky and shrewd Bolshevik conspirator.

Maxim's Return brings the viewer into a new world. From the very first frames – Maxim's appearance with a guitar, as always singing a song, which this time turns out to be a password to the underground secret rendezvous – the viewer understands that he no longer has before him Till Eulenspiegel, but a Bolshevik conspirator. At the same time the hero argues skilfully with the Mensheviks, who are doing everything they can to break up the workers' strike. Maxim's task is to uncover and smash their insidious ideas. Kozintsev described the 'arrangement of forces' in the scene of the argument between the Bolsheviks and Mensheviks thus: 'Among the bustling and twinkling Mensheviks – the quiet and clever Maxim with his cunning eye.'[70]

This 'cunning eye' – Maxim's basic physical characteristic – is also the fundamental attribute of the Bolshevik. This is conspiracy in reverse, so to speak, conspiracy in a mirror. Whoever the hero of *Maxim's Return* may be (a debater, a 'theoretician', an 'organiser of the masses', a lover), he is, above all, a conspirator. The plot of the film moves around the conspiracy against the distribution of military orders, as well as the secret planning of 'the revolutionary act of the workers' and discovery of the secret (in a scene in which Maxim plays 'a slightly dopey lad from Russian fairytales'[71]) and the underground organisation of the strike. All this goes back to the actions of the underground Bolshevik committee, and from there leads to the Bolshevik faction in the State Duma, so that the situation develops as a kind of microcosm of the great political conspiracy happening throughout the country.

In *Maxim's Return* not only a new Maxim, but also a new enemy awaits the viewer; spies and secret agents are replaced by Mensheviks and Duma deputies.

Cossacks and policemen appear as the 'last bulwark' of the tsarist regime, like a force standing behind the mill and factory owners, the Duma and its appeasers, the Mensheviks. Moreover, the latter are depicted in deliberately caricatured fashion. If these are Mensheviks, who call themselves 'theoretical people', 'old Marxists', 'old Social Democrats', then their political actions as 'appeasers' and 'traitors to cause of the working class' are frankly mocked (at the end a Menshevik of Jewish intellectual appearance is even transformed into . . . an officer in the tsarist army); if this is the 'Black-hundred Duma', then here with easy familiarity many of the deputies are depicted as a raving crowd of angry hooligans, hysterically banging tables with their fists, whistling and shrieking in a heart-rending manner, swinish, fat and with cigars in their mouths.

This whole variegated, caricatured crowd of enemies, sometimes protecting the 'rotten tsarist regime' by themselves, sometimes insinuating themselves right into the workers' movement, demands both new protagonists for the party and . . . total disguise. Every word and action here has a double meaning: Maxim's crafty, screwed-up eyes, the Mensheviks' cunning, the underground committees, drowning in tobacco smoke, the viewer, entangled in all the names. (Maxim sometimes becomes Pavel, at other times Fyodor, sometimes a name-less worker, other times a soldier.) Songs turn out to be passwords in disguise. A Bolshevik (that is, Maxim) acts in such a way that the old worker, not knowing what lies hidden behind his behaviour, does not know how to char-acterise him, leading to his erroneous description of the hero: 'a billiard-player, a drunk and a womaniser'. All this engenders a new semantic space. There is no longer a place for the world divided into the sacred and profane of *Maxim's Youth*. The sacred world is now entirely permeated with sarcasm; the playful-ness and ease with which the Bolsheviks carry out their conspiratorial work, the cheerfulness and resourcefulness with which Maxim either deceives the 'enemies of the working class' in an almost clown-like fashion, plays the fool, or winds the Mensheviks around his little finger, all bring to the revolutionary battle itself (with its sacrifices, heroic demonstrations with renditions of the 'Marseillaise', deaths on the barricades, martyrdom, touching concern for each other and so on) a strong share of profanity.

The narrative unity of this world is supported by total organisation. Explaining to the workers the essence of the strikers' fight against the military orders (the factory owners secretly transferred them from the business plagued by the strike to another factory), Maxim says: 'They've made arrangements, and we must make arrangements as well.' This network of conspiracy perme-ates the whole plot of the film. 'Below' we see the actions of Maxim, 'an ordi-nary fighter for the party', who organises the workers, and investigates in drinking dens the mystery of the secret military orders by making an office clerk drunk. He is linked with *Pravda*. The newspaper is the next stage of the uni-versal 'conspiracy'. It avoids the 'turnpikes' of censorship and is published and distributed semi-underground. Through it the conspiracy is disseminated to all the factories, raised, finally, to state level, becoming the subject of discussion in the Duma, and growing into the battles on the barricades in the capital.

The Bolsheviks organise the masses. The masses are in their own right the product of the organisational (that is, strictly, conspiratorial) activities of the Bolsheviks. Without them there would have been no masses at all. The strike, spilling into mass demonstrations with barricades and street battles, was the culmination of the Bolsheviks' underground organisational work. The struggle organised by the Bolsheviks becomes the mirror image of the old tsarist regime. To the state yoke (organisation) the Bolsheviks reply with insurrection (organisation): 'They've made arrangements and we must make arrangements as well' – conspiracy must be answered with conspiracy. Here, in comparison with *Maxim's Youth*, the scope is staggering; in both films the workers' demonstration is the culmination, but in the first this takes the form of the crushing defeat of a peaceful demonstration (the funeral of a worker who died in the factory) and prison, while in the second we have the workers' victory, having driven off the Cossacks, built barricades and fought with the police in open skirmishes. The scale of the demonstrations and the bitterness in the two parts of the film are incomparable, but had, of course, to show 'the growth of the Bolshevik party's influence', although it was more a reflection of the times when the films were made.

Maxim's Youth was made in 1934, during the period of the brief Stalinist thaw, while *Maxim's Return* came out in May 1937, when the political order had become a great deal more powerful. Thus, it is clear that one of the aims of the directors was to provoke disdain and revulsion towards the Russian Parliament (from which was subsequently formed the first democratic Provisional Government in Russian history). In the year in which the film came out, right after the introduction of the Stalin constitution, the deputies of that Duma either escaped abroad, or were shot or ended up in the labour camps. But this treatment of the political elite of the country, represented in caricature in *Maxim's Return*, would not arouse any pity among Soviet viewers because, as one critic noted, the primitive roars of Russian democracy in the Duma fully justified the sentencing of 'enemies of the people'.

The final part of the trilogy, *The Vyborg Side*, which came out in 1939, contained another 'historical allusion'; the central scene of the trial of the people who had pillaged the wine cellars was constructed as an unconcealed caricature of 'bourgeois trials' (with their procedures, legalese, representation by lawyers). In answer to the appeal of the grotesquely depicted lawyer to observe 'legal norms', the hall, filled with 'the Vyborg proletariat', asks in one voice: 'Are they bandits or not?' All the lawyer's cunning constructions collapse before this question, the answer to which is given by Maxim:

> Judge them, citizens of the jury! The lawyer called upon you to judge either according to your conscience, or according to the law. But I say judge according to both your conscience, your revolutionary conscience,

and the law, the higher laws of the October Revolution. And according to your conscience and the law, I say to you, citizens of the jury, and to you, comrades, to these people and those who sent them – show them no mercy, destroy them!

For the viewer who had just lived through the show trials, this object lesson in the 'revolutionary court' was essential. To make matters clearer, Maxim addresses the pillagers themselves with literally the same questions which the prosecutor Vyshinsky had addressed to the accused in 1936–7:

> Before the face of the people, I ask you: Who sent you? Whose money was it, where were you hired? Who is hiding behind your back? . . . Give their names! Silence? Then you should not expect, nor will you be shown, any mercy!

In effect, the Moscow show trials, nearly twenty years after the events depicted in *The Vyborg Side*, had to be seen as the trials of 'those who gave the orders'.

The 'ones who gave the orders' were themselves now rearranged in a new order of importance; at the surface of the plot are the sabotaging bank employees. With the money stolen from the bank they hire pogromists and anarchists, who incite the unconscious masses to pogrom and mutiny. The money is also paid to activists from non-Bolshevik parties (SRs and Mensheviks) and officers in the tsarist army, who are preparing a military coup in Petersburg and the murder of Lenin, and who want to occupy the Tauride palace during the opening of the Constituent Assembly (about which the deputies themselves have been very well informed). This is a global conspiracy, which Maxim in the film is occupied with disentangling; his appointment may be to the post of head of the Central Bank, but he proves himself in the field of investigation, with the arrest of the conspirators and pogromists and the revolutionary courts. Maxim here is, above all, a Chekist.

The Vyborg Side is only in part the story of Maxim. It is already not so much a biographical film as an epic one, less a novel than an epopee. Beginning with the final phrase from *Lenin in October*, it belongs strictly to the 'October films', at the centre of which lie the 'leaders of the revolution': Lenin, Stalin, Sverdlov. The focus is changed from the biography of Maxim to 'epoch-making events'. The *Bildungsroman*, transformed into the novel of ordeal, is petrified in the epic events of the first days after the October Revolution of 1917. The emotionalism which accumulates towards the end of the film brings it closer to Romm's two-parter than to the story of Maxim.

In fact, Kozintsev and Trauberg were moving further and further away from the traditions of revolutionary cinema. The latter, above all, was aimed at mobilisation. In the trilogy the aims were completely different. During the discussion of *The Vyborg Side* on Radio Freedom, Christine Engel drew attention to the directors' strange penchant for the theme of dreams. (It is worth noting that this theme was also important in Romm's two films, in which Lenin is constantly talking to the worker Vasily when the latter is half-asleep.) In *Maxim's Youth* dreams already play an important role; one of the main characters is constantly having prophetic dreams which almost literally foretell coming events.

> If you look at the cinema as a collective dream [Engel said], a question arises: precisely what dream did the viewers have when they were watching Maxim then? And what dream do they have today? When a film was presented, the viewers were instilled with a feeling of the safe overcoming of all conflicts. As if the time of internal hesitation and external shock had ended and would never return. This feeling is communicated by establishing a direct, so to speak, link of kin between Maxim and the leaders – Lenin and Stalin. Maxim as the synthetic embodiment of the revolutionary hero from the common people – the youngest member of a new sort of holy family, the son of two fathers. This is where the collective grows together with the leaders, the gaze is switched from the brothers to the leader-fathers; this closing in can be traced in both top-down and bottom-up movements. Remember who in the film watches over whose sleep. The revolutionaries watch over the children's sleep, Maxim over Natasha's, Lenin and Stalin over Maxim's. Guarding sleep turns into an important metaphor. You – children, women, revolutionaries from the common people, in a word, everyone who belongs to the good part of the people – can sleep in peace, we will watch over you. Later there would be the popular song 'Our beloved city can sleep in peace . . .' The Maxim trilogy works like a lullaby. The link from the bottom up, on the other hand, gives the feeling of the unlimited possibility of socialist development. Maxim as successful revolutionary, Maxim as successful billiard player, Maxim as the commissar of the State Bank. This encourages the feeling that we can cope with everything without any effort; all we need is simplicity, optimism and good-natured cunning. It is precisely this mechanism of identification that has led some viewers today to yearn so strongly for this former picture of the world, in which nothing was demanded of them and they were simultaneously offered a choice between fairytale possibilities – like Ivan the fool.[72]

And not just 'today's viewers'! 'Yearning for Maxim' began immediately after the release of the final part of the trilogy. After *The Vyborg Side* viewers demanded an endless sequel:

> Dear comrades Kozintsev and Trauberg . . . How can it be that you, such incredibly intelligent people, do not wish to understand the viewer's psychology? You created Maxim. We are eternally grateful to you. But, forgive us, now he is ours! Because we, the viewers, love him! So what right do you have to send him off to the front and give no possibility of

waiting for his return? . . . Surely Maxim has not gone forever? Return him to us!

demanded one female viewer from Irkutsk. 'We, the Soviet viewers, want to see the further life and works of Maxim,' demanded a certain A. Korsak from Akimovka station in the Ukraine, suggesting several plots for further episodes – 'Maxim the builder', 'Maxim the economic planner'. The author of another letter asserted:

Viewers do not want to say goodbye to Maxim and ask the directors to make another film about the Maxim of today . . . Maxim is living in our times. He is the director of a large factory, the chairman of a trust or a people's commissariat. He is as ardent and calm in fulfilling the work of the State as he was in the fight against the enemies of the people. He has grown grey in battle, and to his Order of the Red Banner is deservedly added the Order of Lenin. The Soviet people elected him a deputy and sent him to the Supreme Soviet.[73]

At the end of the 1930s the directors received thousands of such letters. And not just in the thirties. Letters (collective letters!) continued to arrive in the mid-1960s:

Comrade Kozintsev, make a sequel to the Maxim trilogy, show Maxim's revolutionary dynasty. Let it include the Great Patriotic War, post-war reconstruction and, finally, Siberia, virgin soil, tents and snowdrops . . . We adults have grown up, matured across the whole country. So let the young Maxim of our time step on to the screen, into our interesting, rich life.[74]

But he took no further steps. His time in the trilogy was limited to the 'era of reaction' (1910), the 'new revolutionary ascent and the eve of the First World War' (1914), and October (1917). The era of the revolutionaries was over. The era of 'state-building' had begun. Maxim, the fellow from the workers' settlement, the underground revolutionary, is transformed into an agent of the Party and the State, into a Chekist, and in this capacity he battles with the anti-Soviet underground in *The Great Citizen*, but in effect, Shakhov-Kirov himself is Maxim after *The Vyborg Side*. (A Leningrader, in 1925, the time depicted in the first part of *The Great Citizen*, he could have been secretary of one of the city's regional committees.) Kozintsev later wrote about the impossibility of prolonging Maxim's on-screen life: 'It was impossible to do that. He could not grow old, as the youth of the Revolution could not grow old. He remained like that forever . . . We could not have taken a textbook approach to the study of its history.'[75] Why? Because at that time (owing in part to the efforts of Kozintsev himself), the Revolution no longer had a history . . .

Maxim was a guest from the future. It was with precisely such lads from the settlements that the Party began to be filled in the 1930s. They needed a pedigree. The elite of the Bolshevik intelligentsia, doomed to extinction at precisely the time when the trilogy was being released, were subject to replacement by the Maxims. This new 'working class', formed in the ruins of the villages cleared of peasants in the years of collectivisation, needed to see itself on screen. It was necessary to replace the historical Bolshevik with a mythical one, having accommodated the Stalinist nomenclature promoted from 'the workers' (yesterday's peasantry, arriving from the outskirts) in 1910–17 and passed them off as major players in the Revolution. So that in a significant sense it was not that Maxim had no future in 1937, but rather that Maxim in 1937 had obtained an imaginary past! The filmmakers proved to be ideally suited for such a task; they were too young to know the pre-revolutionary past. They plainly did not even know pre-revolutionary Petersburg; in 1910 (the time depicted in *Maxim's Youth*), Kozintsev was five years old and Trauberg eight. Not surprisingly, they created their pre-revolutionary Petersburg from old magazines and Pudovkin's stories.

Kozintsev did not hide his intentions: 'We wanted to create a legend,' he said during the discussion of *Maxim's Return*.[76] Maxim is the embodiment of the founding myth of the Revolution, of the 'pure conscience and burning heart of ardent revolutionaries'. But work on the picture went on for eight years (and what years they were!). During that time the revolutionary myth underwent a complete transformation. The directors saw their task as overcoming the pompous heroisation of the Revolution and revolutionaries. But if the new era needed the Revolution in its strictly political-pragmatic aims to legitimise the regime, then it decidedly did not need the revolutionaries.

And that is why Maxim could not have a future. That is why his creators abandoned him in 1917 (although the character was exploited both in *The Great Citizen* and later, during the war). The writer Konstantin Simonov proposed continuing Maxim's story to Kozintsev in 1948. Kozintsev replied:

> I think that our former hero deteriorated from film to film. Perhaps the films themselves became a little better, but the hero kept on losing his charm. By the end it all turned out very badly with him [Maxim]; Ermler put him in *The Great Citizen* and I simply didn't recognise him.[77]

Maxim could be recognised, of course, not only by his name, but also by Chirkov's cunning squint. But this was already the party functionary with neatly trimmed moustaches into which Ermler had transformed Maxim, and into which Maxim inevitably had to be transformed by the very 'logic of the historical process'. Either that or become 'labour-camp dust' (like many of the old Bolsheviks, whose memoirs had given birth to Kozintsev and Trauberg's hero). The further evolution of Maxim was not in the directors' field of vision when they thought up and made the films; at that time Maxim's fate was clear.

But the former FEKSists thought not so much in terms of history as in terms of types. The transformation of the commissar into a bureaucrat, even at the time of the release of the first part of the trilogy, had in effect already been accomplished. Maxim changed with the era: 'The mischievous, desperately audacious, naturally gifted lad from the Petersburg suburbs is transformed from the start into an organised, disciplined, underground man, and then, after the victory of the revolution, into a buttoned-up manager-comrade.'[78]

Who was that hero in the second half of the 1930s, when the trilogy was triumphantly processing across the screen? Above all, not only the legitimised Stalinist guard, but also the legitimised Stalinist bureaucracy promoted from the working class, the new Maxims – cunning lads coming to replace those who had created jobs for them in banks that had been 'liberated for the people' in 1917. Maxim enters the Revolution at the time of the rout of the old generation of revolutionaries and the arrival of the new generation of the revolutionary proletariat. The irony, however, lies in the fact that the trilogy itself came to viewers in the era of the rout of the old generation of revolutionaries and the arrival of the new generation of the Stalinist conscription, people with a completely different, as was said in those years, 'class physiognomy'. The picture turned out to be contrasting; if, at the beginning of the 1910s, the repressions only kindled the flames of the struggle, then a quarter of a century later this long since extinguished fire was transformed into a myth which legitimised new repressions. The basic ideological aim was, nevertheless, fulfilled; it was important for the new regime to appropriate this history so that the biography of the revolutionary became a collective biography of the new Stalinist nomenclature. A review in *Izvestiia* summed it up: 'Maxim is one of the most popular heroes of our cinema. For millions of citizens of the Soviet country he is the artistic generalisation of the biography of the best representatives of the generation of victors.'[79] Thus the appearance of Maxim in Ermler's picture is also well founded: 'because viewers are already familiar with Maxim's previous biography, the path he has followed, they believe in their favourite, they know that he will justify their hopes and expectations.'[80]

The transformation of Maxim also reflected the transformation of Soviet art itself; initially naïve, simple-hearted, idealistically believing in the Revolution, he knows who his enemies are and who he hates (bosses, secret agents, the police). In *Return* he is already a mature revolutionary, and the earlier naïve youth is only the mask of an experienced and cunning underground man. Accordingly, he has new enemies – Menshevik-'splitters', the opposition. In *The Vyborg Side* there is not a trace of the earlier mischievous lad. He is a severe and threatening manager of the 'dictatorship of the proletariat', dressed in leathers. Accordingly, his enemies are transformed not only into class opponents, but into traitors to the nation. Maxim addresses the clerks at the bank with the words: 'Are you the Russian people? You have German surnames, you've associated with English spies, and dreamed of taking orders from the Japanese.' Finally, in a film about contemporary life (*The Great Citizen*),

Maxim is a member of the Central Control Commission, unmasking the activities of the counter-revolutionary opposition.

So ended the history of the Soviet Till Eulenspiegel. The hero of a popular folk tale was transformed into a character from the *Short Course*.

The flair for creating types did not betray the FEKSists. They unerringly found the type of 'professional Bolshevik' who was victorious over the revolutionary intelligentsia. And that is why he fitted in so well. The leader recognised in Maxim the type he needed. After the viewing of *Maxim's Youth*, in the silence that had descended, Stalin raised a toast to success: 'Maxim is good! Maxim is good!' One of the directors fainted. A few days later the film was released.

Revolution as Conspiracy Drama: Romm's 'Leniniana'

Amongst many other problems, for the reader of Soviet newspapers in 1937 problems of a strictly artistic nature could also arise: how to imag-ine (literally, 'embody in images') all the treachery, betrayal, conspiracy, bribery, attempted assassination, diversion, incitement and so on attributed to the accused in the show trials; how to imagine the width, breadth and depth of the treachery, which explained why not only Party leaders but millions of people across the whole country, one's neighbours, friends, acquaintances, family, were being repressed. Romm's films did not simply illustrate the transcripts of the investigations, but formed what we could call mass conspiratorial imagination. If in the Maxim trilogy the underground was the pivot of the plot, then in Romm's two films about Lenin and subsequently in Ermler's *The Great Citizen*, conspiracy became, finally, the style-forming dominant. One could say that in place of Eisenstein's overt intellectual montage, in Romm and Ermler conspiratorial montage comes in. If intellectual montage was to have directly screened concepts, then the conspiratorial montage directly screens plot – its logic, atmosphere, emotional and conceptual aura. In Romm it was as yet only an interframe conspiratorial montage. In Ermler it was not longer just interframe, but also intraframe.

In the first episode, *Lenin in October*, Trotsky, Zinoviev, Kamenev, the Mensheviks and the SRs are the objects of Lenin's hatred. They had only just been sentenced to death, and the film became a kind of illustration, justification and substantiation of the death sentence. Lenin says directly in the film that 'Trotsky, Kamenev and Zinoviev's proposal is either absolute idiocy or absolute treachery.' The latter motif is reinforced when Kamenev's article appeared in *Novaia zhizn'* (*New Life*), in which he, in Lenin's words, 'betrayed the Party, the Central Committee's plans': 'Base, despicable treachery', rages Lenin. 'Bandits!', the leader exclaims from the screen at the very time when condemnation of these 'bandits' was spread over the pages of the newspapers. Meanwhile, in that infamous interview in *Novaia zhizn'*, Kamenev (Zinoviev was brought in here to give the 'complete picture') not only did not betray any secrets, but gave the appearance of there being no secrets at all, declaring that the Party had not taken any decision about the uprising and that he and others were in principle against seizing power by force. Not surprisingly, when Lenin demanded that they both be punished (for some reason Zinoviev as well) for treachery, the Central Committee voted against him. It therefore remains unclear what Lenin was reading in the newspaper. On the other hand, it is perfectly clear why the film begins with Lenin's arrival in Piter from Finland. The fact of the matter was that from 6 July 1917, after the unsuccessful Bolshevik uprising, Lenin was forced to hide (together with Zinoviev) in Petrograd, then on the Gulf of Finland, and then in Finland itself. He only returned to Piter on 7 October. For this entire period the Bolsheviks were being led by Trotsky.

Having returned to Russia from Germany in the famous sealed carriage, Lenin was declared 'a German spy'. Thus the espionage theme was right at the surface. The way it is worked out in the film, however, is interesting. In *Lenin in October* we are reminded, of course, that Lenin is 'a German spy'. (When a passer-by asks whom they are looking for, the soldiers reply: 'Who knows . . . some sort of German spy . . . Olenin or something.') Moreover, the very representatives of the authorities are delegitimised through their connections with the British embassy. It is amusing, moreover, that what was perceived by viewers in 1937 as 'state treachery' could simply not be anything like that in 1917; the Provisional Government was in close contact with the allies' diplomats (and not the Germans at all). Meanwhile, the fact that at the beginning of October 1917 the British were allies, while the Germans were enemies, is completely ignored; the film contrasts the rumours about Lenin as a 'German spy' with the 'espionage' of the Government in favour of . . . Russia's allies.

Conspiracy is depicted via a chain of 'customers' and executors. The British ambassador plays the role of the 'customer'. He mixes with 'landowners and capitalists' (the Provisional Government), who are ready for anything:

> Please! Give up half of Russia? Take it! The Caucasus to the English? Go ahead! The Ukraine to those . . . well, we know who! . . . let them gobble it up! We agree to everything. But give me a man! Give me a man I could believe in! Give me a real oppressor! Yes, yes! An oppressor! . . . An oppressor, a hangman, a dog!!

These monologues could quite easily have been uttered by the defendants at the show trials of 'spies' such as Bukharin who, it was said, 'sold out the Motherland wholesale'. The first line of the conspiracy was marked out, although not fully clarified.

Conspiracy can only take its course in a space of illegitimacy, and therefore the Provisional Government is logically delegitimised. The sources of legitimacy in the film are played by 'the masses of workers, peasants and soldiers' represented in the Soviets. In so far as the Provisional Government had lost control over the Soviets, it ceased to be legitimate. The Soviets, meanwhile, also contained SRs and Mensheviks. Therefore it was precisely they who were to become the next target. The 'landowners and capitalists', together with Britain, could only give money, but could not do anything directly. In the British ambassador's office the following noteworthy conversation takes place between two ministers of the Provisional Government: Tereshchenko declares: 'Above all we must disarm the factories.' Konovalov replies: 'It will be easiest of all for the SRs and Mensheviks to do that.' Thus SRs and Mensheviks, summoned to the ambassador's office and defined as direct agents of conspiracy, appear on the screen. But it turns out that they are both illegitimate (that is, they do not have the support of 'the masses'), and relying on the help of military adventurers and police detectives. Thus the conspiracy comes full circle; involving practically all political spheres and all levels and links in the chain of the state machine, it is transformed into a conspiracy of the State against the people. In this context, the Bolshevik conspiracy must be perceived not as anti-State, but as salvationary, and as the only legitimate conspiracy; the State, scheming against the people, loses all legitimacy and is liable to destruction, with the aim of replacing it with the new, Soviet, socialist, popular and therefore legitimate State.

The appearance of 'representatives of the democratic parties' (the Mensheviks and SRs) becomes an important component in the picture; political paranoia demands not only all-encompassing conspiracy, but also an internal enemy. This 'invasion from within' (the image of the 'fifth column' which was cultivated in Soviet mass consciousness during the years of the Great Terror) is in effect materialised in the office of the ambassador, who speaks 'diplomatically', although in broken Russian, but also 'metaphorically':

> Russia must have a certain order. Order which to make openly now does not seem possible. But look at the people – the Greeks – how they could not take the city of Troy and how they made the Trojan horse, and filled up its middle with infantry. We have to find such an empty horse. We need a screen . . . and that's the democratic parties. They can stop the disorder, and then you can leave your empty horse.

And although the authors of the film were striving for a sense of parallelism, the critics were not always satisfied with the balance of the two opposing underground worlds on which the film rested: 'The film contains the rudiments of a supplementary plot outline,' wrote Yurenev:

> This is the action of the police agent, who is always attempting to discover Lenin's location, in order to organise his assassination. Apparently the directors would not commit definitively to rejecting traditional plot devices, and tried to construct a thread of counter-action, resorting to the rather hackneyed device of the detective. This is a fault in the film.[81]

Various stylistic means in the presentation of the two 'counter-conspiracies', however, compensate for this failing; if the activities of the counter-revolutionary underground are given via the complete self-exposure of the enemies of the Revolution, then the activities of the Bolshevik underground in *Lenin in October* are, on the contrary, full of magic and mystery.

Here, above, all it is worth referring to Lenin's 'mute' conversations with Stalin. The first time we see the worker Vasily, who is guarding Stalin, he is sitting on the steps of a porch outside a house on an out-of-the-way street. Whistles from a steamer can be heard. Vasily goes out on to the roadway. There is a caption, which reads: 'Lenin's discussion with Stalin lasted four hours.' Vasily, chilled to the bone, sits back down on the porch. Next time the 'leaders'' conversation again takes place behind closed doors, with familiar silhouettes moving behind glass shutters. Here the very means of presenting political events draws attention to itself – their secret and inarticulate nature. On the other hand, the 'internal enemy' is not shown either; 'the opposition' does not get a single word in the film. The focus is precisely on Lenin in October.

It is well known that the famous session of the Central Committee at which the decision to foment the uprising was taken was stormy, with heated discussion. The first draft of the screenplay was to have shown this discussion, of which in the final picture nothing remained except Lenin's speech. The scene is transformed into a monologue by the leader. Lenin himself is depicted as a 'conspirator against his own will'; the underground is contra-indicated by his open character. It is as if Lenin 'estranges' the underground, where, it seems, only Stalin and Dzerzhinsky feel at home.

In *Lenin in October* the absence of a legitimate space is keenly felt. And only the inclusion, after work on the film had already finished (at Stalin's direct order), of the scene of the storming of the Winter Palace and the arrest of the Provisional Government spawns this legitimacy. The space of conspiracy proves to be absolutely total – in the picture there is literally not a single 'non-underground' scene. The entire film – scene after scene – unfolds in the underground: on the train which brings Lenin from Finland, and in the ambassador's office, where ministers gather in the hope of aiding the fight against the Bolsheviks; in the getaways from secret rendezvous, in the apartments themselves, where Lenin is hidden and secret meetings of the Central Committee are held, and in the factory sections where the workers organise the militia; in army divisions where Bolshevik agitators act almost openly, in offices (right to the very highest, from the head of the General Staff to the Provisional Government's meeting room at the Winter Palace), and in the trenches at the front, where the soldiers read Lenin's letter. Even such a public place as the street is a conspiratorial space; it is always shown at night, with Lenin moving about in disguise, endless encounters between the persecuted, unrecognised, and their persecutors, pursuits, everybody having their documents checked, and sleuths darting about. Underground work seeps into every corner.

It is difficult to breathe in this illegitimate space, and this is why the film rushes headlong to the denouement, where at last a legitimate space is found – Smolny. This headquarters of the conspiracy are miraculously transformed into the only legitimate space. Significantly, the final scene where Lenin proclaims the victory of 'the workers' and peasants' revolution, the necessity of which the Bolsheviks were constantly talking about', at Smolny, is preceded by the scene at the Winter Palace, where even while it is being stormed ministers are trying to forge links with 'embassies'; that is, right until the last minute they are busy 'betraying national interests'. Lenin's refusal to disguise himself after his arrival at Smolny is also notable. To someone's comment that he ought not to throw away his wig, as it might come in useful, Lenin replies: 'No, old chap, the Bolsheviks in Russia will have to hide no more. We are taking power in earnest and for a long time.'[82]

Thus in the finale of *Lenin in October* a kind of unmasking of the political sphere takes place. The world, divided into two conspiracies, State and Bolshevik, is in the end united into a single whole – only, however, so as to disintegrate definitively in the next picture, *Lenin in 1918*, which in the first place was called *Assassination* (*Pokushenie*), and is based entirely on the 'conspiracy plot'.[83] In contrast to the first film, in which both poles of the opposition were to be found underground, the space of legitimacy here is widened (the Bolsheviks' activities are presented as exclusively supported by the 'broad masses of the people'), but the counter-revolutionary underground is also significantly widened. To the previously limited group of ambassadors, SRs and Mensheviks, are at this point added 'left communists' and other oppositionists, who were now, in the course of the Moscow trials, accused of being 'enemies of the people', and of having made attempts on Lenin's life straight after the Revolution. Infernal 'dark forces' are at work everywhere here:

> A *kulak* comes to declare to Lenin war not on life, but to death. The British ambassador Relton-Konstantinov weaves a cunning web of villainy, bribery and attempted assassination. In one of the counter-revolutionaries' dark alleys the trembling hands of Fanny Kaplan finger poisoned bullets. Bukharin, and foreign spies, and Trotsky, and White Guard officers, were all ready to commit treachery and murder.[84]

Lenin in 1918 was made during the period of the Great Terror and its release in 1939 had to serve as justification for it. It is the true screen adaptation of the *Short Course*. The picture's allusive nature was so transparent that Eisenstein, who transformed the historical allusiveness of his final pictures into an aesthetic principle, did not even try to hide the fact that the year in question was not 1918, but 1936–8. In the pages of *Izvestiia* he wrote that in the picture:

> [T]hroughout the kingdom of nobility, straightforwardness and humanity a web is twisted by the dark threads of the misanthropy of those to whom the victorious path of the proletariat is alien, hated, hostile. And the dark forces of counter-revolution also combine into a single clot – in the terrible figure of Fanny Kaplan. She replicates the whole despicable

order of enemies – from Bukharin to the *kulak* in the countryside, to the obvious and open actions of the opposition.[85]

Directly connecting history to the present, Eisenstein said:

> Kaplan shoots at the screen. And before our eyes stand dark nights of great sorrow over the body of Lenin.
>
> On the screen Gorky visits the sick Lenin, and before us we see the days when the murderers who were guilty of a terrible act – the murder of Gorky – were exposed.
>
> And with anger and ire our eyes turn to that circle of enemies who every day and every hour are searching for the opportunity to strike a blow against our glorious country, as it moves from socialism to communism.[86]

Criticism focused on the new stylistics in the production of history; in place of the symbolisation of October in Eisenstein and Pudovkin, the historicisation of the Revolution is introduced. It was explained by the necessity of verifying the historical schema laid out in the *Short Course*. Therefore criticism emphasised the 'historical correctness' of *Lenin in 1918*. One critic pointed to 'the consistency of events in the picture, proved by documentary evidence, the historical accuracy of every detail'.[87] Another asserted (and one has to admit that the assertion was very well grounded) that 'the future generation will learn about history from the film *Lenin in 1918*.'[88] A third claimed that in *Lenin in 1918*:

> [C]oncrete living reality appeared before the artist with the stern and severe face of historical truth. And this truth was not located at a great temporal distance, it was not separated and curtained off by the dust of centuries, permitting free treatment and living, although discursive, conjecture; no, history was roaming about in art, still breathing the heat of recent battles, still shedding hot blood, still alive in the memory of living contemporaries.[89]

This did not mean, of course, the 'blood' shed by the victims of the Great Terror, which was indeed 'still warm'. But the historical references were as clear to the viewer as they were to the critic:

> In spite of the fact that the film is telling the story of events twenty years past [one of them wrote], every frame of it, every episode is full of the power, energy and passion of today's Soviet times. It is full of those living feelings, by which every person in our country lives; the love and hate our hearts contain – this is the love and hate which is also at work today in the activities of the Bolshevik Party and every one of their fighters.[90]

'Today's Soviet times' were bloody. The apologia for violence in Romm's Lenin films (and in particular *Lenin in 1918*) was, undoubtedly, simultaneously both a consequence and a justification of the Great Terror, while the time of War Communism and the 'Red Terror' was directly related in the picture to the Terror of 1937. The film presented itself as a link in the chain of evidence which proved the necessity of political terror; it depicted a country in which a conspiracy gigantic in its breadth and depth was ripening and being fed from within. Not only foreign secret services were involved, but also Lenin's closest comrades-in-arms, those regarded as the 'Leninist guard' (Trotsky and Bukharin). Its aim was the murder of Lenin. Some unbelievable plot devices were inserted in the film. Thus, the worker Vasily, having found out about the planned assassination attempt, goes to 'warn Ilyich'. When Lenin has already left for that fatal meeting at the Mikhelson factory, Vasily runs out into the Kremlin yard and Bukharin points him in the wrong direction. It is precisely because of this that he fails to prevent Kaplan's fateful shot.

The screen still today blazes with a threat. Its origin lies in the temporal interval; between 1937 (when the first of the two films was released) and 1939 (when the second came out) lay 1938, the year of the publication of the *Short Course*, which was summed up by the events of 1936–7, creating a historical narrative which legitimised the Great Terror. In the *Short Course* we are advised that, 'In 1937, new facts came to light regarding the fiendish crimes of the Bukharin-Trotsky gang', that:

> [T]he trials showed that these dregs of humanity, in conjunction with the enemies of the people, Trotsky, Zinoviev and Kamenev, had been in conspiracy against Lenin, the Party and the Soviet State ever since the early days of the October Socialist Revolution,

that unheard-of villainies and unprecedented crimes against the people and the leaders 'over a period of twenty years were committed, it transpired, with the participation or under the direction of Trotsky, Zinoviev, Kamenev, Bukharin, Rykov and their henchmen, at the behest of espionage services of bourgeois states.'[91] All this 'knowledge', brought in by the show trials and reinforced in the *Short Course*, allowed a picture to be painted in the second film of total conspiracy, in which Trotsky and Bukharin, *kulaks* and Left SRs, foreign embassies and spies were all involved.

It turned out, however, that just as *Lenin in 1918* would have been impossible without the *Short Course*, the *Short Course* itself was greatly reinforced by Romm's picture.

> The list of crimes is inexhaustible [wrote one review of the screenplay of *Lenin in 1918*] and each of the enemies' actions in the screenplay became a piece of evidence, a fact not only of art, but of history. History and the victorious people have pronounced their sentence. The picture asserts the general human wisdom of the act of ruthlessly exterminating these rabid dogs who have been giving off their poisonous saliva for many years.[92]

The central theme of *Lenin in 1918* is formulated by Lenin himself in his conversation with Gorky at the beginning of the film: 'What should we do with our enemies?' Set forth before the viewer there is a certain argument which never took place between Lenin and Gorky on the subject of Gorky's *Untimely Thoughts* – about humanism. To Gorky's reproaches of 'excessive severity', Lenin replies: 'Severity nowadays is an essential condition of battle. Such severity will be understood . . . We are being suffocated from all sides.' The foundations for this theme of 'suffocation' are laid in the very 'frame'; the film opens with a representation of the map of the Soviet Republic in 1918. From all sides it is narrowed until all that remains are little islands (Petrograd, Moscow, Tsaritsyn): 'Soviet Russia is in a ring of fire.' The caption reads: 'Such was the map of our motherland.' At the end of the film we see an 'unfurling' map; the Red Army is squeezing the enemy, breaking apart the 'ring of fire'. But the main source of 'suffocation' is the ever-expanding conspiracy. Strictly speaking, the whole film is constructed of interlacing scenes in the Kremlin and scenes in the underground, where brutalised spies, diversionists, SRs and Mensheviks, the remnants of the 'deposed classes', are preparing the 'vile treachery': bribing the Kremlin commandant, preparing the murders of Uritsky, Lenin, Dzerzhinsky and other 'leaders' (amusingly, the mythical attempt on Stalin's life, which the defendants at the show trials were accused of planning, is not depicted in the picture), sowing seeds of discontent in cities and the countryside.

One should remember that Romm's two films about Lenin not only structured the political imagination of the masses, but also included its ready-made structures. Both films were what we would call box-office successes; *Lenin in October* and *Lenin in 1918* were both triumphs of film distribution at the time. What guaranteed the popularity of these official films that had been 'made by order'? In essence, the same thing that made *Chapaev* popular: the tireless interest of the audience in detective stories – with a beloved, fascinating, popular hero (who here was Lenin himself[93]) overcoming fate, with pursuits, conspiracies and murders around every corner. In a word, these were not simply film-ideologemes, but true cinema for the viewers; Romm's two films, undoubtedly, belonged to the same 'popular' cinematography of the 1930s to which *Road to Life*, the trilogy about Maxim, and *Chapaev* all belonged.

This support of the mass of viewers also defined the success of Romm's films. It was here for the first time that Stalin was played on screen, that Lenin was the central character, and that Dzerzhinsky, Sverdlov, Voroshilov played their parts . . . In a word, the whole Soviet heroic pantheon was brought to life. This reinforced the effect of 'veracity' and cultivated a particular impression in the viewer. The latter can be judged by the behaviour of extras participating in the shoot. Thus, we know that during shooting of the scene of the meeting at the Mikhelson factory, the extras playing the masses took Shchukin's passionate speech for Lenin's speech and accompanied it with a storm of unfeigned raptures, at the end of the scene straining to carry Shchukin in their arms (which did not correspond to the screenplay at all). And when Kaplan's shot rang out in the yard and Shchukin fell down, the extras were seized with genuine horror (women were crying, some were really hysterical, and one person even fainted!), the men threw themselves at 'Kaplan', 'ready to rip her into pieces. And great efforts were needed on the part of the administration to save the actress from enormous troubles.'[94] Kaplan became the true incarnation of the enemy. Thus Eisenstein was not afraid to place the two opposing images in *Lenin in 1918* in direct comparison, declaring that 'the brilliant achievements of the second film' were precisely these two – Lenin and Kaplan.[95] Critics also wrote of the 'civic act, the artistic heroism of N. Efron, playing the role of Kaplan',[96] and asserted that 'N. Efron, heroically overcoming feelings – as a Soviet citizen and a Soviet actress – of repulsion towards the image, understood its fundamental importance for the viewer.'[97]

In general, the culminating scene of the attempted assassination which so stunned Eisenstein was shot in a very expressive style, and became the true summit of Volchek's camerawork. The semi-darkness of the factory section where Lenin was speaking, and the gloomy landscape of the factory yard, a storm brewing, where the assassination attempt takes place, 'the miserly expressiveness of the lighting', of which Romm spoke,[98] created a backdrop against which the denouement of the Revolution's conspiracy drama was played out. On the screen we have Lenin leaving the factory section; first we are given a shot of the whole section, and then a close-up of Lenin surrounded by workers, after which there follows a general scene and a panorama lowering down. The scene of the assassination attempt itself is given in the opposite way; the panorama goes upwards from the group of workers and draws in the whole scene of the assassination attempt, Lenin lying injured and the crowd surrounding him. There then follows the scene of the punishment of Fanny Kaplan, which Romm himself used in a lecture at the All-Union State Institute of Cinematography as an example of successful direction. A huge crowd flooding the entire screen turns on the terrorist and tries to rip her to pieces; only a small group of workers surround her, not allowing 'the people' to seize her by the hair and tear her apart. This was a scene of mob rule, with the viewers joining in, by 1939 having already learnt to express their fervent desire 'to destroy the enemies like rabid dogs'.

Of course, Lenin himself understood best of all the meaning of what was going on:

> Soviet power is surrounded by enemies. The *kulak* uprisings are being fed by money from the SRs and Mensheviks . . . Counter-revolution declared the White Terror to us. The further we move ahead, the more decisive will be the resistance of the dying classes. This corpse cannot be boarded up in a coffin. With its decay it stinks and poisons everything around it . . . Traitors judged by the will of the people will be ruthlessly destroyed . . . The working class will respond to all enemies of the Revolution with merciless terror. Tighten the ranks!

With such words the leader addresses the workers before the very attempt on his life. These words, placed on his lips, upon which the 'Red Terror' was based, are as if taken directly from the pages of Soviet newspapers at the end of the 1930s. At the same time we have before us a clinically pure case of political paranoia. All its key motifs – isolation, total conspiracy, the logic of the struggle, the dehumanisation of the enemy and so on – are apparently gathered together on purpose in Lenin's speech.

At the end of the picture there is a significant scene; Dzerzhinsky reveals a provocateur who has 'penetrated to the very heart of the Revolution' in the ranks of the Cheka. During his interrogation this provocateur seizes a revolver and shoots at Dzerzhinsky. At the sound of the shot a guard runs in and kills the traitor on the spot. Dzerzhinsky is furious: 'What have you done!? Do you understand what you've done?!' he screams at the guard, who has destroyed a priceless source of information. We have to understand the scene as meaning that we now had to wait twenty years for the enemies who had 'penetrated to the very heart of the Revolution' to be exposed. Dzerzhinsky's despair has no limits, but viewers can sigh with relief; they know how this drama ended, they participated in the retribution, they were witness to the triumph of justice. Having survived the Great Terror and lived until 1939, when *Lenin in 1918* was released, they generally had more than a little justification for breathing a sigh of relief.

THE POETRY OF THE INTRA-PARTY STRUGGLE: ERMLER'S *THE GREAT CITIZEN*

During the second Moscow show trial of the 'Right-Trotskyist Centre' (Pyatakov, Radek, Serebryakov, Sokolnikov and others), the screenplay for *The Great Citizen* lay on Stalin's desk. In a letter to Ermler, the leader suggested changing the structure of the screenplay from being 'gripping' (with the murder of Shakhov as the culmination) to ideological – as a 'struggle between two programmes' (one of which, 'for the victory of socialism in the USSR', was supported by 'the people', the other, Trotskyist, programme, 'for the restoration of capitalism in the USSR', rejected by them). Thus, Stalin proposed, 'the screenplay should be redone, making its content more contemporary, reflecting everything fundamental that was revealed in the Pyatakov-Radek trial.'[99] Three days after Stalin's letter to Ermler with these orders was dispatched, Pyatakov and the rest of the accused were shot.

The film was in all senses topical. The orders about the screenplay were given by Stalin in breaks between reviewing lists of executions, while the film crew worked practically following in the footsteps of the firing squads: 'Life continually brought in its correctives to the living canvas of the screenplay', wrote the screenwriters in the pages of the newspaper *Kino* (*The Cinema*).

The brilliant work of the organs of the NKVD was writing new victorious pages in the case of the ultimate defeat of the Trotskyite-Zinovievite and Bukharinite scum. And on this basis we tried more profoundly and correctly to expose and add to the characters of our cast.[100]

Stalin himself was turning 'the glorious victories of the organs of the NKVD' into the pages of a historical narrative, working at this very time on the *Short Course*. Thus the theme of history here becomes just as central. It is precisely what the two main enemies in *The Great Citizen* talk about during their final meeting:

> Kartashov: Only he whose works will go down in history has the right to live.
> Borovsky: Well, we, it seems, have been thrown out of history.
> Kartashov: Nothing of the sort! They're trying to drive us out! But we will still fight them! We will still fight for our place in history!

The final act of the 'fight' is the murder of the 'Great Citizen' Shakhov-Kirov. He is killed by Bryantsev, a former Trotskyist who after the rout of the opposition becomes . . . director of the Museum of the Revolution. Already in itself the choice of the position (approved by Stalin!) for the Trotskyist-murderer and chief villain is demonstrative; Stalin's relation to the previous history of the Party is well known. One could say that Shakhov-Kirov, this Bolshevik-Stalinist, as he is presented in the picture, is killed by this 'history' itself.

Stalin consistently combined two functions: consultant to film directors and director of the show trials of the 'ardent revolutionaries' who seemed dangerous to him even as museum exhibits. These two functions intersected in an odd way. Thus, in the letter about *The Great Citizen*, Stalin motivated his demand for the depiction of Kirov's murder to be removed by saying that 'one terrorist act or another pales into insignificance before the facts that have been revealed by the Pyatakov-Rykov trial.' The leader's cryptogram can be deciphered only in the sense that it was not so much the terrorist act itself that was important as the conspiracy which preceded it: those same 'facts' which were supposedly 'revealed', or more exactly were thought up in the same office in which the leader edited film scripts.

More than anything, *The Great Citizen* was a political act. The film was created as the most important visual evidence of the guilt of the accused in the Moscow show trials. The aim of this picture was the legitimisation of the Great Terror as retribution for an innocent victim – the death of a Bolshevik saint.

As the film's makers wrote, 'the picture about Kirov became for us a picture of the "Kirovian" attitude to the people, the "Kirovian" world view, the "Kirovian" struggle. The picture about Kirov became for us a picture about a Bolshevik.'[101] (There would not be a single review which did not point to Kirov as the prototype of Shakhov.) Why did Stalin reject the idea for the film, in which Kirov would have appeared as a historical figure?[102] After the appearance on the screen of the 'living' Lenin, Stalin, Sverdlov and even the historical figure of Pyatakov, one might have supposed that the appearance of the 'real' Kirov would not have caused any surprise. However, it was precisely in this case that Stalin needed an 'artistic generalisation' and not the solitary figure of Kirov. Kirov was indeed a special case; in the final analysis, the attempt on Lenin's life was only a historical episode (although a terrible one) in the accusations of the era of the Great Terror, whilst Kirov's murder was the main grounds for mass terror. In other words, he was not so much 'solitary' as 'typical' (the remaining leaders could not be typical – they were unique); such Kirovs (and consequently, enemies as well!) were many in number – in every province and region. (For this reason we are not told of which region Shakhov is Party Secretary.) The main task was for the hero to be both 'Kirov' and a type simultaneously.

Be that as it may, the genre of the new picture was designated as 'a tragedy', which also separated it from the stream of historical Party films. Kozintsev wrote of his idea for the trilogy about Maxim: 'We need a real epopee – with no pomposity, with no false pathos, without people shot from below who walk like statues, we need an epopee of the colossal scope of the theme.'[103] But he also asserted that he wanted 'to create a biographical novel'.[104] Did the trilogy become an epopee or a novel? 'Not an enormous canvas, not a memorial, not a history of the party, not a chronicle – we wanted to give the movement of the era in the apparently "private life" of a man without a famous name', wrote Kozintsev.[105] And although the shift towards the 'revolutionary epopee' was already noticeable in *The Vyborg Side*, the trilogy all the same remained a 'novel'. By every indicator, *The Great Citizen* was the total antithesis of the trilogy about Maxim; it was precisely a 'canvas', precisely a 'memorial' (to Kirov), precisely a 'history of the Party' (certain episodes from the film look like illustrations of the corresponding chapters in the *Short Course*), full of people with 'famous names' and without a 'private life' (both Shakhov-Kirov and his enemies). The 'loathsome prose' of the anti-Soviet underground lies adjacent here to the heroic poem of the public activities of the 'great citizen' Shakhov.

Surprisingly, it was precisely Shostakovich's music for the finale of *The Great Citizen* (to the tune of the song 'You fell as a martyr in the fatal struggle') which linked Ermler's picture to *Maxim's Youth*, in which Shostakovich also used this song. But if in the first film (before the start of the Great Terror) the revolutionary funeral song was perceived as a direct projection, then when the second part of *The Great Citizen* was released, in 1939, hot on the heels of the dreadful era of the Terror, this song was perceived entirely differently; both the Shakhovs and the Pyatakovs fell as martyrs in 'the fatal struggle'.

The music for *The Great Citizen*, which became, according to both cultural historians and musicologists, to an even greater extent than Shostakovich's famous Fifth Symphony, 'the musical apotheosis of the year 1937 in art', was 'not so much a counter-point, as its [the Fifth Symphony's – E. D.] word-for-word commentary'.[106] Ermler's screenplay itself, writes Maksimenkov:

was full of verbalised tragic symphonic motifs, which found full expression in the music for *The Great Citizen*. In the nation-wide mourning [for Kirov – E. D.], which lasted for several years, there was space for the expression of the whole gamut of ideas, emotions and feelings. There was no primitive monochromaticism in the Stalinist Terror, nor could there be. The polyphony swam with shouts, weeping, howls, chanted slogans, bursts of applause, toasts and curses, drawn-out steam-ship and factory hooters, volleys of gunfire, ambulance sirens.[107]

In fact the most important factor which allows *The Great Citizen* to qualify as 'almost the main, programmatic film of pre-war Stalinism'[108] is its incredible 'lyricism', which almost becomes self-exposure. The poetry of the Party struggle in the eyes of the viewer is transformed into such an act of laying bare the hidden mechanisms of the Stalinist Terror that the film can be seen as the enormous Freudian slip of Stalinist culture.

The fundamental task of Ermler's film was reduced to projecting and externalising, in a maximally effective way, a paranoid view of the world on to the whole of society, with the aim of mobilising it, by means of strengthening its feelings of anxiety, defencelessness and loss. In the final analysis internal danger is limitless, whilst external danger seems limited and can be removed via an attack on the enemy. The strictly Soviet problem, however, consisted in the fact that the Stalinist attack on the Bolshevik old guard did not answer the fundamental principle of this type of externalisation: 'The more "different" the stranger in our midst, the more readily available he is as a target for externalization.'[109] This led to the pressing need to make the Leninist guard 'different'. At the same time, if the actions of the paranoiac are understood by him as a reaction to the actions of the enemy (conspiracy must be fought with conspiracy, organisation with organisation and so on), then the image of the enemy should be seen above all as the mirror reflection of the paranoiac: his motives, fears, desires and anxieties.

The culmination of the first part of *The Great Citizen* is the meeting of the 'Red Metalworkers', where the opposition is, finally, exposed and defeated. It is constructed on two counter-conspiracies. At one extreme we have the oppositionists. Borovsky, calming Kartashov down, says: 'time, the people, and the Party apparatus are in our hands', control over the composition of the participants of the meeting and the presidium are in 'our people's hands'. Borovsky is depicted here as a true master of Party intrigue. One could say that he is playing here . . . Stalin, who, as we know, came to power via control of the 'Party apparatus' and manipulation of 'the masses in the party' (Stalin's famous words to the effect that in an election it is not the allocation of votes that is important, but who organises the counting). Transferring these characteristics on to Borovsky, he so to speak fashions his own self-portrait. This is exactly how the oppositionists' letters and conversations about the 'physical elimination' of political opponents seems – it was exactly this that occupied

Stalin incessantly in his post as General Secretary, and which constituted the major part of his political activity.

At the other extreme we have Maxim, organising an underground meeting of communists in an apartment belonging to one of the workers under the cover of a 'wedding'. This episode in effect reproduces the scenes of underground gatherings from the trilogy about Maxim; the hero behaves in 1925 exactly as he behaved in 1914. And he now speaks of the oppositionists in exactly the same terms as he used to explain the subversive activities of the Mensheviks:

> All this is both simple and complicated at the same time. Simple because all their cunning strategies and conspiracy – yes, conspiracy – are sewn in white thread. And complicated because it is not *kulaks* doing this, not Curzons, not officers in epaulets, but people who call themselves comrades, members of the Party . . . bowing down in the name of the Party, in the name of Lenin, bowing down before the truth of the Central Committee, they are trying to bring their delegation to the congress in order to battle against the Central Committee in your name. Think about what a Jesuitical tactic this is: without proclaiming their programme, forcing their way into the congress, scraping together a majority by any means, so as to take possession of the heart and mind of the revolution – the Central Committee of our Party.

(In essence, this is precisely what Stalin did in the post of General Secretary in the era of the struggle against the 'opposition' in 1923–7.)

What is interesting here, however, is the paranoid discourse itself: conspiracy, treachery, invasion from within. (Addressing the workers, Maxim talks directly about the opposition: 'Comrades! They are planning the greatest crime against the Central Committee, against the people!' Shakhov at the same meeting calls them 'a bunch of cheats, a bunch of conspirators'. The oppositionists, in their turn, accuse Shakhov of . . . 'fighting for a faction'.) Kartashov, whose image oddly manages to combine Kamenev and Bukharin, speaks of the opposition's tactics in the battle against the Central Committee (events in part one take place in 1925–7): 'The ancients were no worse than us sinners, they knew the value of military valour, and for them the cunning Ulysses was no less a hero than Achilles or Hector.' Borovsky asks: 'How are we going to do it? The Greeks entered impregnable Troy in a wooden horse.' Kartashov replies, just like the British ambassador in *Lenin in October*: 'Yes, exactly in that, in that. In a good old wooden horse. Tactics. New tactics. Under their slogans to our ends.'

It is precisely in the activities of the opposition that Stalin's tactic is revealed of using one group against another in his progress towards the seizure of power. In relation to the opposition the absence of principle in this tactic is emphasised. (First they fight against Trotsky, then join up with him, then they 'sell themselves' to foreign intelligence services.) Kartashov first voices Trotsky's theses (socialism cannot be constructed in one country without a world revolution, a 'Thermidor', a process of degeneration, is taking place in the party), then sounds like a real 'diversionist'. In a word, the oppositionists can have no political views. One could say that they are not only fed by Machiavellian fantasies, but are also as unprincipled as . . . Stalin himself.

This 'unprincipled' nature of the opposition was important to Stalin (in part one of the film), in so far as this was the shortest route to their rebirth (in part two, which tells the story of events in 1934) as a 'band of criminals, spies and diversionists'. Thus when Pyatakov declares the necessity of ending the fight with the workers' initiative and moving on to diversion and terror, he voices Stalin's explanation for why the enemy needed the death of Shakhov-Kirov:

> We've lost! Accidentally, you say?! No, not accidentally! We, the leaders, have to understand that this is a will which can be overcome only at the point of a bayonet, only by a twelve-inch shell, only by high-explosive bombs and battalions of soldiers, which we do not have. And we have to have them whatever happens, at any cost. I have again received a letter from Trotsky. He is extremely dissatisfied with our sluggishness, our inertia. And he's absolutely right. Well, tell me, please, he's over there making agreements with big people, drawing whole states into the game, swearing to Marx, God and the devil that we're the power, but we're fussing over trifles. We have, in the end, to become real politicians, we have to create the impression that we're the power. In short, we need to carry out some effective measures!

Thus he is in effect given the task of organising both a diversion at the canal construction site and the murder of Shakhov.

And here we come up against the question of the motives for the oppositionists' actions. The film gives several answers to this question; they simply thirst for power, they are fighting for their 'place in history', they fear they will be 'written off'. All this suggests a significant helping of idealism in the oppositionists. (It is not for their place in history that they are risking their lives, living in terrible conditions in the underground and in constant fear!) Their 'struggle' itself, accompanied by ceaseless mutual remonstrations to 'act' in the name of an 'aim' that is already 'close by', looks like pure hair-brained scheming (they themselves no longer believing in anything). Meanwhile, these idealists and hare-brained schemers are depicted in the film as cold-blooded murderers and cynics who have gone to pieces.

This apparent inconsistency is the pure product of the transfer; the failure to meld the aims of the enemies' activities with their psychological profiles is explained by the failure of the projection. Their cold-blooded cruelty, cynicism and politicking are a projection of Stalin; their idealism and hair-brained scheming are a projection of the construction of 'the enemy'. (Such must the enemy be, not having 'the support of the masses', not having a 'historical perspective'; he is doomed.) His image is created out of these non-coinciding projections.

According to the *Short Course*, the opposition had no principles; the source and aim of their actions combined in the struggle for power. And although the reflected world of the Stalinist political fantasy was only the projection and externalisation of Stalin's phobias and desires, the former Bolshevik underground revolutionaries, transformed into underground counter-revolutionaries, turned out to be the first people at the centre of the action on the screen. The device was laid bare effectively. In *The Great Citizen* the essence of the verbal squabbles of Stalinism, which had always previously been mystified, were revealed, in reverse; behind the battle against political 'platforms' and 'deviations' stood a personal battle, and the battle for power took its course in effect in the form of an 'ideological battle'. So the puzzle of *The Great Citizen* consists only in the question of why Stalin, who personally formulated the conception of the future film, considered it necessary to adapt this, perhaps most explosive, plot line from the *Short Course* for the screen.

The Great Citizen played a considerable role in the intensification of mass paranoia. It contains an unbelievable number of enemies, traitors and conspirators. (It is notable that here the enemies act, so to speak, on multiple levels, moving from one underground to another.) Thus, there are powers who act via Pyatakov-Kartashov-Borovsky, but in parallel there are acting some sort of diplomatic residents from the foreign secret services, who, as becomes clear, do not know of each other's existence. Stalin was, as it were, illustrating the narrative he invented himself for the second show trial on the case of the 'Parallel Anti-Soviet-Trotskyite Centre'. (This parallelism is lodged in the very plot.) The result is that the viewer has a right to suspect treachery, double-dealing, sabotage and a tendency to counter-revolution in everybody. (It seems that practically every communist who appear in the film could turn out to be a spy or diversionist.)

Therefore, when these 'bandits' needed to be exposed and driven out, the film's makers had to resort to a non-trivial device – bringing into the film Maxim, the 'rock-solid Bolshevik' from Kozintsev and Trauberg's trilogy, who (thanks to viewers' familiarity with his biography) could not be suspected of counter-revolution. It seemed it was only possible to trust an imaginary character. Appearing like a *Deus ex machina*, Maxim is transformed into a 'real historical character' by default. One critic wrote:

> An imaginary hero, Maxim finds reality, which allows him to stand alongside historical figures such as Chapaev. It is no accident that the makers of *The Great Citizen* bring Maxim into the action as a well-known character. His name gradually acquires the character of a Party nickname. And in *The Great Citizen* it already sounds like an honoured rank, like a title.[110]

We should note in passing that *The Vyborg Side* and the second part of *The Great Citizen* were released simultaneously, in 1939. Maxim was transformed in the final picture of the trilogy into the commissar of the State Bank, to which he was appointed straight after the Revolution by Sverdlov. The irony lies in the fact that the prototype for Maxim – that is, the real commissar of the State Bank, appointed by Lenin straight after the October Revolution – was . . . the chief enemy and the only 'real historical character' from *The Great Citizen* – none other than Georgy Piatakov himself.

The Great Citizen differed from the general run of films in the 1930s in that it was not simply a film which showed enemies (enemies became a necessary attribute of the majority of films in those years), but a film about enemies. It was precisely this which, according to *Pravda*, was its main contribution: 'In not a single film which depicted the enemies of our people – Trotskyite murderers, provocateurs, adventurists, saboteurs – did we see such penetration by the actors into the psychology of the abominable "depths" as we did in this film.'[111] As one review noted, even 'Maxim, and not only Maxim, but Pyotr Shakhov as well, were only the means for unmasking, exposing the repulsive figures who filled the whole fundamental line of the development of the action.'[112] Characteristically, as in the situation with Fanny Kaplan, who shot Lenin in Romm's film, here as well 'actors refused to play the enemy. They were afraid of this role, afraid of the viewer's hatred. And we are grateful to I. N. Bersenev, who courageously and directly, correctly understanding the artistic task, took on this seemingly thankless role,' wrote the filmmakers.[113]

Maya Turovskaya has drawn attention to the fact that, whether by accident or not, the actor who played the main enemy in the film was Bersenev. In his prerevolutionary past, in a famous and much-discussed production by the Moscow Arts Theatre of *Nikolai Stavrogin*, an adaptation of Dostoevsky's novel *The Devils*, this actor played the role of the main 'devil', Pyotr Verkhovensky. His acting was one of the brilliant achievements of the production, which provoked Gorky's famous articles against Dostoevsky. Thus, we see not only the source from which the director derived his style and devices, but also how the new 'enemies' received their pedigree and class from the great tradition of the Russian classics.[114] And Dostoevsky's main 'devil' was paradoxically transformed for the twentieth anniversary of the Revolution into one of Lenin's comrades in arms, be that Kamenev or Bukharin.

However, the filmmakers did not hide the link with Dostoevsky's novel.[115] Indeed, strictly speaking, *The Devils* was the first 'historical-revolutionary novel' in Russian literature, and therefore its 'genre memory' is aroused every time Russian and Soviet art turns to underground people; Dostoevsky's experience here cannot be avoided. As regards *The Great Citizen*, even critics were obliged to acknowledge that 'many episodes in part two were treated too gloomily. The authors said that in their depiction of the enemy underground they proceeded from Dostoevsky's *The Devils*. That could not but tell stylistically certain episodes.'[116] But not only stylistically – Dostoevsky lives in the very fabric of the picture. (Thus Borovsky, who has only just entered the underground, explains the 'sweetness of the underground' to Bryantsev by all but quoting Dostoevsky: 'What could be stronger than a secret force, which nobody suspects?')

Having played Verkhovensky and having agreed to take on the role of Kartashov, Bersenev wrote:

> My work on the role was defined by that profound hatred which every honest Soviet citizen feels towards the enemies of his motherland. And the more I hated Kartashov, the more profound and keen became my desire to expose him, to show the viewer how he could dissemble, lie, deceive and betray . . . It was personally difficult and unpleasant for me to take on the role of an enemy of my motherland, one of the most loathsome representatives of the Trotskyite-Zinovievite band [note that he is speaking of an invented character! – E. D.]. My repugnance towards Kartashov was so great that in the first instance I decided to give up work. To give up being an actor. But when I thought about my duty as a citizen, when I thought about how an artist, an actor can respond to the Party's call for vigilance, I understood that a fine, truthful depiction of the enemy, exposing his activities, was as much a citizen's and a Soviet actor's duty as the creation of the images of the heroes of our country.[117]

And critics were simply hysterical:

> Skilfully hiding from the vigilant eye of the Soviet intelligence services, the insignificant statistician Borovsky, former active Trotskyite and now head of the stinking underground, is at work. This person will stoop to any vileness to achieve his filthy aims. A double-dyed cynic, pretending to be a zealot and an ascetic, he is a poisonous and cunning snake.[118]

This critique, from the army newspaper *Krasnaia zvezda* (*Red Star*), was echoed in the pages of *Pravda* by Semyon Tregub:

> They are doomed. And however the arch adventurist and double-dealer Kartashov tried to lie and keep his spirits up, however calm on the surface and convinced of his own invulnerability was the experienced provocateur Zemtsov, they could not hide from themselves the stark truth: they had no future. You feel this particularly strikingly in the Jesuitical degenerate Borovsky. He is a total hybrid of malice and despair.[119]

Another critic wrote of Borovsky as 'a type of real, professional counter-revolutionary. He is an enemy of the people. He is, so to speak, the quintessence, the clot of Trotskyite banditry.'[120]

The directors asserted that actors, in refusing to play enemies, were simply afraid. Can one condemn them for that? The intensely morbid, almost hysterical (as is evident from the utterances of Bersenev and the critics) attitude to the images of Trotskyites created in the picture a fine political-psychological balance, the violation of which (as all members of the 'film crew' – from directors to actors – understood) could be literally fatal: 'From the first days it became clear', wrote Bersenev, 'what complex artistic-political problems faced the entire collective. Any error by an individual performer in a positive or negative role could alter the correctness of the political line of the work and render the whole picture mistaken, worthless.'[121] And, one should add, put the lives of quite real people under threat. (It is worth noting that during work on the picture four members of the film crew were arrested, two of whom died.)

The climate on the set was depressing. Infected by the detective story passions and paranoid fantasies raging on the screen, the filmmakers described work on it as a continuous battle against sabotage. (Exactly at this time the management of Lenfilm, headed by Adrian Pyotrovsky, was routed.)

> They would not let us film. For six months we fought for the production of *The Great Citizen*. We received a graphic lesson in the class struggle from the experience of the production of our own work. The saboteurs who have today been exposed in the leadership of the Lenfilm studios employed the most diverse means to wreck the production. They did not let us shoot the screenplay because it supposedly needed more work; they prevented us shooting the screenplay by putting in doubt its political topicality. Finally, it was put about that the screenplay was counter-revolutionary. And they even ordered articles to be written about this for the studio newspaper. They were counting on us not being able to endure it, hoping we'd give up, reject the project ourselves, because to prohibit the production directly was something the enemies of the people feared, they could not do.
>
> And when we did not give up on the film, when we insisted on it going into production, pure suppression of the production began. They would not give the film any money, they would not give any actors, they would not allow us to make drafts, to form a crew.

And so, the film 'was created in the struggle against the saboteurs in the management of Lenfilm'.[122]

The attitude towards Ermler's film described here fits in completely with the general picture of cinema production in those years. An editorial article in the country's main film journal, *Iskusstvo kino* (*The Art of the Cinema*), in the September issue for 1936 summed up the trials of the 'gang of counter-revolutionary terrorists and hired killers of the Gestapo' that were only just reverberating, and called for 'vigilance on the cinema front'. Having exposed 'rightist-leftist scum' in Soviet cinema production, the journal wrote:

> With every film Soviet cinema is obliged to fight for increased vigilance . . .
> Ermler's new work must be brought into production as soon as possible.

The Main Administration of Cinematography and the Lenfilm studio are obliged to guarantee the decorated director maximally favourable conditions for artistic work on the film, which Soviet viewers are awaiting with impatience.[123]

Here we should, of course, make an amendment to the figure of the 'decorated director'. Fridrikh Ermler was himself in his youth a Chekist (whence the understanding characteristic of his films of the political struggle as a conspiracy; thus, at the centre of *The Peasants*, the film which preceded *The Great Citizen*, an enemy is also exposed). But 'former Chekists' do not exist. At the end of his life, in greetings sent to his former KGB colleagues on 9 May 1965, on the twentieth anniversary of victory, Ermler wrote: 'My biography fits into three paragraphs: Communist, Chekist, Artist. In the Cheka my Party-mindedness, my consciousness, my philosophy were formed. The Cheka educated me.'[124] This was the absolute truth. Ermler was a true 'Cheka-artist'. And nowhere more so than in *The Great Citizen*.

The situation on the set of *The Great Citizen* hardly differed at all from work conditions at the Mosfilm studio on Romm's Lenin pictures; both rank-and-file studio workers and higher management, including Boris Shumyatsky, were arrested, which Romm knew only too well, himself preparing to be arrested at any moment. At the studio itself mysterious events were occurring; someone chopped the lighting cables in half with an axe, someone broke the glass on the light fittings with a crow-bar, someone substituted the negatives. These were examples, as was said at the time, of 'patent sabotage'. Romm himself was unable to understand for whom this could be necessary. However, if one takes into account the fact that the shoot was carried out under the ever-watchful gaze of the NKVD, of the very department which worked out a scenario for the breakdown of the filming of this in all respects politically important picture, then it becomes clear where one should seek the sources of this sabotage.

The 'integrity of the individual', as he is declared one-sided and incapable of change, becomes the source of the threats emanating from the film. (The paranoid view of the world also suggests exactly the presence of duo-tone films.) The task in the depiction of both the hero and the enemy is the same – to achieve:

a complete merging of the psychology, character and political behaviour of the character . . . to show that in the images of the characters the psychological and political lines, the moral appearance of a person and his Party identity constitute an indissoluble whole.[125]

The direct dependence of political behaviour on moral qualities allows one to understand why the terrible 'human' and 'moral' attributes of the enemies lead to their destruction. And in fact, if 'the psychological and political lines, the moral appearance of a person and his Party identity constitute an indissoluble whole', then the firing squad is the only adequate reaction to the incorrect 'political line'. In the end, 'the Trotskyites, Bukharinites, Zinovievites', as one reviewer explained, 'are the vanguard of the counter-revolutionary bourgeoisie and, naturally, in this vanguard there are people in whose characters all the most repulsive features of bourgeois politicians appear in their most concentrated, hyperbolised, monstrous form.'[126] Dividing the latter into 'theoreticians' and 'practitioners' of terror did not help them either. This 'subterfuge' was easily unmasked (one of the main tasks of the show trials) in the picture:

> For all the differences between these characters, they are but two sides of the same coin. Kartashov plays the role of the theoretician and Borovsky is the practitioner. But did not Bukharin persistently try to play the role of theoretician in his trial, only then to be forced to acknowledge that he was the most ordinary 'practitioner' of espionage, organiser of diversionist and insurgent groups, initiator of terrorist acts?[127]

This conviction that personality and political conduct were indissolubly linked in particular presented psychological problems. 'Our task', wrote Ermler, 'was to show the enemy correctly not only in his political, but also in his psychological essence. But how do you penetrate into the dark underground of the enemy's psychology, which is so skilfully conspiratorial?'[128] Ivan Bersenev, who, as we already know, felt 'profound repugnance' towards Kartashov, could serve as an example. The actor, Ermler recalled:

> saw, understood, and with all the passion of an artist and a Soviet citizen hated Kartashov the enemy, Kartashov the traitor . . . Kartashov is crafty, cunning, wily, but doomed and internally ravaged. Hence his uncertainty, the minute trembling in the tips of his fingers, his nervous gait and nausea. Ivan Nikolaevich [Bersenev – E. D.] told me that in the scenes of the clash with Shakhov, when Shakhov was pinning him against the wall, when there were no more words of retort, Ivan Nikolaevich suddenly became tired, felt a strange nausea, could not catch his breath and was very thirsty.[129]

One could say that the actor experienced the same feeling of 'growing accustomed' that Flaubert experienced while describing the poisoning of Madame Bovary. The central question, however, is elsewhere: how did the anti-Soviet underground differ from the Bolshevik underground? The counter-revolutionary underground (before the Revolution), as Gorky showed, was just as 'repulsive' and nauseating', but the revolutionary underground, as Dostoevsky showed before him, was no less terrible. Is it possible to explain the arising differences in strictly ideological terms? Soviet criticism asserted that it was in no way a question here of ideology, but of a truly genetic predisposition of people towards good or evil: 'A repulsive person finds his typical features and becomes not only a repulsive person, but a historically conditioned repulsive manifestation', because of 'the membership of a given figure to the camp which stood up in defence of a historically doomed cause', while 'in such conditions there is no place for the psychological neutrality of specific features of the human personality.'[130]

Sweeping aside individual psychology (which can, at least, 'change', as was then asserted, by means of 'reforging'), this cinema created an infernal villain who turned out to be on the other side of the barricades of the incessantly 'aggravating class struggle'. Precisely 'as a people', not one of these negative characters can be positive, simply because they are all scoundrels from birth, whilst Shakhov is a shining personality, and therefore a 'great citizen' and a Bolshevik. The director Grigory Roshal described this phenomenon thus:

> A Stalinist, full of friendly clarity and love for people, passionate in his loving heart, carrying within him the sunny joys of our era, Shakhov is splendidly handsome with the beauty of the new communist image. His clash with the gang of scoundrels that had lost its senses and was forging a new chain of treachery in the new, bright Stalinist world – this great clash came to a victorious conclusion in spite of the death of Shakhov.[131]

One can therefore conclude that the personal and political qualities of a person were completely interdependent, and that the oppositionists were shot because they were . . . scoundrels.

One critic wrote that:

> [T]he ideological and artistic strength and significance of the film *The Great Citizen* consist above all of the fact that it gives an exhaustive analysis of the historical meaning of the political struggle of that time . . . The conduct and actions of these characters flow from the historical laws governing the events that were taking place.[132]

In other words, psychology retreats to the background. People prove to be chained to the gallery of 'historical laws', playing pre-written roles.

On the other hand, 'truthfulness' demanded seeing in the characters not some 'representatives of various camps' or other, but precisely psychologically authentic figures:

> Pyotr Shakhov and his enemies in no way 'represent', 'symbolise' or embody this or that socialist group. None of the main characters in *The Great Citizen* is a 'symbol' or 'personification'. They live independent lives. These images possess complete internal logic . . . A man who possesses such wonderful moral qualities as Shakhov can find a use for his abilities, his aspirations, only within the ranks of the Party, which brings happiness to mankind. And, on the other hand, the vile diversionary, destructive activities of the Trotskyite-Bukharinite agents of capitalism can

be carried out only by people who have reached such a state of moral disintegration and savagery as Borovsky and Kartashov. Politics and morals coincide exactly in *The Great Citizen*, or, rather, they are simply indivisible.[133]

By virtue of this 'indivisibility', enemies turn out to be enemies straight from birth; Shakhov and Kartashov 'are two types of people who can have nothing in common with each other.'[134] Terror in relation to enemies is not only well grounded, but also inevitable; their very fate, which transforms their 'morals' into 'politics', made them a target for 'just retribution'. Political views are only the derivatives of personal qualities. Thus 'psychologised' politics transforms every viewer into the potential object of 'the anger of the entire people'.

'In *The Great Citizen* Ermler brought together people who organically belonged to the bourgeois world, although they disguised themselves with Soviet faces, among socialist people.'[135] The key word here is 'organically'. In it a threat can be read; the 'sword of popular anger' inevitably comes down on the heads of those who 'belong to the bourgeois world' and 'disguise themselves with Soviet faces', but this 'belonging' (and with it the need for disguises) proves to be extra-rational, independent of man's will, 'organically' given to him. It remains only for the viewer to await the results of the analysis of his own 'organics'; everyone finds themselves under suspicion.

Everyone writing about *The Great Citizen*, even in the post-Soviet era, has noted that this film, more than others, revealed a reliance on the rational characteristic of Stalinist culture (in contrast to the reliance on the irrational in Nazi propaganda), in common with the opinion of criticism in the 1930s that *The Great Citizen* was a 'political film-dispute'. Criticism proceeded from the idea that this was a 'political picture': 'In the picture social, political links between people predominate', the film shows 'people completely and utterly immersed in a tense political struggle.'[136] But was it in fact that? Yes, here they are talking exclusively and only about politics, yet the aim of this cinema was not in the slightest to draw viewers into the field of political relations and connections, but exactly the opposite: to frighten them off. Ermler's 'political cinematography' was part of the depoliticising culture of the 1930s, a culture directed towards the alienation of politics, whereas, on the contrary, political cinematography (as in the case of, for example, early Soviet revolutionary cinema) is not an analysis of the nature of political confrontation, of social conflict, but above all an appeal to the viewer, propaganda and agitation.

Ermler never tired of repeating, in connection with *The Great Citizen*, that he was 'carried away by the emotion of political speech'.[137] But the issue here is not so much in the pathos and the content, as in the very fact of the speech. It is not a question of everybody in the film talking all the time about politics, but of the fact that in the film the only thing they do is talk. They talk ceaselessly. (It is no accident that political revolutionary cinema was silent.) Critics even wrote of the style of *The Great Citizen* as the 'aesthetics of the Party meeting', while conflict in the picture was defined as a 'system of confrontations'.[138] Be that as it may, 'talking pictures' presented filmmakers with more than a few strictly aesthetic problems. The scriptwriters understood that they were entering:

> an as yet undiscovered area of cinema – the area of purely talking pictures. We ourselves were horrified at the abundance of text in the screenplay, we tried to shorten it, it seemed illegitimate to us to make a picture like that, as we did not yet understand that in this thing called speech there is a fundamental element of play.[139]

How was it working with speech, with this new material (not medium, but precisely material!) in cinema?

> We did not know of any works of art that could serve us as models. They were nowhere to be found. And we turned directly to documents – to transcripts of Party congresses, newspapers, to concrete living material. In the speeches of Stalin, Molotov, Dzerzhinsky, Kirov, Ordzhonikidze we found what we were looking for . . . The attentive viewer of the picture would easily detect in the characters' words the same formulae which were heard at Party congresses . . . The viewer of our picture has to follow not only the characters' actions, but also, and most importantly, their words, to listen carefully, to read the text of the picture,[140]

said the screenwriters. (It is worth noting that, with the help of Stalin himself, they skilfully mastered his mode of polemic – with distortions, quotations taken out of context, political labels and so on.)

And after all, the fundamental discoveries lay precisely in the sphere of film aesthetics. Being 'talking pictures', Romm's and in particular Ermler's films, based on huge conversation scenes, led both directors to discover a 'deep *mise en scène*', when in order to avoid splitting up the action, 'the actors themselves, coming out of the depths into the foreground, alter the scale of the portrayal. They montage the film on the move, so to speak, moving along the longitudinal axis of the frame.'[141] Montage is dying before one's eyes. In its place comes 'the new principles of "deep *mise en scène*", which answer the aims of the unceasing actors' play in material of the political dialogue'.[142]

The device of turning a 'talking film' into entertainment was appraised by critics immediately. Already after the release of the first part of *The Great Citizen*, one reviewer wrote:

> Ermler has found new, until now little known principles of cinematographic montage . . . This montage is constructed on a meticulous, intricately sharpened composition of planes, on the exceptional smoothness

of montage transitions . . . The cameraman A. Koltsaty, with his natural placing of light-sources, his skilful apportioning in the frame of fundamental images, and soft ink smudges of the secondary ones, achieved an unusual clarity of design, a fine communication of the director's ideas in all their detail.[143]

Nor did the creators of the film hide their 'secret'. They wrote that,

[T]he usual methods of filming and montage only corrupt the screenplay. With analysis of every scene it became obvious that the jerkiness of montage with the transition from shot to shot destroys the continuity of both the acting and the text. We had to seek new methods of work. They were found in the fact that the camera ceased to 'jump' from shot to shot, but followed the actor, creating the continuity of movement the director needed. This work defined the construction of the frame, the angle of the shot, the *mise en scène*.[144]

This example could serve as another piece of evidence to the effect that, as Victor Shklovsky asserted, it is entirely unimportant for art exactly which flag is flying over the fortress. So that even such a 'cannibalistic film' as *The Great Citizen*, as one viewer commented during a discussion of the film on Soviet television during the era of *Perestroika*, could introduce a truly great discovery into cinematography.

However, during discussion of totalitarian cinema in those years of *Perestroika*, Leonid Kozlov drew attention to the fact that Stalinist cinema's departure from the principles of revolutionary montage was in a paradoxical way accompanied by a reinforcement of the propaganda potential of this art in the 1930s. André Bazin:

cautioned against the danger of manipulating the viewer's psyche by means of montage. In opposition to the principle of 'montage' cinematography Bazin, relying on the experience of American cinema in the 1940s, placed a different system of cinematographic poetics, based on the predominance of protracted, uncut montage patterns with deep *mise en scène*. Bazin interpreted this system as being more realistic in relation to actuality and – which is very important – as being the most human and 'liberal' in relation to the viewer.

There is one film which Bazin did not see, and in which the notorious principles of scene-episode, deep *mise en scène* and drawn-out montage segments were brought to perfection.

It contains in all 150 scenes per hour. This film, forestalling post-war Western cinema and, if you like, to the highest degree 'liberal' in its poetics, was created in the USSR at the end of the 1930s. Its title is *The Great Citizen*.[145]

One critic of the 1930s was right: 'The decisive, defining role is played in the film by the word. The success of *The Great Citizen* is defined by the high quality of the text', and 'the words and speeches of the characters are their actions.'[146] The double-dealing of the 'enemies of the people' is destroyed by a word:

> Kartashov, Borovsky and their accomplices use the word as a disguise, as a smoke screen, as hidden poison. On the lips of Shakhov and his friends the word is a means of exposing the enemy, a means of expressing noble ideas. This is why the Bolshevik word is victorious.[147]

It was no coincidence that criticism endowed the word with so much significance. In fact, what was important was not the word at all, but what stood behind it: the fatal predisposition of the personality towards one type of conduct or another, the 'feeling' it aroused.

The characters do not even need to enter into direct interaction. Thus in part two the opponents never once see each other, but an uneven battle takes place between them; 'Kartashov, Borovsky and their accomplices' act secretly, while Shakhov acts in public. They know everything about him, but he knows nothing about them. (Thinking about enemies, Shakhov echoes exactly this point: 'We know nothing about them', 'We don't yet know', and so on.) His doubt as to whether the matter runs much deeper than a simple attempt to kill him is expressed by him thus, for example: 'If there are stupid enemies who are hunting for regional Party secretaries, maybe there are also clever enemies who are acting otherwise.' Shakhov and the underground counter-revolutionaries are like two mirrors placed at such an angle that one reflects the other, but not completely. On this paradox of the plot, the filmmakers wrote:

> If Kartashov and Borovsky are conducting a complex, cunning plan to fight against the Party and the people, if they realise their aims, by exploiting human backwardness and the vestiges of capitalism in the consciousness of people, then Shakhov defeats them with direct blows – simple blows which paralyse the seeming complexity of the enemies' thoughts. Shakhov is based on Bolshevik practice, on the practice of Party work. He defeats enemies with self-criticism, the promotion of new cadres, and control.[148]

One could say that Shakhov 'defeats' them without himself knowing it. His strength is not in his knowledge but in his 'Bolshevik practice'.

Shakhov did not need specifically to fight against the conspirators; this very 'practice' contains an antidote to the enemies' intrigues. The magic of this 'practice' comes, in fact, from 'theory':

> We were trying not to illustrate our reality, we were trying to understand it, to understand it on the basis of studying Stalin's works. We were trying

to trace the course of his thoughts, the birth of his conclusions and prognoses . . . The idea of the clash of our heroes, their psychological characteristics – all that arose from the study of Stalin's speeches and papers.[149]

These were those same speeches and papers in which Stalin branded the double-dealers, traitors, bandits and diversionists. This entire symphony of hatred sounded out in the pages of both the transcripts of the Moscow show trials, corrected by Stalin, and the *Short Course*. The film's makers knew where to find answers to 'vital artistic questions':

> Our task was in a psychologically truthful way to show the enemy not only in his political, but also in his psychological essence – to expose the double-dealing which had become his political principle, to expose his adventurism and his treacherous essence.
>
> In what forms, in what characters should we invest this? How should we penetrate into the psychology of the enemy, how should we understand his thought processes, when the dark underground of his psychology is closed off even to himself?
>
> We found the answer in Stalin. The psychology of this political rabble was exactly defined by Stalin.[150]

In the reflected projections of the Stalinist era the filmmakers could scarcely have suspected how mortally close they were to the truth. Thus 'Bolshevik flair', and not the word at all, comes to the aid of Shakhov. The word in this 'talking cinema', on the other hand, betrays. Thus Shakhov does not know that Andreev is linked to Borovsky, but he knows, as one reviewer wrote:

> what ethical norms must define the conduct of a builder of socialism, he knows socialism can be built and defended only by people with a pure conscience, and that, on the other hand, people who are defective and depraved are the bearers of the remnants of capitalism, whom capitalism can use.

It is precisely this that exposes the second secretary of the regional committee, Zemtsov: 'Zemtsov's moral putrefaction helps Shakhov to see the enemy in him.' With 'true Bolshevik flair'[151] he unmasks the provocateur Zemtsov. The 'filthy accusation' thrown by Zemtsov,

> betrays him from head to toe, although there is hardly a single piece of evidence against him. It betrays him because in an instant, in two or three of Zemtsov's replies, his 'soul' is exposed to Shakhov, the mechanism of his provocative, politicking, hostile way of thinking, the psychology of a rogue who forced his way into the Party with the filthiest and basest aims.[152]

And so, each time 'Bolshevik flair tells him a great deal.'[153]

According to Oksana Bulgakowa's subtle observation:

> [F]or all the importance of the word, it is not this which carries the idea in the film . . . Although the film consists for the most part of arguments, meetings and speeches, it completely avoids discussion and dialogue. Shakhov argues over the course of four hours with his political opponents, competes with them like an orator before different audiences, but not a single speech uttered in the film is argumentative, and divergences in political and economic programmes are not concretised. At the very moment when the characters finish their rhetorical introductions and approach concrete proposals, the scene suddenly stops and the speech is cut. Not a single phrase from the newspapers or letters is seen in the frame as a full text. Sentences are cut short, they are indications and hints of unpronounced and unpronounceable 'meaningless splashes of ideas' . . . Understanding and recognition (of who is one's own and who is an enemy) is achieved, in the final analysis, not via the word, but via 'intuition', intonation, song. The hero (Shakhov) 'scents' who is an enemy, and this defines a strange type of cut-off dialogue . . . The audience also understands in its core, via intonation and physiognomy, but not via speech, who is their own and who is not.[154]

From this 'scent' a threat emanates. If the enemy is exposed not on the basis of rational explanation, but by 'scent', then anyone can turn out to be an enemy (including everyone sitting in the auditorium). One should also bear in mind that the very problem of the relationship of rationality and 'spirituality' is central to the paranoid mind-set, which is always based on logic. This logic is, however, so defective that it forces psychologists to speak of the spiritualism of the paranoiac; he is a rationalist, but his rationalism is based on 'feeling'. On the other hand, rationality is projected by him on to the forces of evil, which weave a 'network of conspiracy'. In spite of the 'obsession with systematizing everything', they are 'motivated by irrational drives'.[155]

The very 'sublime object' of adoration, Shakhov-Kirov, turns out to be irrational. Thus, one critic found the almost mystical 'spiritual similarity' of Shakhov to Kirov much more important than the surface similarity:

> In spite of the almost complete absence of similarity in appearance, Soviet viewers recognise in Shakhov the features of the image of Sergei Mironovich Kirov, who is dear to all our people. The sincerity and greatness of civil feelings, the beautiful skill of the artistic performance, which penetrates into the inner world of the image, or rather, his artistically correct representation – this is the tool which helped to create the similarity of Shakhov to Kirov.[156]

STALINIST CINEMA AND THE PRODUCTION OF HISTORY

Thus in his hunt for the enemy there is no point in Shakhov listening to enemies' speeches, to convince him or otherwise. The word here is powerless, as the rational basis for the idea that before us we have an enemy is powerless:

> The very idea that there is an enemy before him arises in Shakhov's consciousness almost instantaneously, in no way as a result of the influence of obvious and unarguable evidence, but because in both the conduct and psychology of these people he unexpectedly runs up against features which represent to him something organically alien to the psychology and morality of the Soviet man. We are talking here not of any appreciable features, but rather of a few details which immediately create an unpleasant impression on Shakhov, which immediately arouse an negative emotional reaction in him.[157]

This reaction is always correct.

Critics were delighted by the fact that 'in his evaluation of political phenomena Shakhov adopts terminology which was as if borrowed from some sort of system of ethics, from some sort of study of morality.'[158] But this moralisation of politics had an absolutely definite aim: widening the zone of political responsibility to its greatest possible extent, so that the 'ordinary viewers', who might have supposed that these political passions and events bore no relation to them (if they were not factory directors or regional party secretaries), had to understand his error. It was at them that Shakhov's unmasking moral discourse was aimed, demanding repentance for 'impure thoughts', which would inevitably be turned into 'impure actions'. 'Moral considerations' universalised terror. When 'thoughts' and 'moral purity' turn out to be the criteria for distinction, 'moral considerations' are sufficient to identify the enemy, and for him to be exposed, not even character traits are needed, but 'details which immediately create an unpleasant impression', the blade of the 'sword of the dictatorship of the proletariat' can be felt on the neck of everyone, even the 'tiniest screw'. It is precisely into the soul of the 'simple Soviet man' that Shakhov looks, its most secret corners being open to him.

These, however, are the real fields of battle. It is indeed precisely this 'spiritual' underground that the enemies try to make use of: 'You know how to find in a man such a screw . . . turn it and the man dies. But destroying a man morally is something far greater than simply killing him,' Borovsky teaches his comrades in the underground. 'In every man there are hidden living grievances, suppressed desires, weaknesses, errors, petty passions.' (It is worth noting that Pyatakov, when he appears in the film, suggests that the 'psychological experiments in the spirit of Fyodor Mikhailovich Dostoevsky' carried out by Borovsky are fruitless.) It turns out, however, that this is the world not of 'every' person, but precisely the world of the underground men themselves:

> In the end [one reviewer asserted], this is only autocharacterisation. Neither in Borovsky himself, nor in his whole repulsive milieu has there for a long time been anything 'spiritual', anything ideological. They represent themselves as if they are the embodiment of suppressed desires, grievances, petty passions, weaknesses. Borovsky's theory is nothing more than the theoretical interpretation of his own character, the character of Kartashov, Bryantsev, Sizov. It is the features of his character which have become his programme of sabotage, diversion, counter-revolutionary work.[159]

In this way the psychologisation of the enemies turns them into an 'unprincipled gang of adventurists', and the Party opposition (even in the past) into the 'mob of the scum of society', about which Stalin never ceased talking. On the contrary, everything 'spiritual' is set out on Shakhov's side – to these new people, 'great citizens', 'suppressed desires' are unknown; they do not and cannot have 'grievances, petty passions, weaknesses'.

Three times at culminating points the same tirade is heard in the picture in different ways: in Shakhov's speech at the meeting at the 'Red Metalworkers' in 1925, in his address to the meeting of shock-workers in 1934, and at the end of the picture. The film concludes with a hymn to the destruction of enemies. Over Shakhov's grave the communist Kats pronounces his words of farewell:

> You can deceive one man, you can confuse him, intimidate him, but you cannot deceive thousands of Bolsheviks, thousands of communists, that can never be! The Bolshevik Party is building a new life, realising the age-old dreams of mankind, and everyone who tries to stop our work the people will destroy! And the people, the victorious people, has destroyed them, is destroying them, and will destroy them! Sacred mercilessness to the one in the name of the happiness of millions – that was the idea by which Shakhov lived, which he shouldered, and for which he was treacherously killed . . . He had great belief, great love and great hatred. And he has bequeathed to us this great hatred towards our enemies, great faith in our victory and great love for the people, for the party, for Stalin.

What was projected on the screen was, so to speak, reflected and returned by the auditorium: 'two of the strongest, two of the most passionate feelings of aspiration for the screen: love and hatred,' as one reviewer summed up his impressions.

> Love for one's own Soviet land, for the Leninist-Stalinist Communist Party, for the people, for the working class and its best sons – the Soviet man. And therefore, hatred, angry, limitless hatred for the cruel, deep-rooted enemies of the Soviet motherland, for the filthy, loathsome traitors, for the poisonous, snake-like rabble which has been spawned by all these Trotskys, Bukharins, Zinovievs and Yagodas.[160]

But in the end, the strongest feeling which seized the viewer of *The Great Citizen* was not mentioned by the reviewer: fear. A deadly threat radiates from the screen.

The viewer unmistakably defined the picture's place in the media space of the end of the 1930s; this was a visual adaptation of the show trials, on which the newspapers and radio were reporting every day. To see it meant a great deal.

> The picture *The Great Citizen* [wrote another reviewer] was released at the time when the whole country, the entire Soviet people, gripped by a terrible and shattering hatred, was judging the contemptible scoundrels of the 'Right-Trotskyite bloc'. The picture was seen by millions of Soviet patriots at the same time as in the October Hall of the House of Soviets the prosecutor of the USSR, in the name of the free peoples of our great country, was summing up the legal case against the unparalleled crimes of the vile traitors . . . Viewers look at the screen and can already imagine Kartashov sat in the dock, Kartashov, exposed in his work as a spy, guilty of diversion and murder. They look at the screen and are taught to hate and expose the Kartashovs, the concealed, lying, disguised bandits, who have eclipsed with their unparalleled crimes all the scoundrels, traitors and hypocrites who have ever existed on earth. They look at the screen and know that the picture is telling them an essential truth.[161]

These films far from accidentally aroused not one but two feelings – not only hatred, but also love. These films were not by accident dedicated to the fascinating leader of the Revolution, Lenin, and to the noble and pure Bolsheviks, Maxim and Kirov. (The film about the 'great enemy' was, after all, called *The Great Citizen*!) In the name of self-preservation the viewer had to love these amazing people. They were specially created objects for the sublimation of fear. The more bloody the era became, the greater the place occupied by the underground in mass imagination; from *Maxim's Youth* to the second part of *The Great Citizen* the balance of these scales was shifted to the side of the enemy underground, whilst yesterday's underground revolutionaries turned out to be submerged in the 'stinking world of counter-revolutionary rabble'. But the more powerful the squalls of hatred, the higher the waves of love rose. These two 'most powerful feelings' merged into one; the screen turned the deadly threat it was emanating into a *perpetuum mobile* of fear, a true source and instrument of terror. And in this consisted the 'essential truth' of these menacing pictures.

NOTES

1. Cited by Dmitrii Volkogonov, 'Stalin', *Oktiabr'*, 1988, No. 11, p. 87.
2. Viktor Shklovskii, *Za 60 let*, Moscow: Iskusstvo, 1985, p. 58.
3. R. Iurenev, *Sovetskoe kinoiskusstvo tridtsatykh godov*, Moscow: VGIK, 1997, p. 7.

4. Oksana Bulgakova, 'Sovetskoe kino v poiskakh "obshchei modeli"'. In H. Gunther, E. Dobrenko (eds), *Sotsrealisticheskii kanon*, St Petersburg: Akademicheskii proekt, 2000, pp. 153–4.

5. I. Vaisfel'd, 'Zamechatel'nyi fil'm'. In *Lenin v Oktiabre*, Moscow, Leningrad: Iskusstvo, 1938, p. 6.

6. G. Roshal', 'Obrazy i aktery'. In *Dvadtsat' let sovetskoi kinematografii. Sb. st*, Moscow: Goskinoizdat, 1940, p. 58. Emphasising the trilogy's 'realism', Boris Alpers wrote: 'Here everything is real, made from authentic material . . . Not only Maxim, but also the secondary characters appear on the screen like people who really existed at one time. Of course, Turaev was just such a person . . . With just such gestures and intonations he pronounced from the Duma tribune his speech in defence of the workers . . . The girl Natasha was also just such a person . . . That elderly worker also really existed . . . The authors of *Maxim's Return* (*Vozvrashchenie Maksima*) went down the path of profoundly realistic art.' Boris Alpers, *Dnevnik kinokritika: 1928–1937*, Moscow: Fond 'Novoe tysiacheletie', 1995, p. 169.

7. N. Kovarskii, 'Fridrikh Ermler'. In *Velikii grazhdanin. Sb. materialov k kinofil'mu*, Leningrad: Lenfil'm, 1940, p. 39.

8. E. Grigor'ev, *O fil'me 'Lenin v 1918 godu'*, Moscow: Gosfil'mizdat, 1939, p. 17.

9. Cited by N. Maslov, ' "Kratkii kurs istorii VKP(b)" – entsiklopediia i ideologiia stalinizma i poststalinizma: 1939–1988 gg'. In *Sovetskaia istoriografiia*, Moscow: RGGU, 1996, p. 258.

10. Ibid., pp. 258–9.

11. Ibid., p. 259.

12. O. Nesterovich, 'Dramaturgiia istoriko-revoliutsionnogo fil'ma', *Iskusstvo kino*, 1939, No. 7, p. 25.

13. Ibid., p. 25.

14. See 'Kino totalitarnoi epokhi', *Iskusstvo kino*, 1990, No. 3, pp. 103–6.

15. Liliia Mamatova, 'Model' kinofil'mov 30-kh godov: genii i zlodeistvo', *Iskusstvo kino*, 1991, No. 3, p. 94.

16. Robert Tucker, 'Stalin, Bukharin, and History as Conspiracy'. In Robert Tucker, *The Soviet Political Mind: Stalinism and Post-Stalin Change*, New York: Norton, 1971, p. 54.

17. Feliks Chuev, *Sto sorok besed s Molotovym*, Moscow: Terra, 1991, p. 84.

18. There is a large body of literature on the problem of political paranoia. Among the most interesting works one should refer to R. Waelder, 'Characteristics of Totalitarianism'. In W. Muensterberger, S. Axelrad (eds), *The Psychoanalytic Study of Society*, New York: International University Press, 1960; D. J. Finley et al. (eds), *Enemies in Politics*, Chicago, IL: Rand McNally, 1967; David B. Davis (ed.), *The Fear of Conspiracy: Images of Un-American Subversion from the Revolution to the Present*, Ithaca, NY: Cornell University Press, 1971; Richard O. Curry, Thomas M. Brown (eds), *Conspiracy: The Fear of Subversion in American History*, New York: Holt, Rinehart & Winston, 1972; W. C. Langer, *The Mind of Adolf Hitler*, New York: Basic, 1972; F. Fornary, *The Psychoanalysis of War*, Bloomington, IN: Indiana University Press, 1975; R. Koenigsberg, *Hitler's Ideology: A Study in Psychoanalytic Sociology*, New York: Library of Social Science, 1975; Seymour M. Lipset, Earl Raab, *The Politics of Unreason: Right-Wing Extremism in America, 1790–1977*, Chicago, IL: University of Chicago Press, 1978; Richard Hofstadter, *The Paranoid Style in American Politics and Other Essays*, Chicago, IL: University of Chicago Press, 1979; Robert Eringer, *The Conspiracy Peddlers*, Mason, MI: Loompanics Unlimited, 1981; M. Vovelle, 'Ideologies and Mentalities'. In R. Samuel, G. Jones (eds), *Cultures, Ideology, and Politics*, London: Routledge & Kegan Paul, 1982; S. Keen, *Faces of the Enemy*, New York: Harper & Row, 1986; V. Volkan, *The Need to have Enemies and Allies*, Northvale, NJ: Jason Aronson, 1988; J. A. Aho, *This Thing of Darkness:*

A Sociology of Enemy, Seattle, WA: University of Washington Press, 1995. Work on the problem of political paranoia also regularly appears in the journals *International Journal of Group Psychotherapy* and *Political Psychology*.

19. Robert Robbins, Jerrold Post. *Political Paranoia*. New Haven, CT: Yale University Press, 1997, p. 12.
20. See A. Ulam, *In the Name of the People: Prophets and Conspirators in Pre-Revolutionary Russia*, New York: Viking, 1977.
21. Robbins, Post, *Political Paranoia*, p. 265.
22. On the conception that the idea of conspiracy and the paranoid imagination are fundamental aspects of the internal life of the masses, see Elias Canetti, *Crowds and Power*, New York: Noonday, 1984, pp. 22–4.
23. Robbins, Post, *Political Paranoia*, p. 43.
24. V. I. Lenin, *Polnoe sobranie sochinenii*, 5th edn, Vol. 6, Moscow: Politizdat, p. 9.
25. Fridrikh Ermler, *Dokumenty. Stat'i. Vospominaniia*, Leningrad: Iskusstvo, 1974, p. 84.
26. Aleksandr Karaganov, *Grigorii Kozintsev: Ot 'Tsaria Maksimiliana' do 'Korolia Lira'*, Moscow: Materik, 2003, p. 86.
27. Feliks Dzerzhinskii, *Dnevnik. Pis'ma k rodym*, Moscow: Molodaia gvardiia, 1958, p. 53.
28. Grigorii Kozintsev, 'Glubokii ekran'. In G. Kozintsev, *Sobranie sochinenii v 5 tomakh*, Vol. 1, Leningrad: Iskusstvo, 1982, p. 232.
29. Grigorii Kozintsev, '*Chernoe, likhoe vremia . . .*': *Iz rabochikh tetradei*, Moscow: Artist, 1994, p. 99. This extract was written by Kozintsev for *Glubokii ekran*. In 1970, when the book was already at galley proof stage, the passage was removed by the censorship. In 1981 it was restored by the editors of Kozintsev's collected works.
30. Kozintsev, *Glubokii ekran*, p. 207.
31. In 1933 the filming of *The Bolshevik* (the picture's first title) was suspended after sharp criticism by Andrei Bubnov. The film, however, was supported by Alexei Stetsky (and, consequently, the cinematographers' leadership) and on 14 February 1934 it went into production as *Maxim's Youth*, although Bubnov spoke out against the new version of the screenplay. Stetsky personally gave instructions for the alterations of the screenplay. But then, after filming had already begun, a series of new comments followed, on the basis of which Boris Shumyatsky demanded that the directors 'quickly, without creating stoppages in the filming, develop the dramatically integral and artistically grounded improvements. This instruction should be taken by you and the studio as a directive and be implemented speedily and to the letter.' *Perepiska G. M. Kozintseva: 1922–1973*, Moscow: Artist. Rezhisser. Teatr, 1998, p. 25.
32. Kozintsev, *Glubokii ekran*, pp. 208–9.
33. Karaganov, *Grigorii Kozintsev: Ot 'Tsaria Maksimiliana' do 'Korolia Lira'*, p. 83.
34. Ibid., p. 87.
35. L. Trauberg, *Fil'm nachinaetsia*, Moscow: Iskusstvo, 1977, p. 125.
36. Kozintsev, *Sobranie sochinenii: v 5 tomakh*, Vol. 1, p. 366.
37. Ibid., p. 405.
38. *Trilogiia o Maksime*, Moscow: Iskusstvo, 1981, p. 39.
39. Kozintsev, *Glubokii ekran*, p. 210.
40. Oksana Bulgakova, 'Bul'varizatsiia avangarda – fenomen FEKS', *Kinovedcheskie zapiski*, 1990, No. 7, p. 45.
41. From lectures on totalitarian cinema given at Duke University, USA, Spring 1993.
42. Barbara Leaming, *Grigori Kozintsev*, Boston: Twayne, 1980, p. 60.
43. Kozintsev, *Sobranie sochinenii: v 5 tomakh*, Vol. 1, p. 372.
44. Kozintsev, *Glubokii ekran*, p. 232.
45. Cited by N. Klado, 'Trilogiia o Maksime', *Iskusstvo kino*, 1939, No. 4, p. 51.
46. Kozintsev, *Sobranie sochinenii v 5 tomakh*, Vol. 1, pp. 427–8.

47. Kozintsev, *Glubokii ekran*, p. 221.
48. Grigorii Kozintsev, 'Otryvki iz knigi o kinoaktere', *Iskusstvo kino*, 1938, No. 1, p. 34.
49. Ibid., p. 34.
50. G. Adamovich, 'Iunost' Maksima' (Poslednie novosti (Paris), 1936, 17 July), *Kinovedcheskie zapiski. 2000*, Issue 48, pp. 126–7.
51. Grigorii Kozintsev, Leonid Trauberg, 'Nash fil'm', *Kino*, 1937, 5 May, p. 3.
52. Trauberg, *Fil'm nachinaetsia*, p. 66.
53. Ibid., p. 66.
54. *Trilogiia o Maksime*, Moscow: Iskusstvo, 1981, p. 247.
55. Cited in *Russkii illiuzion*, Moscow: Materik, 2003, p. 129.
56. 'Diskussiia v Len ARRK', *Kino*, 1935, 15 February, p. 3.
57. Ibid.
58. Leonid Trauberg, 'Aktery narodnogo iskusstva', *Izvestiia*, 1940, 15 February, p. 3.
59. Grigorii Kozintsev, *Sobranie sochinenii: v 5 tomakh*, Vol. 1, p. 382.
60. Ibid.
61. Kozintsev, *Glubokii ekran*, p. 219.
62. M. Bleiman, 'Novatorskii fil'm', *Iskusstvo kino*, 1939, No. 2, p. 13.
63. Maksim Gor'kii, *Sobranie sochinenii: v 30 tt*, Vol. 27, Moscow: GIKhL, 1954, p. 435.
64. Kozintsev, *Sobranie sochinenii: v 5 tomakh*, Vol. 1, p. 404.
65. Ibid., p. 405.
66. Alpers, *Dnevnik kinokritika: 1928–1937*, p. 168.
67. S. Dreiden, 'Maksim-Chirkov', *Kino*, 1937, 23 May, p. 2.
68. S. Tsimbal, 'Obraz Maksima', *Iskusstvo kino*, 1937, No. 7, p. 26.
69. From 'lisa' (fox), denoting his cunning (translator's note).
70. Kozintsev, *Sobranie sochinenii: v 5 tomakh*, Vol. 1, p. 419.
71. Ibid.
72. <http://www.svoboda.org/programs/cicles/cinema/russian/ReturnOfMaxim.asp>. Radio Svoboda, Russkaia kinodvadtsatka: 'Vozvrashchenie Maksima' i 'Vyborgskaia storona'. Accessed 15 March 2006.
73. *Trilogiia o Maksime*, Moscow, 1981, pp. 363–4.
74. Ibid.
75. Kozintsev, *Glubokii ekran*, p. 228.
76. *Trilogiia o Maksime*, p. 247.
77. Kozintsev, *Sobranie sochinenii: v 5 tomakh*, Vol. 1, p. 405.
78. Karaganov, *Grigorii Kozintsev: Ot 'Tsaria Maksimiliana' do 'Korolia Lira'*, p. 112.
79. M. Dolgopolov, 'Maksim', *Izvestiia*, 3 June 1938, p. 4.
80. Ibid., p. 4.
81. R. Iurenev, *Sovetskii biograficheskii fil'm*, Moscow: Gokinoizdat, 1949, p. 189.
82. On the status of the space in which the Soviet 'founding myth' was realised, and on the role of the word and the visual image in this process, see Mikhail Iampol'skii, 'Lenin provozglashaet Sovetskuiu vlast' (Zametki o diskurse osnovaniia)'. *Novoe literaturnoe obozrenie*, 26 (1997).
83. M. Zak, *Mikhail Romm i traditsii sovetskoi kinorezhissury*, Moscow: Iskusstvo, 1975, p. 91.
84. R. Iurenev, *Sovetskii biograficheskii fil'm*, p. 197.
85. Sergei Eizenshtein, 'Lenin v nashikh serdtsakh'. *Izvestiia*, 1939, 5 April, p. 4.
86. Ibid., p. 4.
87. S. Tsimbal, 'Obraz Lenina v kino', *Iskusstvo kino*, 1938, No. 1, p. 14.
88. O. Nesterovich, 'Dramaturgiia istoriko-revoliutsionnogo fil'ma', *Iskusstvo kino*, 1939, No. 7, p. 25.
89. Il. Trauberg, 'Rasskaz o velikom vozhde: O stsenarii "Lenin"'. *Iskusstvo kino*, 1939, No. 1, p. 7.

90. Tsimbal, 'Obraz Lenina v kino', p. 14.
91. *Istoriia VKP(b). Kratkii kurs*, Moscow: Gospolitizdat, 1938, p. 331.
92. Trauberg, 'Rasskaz o velikom vozhde', p. 12.
93. Romm himself often asserted that his main and only task was to make Lenin on the screen beloved by all the people.
94. N. A. Lebedev, *Shchukin–akter kino*, Moscow: Goskinoizdat, 1944, p. 129.
95. Eizenshtein, 'Lenin v nashikh serdtsakh', p. 4.
96. Zak, *Mikhail Romm i traditsii sovetskoi kinorezhissury*, p. 103.
97. Il. Trauberg, 'Proizvedenie mysli i strasti: *Lenin v 1918 godu*'. *Iskusstvo kino*, 1939, No. 3, p. 37.
98. Mikhail Romm, 'Rabota Shchukina nad obrazom Lenina'. In *Obrazy Lenina i Stalina v kino*, Moscow: Goskinoizdat, 1939, p. 30.
99. A. Latyshev, 'Stalin i kino'. In *Surovaia drama naroda*, Moscow: Politizdat, 1989, pp. 495–6.
100. 'Utverzhdenie politicheskogo zhanra. Beseda s avtorami stsenariia *Velikogo grazhdanina* M. Bleimanom i M. Bol'shintsovym', *Kino*, 1938, 28 February.
101. M. Bleiman, M. Bol'shintsov, F. Ermler, 'Rabota nad kartinoi'. In *Velikii grazhdanin. Sb. materialov k kinofil'mu*, Leningrad: Lenfil'm, 1940, p. 5.
102. On the preparations for making such a film, see *Istoriia sovetskoi politicheskoi tsenzury: Dokumenty i kommentarii*, Moscow: ROSSPEN, 1997, p. 481.
103. Grigorii Kozintsev. *Sobranie sochinenii: v 5 tomakh*, Vol. 2, Leningrad: Iskusstvo, 1983, p. 15.
104. Ibid., p. 15.
105. *Trilogiia o Maksime*, Moscow, 1981, p. 22.
106. See Leonid Maksimenkov, *Sumbur vmesto muzyki: Stalinskaia kul'turnaia revoliutsiia 1936–1938*, Moscow: Iuridicheskaia kniga, 1997, pp. 131–5. See also Sof'ia Khentova, *Molodye gody Shostakovicha*, Book 2, Leningrad: Sovetskii kompozitor, 1980, p. 222.
107. Maksimenkov, *Sumbur vmesto muzyki*, p. 132.
108. Ibid., p. 131.
109. Robins, Post, *Political Paranoia*, p. 92.
110. L. Belova, *Ocherki istorii sovetskoi kinodramaturgii*, Moscow: Iskusstvo, 1978, p. 188.
111. S. Tregub, 'Velikii Grazhdanin', *Pravda*, 1939, 29 October, p. 4.
112. I. F. Popov, *Problemy sovetskoi kinodramaturgii*, Moscow: Goskinoizdat, 1939, p. 54.
113. M. Bleiman, M. Bol'shintsov, F. Ermler, 'Rabota nad stsenariem', *Iskusstvo kino*, 1938, No. 4–5, p. 31.
114. From Maya Turovskaya's course on totalitarian cinema at Duke University, Spring 1993.
115. Ermler said, 'We had to some degree Dostoevsky's *The Devils* standing behind us.' See: 'Stenogramma obsuzhdeniia rezhisserskoi kollegii kinostudii "Lenfil'ma" stsenarii F. Ermlera, M. Bol'shintsova i M. Bleimana "Velikii grazhdanin" 21 iiulia 1936 goda. (Publikatsiia, predislovie i kommentarii N. S. Gornitskaia i L. B. Shvarts)', *Kinovedcheskie zapiski*, No. 63, 2003, pp. 148–68.
116. D. S. Pisarevskii, S. I. Freilikh, 'Sovremennaia zhizn' sovetskogo obshchestva v fil'makh vtoroi poloviny 30-kh godov'. In *Ocherki istorii sovetskogo kino: v 3 tomakh*, Vol. 2, Moscow: Iskusstvo, 1959, p. 108.
117. I. Bersenev, 'Obraz vraga', *Iskusstvo kino*, 1938, No. 4–5, p. 33.
118. Iu. Sevruk, 'Velikii grazhdanin', *Krasnaia zvezda*, 1939, 29 October, p. 4.
119. S. Tregub, 'Velikii grazhdanin', *Pravda*, 1939, 29 October, p. 28.
120. F. Karen, 'Nenavist' k vragu', *Iskusstvo kino*, 1937, No. 1–2, p. 16.
121. Bersenev, 'Obraz vraga', p. 33.
122. M. Bleiman, M. Bol'shintsov, F. Ermler, 'Rabota nad stsenariem', p. 31.
123. 'Vyshe bditel'nost'!' (Editorial), *Iskusstvo kino*, 1936, No. 9, p. 3.

124. Fridrikh Ermler, *Dokumenty. Stat'i. Vospominaniia*, Leningrad: Iskusstvo, 1974, p. 328.
125. N. Kovarskii, '*Velikii grazhdanin.* Stat'ia pervaia', *Iskusstvo kino*, 1939, No. 11, p. 31.
126. Ibid., p. 32.
127. Ibid., p. 33.
128. Ermler, *Dokumenty. Stat'i. Vospominaniia*, p. 146.
129. Ibid., p. 146.
130. Popov, *Problemy sovetskoi kinodramaturgii*, pp. 53–4.
131. Roshal', *Obrazy i aktery*, p. 59.
132. V. Grachev, *Obraz sovremennika v kinoiskusstve*, Moscow: Goskinoizdat, 1951, p. 18.
133. I. Grinberg, 'Priamo na predmet', *Teatr*, 1940, No. 3, pp. 46–7.
134. Ibid., p. 47.
135. N. Otten, 'Strastnyi khudozhnik: Zametki o tvorchestve Fridrikha Ermlera', *Iskusstvo kino*, 1939, No. 10, p. 37.
136. S. Tsimbal, 'Partiinyi fil'm', *Iskusstvo kino*, 1938, No. 4–5, p. 27.
137. F. Ermler, 'Neskol'ko slov o proshlom i budushchem'. In *Dvadtsat' let sovetskoi kinematografii. Sb. statei*, Moscow: Goskinoizdat, 1937, p. 33.
138. Ermler, *Dokumenty. Stat'i. Vospominaniia*, p. 8.
139. M. Bleiman, M. Bol'shintsov, F. Ermler, 'Rabota nad stsenariem', p. 30.
140. 'Utverzhdenie politicheskogo zhanra. Beseda s avtorami stsenariia "Velikii grazhdanin" M. Bleimanom i M. Bol'shintsovym', *Kino*, 1938, 28 February, p. 3.
141. Zak, *Mikhail Romm i traditsii sovetskoi kinorezhissury*, p. 95.
142. Ibid., p. 95.
143. B. Kattel', 'Velikii grazhdanin', *Kino*, 1938, 14 February, p. 3.
144. M. Bleiman, M. Bol'shintsov, F. Ermler, 'Velikii grazhdanin', *Kino*, 1938, 23 March, p. 3.
145. 'Kino totalitarnoi epokhi', *Iskusstvo kino*, 1990, No. 3, p. 109.
146. I. Grinberg, 'Priamo na predmet', p. 47.
147. Ibid., p. 48.
148. Bleiman, Bol'shintsov, Ermler, 'Rabota nad kartinoi', p. 9.
149. Ibid., pp. 11–12.
150. Ibid., p. 13.
151. N. Kovarskii, 'Velikii grazhdanin. Stat'ia pervaia', *Iskusstvo kino*, 1939, No. 11, p. 34.
152. Ibid., p. 35.
153. Grinberg, 'Priamo na predmet', p. 52.
154. Bulgakova, *Sovetskoe kino v poiskakh "obshchei modeli"*, p. 155.
155. George Johnson, *Architects of Fear: Conspiracy Theories and Paranoia in American Politics*, Los Angeles, CA: Jeremy P. Tarcher, 1983, p. 240.
156. S. Kara, 'Obraz velikogo grazhdanina', *Iskusstvo kino*, 1940, No. 1–2, p. 12.
157. N. Kovarskii, '*Velikii grazhdanin.* Stat'ia pervaia', p. 38.
158. Ibid., p. 36.
159. Ibid., p. 38.
160. M. Kozakov, 'Velikii grazhdanin', *Iskusstvo kino*, 1938, No. 4–5, p. 24.
161. S. Tsimbal, 'Partiinyi fil'm', *Iskusstvo kino*, 1938, No. 4–5, p. 27.

INDEX